Any Sound You Can Imagine

MUSIC / CULTURE

A series from Wesleyan University Press

Edited by George Lipsitz, Susan McClary, and Robert Walser

PAUL THÉBERGE

✳

Any Sound You Can Imagine

MAKING MUSIC/CONSUMING TECHNOLOGY

✳

WESLEYAN UNIVERSITY PRESS

Middletown, Connecticut

Published by Wesleyan University Press,
Middletown, CT 06459
www.wesleyan.edu/wespress

Printed in the United States of America   5   4   3
CIP data appear at the end of the book

Originally produced in 1997 by Wesleyan/
University Press of New England, Hanover, NH 03755

ISBN for the paperback edition: 978–0–8195–6309–5

Wesleyan University Press is a member of the Green Press
Initiative. The paper used in this book meets their
minimum requirement for recycled paper.

Contents

Illustrations

✳

Acknowledgments

✳

This book began as a Ph.D. dissertation in the Department of Communication Studies, at Concordia University, in Montréal. The initial study would not have been possible without the help and encouragement of a number of individuals who it is my pleasure to thank here. First and foremost, I thank my adviser, Martin Allor, for his support and guidance throughout my graduate studies in the Department of Communication Studies at Concordia and during my dissertation research. Others who offered guidance, criticism, inspiration, and support at early stages of the research include Steven Feld, Department of Anthropology, University of Texas, Austin, and Simon Frith, director of the John Logie Baird Centre, Strathclyde University, Glasgow; I am indebted to them both. For financial support throughout my studies, I am grateful to the Social Sciences and Humanities Research Council of Canada.

Apart from academic guidance and financial aid however, there are other individuals to whom I owe a personal debt of thanks for their encouragement, patience, and moral support during the long months of research and writing. I owe the greatest thanks to my wife, Carol Wainio, for her constant love and support during my moments of doubt, confusion, and frustration. Others who have been of particular help through various discussions of the material and through their support of my work during these past few years include a number of close friends and colleagues, especially Lorna Roth, Lon Dubinsky, Sarah Thornton, Keir Keightley, Kim Sawchuck, John Shepherd, Will Straw, and Bill Gilsdorf.

While gathering background information, I conducted a number of interviews in person or by telephone with key individuals in the music instrument and publishing industries. I was also fortunate enough to arrange on-site visits and interviews with individuals at the Ensoniq Corporation, Malvern, Pennsylvania, and at the studios and research facilities of the Yamaha Communication Center in New York City (two days each in November 1990). Some initial recording studio observation and interviews with musicians and recording engineers were conducted in Glasgow, Scotland, during the fall of 1989 and, later, in Montréal and Ottawa (a complete list of interviews can be found in the Background Sources). I am grateful to all the interviewees for the time they spent with me and the insights they shared. My understanding of the musical instrument industry and the processes of contemporary music production have been greatly enhanced by their contributions.

During the interviews it was my hope that my interview subjects would speak as candidly and as freely about their interests and concerns as possible, and for this reason I have allowed their comments to remain, for the most part, anonymous. In a few cases, where individuals spoke on behalf of their organizations, I have cited them by name; I have done so with their permission. In most other instances, however, individual quotations are identified by pseudonym.

I have also had the privilege of teaching Sound Production in the Department of Communication Studies at Concordia, and through my many casual conversations with graduate and undergraduate students I have acquired a sense of some of the musical and technical preoccupations of these young enthusiasts. Portions of the book have been presented in public in the form of conference papers and journal articles. I have benefited greatly from the comments of students and colleagues too numerous to mention here.

Finally, I would like to thank the editors and staff of Wesleyan University Press, as well as series editor Rob Walser, for their help and patience during the preparation of this book. Sheri Zernentsch, a graduate student in the Department of Communication Studies at Concordia, helped with the proofing and editing of the final manuscript; her comments and suggestions have helped clarify some of my arguments and made the text more enjoyable to read. Illustrations for the book were photographed by Allan Edgar in Montréal.

September 1996   P.T.

CHAPTER ONE

Introduction
Technology, Consumption, and Musical Practice

✳

Listen, don't get me wrong. I think this stuff is great, and I use it
every day, but I just know that it's killing music.
(Michel, a Montréal musician talking about his home studio in 1989)

The sentiments expressed in Michel's statement are not uncommon. I have
heard or read similar statements made by countless other musicians, music
critics, and fans whenever new technology in music is discussed. A common lament of the past decade has been that, despite the apparent power
and diversity of new musical instruments and recording devices, everyone's work was beginning to sound the same. Musicians complained that
the limited range of sounds built into some drum machines and synthesizers virtually forced them to write music in a particular style. *Rolling
Stone*, taking a typically reactionary stance, dubbed the entire period of
the late 1970s and early '80s as the era of "push-button rock" (no. 461,
November 21, 1985, p. 89).

But this homogeneity has not always been the case. During the 1960s,
rock guitarists such as Jimi Hendrix and Pete Townshend experimented
with distortion and feedback, creating excitement around new sounds and
electronic effects. At the same time, the multitrack studio was quickly becoming the testing ground for new ideas in pop music for mainstream
artists ranging from Phil Spector to the Beach Boys and the Beatles. By
the time Keith Emerson made his mark with a piercing synthesizer solo
on the number one hit "Lucky Man" in 1971 (*Emerson, Lake, and Palmer*,
Cotillion SD9040) and Stevie Wonder began laying down funky Moog
bass lines on records such as *Innervisions* (1973, Motown T326L), there was
a general feeling that the synthesizer would be welcomed as a mainstream

instrument in a number of different pop genres. It was only during the late 1970s, with the widespread reaction against Disco music, that electronic musical instruments began to be regarded with scepticism.

I have always felt uneasy with this state of affairs and with many of the recent observations and declarations about the role of new technology in popular music-making (positive and negative). One often senses un-examined assumptions regarding the "authenticity" of music and musical expression and, by extension, the implication that "technology is some-how false or falsifying" (Frith 1986: 265). But Michel's apparent conflict with technology cannot be fully explained by simple recourse to romantic notions of personal expression and "authenticity." After all, Michel readily admits that he *does* use technology in his musical practice—"every day"— and that *is* precisely the problem. Indeed, there is a sense of melodrama implied in his death knell for music that belies his own involvement with technology, his own compulsive need to adopt and make use of the latest musical gear available.

There are a number of levels at which one can come to a better under-standing of the dilemmas faced by contemporary musicians in adopting new technologies. The first operates at the level of musical practice itself: Despite the mechanization of musical reproduction through sound record-ing a century ago and despite the obvious importance of instruments such as the electric guitar in popular music-making, most musical instruments and performance practices have been, until relatively recently, insulated from the effects of major technological innovation. In this regard, even the electric guitar cannot be considered as fully "electronic" in either its design or its playing characteristics. Most traditional musical instruments exhibit relatively simple design principles, their sound mechanisms rely on a more-or-less direct relationship between player, technique, and instru-ment, and, for musicians, these characteristics foster a subtle yet complex relationship between musical instruments and musical concepts.

The technical basis of digital synthesizers, samplers, and drum ma-chines, on the other hand, is radically different. Their design principles rely less on acoustics than on electronics and digital logic, and their sound-producing hardware is completely independent of the user "interface"— the device that allows them to be played. Given these fundamental differ-ences, the speed at which these new instruments have been adopted as a part of general practice in the production of popular music has undoubt-edly contributed to a sense of unease with technology.

But there is also a deeper and broader level at which the relationship between music and new technologies must be addressed. Digital musi-cal instruments are hybrid devices: when one plays (or programs) a drum machine, synthesizer, or sampler, one is not only engaged in the production of sounds and melodic or rhythmic patterns but in their technical *re*production as well. Popular musicians who use new technologies are not simply the producers of prerecorded patterns of sounds (music) consumed by particular audiences; they, too, are consumers—consumers of technology, consumers of prerecorded sounds and patterns of sounds that they rework, transform, and arrange into new patterns. Recent innovations in musical technology thus pose two kinds of problems for musicians: On the one hand, they alter the structure of musical practice and concepts of what music is and can be; and, on the other, they place musicians and musical practice in a new relationship with consumer practices and with consumer society as a whole.

Take, for example, the case of drums, drummers, and drum machines. Rhythm is the backbone of many genres of popular music in the twentieth century, yet there is perhaps no more "primitive" a technology than the traditional drum—a membrane stretched across a circular frame that is beaten with a wooden stick. Even relatively recent innovations in drum construction, such as the substitution of synthetic heads for animal skins—an innovation thought to be of considerable importance to drummers from the late 1950s onward—have not altered the basic character of the instrument. The technique required to play a set of drums involves a rhythmic coordination of both mind and body, including a highly complex independence and interplay between the limbs and overall physical balance that is acquired only after long hours of physical disciplining over a period of years. The ability to play with a group of musicians also assumes that one has learned, through practice, a repertoire of rhythmic patterns appropriate to a specific style of music. Learning to play a musical instrument—in all its technical, cognitive, physical, and social dimensions—contributes to a musician's overall sense of musical style and, as I will argue later in this book, their listening habits as well.

The drum machine, on the other hand, bears no resemblance to traditional drums and drumming practice. The instrument has no direct, physical sound-producing mechanism; instead, it reproduces digital recordings of drum and/or synthesized sounds that are stored in its memory. It can be played, or programmed, with a series of buttons on its front panel, a keyboard, or a computer, and requires none of the physical coordination and discipline of a drummer. Finally, most drum machines not only contain drum sounds but also include preset rhythmic patterns, programmed in a variety of musical styles, that can be freely combined to create the rhythm track for a song. As a result, one's sense of musical style and language can be relatively more abstract in nature (e.g., as with the often-cited concern for the number of beats-per-minute in the production of dance music) and more mediated in origin.

What is at stake here is not simply a change in technology—the substitution of one set of materials for another—but rather a form of *practice*, where "practice" is taken to mean a form of knowledge in action (Bourdieu 1990). In this sense, learning to play a traditional musical instrument, especially in genres of popular music where notation plays little or no role in the composition of music, cannot be reduced to a simple acquisition of musical "skills." It is also a process in which one learns both how to make and *listen* to music, and to thereby conceptualize music in specific ways: "A lot of people, when they program machines, they don't *think* like a drummer would play" (Dennis Chambers, *Musician* 116, 1988: 103; emphasis added).

At a second, broader level, the use of not only prerecorded sounds but also prefabricated rhythmic patterns has become an all too common practice among many musicians who rely on new technology in the production of popular music. Entire collections of sounds, rhythmic "grooves," bass lines, and melodic phrases, recorded in a variety of musical styles, have been made commercially available to satisfy the electronic musician's need for raw material. Often, well-known session musicians or star performers have been engaged to create these collections, and specialized musicians' magazines regularly review them in the same way that general interest music and audio magazines review records. The conventional dividing line between production and consumption has thus become increasingly blurred.

These comments regarding new technology are not meant to disguise the extent to which popular music is already firmly rooted in technology. The microphone, electrical amplification, and tape recording have long been essential to its production; indeed, they are an important part of the overall "industrialization" of popular music that has taken place during the twentieth century (Frith 1988). Howard Becker has argued that an entire industry developed during the 1960s and '70s to service the needs of rock musicians for new musical instruments and accessories (1982: 309). By suggesting that this industry is somehow "at their disposal," Becker, however, ignores an important aspect of the relationship between instrument manufacturers and musicians: the fact that musicians have increasingly become *consumers* of technology. Their relationship with manufacturers is thus one of mutual dependency: Technological innovation is, in this sense, not only a response to musicians' needs but also a driving force with which musicians must contend.

In the past, the evolution of musical instrument design was a relatively slow process. Today, in the fast-paced electronics and computer industries, technological obsolescence is both the rule and the rationale for increased consumption. Certainly, musicians are not completely ignorant of this problem. There appears to be a growing awareness among many musicians that their artistic practice has become deeply implicated with a particular version of the notion of technological "progress" and that along with this ideology comes a number of disturbing musical, economic, and political dilemmas. These dilemmas are particularly acute in popular music. Over the past forty years, with the introduction of inexpensive electric and electronic musical instruments, multitrack recording equipment, and, more recently, digital keyboards, processors, and computer-based recording and editing systems, popular music has become increasingly integrated with technologies of sound production and reproduction. More importantly, the creation of these new technologies has taken place within the high-intensity market context of contemporary capitalism. An understanding of the various issues relating to music and technical innovation cannot be separated from a broader analysis of contemporary social and economic relations.

This book is about the role of recent digital technologies in the production of popular music. It is about the industries that supply these technologies, the media that promote them, and the meanings they have for the musicians who use them. My concern here is not only with the impact of high technology within a particular field but with technology as a specific type of consumer product and technology as part of the broader phenomenon of consumerism in the late twentieth century. An examination of the dynamic interplay that exists between technology[1] and contemporary modes of production, distribution, and consumption, and the manner in which this interplay has become an integral part of contemporary music-making, is thus a central concern of the book.

The key case material for this study is drawn from the 1970s and '80s when microprocessor technologies were first introduced into the design of electronic keyboard instruments. The period between 1983 and 1988 is of particular interest here, because, with the advent of the MIDI (Musical Instrument Digital Interface) specification, both the marketplace and the very nature of electronic music production were completely reorganized. This particular moment marks not only a significant period of innovation in the design, marketing, and use of electronic musical instruments but also, I will argue, a watershed moment in the history of popular music-making as regards the very relationship between production and consumption.

Indeed, what concerns me most is the manner in which popular musicians have become "consumers of technology." By this expression I do not simply mean that musicians have become consumers of digital musical instruments and recording devices as consumer objects; but rather, they have, in various ways, aligned their musical practices with a kind of behavior akin to a type of consumer practice—a practice altogether different from earlier relationships between musicians and their instruments as a means of production.

Such a claim, however, begs the question of how one might conceptualize, study, and interpret the relationships between musical practice, technology, and culture. Traditional musicology offers little assistance in this regard: The analytic study of musical technologies, sometimes referred to as "organology," is usually restricted to the simple classification of musical instruments, histories of instrument building, and accounts of the development of playing techniques. The relationship of musical instruments to musical style and genre, let alone the broader cultural significance of any given instrument or family of instruments, generally lies outside the scope of this discipline. Perhaps only in ethnomusicology has there been any systematic attempt to integrate the study of musical instruments within the overall study of music and culture; but, insofar as the domain of ethnomusicology has, for the most part, been restricted to the study of the so-called "traditional" musics of non-Western cultures, little of this work can be applied in any direct way to the complex workings of contemporary industrial culture.

Adopting musicological approaches to the study of recent technology and culture is problematic in other ways as well: in conventional musicology, the analysis of musical style, as revealed through the detailed study of musical scores and the canonization of individual genius, has long taken precedence over the study of social processes and material culture (Kerman 1985: 31–59). Most accounts of electronic music written from an academic perspective have adopted the positivistic orientation of musicology. They have emphasized the detailed history of relatively obscure musical inventions and the (often equally obscure) compositions from the classical avant-garde that have been created with those inventions.[2] Such accounts remain firmly within a tradition of histories of "great men" and their accomplishments in technology and art. Indeed, there is a kind of symmetry in these accounts where inventors and their machines share a certain (though subsidiary) glory with avant-garde composers and their music. In most cases, even the rigors of conventional musical analysis are eschewed in favor of discussions of technical and compositional strategy, thus placing an almost one-dimensional focus on the twin elements of technology and technique.

With few exceptions, the technologies and techniques of popular music have been ignored or denigrated in these histories.[3] In Schrader's *Introduction to Electro-Acoustic Music* (1982), for example, only a single paragraph is devoted to the Hammond Organ and its inventor, Laurens Hammond, although, by Schrader's own admission, it "has been one of the most commercially successful electro-acoustic instruments" (p. 68). The only reason for giving such brief attention to what might otherwise appear to be an important innovation in the history of electronic musical instruments is the following statement: "Although it has been widely used in popular music, the Hammond Organ has been all but ignored by composers of art music" (ibid.). Similarly, the adoption of synthesizer technology by popular musicians during the 1970s, a phenomenon that completely reoriented the technical design of synthesizers toward real-time performance capability, is dealt with by Schrader in three short paragraphs and a few instrument photos. Indeed, the photos take up more page space than the text itself (ibid.: 139–41). In these ways, the history of electronic instruments and music has become overly biased by narrow stylistic allegiances rather than openly addressed as a musical phenomenon of the broadest cultural significance.

Outside of musicology, and in popular music scholarship in particular, the technologies of sound reproduction have been regarded as playing a central role in the production and consumption of popular music, especially popular music of the post–World War II period. Because of the predominantly sociological perspective of many pop music commentators, the attention given to industrial organization and structure, at least for the recording and broadcast industries, has been more fully developed.[4] Strangely, however, although electronics corporations that have a direct stake in the recording industry, such as RCA, Philips/Polygram, and Sony/CBS, have received a large amount of critical scrutiny, considerably less attention has been given to the broader spectrum of industries that produce musical instruments, sound recording technology, hi-fi equipment, and amplifiers.

Most popular music scholars have chosen, instead, to focus on either specific *uses* of technology in production and consumption or on the aesthetic and ideological conflicts about the introduction of new musical instruments.[5] To a certain extent, these discourses can be regarded as critical elaborations on, or critiques of, dominant concerns, expressed not only in "common sense" rock sociology but also by fans and the popular music press, as well. In neither case, however, has there been a sustained analysis of the social and industrial contexts in which technical innovations in music-making and instrument design take place.

If electronic technologies do play an important role in the production and consumption of musical sounds, then a better understanding of the organization and dynamics of the musical instrument and electronics industries may offer new insights into the relationship between technology and musical practice, sound reproduction, and musical style. As this statement implies, however, such an understanding requires more than the study of a single industry: The musical instrument, electronics, and recording industries are all more or less distinct but also linked in significant ways. Differences in size, markets, pressures, and competitive strategies must be taken into account without losing sight of their complementary and sometimes contradictory roles in the larger complex, which might be referred to as the "music industries."

The problem remains of how adequately to conceptualize the nature of the technical, social, economic, cultural, and musical phenomena at hand. An examination of the musical instrument and electronics industries themselves, no matter how complex or richly detailed, cannot ultimately reveal the relationship of recent technical developments in musical instrument design to general social and historical conditions, nor can it illuminate the specific shifts in musical practice that have been both a contribution and a response to these developments. The present study has been conducted in a manner that is consistent, both in its general orientation and with regard to a number of specific insights and theoretical approaches, with the discipline of "cultural studies" as it has emerged during the past few decades, first in Britain and then in North America and elsewhere. The discipline itself, however, if a recently published anthology is any indication, is extremely diverse in its objects of study and in its virtual "bricolage" of theories and methodologies (Grossberg, et al. 1992: 2–3).

A good point of departure is to review some of the foundational work within the field of cultural studies as laid by Raymond Williams (1958, 1974, 1977, 1981). In his book *Culture* (1981), Williams outlines his approach to what he calls a "sociology of culture." For Williams, such a project comprises several areas of concern. These include, among others, the study of "institutions" (in this book, the study of the musical instrument industry), "formations" (more or less conscious movements or associations of individuals, such as, in this instance, so-called "user groups"), the social relations of specific "means of production" (as in the social relations in the multitrack recording studio), and "forms" (the analysis of musical works in terms of both their internal characteristics and in their broader social dimensions). Though initially isolated for the purposes of study and analysis, these various areas of concern, Williams argues must ultimately be brought together and understood as elements in a "complex unity": "Indeed the most basic task of the sociology of culture is analysis of the interrelationships within this complex unity: a task distinct from the reduced sociology of institutions, formations, and communicative relationships and yet, as a sociology, radically distinct also from the analysis of isolated forms" (Williams 1977: 139–140). For Williams, then, a sociology of culture must attempt to overcome the limitations of both conventional sociology and bourgeois aesthetics in order to understand cultural production as "a whole and connected social material process" (ibid.: 140); as such, a sociology of culture is at once a sociological *and* an aesthetic enterprise.

In adopting Williams's general approach to the sociology of culture, I want to extend one of his concepts. Williams describes cultural "formations" as a diverse set of possible associations, ranging from the medieval bardic orders and the highly organized craft guilds to the much more loosely defined artistic "movements" or "schools" of modern art and literature. The latter may include organizational structures based on "formal membership," less formal structures based around "collective public manifestations" (as in the case of specialized periodicals or exhibitions), or those represented by no formal, sustained relationships at all but, rather, by various temporary forms of "group identification" (Williams 1981: 57–69). Williams makes clear that the increasing number of cultural formations in the modern period is the result of shifts in market forces and, hence, the very conditions of artistic production. Furthermore, artistic or cultural formations can be located within larger "social formations"—religious, political, or intellectual in nature—to which they may adopt, at different times, a supportive or an oppositional stance (ibid.: 75–76). It is this more general notion of a "formation"—as a background or contextual element—that I wish to adopt here.[6]

The specific, three-part scheme of analysis and presentation adopted in *Any Sound You Can Imagine* has been derived from an extended essay entitled, "Object as Image: The Italian Scooter Cycle," written by another well-known figure in cultural studies, Dick Hebdige (1981). In this essay, Hebdige focuses on the constantly shifting cultural significance of the motor scooter and its relationship to the post-war rise of consumerism. Hebdige creates a kind of "cultural biography" (Kopytoff 1986) of the motor scooter by considering it not as a singular object but as several objects existing at distinct "moments": the moments of design/production, mediation (marketing and promotion), and consumption/use (ibid.: 45). Each "moment" is independent, housed within specific structures yet caught up in "networks of relationships" with the other two moments and within larger networks and contexts. No single moment can be considered as a completely "determining instance" dictating the meaning of the object at other moments or in other social contexts (ibid.). For the researcher, the consideration of each individual "moment" demands its own set of theories and analytic tools while, at every point, the entire network of relationships needs to be kept firmly within view.

To a large degree, Hebdige's approach to the phenomenon of the motor scooter drew on a familiar set of tools—a combination of semiotics and subcultural analysis—that had characterized his earlier work (1979) and that of a number of other individuals involved in British cultural studies during the early '70s (e.g., Hall and Jefferson 1976). My interests here have less to do with "style" or "subcultures," per se (although the book does touch on such issues), than with shifts in the technological basis of musical instrument design and in industrial organization; in patterns of association, apprenticeship, and the acquisition of musical knowledge; and in changes in musical practice that both are and are not manifest in musical sounds.

The breadth of study required to investigate thoroughly these various "moments" in the life of a commodity or, conversely, to trace the complex relationships of the cultural formation within which the commodity circulates is formidable and suggests a synchronic strategy, where only the most limited period of time is taken into consideration. As I studied the introduction of new musical instruments during the 1980s more closely, however, I began to understand it as the culmination of a certain technical development—the digitization of keyboard instruments—as well as the beginning of another change—the advent of a fully computerized studio recording apparatus. To a certain extent, I had understood this evolution from the beginning, but its full import did not strike me until my research took me into closer contact with the musical instrument industry itself and I began to consider, in greater detail, the various reactions, positive and negative, to digital instruments among musicians and the press. In short, it became increasingly clear to me that the events of the 1970s and '80s took on an even greater significance when placed within the specific contexts of the history of the musical instrument and magazine trades and within the long-held traditions and conventions of musical practice.

A broad, diachronically based program of research, in addition to the synchronic study of the more recent cultural formation, thus seemed to be called for. Here again, the importance of the work of Raymond Williams became evident, especially what he has referred to as the method of "'epochal' analysis" and his notion of the "dominant, residual and emergent" as dynamic elements within cultural processes (1977: 121–27). This line of reasoning led me to conduct additional historical research and to introduce each of the main sections of the book with fairly detailed accounts of the history of the musical instrument trade (and especially the development of keyboard instruments), of the music press as an area of specialized periodical publishing (and, also, the rise of enthusiasts in the area of communications technologies), and of musical practice as a set of specific skills, techniques, and knowledge in action.

The dangers inherent in such an approach are perhaps obvious enough: The plan of the book is already quite large—including three distinct areas of investigation—and the addition of historical data could easily lead to sacrificing detail and coherence for sweeping generalizations, false comparisons, and the like. But the strengths of the approach, I hope, far outweigh any potential weakness by allowing for a more in-depth understanding of the unique character of the cultural formation in question. In this regard, for example, it seemed absolutely necessary to try to understand the peculiar, fragmented nature of the musical instrument trades, the particular problems associated with musical instruments as commodities, the specialized nature of music periodical publishing, and the specificity of music as a form of artistic practice.

Any Sound You Can Imagine is broken into three separate sections: (1) Design/Production: The Musical Instrument Industry; (2) Mediation: Musicians' Magazines, Networks, and User Groups; and, (3) Consumption/Use: Technology and Musical Practice. Each section begins with a chapter that is primarily historical or theoretical in nature and sets up some of the important background issues to be addressed in subsequent material. The history of the piano—its industrial base, its promotional strategies, and its role in musical culture—supplies a particular focus for most of these chapters.

Because these three areas are interrelated in a variety of ways, inevitably some material will overlap between sections. At times it seemed impossible to keep the three areas entirely distinct; moreover, theoretical arguments and particular historical events had to be broken up between chapters in different sections of the book, creating other discontinuities. I have tried to minimize this problem as much as possible.

Part I is primarily concerned with the problems of technical innovations in musical instrument design. Chapter 2 provides a broad historical background on the nature of the musical instrument trades. Of particular importance in this discussion are two social histories of the piano by Loesser (1954) and Roell (1989). Roell's assessment of the piano industry at the turn of the century and its relationship to the rise of a consumer culture is of special relevance to the study as a whole. Chapter 3 addresses invention and innovation in capitalist markets through a set of examples drawn from the history of electronic musical instrument design. André Piatier's notion of "transectorial innovation" (1987/88) is introduced as a key concept in understanding the dynamics of recent innovations in microprocessor-based musical instruments. Finally, in Chapter 4, the rise of a "cottage industry" devoted to the supply of prefabricated sounds for digital synthesizers and the commercial development of MIDI (Musical Instrument Digital Interface) during the 1980s are discussed. Issues related to the so-called "democratization" of the marketplace are initially introduced here and followed up in greater detail in Chapter 6.

Part II, "Mediation: Musicians' Magazines, Networks, and User Groups," looks at the music periodical publishing industry and other forms of communication and their role in the formation of markets and communities of interest. Although they are seldom cited in a direct manner, much of the background theory and orientation for this section concerning the role of communications in twentieth century consumer culture and the cultural significance invested in consumer objects is drawn from Ewen (1976), Leiss (1976), Leiss et al. (1990), Appadurai (1986), and Kopytoff (1986). Chapter 5 is initially concerned with the history of music periodicals and their relationship to the music industries and to musical consumption in the home. The second part of the chapter focuses on the modern, highly specialized musicians' magazine industry and its role in the definition of markets and the promotion of a (largely male) technical culture around the new instruments of musical production. Chapter 6 follows with a brief discussion of the early twentieth-century phenomenon of "ham radio" operators; my interest here is in the nature of technically mediated communications networks. It then describes the rise of computer networks and "user groups" associated with new musical technologies and, in particular, gives an account of the early activities of the International MIDI Association (IMA). The theories of C. B. Macpherson (1973) are discussed in relation to the IMA's attempts to establish an open, "democratic" process to guide the technical innovation and diffusion of the MIDI specification.

Part III, "Consumption/Use: Technology and Musical Practice," focuses on musicians themselves and the relationship between musical instruments and the concepts and techniques of sound-making. Chapter 7 draws on the literature of ethnomusicology, sociology/anthropology, and, most prominently, on the reflections of David Sudnow (1978) with regard to jazz piano playing. One of the main concerns here is to explore the nature of "practical" (in Bourdieu's terms) versus formal acquisition of musical knowledge; issues concerning the role of notation in Western music are also addressed. Chapter 8 discusses changes in the concept of "sound" in music and their relationship to performance practices and to electronic means of reproduction. The language used by musicians to describe sounds becomes one of the focal points of this analysis. In Chapter 9, the multitrack studio, MIDI sequencing, and the rise of the home studio are considered as part of an overall movement towards the rationalization (Weber 1958b) of musical practice. The changing status of the term "live" in relation to music and technical means of reproduction is also discussed. Finally, some reflections on musical copyright that bring together notions of sound, performance, and reproduction are presented.

The concluding chapter (Chapter 10) pulls together some of the main arguments concerning the nature of what I have described here as a "cultural formation" and argues that the phenomena discussed in the book may be part of a much larger shift in the nature of production and consumption in the late twentieth century.

PART ONE

✳

DESIGN/PRODUCTION:
THE MUSICAL INSTRUMENT
INDUSTRY

✳

CHAPTER TWO

The Industrial Context
of a "Revolution" in Marketing
and Design

✳

> Electric instruments are a departure from nineteenth century tradition. Because they
> depend on physical discoveries of this century, they are often considered the most
> characteristic instruments of our time. . . .
>
> . . . We do not know the destiny of these engineers' inventions, nor can we tell how much
> they will mean to the future of music. For the time being, they surely owe their existence
> to the experimentations of electroengineers rather than to any musical need.
> (Sachs 1940: 447, 448–49)

In his monumental comparative and historical work, *The History of Musical Instruments* (1940), Curt Sachs thus summed up the early history of electric musical instruments. Nearly half a century of technical experimentation had seen little, if any, production of lasting musical significance; certainly the future of electric instruments seemed, at best, marginal. Indeed, Barry Schrader has observed that between 1930 and 1950 alone, over a hundred electro-acoustic instruments were invented; yet few of these experimental musical instruments achieved any kind of success during this twenty-year period, and none are in use today (1982: 68).

The situation, however, could not have changed more drastically during the second half of the twentieth century. During the past forty years, changes in musical styles and tastes and advances in technical design and marketing have transformed electro-acoustic instruments—electric guitars and amplifiers, electronic organs, digital pianos, synthesizers, and signal processors—from idle engineering experiments into what must be regarded as the "most characteristic instruments of our time." An analysis of the forces that have contributed to such a transformation must include both an understanding of what today constitutes a genuine "musical need" and an understanding of technical experimentation as a partly independent driving force behind the development of new technologies. Neither "musical needs" nor the experiments of electroengineers, however, can be entirely separated from market forces—from the industrial requirement for new products and the influence of contemporary advertising and promotion on the formation of consumer needs. An examination of the dynamics of the musical instrument trade—its specific character, economic problems, and marketing strategies—and the role of technical innovation within this industry must thus be considered an important contextual element in the development and adoption of new musical technologies.

The initial impulses that have historically directed human ingenuity toward the development of musical instruments are elemental in character: They include motor impulses—the desire to express emotion through physical movement—ritual functions—the desire to invest sound with symbolic meaning or magical powers—and, later, melodic impulses—the use of instruments to imitate repetitive patterns in speech and song (Sachs 1940: 25–59). Certainly, aspects of these "primitive" impulses continue to play a role in the design of musical instruments. For example, even in electronically produced music, where there exists a clear separation between physical movement and actual sound production and where keyboards of the organ variety amount to little more than a switching device turning predetermined electronic events on and off, there remains a strong interest in supplying musicians with greater levels of touch sensitivity. The on-going search for viable "alternate controllers" is an expression of the desire to bring into play a wider range of physical gestures as a means of initiating and shaping electronic sounds.

In addition to these basic impulses are a variety of motivations related to musical developments unique to the West. Among them is an increased desire for greater timbral variety and expressive range and, above all during the late eighteenth century and throughout the nineteenth, a desire for greater power (i.e., volume). The piano was the instrument most representative of both these tendencies (ibid.: 388–90). Such musical requirements were the impetus behind innovations in piano design—the introduction of cast-iron framing, heavier strings, and hammer actions—during the early nineteenth century (Loesser 1954: 301–4). Furthermore, experiments with electronics in the early twentieth century exhibited a basic continuity with these same desires: "Most eulogies of electric instruments emphasize their unlimited capacity for dynamic power and varied timbre. This is in line with the trend of the later nineteenth century" (Sachs 1940: 449). Indeed, the appeal to unlimited capacity for varied timbre continues to be a major component in promotional hype for digital synthesizers half a century later.

The early formation of these desires are related to historical, social, and cultural factors, such as the gradual shift from aristocratic to democratic social structures from the eighteenth century onward, which precipitated the building of large public concert halls requiring greater volume of sound (ibid.: 388–90). Similarly, with mass culture in the twentieth century, concert promoters in popular music have increasingly turned to sports stadiums and other large venues, thus stimulating the need for powerful amplification systems.

Sachs also cites the rise of a romantic, passionate spirit in art-making following the French Revolution as a factor in the demand for greater timbral variety and dynamic power (ibid.). His speculations come close to identifying what Raymond Williams might refer to as the "structure of feeling" (1977: 128–35) of the period as manifest in its instrumental forms and expressive styles. Although Sachs recognized such social and cultural forces at play in the design of musical instruments and understood the importance of a number of technical innovations in the development of complex instruments such as the nineteenth-century piano, his appreciation of the economic context of these developments, however, is much less acute. Arthur Loesser (1954) and Craig H. Roell (1989), on the other hand, have attempted to view the development of the piano as a complex interplay between commerce and culture: Technical innovations, efficiencies in manufacturing and distribution, corporate finance, market control, merchandising, concert promotion and advertising are all part of their stories about how the piano industry became a central part of musical life in Europe and North America. In particular, Roell's observations of the piano industry in the United States at the turn of the century, its response to and contributions toward the emergence of a consumer culture, offer important insights into the dynamic relationship between music and cultural values.

In this chapter I would like to begin by outlining, in a rather broad fashion, a number of factors that relate to the particular nature, organization, and historical evolution of the musical instrument industry. The first section emphasizes the development of the piano industry during the eighteenth and nineteenth centuries. Though this period may appear to have little direct relevance to the modern synthesizer industry, the history does reveal important issues about the process of technical innovation and the evolving capitalist organization of the industry.

There are other compelling reasons, however, for examining the history of the piano industry within this study. The piano has been unquestionably one of the dominant musical and cultural forces in the West—theoretically, practically, and symbolically—during the past two centuries. Technically, its distinctively mechanical design characteristics made it amenable to modern manufacturing processes; and economically, the category of keyboard instruments, today including not only pianos but also organs, synthesizers, digital pianos, and portable keyboards, has consistently dominated the music instrument trade. The category presently constitutes between 40 and 50 percent of total dollar sales within the industry and has been even greater in the past. Together, these factors have exerted enormous pressure on the manufacturers of new musical instruments and, in large part, may account for the continued dominance of keyboards in digital instrument design.

I now turn to a brief discussion of the contemporary organization of the musical instrument trade, its status as a leisure industry, and its relationship to the electronics and sound reproduction industries of the twentieth century. The observations in this section are intended primarily as background information on the overall commercial context wherein musical instruments are currently produced and sold. Of particular interest to this discussion are the relative size and specialization of various sectors of the musical instrument industry and the resulting interconnection of personal relationships and corporate structures apparently so characteristic of the industry as a whole.

History and Organization of the Musical Instrument Industry

Music in the twentieth century is, to a large degree, a technologically dependent, leisure commodity whose existence is guaranteed by the organized activities of a number of large corporate enterprises and media outlets. As in other areas of commodity culture, rapid changes in musical style, fashion, and technology go hand in hand with contemporary modes of production and distribution. Of course, this commercial tie has not always existed; until about the sixteenth century, most music for entertainment purposes was primarily the preserve of individuals: wandering minstrels, amateur musicians in the home, and the like. The only formal organizations of musical activity in Western Europe prior to this time was the church and the municipal musicians' guilds. Within these institutional frameworks, music served relatively specific religious and social functions, musical styles changed only slowly, and the production, distribution, and use of musical technologies (i.e., musical instruments and early notated scores) were relatively controlled.

In the case of the church, most musical instruments were outlawed from use in religious ceremonies at an early date, and church leaders had even attempted, with relatively little success, to prescribe the use of instruments in secular music as well (Raynor 1972: 23–25). As one of the main institutional patrons of music, the church's early hostility toward instrumental music likely had a profound impact on the development of musical instruments in Europe throughout the Middle Ages. With the possible exception of the lyre, there were virtually no medieval musical instruments that could be considered as European in origin; nearly all instruments of the time were adapted from Asian models (Sachs 1940: 260). As an institution, the church was indispensable in the development of keyboard instruments, however. The early monasteries provided a stable environment for the development of organ technology; only after the thirteenth century did organ building become a secular profession (Weber 1958b: 114–15).

Even in secular music, where musical instruments were certainly widely played during this period, their role remained subservient to the voice in most music-making. As a result of this subservience, secular instrument production was limited, and few standards developed either with regards to their design or their use in instrumental ensembles. In Max Weber's account, it was the early professional organization of the medieval bards and that of the music guilds (at least from about the thirteenth century onward) that provided for the first, relatively fixed markets for musical instruments, thus encouraging their manufacture and early efforts toward standardization (ibid.: 107). As a market, however, the guild musicians tended to be relatively conservative. The nature of guild apprenticeship training encouraged musicians to maintain traditional musical forms and traditional instruments and discouraged experimentation with new musical styles and sounds, even as public taste began to change during the early years of the Renaissance (Raynor 1972: 61–62).

Not until the sixteenth century did instrumental music begin to evolve as a separate, distinct area of musical form in Western music. It was also during the sixteenth century that keyboard instruments began to become popular for vocal accompaniment and as instruments of home entertainment among the aristocracy; they had been preceded in this function by the lute. Not until later, in the seventeenth century as instruments began to be specified in musical scores, did orchestration begin to emerge as a distinct area of musical composition, thus providing the basis for the formation of the modern orchestra.[1]

Because of the small size of the market, however, instrument building remained, throughout this latter period, a specialized, craft-oriented activity supported by little in the way of formal industrial structures in either manufacturing or distribution. Until quite recently, instrument manufacture could hardly be described as an "industry" at all, at least not in the modern sense of the term, and was often no more than a secondary area of activity carried on by persons engaged in furniture making and other craft. In eighteenth-century Germany, for example, keyboard instruments were still made by individual artisans and their assistants, often as a secondary line of production along with other manufacturing:

> Harpsichords and clavichords could not be bought at a "store" or at "warerooms": they were made to the order, and often to the specification, of individual customers. . . . It is unlikely that, before the middle of the eighteenth century, there was enough demand . . . to occupy a craftsman exclusively with the making of them. Usually these instruments were a side line of organ builders or of cabinet makers. It was after 1740 that the demand grew to a point where building them could become an independent trade.   (Loesser 1954: 16)

Even in the area of keyboard instruments, whose history is central to the development of Western music as a whole, the high cost of the instruments and the small size of the market effectively limited their production.

The personal, "made to the order" nature of the instrument trade was reflected in other areas of musical life as well, and the gradual development of musical activity into a broad-based entertainment industry during the late eighteenth and early nineteenth centuries continued to be influenced, and limited, by relatively specialized networks of distribution. According to musicologist William Weber, concert life and music publication were dependent on such networks and on personal relationships between individuals. New compositions were

> sold copy-by-copy through a complex web of ties among composers, musicians, and interested amateurs. Each composer would ask colleagues in different cities to solicit subscriptions to a new composition (whether printed or not) for a small remuneration, usually advertising these agents in periodicals. . . . Trusting relationships were the key to success.   (Weber 1977: 9)

Musicians themselves, acting as "part-time merchants" (Hortschansky 1983), were thus central to the early commercial development of music publishing. As Weber points out, such a personalized method of distribution was, by its very nature, a "self-limiting" system (Weber 1977: 9).

Similarly, in North America, where instruments and printed music were in short supply during this period of history, semi-commercial networks of professional musicians and amateurs were vital to the early development of musical life. For example, historian Helmut Kallmann has described how the development of secular concert music in Québec was dependent on the varied activities of musicians such as Friedrich Heinrich Glackemeyer (1751–1836). In addition to his musical performances and activities as a band director, Glackemeyer was a key figure in musical education and, equally important, in the importation of printed music and instruments (Kallmann 1960: 50–55). Kallmann considers musicians' "auxilliary occupations" in education and trade to be central to the early development of music in Canada.

A gradual transformation in these networks of musical, social, and economic relationships took place when music began to be played by amateurs in the homes of the emerging middle classes in Europe. William Weber claims that the publishing industry was the main driving force behind this transformation during the critical period between 1780 and 1850 and that its growth was aided by a number of factors. These factors included technical developments in lithography, movable type, and engraving; the spread of retail outlets;[2] and the development of promotional and merchandising techniques aimed directly at the emerging amateur market (Weber 1977: 6, 10–11). Thus, as Weber argues, technological innovations combined with changes in distribution and marketing were, from the outset, essential to the early formation of a consumer market for music.

A particularly interesting element in this transformation, which Weber describes as a "quantum leap" from local, personalized relationships to a professionalized, international trade network, is the degree to which these two levels of activity continued to work together in the world of music:

> The personalized commerce and concert life of the eighteenth century never disappeared completely from European musical life. Amateur orchestras today still have an internal structure not very different from those back then. . . . But around them have developed broadly based, impersonal social systems which have come to control these concerts in powerful ways. Indeed, one of the most fascinating aspects of modern mass culture is how it has interlocked with personalized institutions in this manner. (Ibid.: 9–10)

This interlocking of personal networks with bureaucratic and technical systems is still, I argue, an important factor in the music industry.

The transformation of personal relationships into commercial ones is also indicative of broader changes in the social status of musicians in Western culture. Faced with a much less secure employment than that of church, guild, or aristocratic patronage, those who needed to supplement their income from a permanent post or from freelance work often turned to the music trades. Klaus Hortschansky has shown that among the various people who chose to become involved in the music publishing and retail trades during the late eighteenth and early nineteenth centuries, professional and amateur musicians figure prominently; many maintained their musical activities as composers, conductors, or musicians, whereas others used the trades as a means of becoming fully integrated with middle-class society (1983: 207–18). The pianist Muzio Clementi, well known as a composer, performer, and teacher during the classical period, was perhaps one of the most celebrated musicians to turn to the music trades to gain a more secure and respected position in middle-class society. His firm, Clementi & Co., became a well-established piano manufacturing and music publishing concern in England during the early nineteenth century (Loesser 1954: 259–67). According to many of the interviews that I conducted for the present book, apparently a large number of musicians today continue to use the music trades as an escape from the insecurity of a musical career. Indeed, the participation of amateur and former professional musicians at virtually every level of the industry appears to be characteristic of the music trades.

In conjunction with the developments in publishing and concert management, the expansion of piano manufacturing was an especially critical factor in the industrialization and commercialization of music production during the late eighteenth and early nineteenth centuries. Initially, the early European piano makers were dependent upon craft modes of production not unlike those of other instrument makers and the same personal networks of distribution as were characteristic of other areas of musical life. Loesser claims that an average keyboard workshop during the early and mid-eighteenth centuries—consisting of a single master craftsperson and a few assistants—could turn out no more than seventeen to nineteen instruments a year (ibid.: 133, 234). In centers such as Vienna, where public advertising was frowned upon, piano makers regularly turned to piano teachers, offering them a large commission on each instrument sold, in an attempt to market their instruments to prospective buyers (ibid.: 134–35).

The transformation of the craft of piano manufacturing proved to be perhaps more profound than in any other area of musical life. As the eighteenth century drew to a close, the increasing demand for pianos required that production capacity be greatly expanded. Nanette Streicher, who had taken over her father's piano making business in Austria just prior to the turn of the century, appears to have introduced changes to the manufacturing process that enabled her operation to produce close to fifty pianos a year: "Clearly, this could be accomplished only by a considerable enlargement of plant facilities, an increase of working personnel, a fairly rigorous division of labor, and a steady purchase of ready treated materials. It could only be done by an organization approximating what we would call a factory" (ibid.: 133). In England, where industrial manufacturing methods had progressed much more quickly than in Austria, the piano manufacturer Broadwood was producing in excess of four hundred instruments a year by the beginning of the nineteenth century (ibid.: 234). Piano manufacture had thus distinguished itself from all other forms of musical instrument production:

Instruments of the fiddle or pipe species, by their relative simplicity and rarity, might never have tempted anyone to build them by factory methods. But the pianoforte, with its manifold, intricate structure—and especially with its abundance of serially repeated parts—seemed particularly suited to the new mechanical processes. . . . The piano was the factory's natural prey; purely on the basis of its structure, it was the instrument of the time.   (Ibid.: 233)

These passages illustrate the changes that factory methods of production brought about in keyboard manufacture during the early nineteenth century. The piano was the first musical instrument to become the beneficiary of what today is described as a set of "process innovations"—innovations that allow for greater productivity in manufacture, economies of scale, or more efficient distribution. From its earliest incarnation, the piano was designed to overcome the musical shortcomings of earlier keyboards such as the harpsichord—shortcomings in the ability to play loud and soft, deficiencies in overall sonic power, and so on. Initially, it was a series of innovations in technical design, similar to those in hammer design and cast-iron framing, that allowed the piano gradually to displace earlier keyboard instruments. For the most part, these "product innovations" are what have attracted the concern of most musicologists (e.g., Sachs 1940: 391–98). I argue, however, that these innovations in technical design alone cannot account for the unparalleled rise of the piano in Western music history; only in conjunction with *process* innovations—innovations in manufacturing, distribution, and marketing—could the piano have emerged as the quintessential instrument of musical entertainment in the homes of the middle class and as a dominant force in Western musical culture as a whole.

Such a perspective has been adopted in *The Piano in America 1890–1940*, a book in which Craig H. Roell (1989) documents the rise of the American piano industry and its relationship to the emergence of a modern consumer culture. By the middle of the nineteenth century, the United States had already begun to establish itself as one of the leading centers of piano production in the world. Indeed, piano manufacturing in the United States had become a big business: In 1851, some nine thousand instruments were produced (mostly for the domestic market), and, by 1853, the Chickering piano company of Boston had erected the largest single industrial building in the country (Loesser 1954: 495). By the latter part of the century, Chickering, Baldwin, and Steinway were only the most prestigious companies in an industry made up of literally dozens of small manufacturers—or rather "assemblers"—producing pianos from stock parts provided by a growing piano supply industry. The supply industry made it possible for small companies with limited capital to produce pianos for a mass market at competitive prices (Roell 1989: 72–76). In Canada, the growth of domestic piano manufacturing during the late nineteenth century also depended on the ready availability of standardized piano parts, both domestically produced and imported (Kallmann 1960: 196–97).

Increased productivity, however, necessitated an increased attention to marketing and promotion. Many of the small manufacturers distributed their pianos without brand names, and it was a common practice for local dealers to apply their own names or to fraudulently apply the name of a reputable manufacturer to the instruments. To combat the "stencil" piano trade, the larger manufacturers began to emphasize the value of trademarks and to encourage brand name loyalty (a relatively unfamiliar concept in the nineteenth century); to aid this effort, they turned increasingly to national advertising as a means of promotion (Roell 1989: 76). From the beginning of the nineteenth century, artist endorsements and manufacturer-subsidized concert tours had been a regular feature of piano promotion. In this way, art and commerce came together in mutual support of one another on the concert stage: It was customary for manufacturers to hang a sign on their instruments for the entire audience to see (ibid.: 144–46, 150; Loesser 1954: 531–36). Not surprisingly, newspaper and magazine advertisements made prominent use of artist endorsements.

A new feature was added to this form of promotion in the latter part of the nineteenth century. International fairs had become a kind of mass medium for the communication of technological developments, and piano manufacturers began to compete for recognition at events such as the World Exhibition held in London in 1851, the Paris Exposition of 1867, and the Centennial Exposition in Philadelphia in 1876 (Roell 1989: 147). Awards and citations received at these numerous events could then be turned into important indicators of technical superiority in future ad campaigns (ibid.: 147–49). Artistic distinction and the display of technical prowess thus became twin focal points of brand name promotional strategies in the piano industry.

In response to increased competition, the larger manufacturers began a process of integration and modernization through incorporation, increased capitalization, and mergers. Some also used franchised dealerships to gain greater control over distribution. As factory methods led to greater productivity, lower prices, and intense competition, the leaders of the American piano industry thus increasingly turned their attention to corporate and market control as a means of guaranteeing prosperity (ibid.: 83–93). Interestingly, however, attempts to establish monopoly control through the creation of a piano trust failed. Perhaps as a reflection of the piano industry's craft origins, the piano trade remained relatively conservative and highly competitive: Most piano companies during the late nineteenth century continued to be managed by their owners or by their major stockholders and were slow to adopt the modern managerial hierarchies that were quickly becoming typical in other spheres of American corporate life (ibid.: 85).

Despite mass production practices and falling prices, pianos, at least high-quality ones, still represented a sizable investment for both the average retail operation and the consumer. In addition to the measures mentioned above, piano manufacturers and dealers attempted to stimulate sales through credit programs and installment purchase plans (ibid.: 96–97). Installment buying was still a rather novel merchandizing concept during the nineteenth century: The practice had been introduced by the Singer sewing machine company in 1856, adopted by the Baldwin piano company during the 1870s, and spread throughout the piano industry during the 1880s and '90s (ibid.: 100–102, 142–43; see also, Majeski 1990: 31).[3] Organized financing thus became an essential component of the trade both in terms of retail floor-planning and consumer sales. It would eventually become a hallmark of the emerging consumer culture during the early twentieth century, promoting the sale of all "consumer durables" such as automobiles and electrical appliances.

Given the mechanical character of piano design—a feature that made it so well suited to modern factory manufacturing processes—it was perhaps only a matter of time before automation techniques would be applied to its ability to play music as well. The introduction of the automatic player piano around the turn of the century had a major impact on the piano industry and its relationship to the consumer market. A number of points should be made about the introduction of automation in music that are of particular relevance to more recent developments in the design and marketing of electronic and digital musical instruments.

As early as 1825 attempts were being made to design a self-playing piano, most based on clockwork technologies derived from barrel organs, music boxes, and other instruments already common in the eighteenth century (Loesser 1954: 577–79). The technical advance that would eventually make both barrel organs and player pianos more practical, however, came from an unlikely source: the textile trade. It was Joseph Jacquard's use of perforated cards on cylinders to control needlework, introduced during the early nineteenth century, that became the basis of the perforated music roll on automatic pianos (ibid.: 580; see also Ord-Hume 1984: 79–81, 83). It can certainly be argued that virtually all aspects of musical instrument manufacture are dependent on the general level of industrial development attained in a given society, especially craft techniques in metal and woodworking. The early development of automatic musical instruments based on such an unlikely invention as the Jacquard loom must, however, be among the more salient examples of what André Piatier (1987/88) refers to as "transectorial innovations"—innovations generated within a specific industrial sector that find subsequent application in other, often unrelated

Time proves
that there is a
wonderful fas-
cination about
a Kranich &
Bach Player Piano,
steadily increasing in
its charm as the music
lover becomes familiar
with its remarkable possibilities for personal expression,
and justifying its selection in
preference to some other form
of mechanical musical instru-
ment that sells for less but soon grows tiresome.
Half a century of effort by the Kranich & Bach families of
piano builders has made this instrument supreme in tone and
real musical value.

Our "Golden Anniversary" Booklet, for the
guidance of piano buyers, will be sent on request.

JUBILEE PLAYER
Price, $700
(Freight and handling extra)
"The instrument you
will always enjoy."

Personal expression in the mechanical age. This ad from 1915 condenses several essential aspects of the piano trade during the early decades of the twentieth century: the centrality of
the piano in the domestic musical culture of the middle class, the figure of the female amateur
pianist, and the continued appeal to values of "personal expression" in an age of mechanical
reproduction. Note that the pianist's hands do not touch the keyboard.

sectors. In the electronic age, transectorial innovations have become increasingly significant and commonplace. In the case of the early piano industry, the impact of such far-flung technical innovations as the automatic
loom could not have been greater: Player pianos would eventually account
for 56 percent of the industry's production and sales (Roell 1989: 155).

Just as printed music suitable for home entertainment and designed for
amateur players had been an important factor contributing to the sale of
keyboard instruments during the late eighteenth and early nineteenth centuries, an adequate supply of piano rolls containing popular repertoire was
essential to the success of the new automatic piano industry. In a sense,
both sheet music and piano rolls could be considered the "software" com-

ponents of a primarily hardware-driven industry; similarly, in the early days of the recording industry, it was necessary to produce recordings to sell gramophones and phonographs. Unlike sheet music (and very much like records and record players) the technical nature of the automated instruments required a certain degree of compatibility in the rolls and playing mechanisms if they were to be playable on more than one brand of instrument. Clearly, cooperation and not competition was required of the fledgling industry, and, in 1905, four manufacturers combined efforts to create a uniform standard for piano rolls; perhaps no other technical innovation contributed more to the overnight success of the player piano than the achievement of the standard roll (Majeski 1990: 52). Industrial cooperation and standardization thus proved to be essential components in a strategy to both stabilize and stimulate the marketplace.

The enormous success of the player piano, or "pianola" as it came to be known, was not based on technical innovations alone, however. Fundamental changes in cultural values and patterns of consumption had to precede, or develop in tandem with, the new technical capabilities. The pianola was a new kind of musical instrument—an instrument that required no particular skill on the part of the operator. In this sense, the pianola had more in common with music boxes and the newly invented phonograph than with the traditional piano. Roell describes how promotion of the unique capabilities of the pianola resulted in a kind of "contradictory ideology" expressed in advertising campaigns of the period (ca. 1900–1925). The personal sense of individual achievement and creativity characteristically associated with the "producer ethic" of the nineteenth century and most clearly identified with the piano in middle-class Victorian culture was suddenly juxtaposed with an opposing set of values characteristic of the new "mythology of consumerism"—effortless recreation, leisure, and immediate gratification (Roell 1989: 156–59).

The "easy to play" appeal of the instruments became linked to a notion of "musical democracy" (ibid.)—a notion of universal accessibility to culture that would later become an essential component in the consumer mythology associated with the phonograph and radio. This mythology became especially powerful in the United States, where there had long been a tendency towards the division of musical taste along class lines not unlike that found in the musical culture of Europe. According to musicologist Charles Seeger, the efforts of the mechanical music industries to promote the consumption of music in any and all styles—popular, folk, and classical—had a profound leveling effect on American musical taste during the early part of the twentieth century. In Seeger's view, the music industries—what he sarcastically referred to as the "sell-America-music" group—were essentially a "democratizing" agent in American musical culture (1977: 229). In a sense, then, the twin aims of the automatic piano industry—instrument sales and the universal accessibility of music—were the complementary halves of an economic and social ideology.

This relationship between the musical instrument industry and the emerging technologies of mechanical and electronic reproduction is particularly intriguing because it has changed so radically over the course of this century. Initially, instrument manufacturers and retailers did not regard the new technologies as a threat to traditional music-making; indeed, they saw reproductive technology as not only contributing to the democratization of music but also as a stimulus to sales. From the outset, music shops had been among the primary outlets for phonographs, and, by the 1920s, some piano manufacturers were producing both phonographs and radios and selling them through their dealerships (ibid.: 211–12; Majeski 1990: 50–54, 92–99). Music shops even served as outlets for television sets during the 1950s; music retailers eventually got out of the television business not because of ideological opposition but because it put them in direct competition with department stores and mass merchandising outlets, forcing a substantial lowering of their usual profit margins (Majeski 1990: 149–50).

Musical instruments remained the industry's main focus, and, as a consumer product offering instant, repeatable pleasures, an instrument like the player piano soon found itself in competition with all other products of a similar nature (it was eventually outdone by radio during the 1920s). Although promotion of the contradictory ideologies of personal achievement and immediate gratification proved to be very profitable to the industry, such contradictions could not be maintained indefinitely, and the more traditional piano manufacturers—Baldwin and Steinway—returned to the old Victorian values of technical and artistic accomplishment in their promotional activities (Roell 1989: 160–82). The piano industry began to realize that the promotion of music-making in private and public education was both ideologically and economically more appropriate and, in the long term, more effective than direct appeals to modern consumer values. Individually, piano manufacturers and their agents began systematically to exploit local networks of private music teachers and their pupils as sources of prospective sales (Roell 1989: 169–70); and collectively, the industry launched major campaigns to promote music programs in the public schools and to support group instruction (ibid.: 190–91, 203).

Although the piano industry initially participated in, and profited from, the promotion of the new consumer ethic, it soon found itself at odds with the entertainment values of the leisure age. By the time the first commercially viable, electronic musical instruments, such as the Hammond Organ, arrived on the scene during the 1930s, the industry was already becoming sensitive about competition from leisure-oriented commodities such as radio and the automobile. Initially, the electric organ was marketed as the legitimate musical heir to the pipe organ and sold primarily to churches and auditoriums (Majeski 1990: 134); but, after the Second World War, Laurens Hammond began to look for ways to tap into the potentially lucrative home market (the piano industry's traditional turf). He began by developing a new electric organ incorporating a system of accordion-like chord buttons and then launched an "easy-play" ad campaign during the early 1950s to support its introduction into the marketplace: "Trade In Your Silent Piano For A New Hammond Chord Organ. Without lessons, you can play the Hammond chord organ in minutes, even if you can't read music. You'll never have to work on boring scales and exercises" (ibid.: 140). In what must be regarded as an extreme form of collective amnesia about its own promotional appeals during the heyday of the player piano, the piano industry reacted with outrage—not only, one suspects, because of the explicit call to "trade in" the parlor piano but also because of the implication that musical accomplishment was no longer the result of diligent work. Playing a musical instrument could be made effortless, or so it seemed, through the intervention of electronic technology.

The tension between the belief that acquiring musical skills requires concentrated effort (a work ethic) and the marketing requirement that all music-making be seen as a form of entertainment (a leisure ethic) has become one of the more enduring ideological and economic conflicts for the musical instrument trade during the twentieth century, both in its internal and external market relations. With the advent of electronic technologies designed for domestic entertainment, this conflict has become ever more acute. Beginning with radio and followed by high-fidelity stereo music systems, television, video cassette recorders, and computer games, each successive wave of new entertainment technology has been seen by the more conservative elements of the musical instrument trade (especially the manufacturers) as a threat to both immediate sales and to the self-reliant, do-it-yourself philosophy of music-making regarded by many as essential to the long term survival of the industry.

The Structure of the Contemporary Music Instrument Industry

Thus far I have discussed the music instrument industry primarily in terms of the development of piano manufacturing and marketing. Certainly, though, the musical instrument industry cannot be reduced to a single set of characteristics, even when those characteristics are derived from one of its largest sectors. For example, electric guitars have arguably constituted a significant portion of the musical instrument trade since the 1950s, in terms of units sold if not in total dollar sales (guitars are generally much less expensive than most keyboards). With its employment of modern electronics and its focus on the youth market, the electric guitar has also been representative of post-war trends in instrument design and marketing strategies; furthermore, musically and symbolically the electric guitar plays a role in contemporary popular music that is as central as that played by the piano in nineteenth-century Victorian culture. Similarly, band instruments, although their technical design has changed little during the past century, have nevertheless occupied a significant position in secondary school music education programs for many years. The relative stability of the educational market has made the band instrument sector a staple of the industry. As these examples demonstrate, the developments in any one sector of the industry can only be truly appreciated when they are placed within the context of the industry as a whole.

According to a recent assessment of the size and diversity of the music instrument trade in the United States, the industry is a "highly fragmented business," composed of a number of product categories that are "in themselves self-contained industries with their own set of customers, trade practices, and challenges" (*The Music Trades* 138 [10], November 1990: 52). There are, for example, few links between the manufacturers of band instruments, electric guitars, or electronic organs: Each relies on different materials—from wood and brass to electronic circuits—different manufacturing processes—from hand-crafting to assembly-line processes—and different primary markets—schools, young rock enthusiasts, or mature amateur musicians in the home. Partly due to this specialization in manufacturing and market fragmentation, trade journals argue that there are "few, if any, truly dominant players" in the contemporary music instrument industry (ibid.).

Having made this statement, however, *The Music Trades* presents data that tell a somewhat different story. The top five instrument suppliers in North America—Yamaha Corporation of America, Peavey Electronics, Baldwin Piano & Organ Company, Roland Corporation US, and Casio Inc.—accounted for over 25 percent of total retail sales of musical instruments in the United States during 1989. Although the level of concentration demonstrated within the musical instrument trade is considerably less than that within the record industry—where the same number of companies control 80 percent or more of worldwide sales—such concentration is still, I would argue, quite significant. The well-known, Japanese-owned company, Yamaha, with U.S. sales in excess of $370 million, alone accounts for over 10 percent of all instrument sales in the United States. With its vast international holdings and a diverse line of products that includes pianos, organs, wind instruments, digital keyboards, drums, guitars, and sound reinforcement equipment, Yamaha is one of the only companies capable of supplying instruments to virtually all industry sectors. For this reason alone, it must be considered a "dominant player" within the industry as a whole.

Market fragmentation and manufacturing specialization is nevertheless a significant factor in the dynamic balance between large and small companies, which appears to be characteristic of the music instrument industry. For example, Roland Corporation, although it has total U.S. sales of less than one-third that of Yamaha ($120 million), specializes in digital musical instruments and sound reinforcement equipment and is thus a major force within the electronics sector of the industry. Even much smaller companies such as the U.S.-based Ensoniq Corporation, with an even more limited range of digital products and estimated worldwide sales of only $24 million, is still considered to be a significant competitor in the highly specialized market for digital samplers and synthesizers.

Market fragmentation may contribute to the relative "volatility" of individual market sectors: their response to fads, fashions, and changing musical styles, on the one hand, and their susceptibility to the influence of entrepreneurial capital, technical innovation, and unconventional marketing strategies, on the other. During the past century, ukuleles, accordions, and a host of other instruments (including the player piano) have all risen to prominence within the industry, generating huge short-term profits, only to disappear into obscurity a decade later. The guitar had always been a relatively insignificant part of overall sales within the industry, but the popularity of jazz, folk, and especially rock and roll during the 1950s catapulted the instrument to the forefront of the industry with sales in excess of 400,000 units in 1959 (Majeski 1990: 143–46). In an attempt to keep pace with demand, guitar manufacturers expanded production capacity during the early 1960s; but even their most optimistic sales forecasts could not predict the explosive impact of the arrival in the United States of the Beatles. In 1964, following the Beatles's first American tour and their national television appearance on the Ed Sullivan Show, over one million guitars were sold. Even market share among manufacturers within the guitar sector was affected by the popularity of the Beatles. George Harrison's use of Gretsch electric guitars gave them a market credibility that had formerly been reserved only for instruments made by Fender and Gibson (ibid.: 152–54).

The popularity of musical instruments is not only a response to changing musical styles or the simple result of market demand, however. The development of the home organ industry was predicated on a completely different set of criteria. First, some of the technical expertise required for instrument design had to come from outside the traditional music instrument-building craft. In the case of Conn, formerly a band instrument manufacturer, experience with electronics was derived from work on military contracts during the Second World War (ibid.: 142). Similar factors had contributed to the more general rise of consumer electronics, and especially high-fidelity audio equipment, during the 1950s (Read and Welch 1976: 343–52).

Second, no prior market existed for the electronic organ, so essentially sophisticated marketing and promotion led to the creation of one. The "easy-play" idea, already mentioned, became an increasingly important part of ad campaigns for the industry during the 1960s. A host of technical innovations—rhythm units, chord systems, automatic orchestras, and the like—were introduced to complement this basic philosophy. Organ manufacturers also introduced the idea of "trading up" to the music instrument industry. Formerly, large-scale personal investments in instruments such as the piano were meant to last a lifetime. With the home organ, each new year brought new models, features, and accessories with which buyers could be enticed into returning to the music shops. By the end of the 1960s, electronic organs were selling in the hundreds of thousands and had begun to rival even the piano for dominance in the home market (Majeski 1990: 159–60).

Interestingly, the same combination of technology and promotional appeal appears to have prevented the electronic organ from ever attaining status as a legitimate instrument within the more stable educational markets (ibid.: 163). These same factors were no doubt also critical in the ultimate demise of the home organ business as more sophisticated digital technologies were introduced during the early 1980s. Electronics giants, such as Casio Inc., shattered the technical competence and economic dominance of the organ manufacturers by introducing a series of low-cost, portable, digital keyboards into the home market. A newcomer to the music industry, Casio rose to the position of the fifth largest instrument supplier in the United States in less than a decade, based on little more than a single line of musical products. Meanwhile, the sale of home organs, which had constituted some 25 percent of total industry sales throughout the 1970s, fell to less than 2 percent of the instrument trade by the late 1980s.[4]

Such enormous fluctuations in the fortunes of the organ manufacturers must be understood as characteristic of the music instrument industry as a whole. The initial popularity of the home organ and the subsequent success of portable electronic keyboards are testaments to the power of large-scale capital investment in technical innovation and aggressive marketing strategies, when exerted within what amounts to a relatively small industry over all. For example, the entire retail sales value of musical instruments, sheet music, and musical accessories in the United States for the year 1989 was approximately $3.6 billion (by 1995, the figure had risen to $4.9 billion). Reflecting the size of the Canadian market relative to that of the United States, the Music Industry Association of Canada (MIAC) estimated Canadian sales at the wholesale level for 1989 at $284.3 million.[5] When such figures are put into perspective, the industry as a whole must be regarded as exceedingly small. There are literally dozens of Fortune 500 firms operating in the United States that have annual sales greater than that of the combined sales of the entire North American musical instrument industry. A standard joke among American synthesizer manufacturers is that sales for their entire sector of the industry are about the same as those for any reasonably large grocery store in California.

To a certain extent, because of the size and fragmentation of the industry and, perhaps equally important, because of the romantic ideologies of personal expression that have traditionally been associated with musical instruments, the hand-crafted aspect of the musical instrument industry has never completely disappeared, nor has the intimacy of the relationship between musicians and instrument builders. In Canada, for example, some eighty-five firms are currently engaged in the manufacture of music-related products (Allen 1990: 23). Québec instrument maker Paul Champagne, whose hand-crafted guitars are known throughout North America, manages to produce only about fourteen instruments a year; and Sabian Ltd. of New Brunswick, reputed to be the second leading cymbal manufacturer in the world, produces some 200,000 instruments annually, including a series of hand-hammered bronze instruments (ibid.: 31–32). Even instruments such as electric guitars and basses continue to be produced on a limited, commission basis, under handcraft conditions. Synthesizer designer Don Buchla, a leading innovator in the field since the 1960s who has worked closely with a number of individual, avant-garde composers, has eschewed factory production methods and works at what most would consider to be a "garage-level" operation. There apparently is a kind of enduring "fit" that exists between modes of manufacturing and musical performance that is almost entirely aesthetic and ideological in character: The musical instrument passes from the hand of the maker, as it were, to the hand of the musician.

In contrast, the electronics sector of the industry is among the most automated. For example, the Ontario-based company, Yorkville, a leading manufacturer and distributor of musical instruments and sound reinforcement equipment, uses a computer-assisted production system to cut labor costs and to compete in the global market (ibid.: 29). The dialogue between musicians and builders, however, continues to be important, especially during the early period of development for any new instrument. In the digital musical instrument industry, this process has become formalized, and professional musicians and recording engineers are often used as consultants by manufacturers during the design stages of new musical technologies or as "beta testers" prior to the release of new products. The character of the innovation process in musical instrument design is extremely variable, however, and can, in certain instances that will be described later, transcend such simple marketing strategies and alter the basic relationship between manufacturers and musicians.

The role of musicians as "part-time merchants" also continues to be an important characteristic of the retail sector of the industry. Trade magazines continually remark upon the unsophisticated, untrained nature of most retail management and sales staff; their pages are filled with the most basic "tips" on running a business. Often, manufacturers have had to bear the cost of training dealers, not only regarding how to sell their own products but in basic marketing and sales techniques as well. In the field of digital electronics, where specialized knowledge is often required even to operate the instruments, dealer training is an essential part of the suppliers' marketing operations.

Retailers and their knowledge of the needs of local musicians can, conversely, play a role in the process of technical innovation and in the fortunes of the industry as a whole. With most of the technical innovations already discussed the implied source of the innovations has been the manufacturers themselves; however, in his book, *The Sources of Innovation* (1988), Eric von Hippel argues that parts suppliers, distributors, and users can, under certain conditions, become the functional source of new innovations. During the 1960s, when guitar amplifiers had not yet caught up with the demands of rock musicians, retailers were able to fill a void in the marketplace. Building initially on their experience in renting and repairing amplifiers, shop technicians like Peter Traynor, who worked for the Long & McQuade retail outlet in Toronto, began to design their own amplifiers and speaker cabinets. The Yorkville manufacturing operation and the successful Traynor line of amplifiers grew out of these initial beginnings in a retail repair shop in 1963 (see Emmerson 1979; and Rowland 1987). The U.S. giant Peavey Electronics and its innovative line of sound reinforcement equipment appears to have had similar origins in the retail trade (Majeski 1990: 216–17).

The intimacy between retailers and the music scene may be a factor in the success of many individual operations as well. For example, Toronto musician and synthesizer programmer Jim Burgess made a reputation for himself by working with popular performers such as Stevie Wonder during the early 1980s. His musical expertise in the emerging field of digital keyboard instruments and MIDI (Musical Instrument Digital Interface) allowed him to establish what has become a highly successful consulting and retail operation in Toronto, called "Saved By Technology."

Perhaps because of this intimate, almost insular nature of the musical instrument trade (and despite the occasional successes of companies such as Casio), it has not been entirely easy for outside investors and business strategists to exercise influence and control within the music industry. During the boom years of the 1960s and '70s, large corporations viewed the industry as a potentially lucrative source of additional income. Corporations like Macmillan, CBS, and Norlin pursued an aggressive campaign of conglomeration and brought new, professional managers to the industry; CBS alone acquired the piano company Steinway & Sons, Fender Guitars, Gulbransen Organs, and a number of other profitable operations (Majeski 1990: 176–77). Popular music scholars such as Wallis and Malm have made much of this trend and have regarded it as a sign of increasing vertical and horizontal integration within the recording and electronics industries (1984: 282–84). In fact, the influence of these companies was extremely short-lived; within a decade, most of these corporations had left the industry because of their basic misunderstanding of the dynamics of the musical instrument trade and an inability to produce effectively meaningful product innovations (Majeski 1990: 188–89). Another hypothesis, I argue, might also be offered to explain this phenomenon: Perhaps the basic conflict between the producer and consumer ethic that separates the music instrument industry from the record industry made it unlikely, from the outset, that companies like CBS would be able effectively to manage such a wide range of manufacturing and market sectors.

Conclusion

My purpose in this chapter has been to set out, in as broad a fashion as possible, some of the particularities (and, indeed, peculiarities) of the musical instrument trade. Only against this backdrop—the continuing value placed on hand-crafted instruments within certain sectors of the industry, the interconnection of personal and impersonal networks, the striking changes wrought in manufacturing and marketing within the piano and organ industries, the unresolved problem of the producer ethic (i.e., the problem of acquiring requisite musical skills) versus modern modes of consumption (based on automation, reproducibility, and ease of use), and the fragmented character of the instrument industry overall—can the issues of technical innovation and marketing, discussed in the following chapters of this book, be fully appreciated.

I have concentrated much of this discussion on the development of keyboard instruments, especially the piano, for a number of reasons, some of which have already been noted. Beyond these reasons, I also must single out Roell's (1989) insightful analysis of the central economic opportunities and ideological conflicts within the piano industry at the turn of the century and its part in the much larger cultural shift in the nature of production and consumption within capitalism. In the following chapters, I argue that the application of microprocessor technology and the attendant innovations in instrument design, organizational structure, and musical use within the electronics sector of the music industry is a sign of a similar shift occurring during the late twentieth century. Roell's analysis of this earlier cultural formation is thus a key reference point for much of what follows.

There is another reason, however, for this concentration on the piano industry that is perhaps even more immediately pertinent. The use of microprocessor technologies in musical instrument design was first and most significantly developed for keyboard synthesizers during the 1970s and '80s, and, to a certain degree, apparently one of the long-term effects of this development will ultimately be felt within the keyboard sector of the industry as a whole. In a certain sense, the legitimation of microprocessor technology in conventional keyboards is taking place at a rate about equivalent to the pace at which it is currently usurping the traditional markets for pianos and organs, including the educational, church, and home markets.

In essence, microprocessors have entered what might be considered as a further, secondary stage of diffusion within the musical instrument industry. The economic theory of technological innovation described by Douglas Gomery (1976) posits that new technologies are introduced in three separate phases: invention, innovation, and diffusion. In Chapter 3 I will discuss the dynamics of invention and innovation in electronic musical instrument design, and in Chapter 4 I take up Gomery's model in a more explicit manner to describe some of the recent events surrounding the development of MIDI. The developments that will be described in both these chapters, which reached a peak in the synthesizer sector of the industry around 1987/88, were perhaps only the prelude to a more widespread diffusion of microprocessors that has become apparent in recent years. Whereas the number of acoustic pianos sold in North America, especially upright pianos for the home market, has been in a state of almost continuous decline since the late 1970s, the sale of electronic and digital pianos became a significant growth area during this same period.

In what must be regarded as one of the most ironic developments in the recent history of the piano industry, Yamaha has introduced a line of hybrid digital/acoustic player pianos—the "Disklavier" series—wherein a floppy disk and a MIDI-based control mechanism replaces the piano rolls of a century ago. Hoping to recreate the boom years of the pianola by bringing a new kind of consumer to the contemporary piano market, Yamaha has even conducted research into the nature of the early player piano industry and its marketing strategies. The expansion in this area has been significant enough during the early 1990s that the National Association of Music Merchants (NAMM) began to track sales of player pianos as a separate product category: By 1994, sales in the United States had reached almost $46 million.

Perhaps the most pivotal sign of this second stage in the diffusion of digital technologies, however, can be found in recent shifts at both the corporate and retail levels within the industry. Piano manufacturers have recently made alliances with high-tech music firms in an attempt to diversify their product lines and maintain their share of piano markets. The Korean piano maker, Young Chang, for example, has acquired Kurzweil Music Systems, a leader in sampling/synthesizer keyboards; the American piano company, Baldwin, has an agreement with the Ensoniq Corporation for the joint development of digital piano products; and the digital technology used in recent pianos introduced for the home market by the Samick Music Corporation has been supplied by E-mu Systems. The nature of these new corporate relationships was made clear in a statement made by Harold Smith, president of Baldwin: "They [Ensoniq] have exceptional digital technology and we have the ability to package and market a finished product" (*The Music Trades* 140 [2], March 1992: 133). Piano companies, at one time the dominant economic force within the industry and leaders in technical and market innovations, have thus become dependent upon outside interests to supply them with the technical innovations they need but can no longer create on their own. Meanwhile, they continue to concentrate on the things they have learned to do best: manufacturing, promotion, and distribution.

Retailers, on the other hand, have also become involved in this phenomenon by diversifying their market base. Shops that previously catered mainly to young rock and roll musicians have used digital pianos as a means of entering the lucrative home keyboard market. Traditional piano retailers, whose ongoing relationship with their customers was always based on servicing and tuning, have now looked to digital technology as a new form of potential income, based not only on the initial sale of the keyboards themselves but on the subsequent sale of peripheral devices and accessories (*Canadian Music Trades* 12 [4], June/July 1990: 30).

Digital technologies have thus become the basis for an increasing integration within the keyboard industry at virtually every level. Because of the central role played by keyboard instruments in the history of Western music, a better understanding of the nature of the new technologies and the dynamics of recent technical innovation is essential. Such an understanding could shed light on what may be a key historical development within the musical instrument industry and musical culture as a whole.

CHAPTER THREE

Invention and Innovation in Electronic Instrument Design

✳

In September 1978, a project was proposed: to design and build a high-quality all-digital keyboard synthesizer for the commercial market. . . . The proposal was motivated by the successful prototyping of a digital circuit that simulated 32 oscillators. . . . With a working example in hand . . . all that remained was to incorporate the device into a suitable package, program the desired features, and sell it. Initially, it was estimated that this process might take a few months. Two and one-half years and nearly one million dollars later, the resultant product . . . is available for sale. In retrospect, the tremendous number of technological, design, and production difficulties encountered make the original estimates seem appallingly naive.
(Kaplan 1989: 611)

The passage from invention to innovation—the process by which "an idea or a group of ideas [is] transformed into something that is sold or used" (Piatier 1987/88: 208)—is a difficult transition in the development of any technology. This passage has been especially difficult in the history of electronic musical instruments. Literally dozens of electronic instruments were invented during the first sixty years of this century, yet precious few could claim the status of an "innovation"; that is, few ever reached the marketplace, and fewer still achieved anything resembling widespread acceptance among musicians.

In some cases, the failure of these instruments may have been due to a simple lack of business acumen on the part of their inventors. Inventors seldom possess the business skills required to manufacture and market a musical instrument successfully, even one superbly designed. Technical innovation, however, is more complex than simply achieving a proper balance between brilliant design and shrewd marketing strategies. Every step of the innovation process—from conception to financing, research and development, testing, marketing, production engineering, manufacturing, promotion, distribution, and, finally, public acceptance—requires careful planning, coordination, and execution.

The history of electronic musical instruments, however, reveals that surprisingly little attention has been given to the problems of introducing technical innovations to the world of musical culture.[1] Indeed, you must read between the lines, so to speak, in most conventional historical accounts to focus on those transitional moments between invention and innovation, when the key issues of musical instrument design and marketing come to the fore. Only through an understanding of these issues, though, can you truly appreciate the difficulties encountered by the early inventor/entrepreneurs as the synthesizer industry began to emerge during the 1960s and '70s. The nature of the early industry, the collaborations that existed between individual musicians and entrepreneurs, the difficulties in gaining widespread acceptance for the instruments, and the limitations of the inventor/entrepreneurial form of organization are all important factors in understanding the rise and eventual fall of the early entrepreneurs. In this sense, the decade of the 1970s proved to be transitional: Although only a handful of individuals designed what amounted to a whole new genre of musical instruments—the synthesizer—and simultaneously went about the business of creating a new market for their products, another generation of entrepreneurs (and a number of large corporate interests) would ultimately reap the benefits of these early developments. In particular with the introduction of microprocessor technology into musical instrument design, momentous changes took place within the entire structure of the synthesizer industry. These changes placed the synthesizer manufacturers firmly within the dynamics of the contemporary computer and electronics industries, where a much broader set of technical and economic forces characteristic of late twentieth-century capitalism are at play.

Success and Failure in the History of Electronic Instruments

The standard histories of electronic music usually begin with a number of so-called "pioneers" in the field. The tale is a familiar one: Isolated geniuses exploring uncharted domains of science and engineering, inventing brilliant, unique designs for instruments with never-before imagined sounds and capabilities. If they are lucky, their devices come into some limited use among composers of the avant-garde (also cast as geniuses for their ability to realize and master the technical possibilities offered by the new instruments), but they seldom gain any recognition from the public at large. Their failure, when acknowledged at all, is often explained away with the banal comment that the inventor was "ahead of his [her] time." In most of these accounts, the term "innovative" has no precise meaning at all and is usually employed as a simple stand-in for notions of originality, novelty, or inventiveness.

For my purposes here, these tales are far too colored by a thinly disguised romanticism, by their overt admiration for extravagant individual effort, and by the hagiographic intentions of their authors; furthermore, few of these stories take into account the context of invention, for example, the accumulation of scientific knowledge and engineering expertise in a particular field, which often precedes the invention itself, and the musical, social, economic, and institutional forces that help or hinder it. When fully considered, such factors can often make the invention in question seem less the fruit of individual genius than the outcome of a particular interplay of social forces and local initiatives, resulting in an almost predictable (if not always inevitable) sequence of events.

Truthfully, the vast majority of these early devices were, from a practical point of view, probably poorly designed in the first place: idiosyncratic, incapable of functioning in any musical context outside the laboratory, or impossible to manufacture in a cost-efficient manner. Thaddeus Cahill's "Telharmonium," or, as it was sometimes called, the "Dynamophone," serves as a good example. Introduced publicly in New York in 1906, the instrument is often cited as one of the first electrical musical instruments ever built. Virtually an electric generation plant played from an organ-like set of manuals, the huge instrument required thirty boxcars for transport and cost over $200,000 to develop. Despite an initial positive reception in the American press, the Telharmonium was beset with technical difficulties and, furthermore, soon proved to be poorly suited to its main purpose: that of providing music to businesses and individuals over telephone wires from a single, centralized point of transmission.

Even if Cahill had been able to overcome the technical problems of the instrument itself, its potential use in any other, more conventional musical setting would have been highly questionable. Its size alone placed major constraints on its use. The idea of using telephone wires as a system of distribution, however, appears to have been technically ill conceived from the beginning. The wires were hardly capable of transmitting the strength of the required signal, and their use was, in any case, soon made obsolete by the advent of radio. Cahill's enterprise failed within a few years. The Telharmonium did not succeed, then, for two reasons: first, because of basic problems of cost and design, and second, because of Cahill's own limited perception of the role such an instrument could play in musical culture.

Another well-known electronic instrument of the early twentieth century was the "etherophone," more commonly known as the "Theremin," invented in Russia by Leon Termen around 1919. The instrument was small and relatively simple in its design, making use of vacuum-tube oscillator technology. The Theremin possessed a unique sound and playing technique: A pure, sweeping electronic tone was produced whenever the player simply waved his hands in the vicinity of two radio-like antennae. The mysterious playing method added an element of bizarre theatricality to performance and may have accounted, in large part, for the interest the instrument generated as a novelty device.

The same characteristic that gave the Theremin such a unique appeal, however, was also the main drawback in its widespread use as a musical instrument; control over the pitch of the instrument was awkward and imprecise, and the continuous glissando between pitches was equally difficult to regulate. A handful of virtuoso performers did dedicate themselves to promoting the instrument in public, of whom former-violinist Clara Rockmore was perhaps the best known. Despite their efforts, the Theremin was never widely adopted by professional or amateur musicians. It remained essentially a novelty device for many years, which is not to say that the instrument did not achieve a significant level of diffusion in this capacity. Ironically, the instrument's novelty status has been all the more reinforced by its occasionally evocative, though primarily anecdotal, use in science fiction, suspense, and psycho-dramatic films, such as *The Day the Earth Stood Still* or Miklos Rozsa's score to Hitchcock's *Spellbound*, and by its even more rare appearances in popular music as in the Beach Boys's 1966 hit, "Good Vibrations."

The failure of the Theremin to enter into musical practice meaningfully highlights the problem of designing musical instruments so that they bear no resemblance to any existing musical technology, thus requiring musicians not only to adapt to unfamiliar sounds but also to learn an entirely foreign set of performance techniques. Given the investment in time and effort made by musicians in the normal acquisition of instrumental skills, it is not surprising that new technologies are not always readily accepted.[2] Composers of the musical avant-garde have, however, championed such instruments precisely because of their unique sonic characteristics and their implicit rejection of past musical technique. Unfortunately, these modernist attitudes have also been somewhat dismissive of the need, felt especially among performers, for some form of common musical practice and a sense of continuity with their acquired skills, knowledge, and experience.

This point can be further illustrated by the Ondes Martenot, an instrument that bears certain similarities to the Theremin both in its sound generating apparatus and its sonic appeal. Developed in France in 1928, its inventor, Maurice Martenot, was apparently more cognizant of the need to give performers some kind of tactile and visual contact with the instrument. Through a series of design modifications, Martenot eventually arrived at an instrument that used a conventional keyboard plus a number of other, more specialized controlling mechanisms, which together gave the performer wide-ranging expressive control over the sound produced by the instrument. The inclusion of the keyboard, without necessarily limiting the instrument to a fixed pitch scheme, gave the instrument a footing within the experience of most performers and within established modes of composition and notation, allowing it to be integrated easily within both conventional and more adventurous forms of instrumental music.

The Ondes Martenot was never manufactured on a large scale; indeed, it continued to be made entirely by hand until the 1950s, thus limiting its potential market. The instrument was, nevertheless, distinguished among virtually all other electronic musical instruments of the period in that a distinct repertoire of music was created expressly for it, mostly by French composers. It also later found some use in film and commercial music in North America. The instrument is still taught and played in a number of music conservatories, primarily in the French-speaking world, including Québec. In this sense, the Ondes Martenot was more than a mere "invention," a novelty device for the production of strange, electronic sounds: Its fundamental musical characteristics, expressly designed for performance purposes, allowed it to become an "innovation" of considerable musical import, if only within a limited sphere.

From this perspective, however, the most important innovation in keyboard design during the first half of the twentieth century would undoubtedly be the Hammond Organ. First introduced by Laurens Hammond in 1935, the instrument became an instant commercial success, accumulating over 1,400 orders in only a few weeks. It was used extensively in jazz and popular music for almost four decades. The characteristic sound of the B-3 model remains one of the most sought after musical timbres among synthesizer sound designers.

Part of this success was no doubt because Hammond's ambitions were relatively conservative; he did not set out to create a revolutionary new instrument but simply to design a more modern and cost-efficient organ, primarily for church use. Not a musician himself, Hammond worked closely with W. L. Lahey, a church organist, and a number of the more popular musical characteristics of the early instrument were likely the result of this collaboration between musician and inventor. These characteristics are no doubt also responsible for the lack of attention paid to the instrument in most standard histories of electronic music. Although there is certainly some validity to the argument that simply playing an organ, even an electronic one, is not the same as making "electronic music" (at least not in the conventional sense of the term), I argue that altering the timbre of the instrument through its unique draw-bar mechanism, not to mention the later addition of percussive effects, vibrato, chorus, and reverb, is not unlike programming an early analog synthesizer.

Popularity, commercial success, and problems of legitimacy aside, the

Hammond Organ is important in the present context for a number of other reasons. First, the instrument is an example of what might be considered a kind of "transectorial innovation" (Piatier 1987/88). The primary technical innovation of the Hammond Organ was the use of revolving tone wheels, powered by a synchronous motor, as the instrument's basic sound generating apparatus. The synchronous motor itself had been developed several years earlier by Hammond for the purpose of powering electric clocks. The motor stabilized the pitch produced by the tone wheels, thus circumventing a problem that had plagued most earlier designs that made use of vacuum-tube oscillators. The tone wheels have been described as being not unlike those used by Cahill in his Telharmonium, but, because of the availability of electronic amplification, Hammond's wheels could be miniaturized, thus creating an instrument of reasonable proportions.

The fact that Hammond derived his idea for the motor-driven tone generating apparatus from a previous, unrelated invention, however, does not alone make his organ an example of a transectorial innovation; rather, the motor/tone wheel mechanism, reinforced by vacuum-tube amplification, embodies a characteristic wedding of electronic, electro-magnetic, and mechanical technologies that was common throughout the late nineteenth and early twentieth centuries. In a similar way, the shift from the purely acoustical and mechanical design of the early gramophone to the electro-mechanical gramophone of the 1920s and '30s resulted from the application of electrical principles to the powering, amplification, and/or regulation of mechanical devices. Understood in this way, the Hammond Organ is perhaps one of the most characteristic musical instruments of this transitional period in the history of technology—the transition from mechanical technologies to purely electronic devices.

Second, and more importantly, the simplicity of Hammond's electro-mechanical design made it both efficient, durable, and ideally suited to mass-production techniques, which reduced production costs and facilitated the development of the instrument for a large market. The significance of these design characteristics, however, lies not only in their economic value, for what Hammond actually succeeded in doing was combining two or more separate stages in the process of innovation. The tasks of conceiving a new technical device, designing prototypes, and then adapting the design for production purposes are often separate stages in the development of a product, each stage requiring different kinds of knowledge and engineering expertise. Hammond's approach to the development of a tone generating apparatus for his instrument fused design, manufacturing, and product-oriented criteria; in a sense, then, the tone-wheel mechanism combined a product innovation and a process innovation within a single device.

Third, Hammond was as skillful in marketing and promoting his instruments as he was in designing them. Although the Hammond Organ was originally designed primarily for church use (and, indeed, about 35 percent of initial sales were made to churches), it soon became clear that a more lucrative market existed for the instrument among professional musicians and, especially, among amateur players in the home. Through a series of product and marketing innovations—the use of chord buttons, the invention of the small "spinet" organ, the concept of "easy-play," and group instruction—Hammond succeeded in tapping and expanding the home entertainment market. The importance of these innovations goes beyond their simple ability to generate sales; for, if innovation is understood as a *process*, then marketing is one way in which the innovating firm establishes a dynamic relationship not only between itself and its market but also between invention and use.

Mark Vail (1991) has discussed a number of relatively minor innovations and design modifications that were introduced by Hammond's engineers in response to the interests of musicians, outside competition, and changing market conditions: such as the addition of percussive effects, chorus, and reverb to the basic organ tone. Ongoing design modification is critical in the competitive environment fostered by capitalism; every new innovation inevitably generates imitators and competitors, necessitating a program of sustained development and innovation if a firm is to remain profitable, a fact apparently well understood by Hammond. In recent years, patterns of competition, collaboration, and innovation have become increasingly complex, and, as Yasunori Baba (1989) has argued, such patterns within the electronics, microprocessor, and other key industries have fostered the development of what he refers to as a process of "continuous innovation."

A number of other characteristics of market- and technology-driven innovation can perhaps be best illustrated by considering some of the problems of marketplace adaptation of electronic instruments designed within institutionally based research environments. The experiences of the well-known Canadian inventor, Hugh Le Caine, are instructive in this regard because, despite the notoriety that his various inventions have received among composers of avant-garde electronic music, none were ever successfully brought to market.

Perhaps the single most important factor contributing to the character of Le Caine's productive life was his association with the National Research Council (NRC) in Ottawa from 1940 to 1974. Arriving at the NRC during the war years, Le Caine's early work was instrumental in the development of radar and other NRC wartime projects. With the security of working at the NRC, Le Caine was able to devote himself to developing a series of unique electronic musical instruments, at first in his spare time, then, from about 1954 onward, with the support of the NRC.

Le Caine's association with the NRC was also, perhaps, one of the greatest roadblocks in the passage of his instruments from the status of "invention" to "innovation." The contradictory aspects of this association were many. First, Le Caine decided to stay with the NRC after the war because he felt that he could best pursue his creative objectives outside the context of commercial imperatives (Young 1989: 29). Ironically, although this decision may have afforded Le Caine the freedom to pursue problems of interest to him and to produce novel designs for electronic instruments, apparently this strategy was not equally beneficial for producing a coherent program of instrument development. Indeed, Le Caine's output is telling: Of the more than twenty musical instruments and devices built by Le Caine, more than half existed only in the form of a single, original prototype. No instrument was produced in quantities exceeding five units (ibid.: 167–223); furthermore, only a few of these instruments were engineered on the basis of related principles, thus attesting to the eclecticism of Le Caine's approach and the lack of systematic, on-going development of any one instrument type. Even the instruments produced in multiple units often incorporated significant design changes, thus becoming a series of distinct prototypes.

Second, because of the institutional matrix of publicly funded research in Canada and the United States (and, to some extent, because of his own musical interests), perhaps inevitably Le Caine's work drew attention, initially at least, from the university-based music community. The first electronic music studios in Canada—those at the University of Toronto and at the Faculty of Music at McGill University—were established with the assistance of Le Caine and the NRC. To a large degree, these institutional sites served as surrogate markets for Le Caine's research, and, I argue, this association may have ultimately constrained his output as much as any economic pressures of commercial design. For example, among the instruments designed by Le Caine, biographer Gail Young lists a ring modulator that he built at the request of composers at the University of Toronto Electronic Music Studio. Young admits that the ring modulator had been a familiar component of radio technology for decades, that it posed no technical challenge to Le Caine (he built it himself without the aid of his assistants), and that there was nothing particularly innovative in his design (ibid.: 210).[3] In fact, Le Caine apparently found it to be a rather trivial device, useful for generating "odd sounds" at best (ibid.: 135). Although there certainly may have been a number of genuine collaborations between Le Caine and the university community, clearly positive interaction was not always guaranteed; problems of technical and financial support at the fledgling studios as well as the very structure of the relationship between the universities and the NRC appeared, at times, to reduce the latter (and, by implication, Le Caine himself) to the role of simple instrument supplier (ibid.: 136–38, 246).

More important for my argument, Young describes how Le Caine was, from his earliest experiments, interested in developing musical instruments for live performance. The electronic Sackbut, among other instruments, was the product of this desire. For the most part, however, composers of avant-garde electronic music during the 1950s and early '60s had little interest in live performance, and, as clearly implied in Young's text, they apparently ignored Le Caine's efforts to develop instruments like the Sackbut in favor of inventions designed for studio composition (ibid.: 107–9). In this way, their role as a surrogate market had a substantial influence on the direction of Le Caine's research as a whole, a fact he seems to have later realized (ibid.: 146). Ironically, it was the popular music market that would eventually prove to be most receptive to performance-oriented keyboard synthesizers like the Sackbut.

Third, designing one-of-a-kind instruments for a very specific and limited group of clients did not prepare Le Caine for the varied requirements of commercial production, making the transition from invention to innovation even more difficult. For example, when he designed as a hobby, Le Caine appears to have paid little attention to obtaining patents for his devices. His first patent application, made at the suggestion of a colleague at the NRC, was delayed for two years because of technical errors in the legal documents (ibid.: 58). Such oversights could hardly be tolerated in a commercial context where monopoly control over new inventions can be critical to the profitability of a corporation.

An equally important but more subtle problem for commercial operations involves the amount of time and money that can be allotted for research and development before a product must be brought to market, either because of internal financial constraints or because of external competition. By working at the NRC for his university clients, however, Le Caine often had the luxury of working on projects until he was completely satisfied with them, an immediate problem when some of his studio instruments began to attract the interest of commercial developers in Toronto around 1960. After waiting for three years for Le Caine to complete redesigning his so-called "Multi-track Tape Recorder," a keyboard instrument for playback and modification of pre-recorded tapes, the company gave up manufacturing plans, assuming the market for the device would evaporate before a workable prototype could be produced (ibid.: 123–29).

Le Caine later regretted this failure to address a larger market with his invention: "I was too much impressed by the undesirability of 'freezing' the position of the tenuous 'new music' at this stage, and I did not give enough weight to the benefits of making inexpensive equipment available to a large group of potential users with widely differing objectives" (ibid.: 128). Le Caine thus realized, though perhaps too late, that the design process alone does not determine how an instrument comes to embody, limit, or exhaust its musical potential. Indeed, an instrument is never really completed at the stage of design and manufacture at all; it is only made "complete" through its use, often in a variety of different ways and in different musical contexts. An "invention," that is, only becomes an "innovation" once it has been put into the hands of users.

Finally, developing instruments for a commercial market often requires consideration of production issues, even at the initial stages of design. The characteristics and limitations of standard components, ease of assembly, planning for maintenance and servicing, and other factors can pose serious problems for commercial designers that are seldom encountered within research environments (see Kaplan 1989: 620–21; and Rossum 1987: 21). This consideration must have become especially salient for Le Caine when, during the late 1960s and early '70s, he began redesigning the Sackbut with the intention of introducing it to the commercial market. By 1970, an arrangement had been made wherein a Montréal company, Dayrand Ltd., with technical support from the NRC, would produce and manufacture the instrument. Although the company apparently had a strong background in the marketing and distribution of audio equipment, it had little or no manufacturing experience, however. As a result, delays in creating a production prototype were immediately encountered; furthermore, in an effort to make the Sackbut cheaper to manufacture, Dayrand began to propose design changes that, from the point of view of Le Caine and the NRC, would substantially compromise the uniqueness of the instrument.

The evidence supplied by Young suggests that much of the blame for the eventual failure to produce an instrument suitable for manufacturing rested with Dayrand. They neither had the finances nor the experience necessary for the project, and it received low priority within the company (1989: 151–56). Although Dayrand's deficiencies may, in large part, have been truthfully described, Young does not adequately question whether Le Caine's design itself may have posed significant difficulties. Indeed, a number of the unique features of the Sackbut, such as its touch-sensitive keyboard, were uncommon at the time and prevented the use of prefabricated components. Too many such features would likely have made cost-effective production of the instrument virtually impossible. Whereas a high percentage of custom-designed parts may be acceptable in the research environment, efficient manufacturing usually requires that they be kept to a minimum. Adopting design practices that are sensitive to production issues at the outset can sometimes prevent the inevitable compromises that result from the post-hoc application of cost/performance criteria.

At a more general level was the problem of the lengthy, idiosyncratic development of the Sackbut as a whole. The instrument had been invented and redesigned during three separate periods that spanned Le Caine's entire career at the NRC: 1945–1948, 1954–1960, and 1969–1973. With each subsequent prototype (a total of four were produced by Le Caine and his assistants), not only were new features added but new discoveries in the world of electronics required that the entire technical basis of the instrument be substantially modified. For example, during this twenty-eight-year period, electronic components changed from tubes, to transistors, to integrated circuits. Such a protracted and disjointed development no doubt contributed to the complexity of adapting the design to manufacturing processes. Regardless of the responsibilities of the various players in the demise of the Sackbut manufacturing project, clearly everyone concerned seriously underestimated the difficulties involved in developing a production prototype of the instrument.

Ultimately, then, the most critical factor in the commercial potential of both the Multi-track and the Sackbut was time. In the competitive and fast-changing world of electronic instruments, most industry experts agree that a period of no longer than two to three years can elapse before a product must be brought to market. Balancing the pitfalls of launching an instrument before it is technically ready against the potential for competitors to gain an upper hand in the marketplace is an extremely delicate part of commercial decision making that has caused the demise of many otherwise successful and innovative firms. In the case of Le Caine's Sackbut, the competition—early performance synthesizers by Moog and ARP—had already made their market debut.

Synthesizers of the 1970s: The Birth of an Industry

The development of analog and digital synthesizers, and a corresponding commercial market for them, during the 1960s and '70s was largely the result of the activities of a handful of musicians, inventors, and entrepreneurs, often working out of small, make-shift laboratories and manufacturing facilities.[4] The relationship between musicians and engineers was especially important during this period, because through their various collaborations not only were individual devices invented but the design and operational characteristics of an entire genre of musical instruments gradually evolved. The early collaborations between composers such as Herbert Deutsch, Walter (now Wendy) Carlos, and Gustav Ciamaga (of the University of Toronto) and inventor Robert Moog (based in Trumansburg, New York), or that between Morton Subotnick and Donald Buchla (in San Francisco), or the one between John Eaton and Paolo Ketoff (in Italy), have long been understood in the history of electronic music as critical relationships that helped define the very nature of the analog voltage-controlled synthesizer during the 1960s.

The effort involving Moog, however, was critical, for Moog was perhaps as vigorous an entrepreneur as he was talented as an engineer. During the ten years prior to 1964, when he first introduced his modular synthesizers, Moog had already managed to pay his way through graduate school and make a reasonably successful living out of building and selling Theremins on a part-time basis from his own home. This experience, and others like it (not all of them successful), gave Moog a sensitivity to the marketplace that he might otherwise have lacked had he remained only in the service of the university-based music community.

Partly because of this sensitivity and an interest in popular electronic organs, Moog, from the outset, had no reservations about creating an electronic instrument with a conventional organ keyboard as a controller. Buchla, with his closer relationship to the avant-garde, was initially hesitant to take such a step. As popular musicians became more interested in Moog's devices as recording studio and live performance instruments, he turned his efforts away from the large, modular systems designed for laboratory use and toward the problem of creating a synthesizer that would be portable, reliable, and easy to use. The Minimoog, introduced in 1970, was the fruit of this labor and was eventually to become one of the most popular electronic keyboards of the 1970s. I will not describe the instrument in detail here, since it is well documented in both the serious and popular literature on electronic music (e.g., Schrader 1982; Vail 1993).

This popularity was not easily turned into substantial sales figures, however, for no real promotion, distribution, or retail network existed for the instruments at the time. Both Moog and his most powerful rival of the period, ARP Instruments (founded by engineer Alan R. Pearlman in 1969), initially had difficulty convincing music retailers even to carry the new instruments. The early 1970s was thus an important period during which the infrastructure required to create and maintain a dealer base and, hence, a viable market for electronic synthesizers was established. Some degree of legitimacy was apparently achieved by about 1973 when the American Music Conference began tracking the sales of synthesizers as a

when you've got the sound

you don't have to talk about it so much.

The instrument and "the sound" that started it all. The Minimoog was the first synthesizer designed for the popular music market and the demands of real-time performance. For many, it defined the word "synthesizer" throughout the decade of the '70s. Its "warm," rich analog sound continues to be the standard by which digital synthesizer sounds are measured today.

separate category in its annual statistics on the music instrument industry. About 7,000 synthesizers were sold in the United States that year, valued at approximately $8 million, rising to approximately 24,000 units annually during the latter part of the decade.

The development of a small network of independent dealers, often times musicians and/or engineers themselves, has often been ignored as an important factor in the early development, promotion, and distribution of synthesizer technology. In Montréal, for example, musician and composer Otto Joachim was an early enthusiast of electro-acoustic music and set up his own studio during the mid-1950s. He later became an independent dealer of electronic instruments in his spare time and, in this way, helped introduce synthesizers to the local Montréal market. Joachim and enthusiasts like him in cities throughout North America were the first links between the fledgling industry and its consumers.

Beyond simple distribution, the development of a network of independent dealers during this period had significant ramifications for design and technical innovation, especially during this initial period in which the new technologies were transformed into commercial products. Tom Oberheim, inventor of a number of polyphonic synthesizers, expander modules, and other devices during the mid-'70s, began his career in the late '60s building electronic devices for individual musicians he had met while studying physics at UCLA. Later, in 1971, he became a dealer for ARP instruments in Los Angeles and, in this capacity, had direct contact with many popular recording artists and session players in the area, including Ian Underwood and Frank Zappa, among others. It was, in part, through his experience as a dealer and his relationships with these performers that he developed an awareness of the possibilities of analog synthesizers and, equally important, the specific needs of musicians (Darter and Armbruster 1984: 96–97). In a similar way, though somewhat later, musician and electronics engineer Dave Simmons began his industry career as chief service engineer for ARP instruments in Britain during the late '70s; out of this and other experiences he developed his own line of drum synthesizers, which became well known in popular music during the 1980s (Anderton 1988: 77–78). Both these examples bear testimony to von Hippel's theory that the functional source of technical innovations is variable and that any party that stands to benefit from an innovation—as user, manufacturer, supplier, distributor, insurer, and so on—can be regarded a potential source of innovation (1988: 3–4).

As intriguing as some of these individual stories may be, the main focus of my inquiry here is the manner in which synthesizer manufacturing reached industrial proportions during the 1970s, thus setting the stage for the innovations in design and marketing that came to full fruition in the 1980s. During the late 1960s, the "industry" consisted of little more than informal networks of individual engineers and independent dealers working directly with a small number of musicians and enthusiasts. The instruments themselves were often custom designed and produced in make-shift manufacturing facilities. These networks quickly gave way to more formal structures of research and development, manufacturing, distribution, promotion, and artist endorsement. By the mid-'70s, dozens of manufacturers from a number of different countries, including Japan, had entered the marketplace, and synthesizers were quickly becoming an important niche item, carried by larger music shops in most major cities. A number of interrelated factors contributed to the character of industrial maturation.

Some of these factors are no doubt similar to those that occur within any industry as it moves quickly toward mass production capability, whereas others are more dependent upon the general nature of relations within the music instrument industry, on the one hand, and the more specific problems of technical innovation within the highly competitive electronics industry, on the other.

Undoubtedly, the most important factor contributing to the expansion and maturation of the synthesizer industry was the decision by a number of engineers and inventors, such as those already mentioned above, to move away from making unique devices to meet the specialized needs of avant-garde composers working primarily in institutionally based electronic studios and toward the manufacture of affordable, keyboard-oriented musical instruments that could meet the demands of live performance.[5] Among the more immediate effects of such a decision were requiring greater planning in product development and large-scale financing of manufacturing facilities. The various engineer/entrepreneurs responded to these necessities with greater or lesser success during the 1970s, but, ultimately, few of the engineer-owned companies established during this period survived into the 1980s. The failure and/or gradual absorption of these enterprises into larger industrial concerns and the displacement of the individual inventors by engineering teams must be regarded a key sign of the maturation of the synthesizer industry.

In the case of Bob Moog, the initial transition from inventor and entrepreneur to company president was relatively slow compared to the swift and far-reaching changes that overtook him and his company during the early 1970s. Moog had established the R. A. Moog Company as early as 1954 as a part-time business to make and sell his Theremins, and it only became a full-time operation in 1964 when he began producing voltage-controlled synthesizers and components. The company was not fully incorporated until 1968, and its name was changed to Moog Music, Inc., in 1971. The inclusion of the word "music" in the company name was significant since it reflected Moog's decision to design and market the Minimoog as a musical instrument for performers as opposed to a studio production device. In that same year, Moog first displayed the Minimoog at a NAMM trade show; prior to that time, Moog had presented his inventions at the Audio Engineering Society annual meetings.

Not long after entering the marketplace, however, Moog Music was acquired, in 1973, by the Norlin Corporation. Norlin had been formed in 1970 out of a merger between one of the largest music concerns in the United States, Chicago Musical Instrument Corporation (owner of Lowrey Organs and other successful instrument lines), and a foreign holding company, ECL Corporation, who hoped to profit from the phenomenal growth in the musical instrument industry during the 1960s. In an attempt to internationalize the company's operations, ECL installed professional managers and consultants at the head of Norlin. Few of these individuals apparently had any understanding of the musical instrument trade, however, and most of their investments and attempts to develop new products failed miserably (Majeski 1990: 176–78).

Initially, with the financial backing, distribution, and marketing structures of such a large corporation, Moog was able to concentrate on manufacturing and instrument development. Soon he was producing Minimoogs faster than Norlin could sell them and, in 1974, introduced the Micromoog, an even more simplified synthesizer aimed at a lower-priced market. Ironically, though still nominally president of the subsidiary, Moog's position had become that of an employee within the larger corporate structure, and, between 1974 and 1977 (when he left the company), he took a far less active role in the design of new products (Moog 1985: 36).[6]

By this time, product development at Moog Music, and elsewhere, was quickly becoming the province of design teams—a shift that was not simply the result of changing organizational structures but, also, one virtually necessitated by the increasing complexity of the next generation of synthesizer technology. The new instruments were designed for keyboard players, and, since they had achieved a certain degree of popularity, the innovating manufacturers had obviously created a market for themselves; but their continued success would be dependent upon the degree to which they could meet the escalating demands of that new market. The keyboard itself was perhaps a critical factor: traditionally, keyboard players held certain expectations of their instruments, and these attitudes placed a burden on the manufacturers to come up with additional technical innovations. Clearly, for example, the next generation of synthesizers would have to be polyphonic. The early synthesizers could play only one note at a time, and this characteristic frustrated many keyboard players who were used to playing polyphonic instruments like the piano and the organ. Some way would also have to be found to make synthesizer voice changes as quick and easy to execute as choosing a stop on an electronic organ. Programming new voices on the earlier instruments was often laborious and time consuming and, therefore, virtually impossible to execute in live performance contexts. Devising a method of storing pre-programmed sounds for instant recall was clearly on the agenda.

The problem of achieving polyphonic keyboard designs with analog technology proved to be formidable. ARP Musical Instruments developed and patented a complex polyphonic, key-switching design for their instruments that could play two or more notes at a time using a (not always musically useful) high note/low note system of priority logic. At Moog Music, the difficulty of devising a workable polyphonic design of their own using existing technology held up the introduction of the Polymoog for several years. Such difficulties allowed other entrepreneurial firms, starting from a very different technological base, to introduce innovations that neither ARP nor Moog could achieve.

The major breakthrough came in 1975 when Dave Rossum and Scott Wedge, founders of E-mu Systems, introduced a keyboard scheme using microprocessor control and a time-based form of logic. The design was adopted not only by E-mu but also licensed to two other young entrepreneurial firms, Oberheim Electronics and Sequential Circuits, for use with their instruments. Sequential Circuits had made its own entry into the marketplace during the early 1970s by introducing a digital sequencer and a digital device to edit and store synthesizer sound patches. The latter constituted a major step toward solving the second main problem associated with analog synthesizers. Its Prophet-5, introduced in 1978, was the first commercial synthesizer designed entirely for microprocessor control.

The introduction of microprocessor control by companies like E-mu Systems and Sequential Circuits was a critical step in synthesizer design. Not unlike Hammond's use of the synchronous electric motor to regulate the speed of the mechanical sound producing mechanism of his organs during the 1930s, these companies used microprocessor technology to stabilize and control the analog components of the synthesizer and to introduce fundamental product improvements that could not have been achieved using analog electronics alone. Though synthesizers remained, for the time being, hybrid devices—a combination of digital and analog components—the introduction of microprocessor-based technologies represented a type of "technological discontinuity" (Tushman and Anderson 1986: 440–41) in synthesizer design during the 1970s. This discontinuity should further be considered "competence-destroying" (ibid.: 442): The new technology did not build on the type of technical competencies already present within the established companies. This shift allowed the new entrepreneurs to gain a foothold in the marketplace, thereby increasing the level of competition and uncertainty (or "turbulence") in a young and already volatile industry. In essence, the introduction of microprocessors shattered the "technical competence" of the earlier designers of analog synthesizer technology:

I remember that the Moog engineering department was in up to its chin coping with the problems of getting the Polymoog into production. Work on that instrument had already proceeded for more than three years, and there was heavy pressure from headquarters (Norlin) to get it into the stores. To redesign the Poly-moog for microprocessor control would have meant another two-year delay and many more hundreds of thousands of dollars—which, as they say in the business world, was "an unworkable plan." (Moog 1985: 38, 40)

The degree to which the loss of technical competence and increasing market competition affected the industry leaders was staggering: Moog Music managed to produce a microprocessor-controlled synthesizer in 1981, but it was already far too late for the company to regain its former market position; Norlin was forced to liquidate the company in 1985. At ARP, which had become the industry leader in the mid-1970s, a combination of mismanagement, design error, and financial miscalculation led to the spectacular failure of the company in 1981 (Waters 1983). From the standpoint of technical innovation, the entire approach to instrument design at ARP seemed to be at odds with the pace of change in the electronics industry. According to one observer, "A major part of the company's design philosophy was explicitly to recycle circuit boards into new instruments, which left plenty of room for newcomers in the industry, unencumbered by outmoded components and concepts, to take advantage of developments such as microprocessors" (Jim Aitkin in ibid.). During its last years of operation, ARP attempted to design its own microprocessor-controlled synthesizer, but the company went bankrupt before the instrument could be put into production. ARP's instrument, the Chroma, and its design team were eventually sold to CBS/Rhodes, which did introduce the instrument some time later.

The importance of the introduction of microprocessors in synthesizer design was not simply that it led to the downfall of a small number of industry leaders and to the rise of another, more enterprising group of entrepreneurial inventors. Microprocessor control was the first step in the development of commercially produced, digital musical instruments, an event that would precipitate a far more important development—"transectorial innovation" within the electronic musical instrument industry as a whole.

Transectorial Innovation and the Musical Instrument Industry

In an essay published in 1987/88, André Piatier discussed the phenomenon in which innovations developed to meet the needs of a specific industrial sector come to play an important role in the creation of new innovations and commodities in formerly unrelated industries. He refers to this phenomenon as "transectorial innovation" and goes on to argue that it has become an increasingly important factor in the late twentieth century, especially in electronics and biotechnologies (ibid.: 212). Transectorial innovation leads not only to the creation of new products but can also contribute to the diversification of innovating firms and to a transformation in the ways in which industries characteristically organize their operations (ibid.: 223–28). Perhaps more important, the nature of recent transectorial innovation has resulted in a kind of technical interdependence, where "each sector has become more and more dependent for its own development on all others" (ibid.: 209).

I adopt Piatier's concept of transectorial innovation here as a way of understanding developments that have occurred within the musical instrument and audio industries since the introduction of microprocessor technology. Whereas Piatier focuses his discussion on the transfer of technology from one industrial sector to another, however, I expand upon his observations by introducing a set of subsidiary concepts: I refer to the movement, from one industry sector to another, of individuals with particular forms of technical knowledge and expertise as "transectorial migration";[7] and I use the term "transectorial marketing" to describe particular concepts or practices of marketing and promotion that clearly originate in one industrial sector and are subsequently taken up in other areas.

Evidence of transectorial innovation can be identified at a number of levels within the musical instrument industry, and its effects have been as profound and contradictory as they are varied. At the level of technology, the inclusion of microprocessors in musical instruments of the 1970s and '80s placed the manufacturers of electronic keyboards and audio devices in a dependent position with regards to the overall advancement of general-purpose microprocessor technology. At the same time, they had to develop new forms of technical expertise to create their own custom-designed integrated circuits for specific musical purposes. At an industrial level, these two complementary pressures have resulted in, first, a reliance on the general economic success and innovative capacity of the computer industry as a whole and, second, a simultaneous move toward product and market diversification for innovating musical instrument firms.

The capabilities of microprocessors—in terms of raw power, efficiency, complexity of device interconnections, cost, and availability (see Kahrs 1989)—have played an important role in the development of each successive generation of electronic musical instruments since the mid-1970s.[8] Initially, a number of polyphonic keyboards and sequencers of the late '70s were based on the characteristics of early 8-bit microprocessors such as Intel's 8080, Motorola's 6800, and Zilog's Z80. For example, the Zilog Z80 processor was incorporated into the design of E-mu Systems's polyphonic keyboards, Sequential Circuits's Prophet-5 synthesizer, and Roland's MC-4 digital sequencer (Anderton 1988: 44–45). During the 1980s, not only synthesizer control functions but their entire audio production pathways were designed as digital circuits, and this design created a need for ever more powerful processors. To a large degree, synthesizers and samplers can now be regarded as nothing less than personal computers whose operating systems and input/output circuitry have been optimized for musical purposes. Ensoniq's EPS-16 sampler, for example, contains a standard Motorola 68000 microprocessor, the same chip found in computers manufactured by Apple, Atari, and Amiga during the mid-1980s.

Similarly, as digital audio production has become the norm throughout the sound recording industry, the advancement of audio editing and processing technology has become heavily dependent upon the availability of powerful digital signal processors (DSPs). As a result, many of the digital audio "workstations" currently available from a variety of manufacturers make use of the same signal processing chip, the Motorola DSP56001 (also used in the NeXT computer). More importantly, plans for the next generation of workstations, which will integrate both digital audio and video, are entirely contingent upon the availability of even more powerful, parallel processing DSP chips emanating from the computer industry. It comes as no surprise, then, that periodicals devoted to audio engineers now contain articles eagerly greeting the announcement of each new development in computer hardware, with detailed descriptions of more obscure characteristics, such as math capabilities, interrupt functions, and the like.

Clearly, the use of standard, general-purpose microprocessors and more sophisticated DSP chips represents a potential constraint on musical instrument and audio design, since the overall capability of the system is dependent on the characteristics, power, and speed of chips already in widespread use and, hence, cheap and readily available in the computer industry. Such a dependency, however, can also be an enabling factor when you consider that the potential market for musical instruments and audio production devices is relatively small. The availability of off-the-shelf digital components is, in part, what allows technical innovations to occur in the musical instrument industry in the first place, especially at the consumer end of the industry where the costs of design and production must be kept under tight control: "This industry is far too small to innovate dramatically on its own. . . . Prices have come down I think mainly because we have been able to feed off the computer industry. . . . We're going to live off what the computer industry is doing" (Silicon Sam, a synthesizer engineer and chip designer, personal interview).

Consumer audio is another area on which electronic musical instrument designers have become dependent for basic components: "The whole CD revolution is what allowed the digital thing to happen and bring the cost down further because you could get D-to-A (digital-to-analog) converters at a good price" (personal interview, ibid.). The same is true in the digital audio industry where, ironically, the trickle-down theory of technological progress has now, at least in part, been reversed: "It is primarily the high volume of consumer sales which will justify the integration cost of circuitry, thus the professional's digital multitrack recorder will use chips primarily designed for CD players. That is the economics of digital design" (Pohlmann 1985: 22). Transectorial innovation, then, is a vital factor in the continued development of both the digital musical instrument and professional audio industries and, further, must be considered a basic precondition for their very existence.

The musical instrument industry is not, however, simply a parasite that lives off the back of the computer and consumer audio industries. From the outset, innovating music firms have had to commission or develop custom-designed components of their own to meet the specific needs of sound generation, control, and processing. For example, from the late 1970s onward, two companies in particular—Solid State Music (SSM) and Curtis Electromusic Specialties (CEM)—made a substantial contribution to the development of analog (and, later, digital) music technologies by designing and manufacturing integrated circuits (ICs) for musical purposes. Though more expensive than most general-purpose ICs, the application-specific character, degree of integration, and reliability of SSM and CEM chip sets led to their being used in literally dozens of products by a variety of organ, synthesizer, and audio equipment manufacturers (Anderton 1988: 46–52).

By the 1980s, increasing levels of integration and the importance of chip design overall in the development of the next generation of synthesizer technology made it inevitable that manufacturers would begin to develop their own expertise in the design and fabrication of integrated circuits. Large Japanese music companies such as Yamaha and Roland, and even many smaller (U.S.) firms such as E-mu, Ensoniq, and Alesis, have developed the capacity to design and/or manufacture their own large-scale and very large-scale integrated circuits (LSIs and VLSIs). Indeed, the market success of many of the smaller entrepreneurial firms during the 1980s has been based on their ability to innovate in the area of chip design and thereby create products with extensive features and capabilities at a lower cost than can the competition.

This newly developed technical expertise within the music industry has allowed some manufacturers to expand and diversify their operations into new industrial sectors and markets. In this sense, transectorial innovation has not simply been a one-way street:

That's one of the nice things that music does offer: because it is a technically competitive field, there is technology that does happen. You bring in some technology, you mold it and shape it and it turns into something else. But in order to do that you develop chip technology, hardware technology, software technology, manufacturing . . . all those things, so that if you are now in a position to see another opportunity you can actually go after it.   (Silicon Sam, personal interview)

During the 1980s, music companies did indeed "go after it" in a variety of ways. For example, Yamaha, which had established its own facilities for the manufacture of ICs used in its electronic organs as early as 1969, developed its design capabilities in the area of LSI (large-scale integration) and ASIC (application specific IC) technology to the point where, in 1983, it began to develop an entire line of ASICs for outside customers. In this way, Yamaha has not only been able to improve its own product line and keep costs down through in-house manufacturing but has also become part of the supply industry for basic digital components. During the 1980s, Yamaha chips could be found in Atari computers and in a variety of other digital products. Similarly, in 1981, Roland established a separate corporation, Roland DG (Digital Group), for the purpose of exploiting its expertise in electronics and digital technology. The company produces devices such as plotters, modeling machines, and other computer peripherals. Even smaller firms have used their work in music and audio technology as a means of diversifying their products and entering new markets: In 1989, Ensoniq launched an innovative design for hearing aids that, if successful, could give the company a foothold in the large and very lucrative market for medical technology.

To a certain extent, this movement within the electronic musical instrument industry might go beyond simple diversification. Piatier argues that the multisectoral aspect of recent innovation within the electronics and biotechnology fields represents a new kind of "technological strategy." Whereas firms might have once used technology as part of an overall "product strategy" within a single market, technology has now become the core of the firm, the means through which a variety of products can be developed for any number of markets (1987/88: 223–26). Support for Piatier's argument can be found throughout the electronic musical instrument industry. During the late 1980s, for example, Anatek Microcircuits Inc., a Vancouver-based company with close links to suppliers of integrated circuits for the hearing-aid industry and other specialty markets, entered the music market by introducing an innovative and highly successful set of peripheral devices for MIDI synthesizers and computer music systems under the brand name "Pocket Products." Similarly, Brother International, best known as a manufacturer of electronic typewriters, has used its expertise in electronics as the vehicle for a technological strategy that includes the production of computer peripherals, home appliances, and, more recently, digital sequencers for the amateur music market.

What is striking about this phenomenon is that, unlike the early 1970s when large, diversified corporations such as Norlin entered the music market by simply buying up existing music firms, the electronics companies that pursue a program of transectorial innovation do so by making use of their formidable technical expertise to produce a limited range of products for a variety of specialized markets at lower than existing costs. What Piatier describes as a "technological strategy" has been linked by other theorists, such as David Harvey, to a broader transformation in the nature of capital and mass production in the late twentieth century:

Flexible production systems have permitted, and to some degree depended upon, an acceleration in the pace of product innovation together with the exploration of highly specialized and small-scale market niches. Under conditions of recession and heightened competition, the drive to explore such possibilities became fundamental to survival. (Harvey 1989: 156)

Harvey argues that the technological strategy of these highly mobile innovating firms is just one of a number of shifts in the organization of finance, labor, production, and consumption that signals the arrival of a new system of "flexible accumulation." This new system has begun, in the so-called "postmodern" era, to displace the rational, bureaucratic modes of production and management associated with Fordism (ibid: 141–72).

Transectorial innovation in the electronics industries and the technological strategies it fosters clearly could not occur, however, without the existence of fairly large numbers of individuals who, possessing certain types of knowledge and skill, are constantly in search of new outlets for their talents. "Transectorial migration," then, has no doubt been an important factor in the proliferation of digital technologies throughout many industrial sectors. This factor has certainly been important in the field of electronic musical instrument design, where the migration of individuals from the computer industries has been essential to the development of an entire generation of electronic instruments and recording devices.

Perhaps one of the most salient examples of transectorial migration can be found in the U.S.-based Ensoniq Corporation, which made its debut in the music market in December of 1984 with an inexpensive digital sampler called the Mirage.[9] The Mirage itself is noteworthy for marking the arrival of custom VLSI (very large-scale integration) technology within the U.S. synthesizer industry. Its "Q-Chip," a sound chip originally developed for the video game market and further developed for the Mirage, is an example of transectorial innovation par excellence. Ensoniq's founders—

Sampling technology for the masses. Ensoniq took a marketing approach to designing the Mirage sampler: Start with the right "price-point" for the marketplace, then design the technology to fit the price. It also introduced custom VLSI (very large scale integration) technology to the American synthesizer industry.

Bruce Crockett, Albert Charpentier, and Bob Yannes—had previously worked for Commodore International and were largely responsible for several of that company's most successful products: the VIC-20 and the Commodore 64 personal computers. Yannes's work on the C-64 included the design for a sound chip that provided the computer's sound capabilities. After leaving Commodore in 1982, the co-founders planned to start their own computer company, but an overall slump in the computer industry made it difficult to find venture capital with which to establish operations. One of the founders, "a closet musician," suggested musical instruments as a possible alternative to computers, and, after three months of market research, the company decided that its expertise in custom chip design could give it a leading edge in the production of electronic keyboards. The migration of individuals from Commodore to the music industry was thus a clear case of technical expertise looking for a market.

Interestingly, in some of its product literature, Ensoniq does not even describe itself as a music company but, rather, as a "technology company." The company began working on a synthesizer but soon decided that the market for digital samplers would be a more appropriate entry position. At the time, even the most inexpensive samplers cost over $8,000, and the people at Ensoniq were convinced that, with their custom chip designs, they could create a sampler at a much lower cost. In the end, Ensoniq's Mirage was introduced at only $1,695. The product strategy employed in developing the Mirage was one the co-founders "brought with [them] from Commodore" and, as such, can perhaps be considered a form of "transectorial marketing." The team began with a "marketing definition" of the Mirage—a definition that had less to do with what the capabilities of the instrument would be than with what it would cost. Once the appropriate "price point" had been determined, it then became possible to decide what features could be included in the instrument and how they would be technically designed. The latter were certainly no trivial tasks given the economic constraints; the cost versus performance tradeoff inherent in designing a commercial digital instrument results in what has been called "an art of compromise" demanding the utmost creativity, sensitivity, and good judgment on the part of designers (Rossum 1987). At times, even Ensoniq's promotional strategies appeared to have been imported directly from the computer industry: When it launched its second-generation sampler in the late 1980s, it did so with a promotional campaign entitled, "Test Drive an EPS," echoing Apple's "Test Drive a Macintosh" marketing pitch introduced in 1984.

Individuals in a number of other musical instrument companies have also stated that their concepts of product development and marketing often come from their prior background in the computer industry. One reference that serves as a case in point is Guy Kawasaki's *The Macintosh Way* (1990). Kawasaki's book is a light, tongue-in-cheek history of Apple Corporation and a guide to the marketing of high-tech products. In addition, it takes an inside look at computer culture and some of its dominant concerns: the fascination with technology for its own sake, styles of management, the importance of user groups, and the like. The book's content, however, is perhaps less important than its status as a common reference point among a number of individuals in different parts of the music industry; as such, it offers insight into the diffusion of ideas and the workings of transectorial marketing.

The success of Ensoniq's marketing research and its imposition of a precise and relatively fixed "price point" at the outset of the innovation process suggest that marketing expertise may be one of the most essential complementary skills required of the innovating firm. Indeed, because of the complexities involved in developing products for multiple markets, marketing knowledge must be virtually equal in importance to technical knowledge as a requirement for transectorial innovation.

To a certain extent, this revelation is nothing new: Detailed studies of the innovation process show that identification of a need that can be satisfied through technological means is one of the first steps taken by any inventor or organization. In Wasserman's twelve-stage outline of the innovation process, for example, the perception of a need is the second stage in the overall flow of events, preceded only by the establishment of a basic body of knowledge in the appropriate area of science (1985: 9–13). Although Wasserman gives precedence within his overall scheme to the identification of a commercial opportunity, clearly this stage of the innovation process is primarily a point of departure that does not, in any necessary way, determine the manner in which the innovation will be realized. Later stages, such as the conception of the invention, theory of operation, and the development of prototypes, appear to be relatively autonomous; furthermore, Wasserman's outline, which breaks the innovation process into two distinct areas of activity, "invention" and "implementation," does not recognize the degree to which problems anticipated in production engineering might influence the initial design of prototypes or even earlier stages of "invention." Even in his more elaborated model, which explores the predominance of economic pressures on the process as a whole and of various overlaps and feedback cycles between stages, this influence is not addressed (ibid.: 119–23).[10]

Attempts to map the innovation process in more commercially competitive environments than the case study presented in Wasserman's work (e.g., Livesay et al., 1989) have emphasized both the scope and depth of market analysis required to produce successful innovations. Davidow's *Marketing High Technology* (1986) demonstrates that both the evolution of needs in the marketplace and the outside influence of competition have as much influence on the design of new technologies as the interests of engineering teams.

Most important for my argument here, however, is how the speed of technical innovation and the increased pressure to bring new products to market as quickly as possible have had an overall effect on the innovation process, the nature of the devices produced, and the relationship with the consumer. Most industry people agree that a period of about eighteen months to two years is the maximum time that a manufacturer can afford for the development of a new instrument. This time constraint pressures the innovating firm to compress and streamline the various stages of marketing, design, and production such that there now exists an overall fusion of these moments in the life of a new product.

Certainly, the design process is still divided, conceptually at least, into fairly distinct stages—from basic research to product concept, chip design, the development and testing of prototypes, production models, and so on—but, as I have already argued, at a practical level commercial considerations demand that production criteria be regarded at the outset. Such regard requires not only foresight in the selection of components that will eventually facilitate manufacturing (Kaplan 1989) but, also, consideration of cost/performance constraints in the selection of key hardware systems. Because software programming can be extremely dependent on the types of hardware in use, even initial decisions concerning the operational characteristics of the instruments can be influenced by hardware choices. For example, both Rossum (1987) and Mauchly and Charpentier (1987) have described how cost/performance criteria influenced their decisions on the basic approach toward designing digital oscillators in early sampling instruments introduced by E-mu and Ensoniq, respectively. In this way, marketing issues can impact even the most basic levels at which scientific principles are turned into product designs.

The nature of mass production in the hi-tech industries also poses specific problems, and generates particular solutions, in management, quality control, and delivery systems, problems not often encountered in conventional musical instrument manufacture. For example, the complexity of digital instrument design has led a number of companies in the synthesizer industry to adopt the management strategies advocated by W. Edwards Deming (Deming 1981; Deming and Gray 1981; Walton 1990). More sober than the attitudes expressed in Kawasaki's book cited previously, Deming's work provides a managerial framework for planned innovation and statistical techniques for quality control. Only recently adopted in North America, Deming's ideas have had a major influence in Japan since the Second World War, where he is regarded as "the 'patron saint' of Japanese quality control" (Morita 1986: 165). The Deming Award is one of the highest distinctions in product quality that can be awarded to a Japanese company. Similarly, to reduce the risks of overproduction in the highly volatile market for high technology, many smaller companies have adopted "just-in-time" strategies of inventory flow and delivery. The "just-in-time" system reduces the amount of stock held by the company and has been cited by David Harvey (1989) as one of the many strategies contributing to the rise of more flexible modes of accumulation in the post-Fordist period.

In terms of the products themselves, market considerations have created a tendency to introduce "families" of instruments with differing capabilities rather than individual devices. For example, whereas high-end synthesizers like the Fairlight and the Synclavier came in only one basic model, with the possibility of adding various expansions, manufacturers like Roland have used successive product introductions—such as the D-50, D-20, D-110, and MT-32, all based on so-called "linear arithmetic" technology—as a means of distributing design costs over a range of instruments. The technical and financial investment in custom LSI and VLSI chip design often constitutes the largest part of the design effort: It takes a minimum of ten to twelve months to design a single chip (a new instrument could contain several) at a cost of approximately \$250,000 to \$300,000, whereas it might only take six to eight months to design each new product incorporating the chip. To offset these costs, the manufacturer needs to anticipate instrument sales of at least 50,000 to 70,000 units. This method reduces the cost of designing the chip to a mere five dollars per unit, with fabrication costs adding approximately another nine to ten dollars. To generate sufficient returns and reduce the risks entailed in the market failure of any one product, the manufacturer might design chips that can be used in at least three instruments and thus increase the potential lifespan of the chip in the marketplace two to three years. Marketing also requires that hi-tech companies engage in an almost obsessive program of product differentiation to separate their own products from those of their competitors, using, for example, "creative marketing" terms such as "linear arithmetic," "structured adaptive," and "advanced integrated" to describe synthesis techniques (Mauchley and Charpentier 1987: 29). Additionally, as companies diversify their products for different segments of the market, similar marketing strategies must be employed to distinguish their own product lines from one another (Davidow 1986: 37–52).

Above all, the increased pace of technical innovation has resulted in a new phenomenon that has been described as "continuous innovation" (Baba 1989), creating various dependencies between small, creative firms and large, scale-intensive corporations. Evidence from the electronic musical instrument industry suggests that a number of the early innovators in the field have now become "innovation suppliers" (ibid.) to the dominant manufacturers. For example, the creative team behind Sequential Circuits has been absorbed by the Japanese synthesizer manufacturer, Korg, and become the center of their U.S. based research and development efforts. Similarly, Kurzweil Music Systems was purchased by Young Chang (a Korean piano manufacturer) to provide it with the technology necessary to enter the electronic keyboard market; and, both E-mu and Ensoniq have provided technology to larger companies such as Apple Computers, Matsushita Electric Industries, and Baldwin Pianos.

What is often ignored in this scenario, however, is that an increase in the turnover of innovations also requires an increase in the consumption of goods. Insofar as continuous innovation demands continuous consumption, the role of marketing and promotion has been both expanded and intensified in the music industry. The existence of "user groups," so characteristic of the world of computers and, now, electronic musical instruments, thus provides an essential vehicle for continuous, ongoing relations between manufacturers and a group of consumers that might be considered the "opinion leaders" in the diffusion of new musical technology (Rogers 1983: 271–311; Kawasaki 1990: 87–96). Marketing and promotion pervades both production and consumption in high-technology fields, first as a necessary component of successful transectorial innovation and, second, as a precondition for sustaining continuous cycles of innovation.

Conclusion

Electronic musical instrument design has undergone a series of enormous changes during the twentieth century. From a technical and marketing point of view, the idiosyncratic experiments of individual inventors have been superseded by a series of innovative designs that have attempted to combine electronic sound generation with the characteristics of conventional musical instruments (primarily piano and organ-like keyboards). In the early twentieth century, as I have argued, the Hammond Organ stands out as an unparalleled achievement: The simplicity of its design made it ideal for efficient manufacturing, and the conventional nature of its playing mechanism guaranteed its acceptance in the marketplace. To these advantages was added a simple yet powerful means of sound modification—the drawbar system—that gave the user direct access to the tone wheels. Certainly other succesful keyboard instruments followed—the Rhodes electric piano was notable—but none apparently captured the market for musical entertainment in the home like the electronic organ did from the 1950s onward.

Similarly, the shift during the late 1960s and early '70s from modular synthesizer design to inexpensive, performance-oriented keyboards changed the nature of the synthesizer as a musical instrument and paved the way for the later development of polyphonic synthesizers, portable keyboards, digital pianos, and MIDI. Certainly, composers of avant-garde music have tended to regard these developments as retrograde, as impediments to true musical "progress"; but it seems to me that it is precisely because of such "compromises" that electronic means of production have become a broad-based cultural phenomenon during the latter part of the twentieth century. Indeed, by the late 1980s, inexpensive portable key-boards had all but entirely displaced the home organ sector of the industry, and digital pianos were just beginning to threaten the most prized sector of all within the industry—that of the parlor piano.

The development of these more sophisticated keyboards, however, could not have taken place without the advent of microprocessor control during the mid-1970s and, later, of digital sound generation and signal processing. The complexity of the technological and organizational change itself shattered the competence of the early synthesizer developers and brought about permanent changes within the synthesizer industry. The magnitude of this technical transformation, in simple quantitative terms, has been described by software engineer Alex Limberis (1991): Whereas the Minimoog (introduced in 1970) contained about three hundred transistors and took Moog about six months to design, an instrument such as Korg's Wavestation (introduced in 1990) contained the digital equivalent of close to 300 million transistors and occupied some twenty people for a period of over three years.

What Limberis fails to point out, however, is that underlying these changes in technical design is an even more significant shift in the organizational structure of the industry. To a large degree, the days of the inventor/entrepreneur are over. The production of electronic musical instruments is today dominated by large corporate concerns where, because of the huge technical and capital investments required, product development is entrusted to teams of designers, engineers, and marketing personnel. In this context, marketing criteria have come to play an increasingly important role at every stage of instrument development.

The incorporation of digital electronics in instrument design has, furthermore, resulted in an interdependence between various industrial sectors, including the microprocessor, computer, digital audio, and musical instrument industries.[11] The impact of what I have referred to here as "transectorial innovation" on the musical instrument industry has been profound: The industry is now dependent upon developments in other, larger technology sectors for its basic components; it has used its own developing expertise in chip design as a means of product diversification; and it has become a site of speculative investment and market development for innovating high-technology firms from outside the traditional confines of the music arena.

Most important to me here is the manner in which these issues of technology, industrial organization, and markets have contributed to both the particular nature of the current generation of electronic musical instruments and to the simultaneous "production" of musicians as consumers of high technology. Indeed, the adoption of digital technology has had its own peculiar impact on the shape, sound capabilities, and uses of musical instruments and audio products during the 1980s. In the following chapter, I discuss two key developments that were both the result of, and major contributions toward, the digitization of music during this period: the production of MIDI (Musical Instrument Digital Interface) and the rise of third-party sound developers.

CHAPTER FOUR

Consumption and "Democratization"
Digital Synthesizers, Sounds, and MIDI

✳

The number of musicians who own these instruments has increased dramatically. Early last year I went to catch a Korg clinic which was put on by Chuck Leavell at a local music store in Asheville, North Carolina. As his final demo, Chuck played the Korg Poly 800 and blew the audience away. Here was a portable 8-voice keyboard with programmability and MIDI that cost less than a plane trip to the Coast!
The fact that the event took place in North Carolina should not be overlooked. . . .
Before then, you couldn't really buy a synthesizer in Asheville . . . but by 1984, the salesman knew his way around keyboard synthesizers, Chuck Leavell demoed to a hundred or so musicians, and suddenly synthesizers were a musical presence in Western North Carolina. That's what I mean by "democratization."
(Moog 1985: 42, 44)

There has long been a tendency to equate simple technical improvement or the increased distribution of consumer goods in capitalist society with greater levels of freedom and democracy. This tendency has been especially prominent in the blandishments of consumer advertising (every new ball point pen is hailed as a "revolution," in both the technical and social connotations of the term) and has been a fundamental tenet of marketing ideology: "Giving the people what they want" is the most basic, democratic principle of the marketplace. At a somewhat different level is, in recent decades, a similar popular ideology surrounding the introduction of new technologies. From the outset, microcomputers and computer networks have been the focus of a largely uncritical and utopian rhetoric of personal and political empowerment.

In a certain sense, these attitudes are the popular manifestations of a much deeper ideology; after all, the historical link between the emergence of modern industrial capitalism and of democratic institutions in the West is a complex economic and social phenomenon of utmost importance. As an ideology, the assumption that one form of "progress" cannot take place without the other has guided Western development initiatives in the Third

World ever since the collapse of colonialism. More recently in the former Eastern bloc countries, political reform, liberalization of the economy, and greater access to consumer goods are understood to go hand in hand.

It is interesting to trace some of the material effects of such a pervasive ideology. The development of the synthesizer industry during the 1980s offers a concrete example of how such ideas can contribute to both the formation of new services and industries and the definition of the operational characteristics of new technologies. At one level, the "democratization" that Bob Moog refers to in the opening quotation is related to little more than the breaking of the early price barriers that had kept the synthesizer from becoming a broad-based consumer item until the 1980s. During the late 1970s and early '80s, synthesizers were still quite expensive for the average musician/consumer—as much as $2,000 for a monophonic synthesizer, $5,000 for a polyphonic one, and even more for an early sampler. Added to the problem of cost was the fact that, given the limited capabilities of the technology, keyboard players often required more than one instrument to be truly effective in live performance or recording.

From a distribution and retail point of view as well, the market potential of synthesizers was still limited by the relatively "high-end" nature of the instruments. Speaking in 1977, Canadian distributor Marty Golden noted:

No traditional price pyramid has yet developed in the synthesizer field . . . it is not yet possible to find a really wide price range on synthesizers, the way it is with, say, guitars. Starting with the most expensive custom-made guitar, one finds progressively more and more merchandise, the lower the price/quality level is reduced. Only the very top of the pyramid exists now in the synthesizer field.
(*Music Market Canada* 1 [9], October 1977: 12)

The expansion of the lower part of the "price pyramid" took place during the early 1980s, in part because of marketing decisions made by synthesizer manufacturers themselves but also because of falling prices in microprocessor technology, improved manufacturing, and the entry into the field of powerful new competitors, such as Casio Musical Instruments, who introduced new digital keyboards in both the consumer and the musicians' markets. In the professional and semi-professional market, Korg appears to have led the way when it introduced a polyphonic synth, the Poly-6, at just under $2,000 in 1982. Other manufacturers followed Korg and developed new products for the lower-priced market, and, by 1984, Casio was able to introduce the CZ-101, a 4-voice instrument at a cost of under $500 (Moog 1985: 42).

The magnitude of this change in the synthesizer market should not be underestimated: For example, during the entire decade of the 1970s, the Minimoog sold about 12,000 units, whereas Yamaha's DX7, released in 1983, sold over 200,000 units in just over three years. Casio's successes were even more spectacular. Although a relative newcomer to the music industry, the Casio Electronics firm (manufacturer of calculators and other consumer products) had huge financial resources and a proven expertise in the production of microprocessor technology. The company was able to launch a musical instrument division in 1978 and introduce its first portable keyboards in 1980. Although its success in the marketplace was initially slow in coming, by the end of the decade Casio had sold some 15 million instruments—an accomplishment unprecedented in the history of the keyboard industry. Most of these instruments were sold through department stores, outside the mainstream music retail and distribution network. Because of this distribution method and because of its reputation as a supplier of consumer (i.e., hobbyist) musical instruments, only a handful of Casio products ever gained acceptance in the professional and semi-professional musicians' market. The more broad-based cultural role of Casio, however, is nevertheless important: By introducing low-cost synthesizer technology to the home market, it helped broaden the base of the "price pyramid" and has had an immeasurable impact on an entire generation of young amateurs.

The lowering of price barriers is only one factor among several that contributed to the spread of digital musical instruments during the 1980s. In this chapter, I explore two little understood factors that had a considerable impact on the growth of the synthesizer industry during this period. The first concerns the rise, during the mid-1980s, of a small cottage industry that supplies prefabricated sound programs for synthesizers and samplers. This industry is both an effect of the growing popularity of synthesizers and a contributing factor to it: By simplifying the operational characteristics of the technology and eliminating the need for musicians to become proficient programmers, the consumer appeal of the instruments was considerably enhanced. In many respects, the continued success of a number of recent digital instruments has been guaranteed by the widespread availability of prefabricated sounds. At an industrial level, the mutual dependency that results from this phenomenon needs to be fully understood.

Second, I focus on how the evolving synthesizer marketplace during the 1980s guided the design and development of MIDI (Musical Instrument Digital Interface)—widely regarded as one of the most significant innovations in electronic musical instrument design since the invention of the synthesizer itself. Here again, the characteristics of MIDI can be understood as both a response to the nature of the synthesizer market and a contributing factor to its growth during this period. In the second half of the chapter, I demonstrate how the stabilization of the marketplace and the stimulation of consumption was the main raison d'être of MIDI and how cost/performance (i.e., marketing) factors became one of the main technical constraints of its implementation.

Selling Sounds: A Tale of Industries and Cottages

During the mid-1970s, instruments with the ability to store sound programs (or "patches") in computer memory slowly began to appear in the marketplace. Since that time, in addition to internal ROM and RAM banks, a variety of external storage media such as cassette tape, cartridges, cards, computer diskettes, and CD-ROMs have been used. Although initially intended as a convenient way for users to store their own sound programs for instant recall during live performance, manufacturers also found them useful for storing programs that demonstrated the unique abilities of their instruments and thus acted as sales tools at the retail level. More importantly, the very existence of the memory chips and various storage options opened up the possibility for third-party developers to create and market sound patches to synth owners. This market opportunity lay relatively dormant for several years, however, for at least two reasons: First, the internal memories were quite limited, allowing for only a few sounds to be stored in the instruments at any one time; and second, it was assumed there was no real *demand* for prefabricated sounds. Users were considered programmers as well as players, and, following this logic, it was generally believed that they created their own, original sounds to meet their specific musical needs.

By the late '70s, this perception of the synthesizer user had begun to change. The story, as told to me in numerous interviews and as popularly known through various magazine articles (e.g., *Keyboard* 15 [1], January 1989: 68–69, 79), is that several months after the introduction of the Prophet-5 in 1978, the service department at Sequential Circuits began to notice that most of the instruments returned to the factory for repairs still had the factory preset programs in their memory banks. They thus assumed that the majority of users, 80 percent or more, were not actually programming at all but were relying almost exclusively on the presets. As instrument technology became increasingly complex during the early 1980s (Yamaha's popular DX7 is often cited as a case in point) and programming more difficult, the suspicion that most users simply did not program became even stronger. By the end of the decade, marketing departments were estimating that as few as 10 percent of users programmed their own sounds.

This estimation serves as a justification for the necessity and popularity of prefabricated sound programs and the existence of the tiny industry that supplies them. Indeed, the story has assumed the status of a legend, or myth, within the industry, its legendary status supported by the fact that the specific instrument and manufacturer involved often differs in the accounts, but the story essentially remains the same. The particular interpretation of the events has, however, been challenged by at least one prominent musician/programmer that I interviewed. During the late 1970s and early '80s, there was no copyright possible in individual sounds or synthesizer patches; the basis for it, in fact, has only recently been established in the United States (*Keyboard* 15 [2], December 1989: 24–25). According to my informant, he and other programmers would quite deliberately purge the memory banks of their synthesizers before sending the instruments anywhere to be serviced. It is possible, then, that many of the early Prophet-5 users were using the only means at their disposal to protect their work.

Which interpretation is correct is perhaps less important than the changing perception of the user that began to take hold within the industry from this point onward. As far as the manufacturers were concerned, programmability was still important as a status symbol for any serious, professional synthesizer; but ease of use and ready access to "libraries" of exciting, prefabricated sounds would increasingly become the basis upon which new instruments were marketed and sold. For example, during the 1970s synthesizers were often promoted with the idea that they could "create any sound that you can imagine." Both the imagining and the creating, however, were understood to be the responsibility of the individual user. By the early 1980s, in addition to the claims concerning the superior programming capacity of the new generation of digital synthesizers, they were just as likely to be promoted in the following manner:

You Don't Have to Program to Play
The DX7 comes with 32 voices programmed into the 32 internal voice memory positions that are ready to play at the touch of their selector buttons. . . . The DX7 also accepts plug-in cartridges that are loaded with even more preprogrammed sounds. . . . you have 128 voices at your fingertips without programming a single one.   (Yamaha DX Series product brochure, 1983; emphasis in the original)

In a certain sense, then, even if there did not already exist a market for prefabricated sounds, the promotional activities of the manufacturers and the rise of third-party interests certainly would have contributed to the creation of one. Changing perceptions within the industry were thus the first step towards the *production* of a new kind of consumer for digital musical instruments.

Initially, the main source of sounds for new instruments was the manufacturer. Each synthesizer was supplied with a number of preset patches stored in ROM or RAM and alternates on cartridges or other storage systems. These increased in number from only a handful of sounds to thirty-two, sixty-four, and eventually hundreds of patches by the mid-1980s. In some cases, these sounds were created by programmers who were part of the design teams themselves or by musicians hired as full-time product specialists for the companies. For example, John Bowen, a product specialist, and Dave Smith, owner/president and head designer at Sequential Circuits, worked together on the first presets for the Prophet-5 during the late 1970s; and Marcus Ryle, who created a number of the factory presets for Oberheim instruments during the early '80s, was also a product design engineer with the company (*Keyboard* 11 [6], June 1985: 28–32).

Although this practice appears to have been common, especially among the smaller, entrepreneurial companies where engineers often felt they had the necessary technical skills and the most comprehensive knowledge of the instruments to perform such tasks, it soon became clear, even to the entrepreneurs, that designing sounds was better left to individuals who had a more intuitive sense of what was currently most popular among musicians, especially session musicians. By the late '80s, most manufacturers of digital instruments recognized that the production of sounds had become essential to the success of their products—sounds helped sell synthesizers. As a result, they shifted the responsibility for the production of sounds out of the hands of hardware designers and into the hands of their marketing departments or to outside specialists.

To a certain extent, this procedure was first used by the larger, Japanese firms where product specialists and outside consultants from different countries were often involved, from the outset, in creating sounds for their instruments. At first, sounds supplied with some keyboards were different in the Japanese, European, and American markets; but increasingly an effort was made to standardize sound patches in all markets. Like popular music itself, sounds came to be regarded as an "international language" (ibid.: 32).

The role played by musicians in sound production is important: It is one of the ways in which even modern industrial capital must deal, especially within highly specialized markets such as the musicians' market, with individuals at the street level. In virtually every local music scene, the relationships between local retail sales personnel and session musicians, shop owners, recording studios, and instrument distributors are intimate and interconnected in complex ways. Through these networks of individuals, information is relayed back to the manufacturers. For example, Gary Leuenberger, who contributed to the factory sounds used in a number of

Yamaha's FM synthesizers during the early 1980s, was also a shop owner in the San Francisco area where his contacts with other dealers, customers, and professional studio musicians became a source of direct feedback on the acceptance of specific sound programs. This feedback was later incorporated into the creation of new sounds and into new product developments at Yamaha (ibid.: 31). Similarly, in Montréal a number of individuals associated with Erikson Music (a Canadian distributor) have had direct input into product development at Korg and, under the trade name of "Oktal," have created a number of sound librarian, sequencer, and other computer software products that are distributed internationally through an exclusive arrangement with Korg. In Toronto, Jim Burgess, synthesizer programmer, session musician, and owner of a retail operation called Saved By Technology, has acted as a consultant not only to manufacturers but also to the Ontario School Commission in developing secondary school music programs and teacher training in new technology. In these ways, local networks of dealers, musicians, and enthusiasts often become the source of innovative ideas for future product developments at the manufacturing level, on the one hand, and the nodal point for the distribution of new technologies and new concepts of music-making, on the other.

Activity at the local level, in fact, was apparently the initial impetus behind the development of a growing trade in sound programs during the early 1980s. Individual programmers working in studios or out of local retail operations began to sell their own, original synthesizer patches to the musicians they worked with or to customers coming into the shop. Around 1984, this activity began to gain a more national profile as classifieds and display ads for sound patches started to appear in musicians' magazines such as *Keyboard*. These early suppliers were often no more than single-person enterprises operating out of private homes and apartments. One early programmer and computer software developer told me that, at the beginning, he worked out of his home and would sometimes entrust his five-year-old daughter with the task of duplicating diskettes to meet the influx of new orders.

Independent suppliers of prerecorded instrument samples were among the only significant exceptions to this rule: Because of the costs in hiring musicians and booking time in professional studios to create original instrument samples, sample makers are more likely to be part of larger corporate concerns. Most manufacturers of digital samplers have, in fact, taken it upon themselves to record and release large sample libraries in support of their instruments. In Canada, the most prominent independent suppliers of sample libraries during the mid-1980s were Sound Ideas, based in Richmond Hill, Ontario, and McGill University Master Samples (MUMS) in

Montréal. The corporate/institutional base of these two enterprises should not be ignored. Sound Ideas was, and continues to be, a leading supplier of prerecorded sound effects for film and video post-production. The link here is interesting since the only real precedent for producing and marketing collections of individual sounds lay within the film industry, not the music industry. In the case of McGill University, the newly installed sound recording program within the Faculty of Music provided a ready-made technical infrastructure for such a project. The MUMS project itself offered a limited commercial justification for the program's further development.[1] By the 1990s, however, even sample libraries were being created and distributed by smaller-scale operations: the Roland Corporation, for example, works closely with no fewer than eighteen third-party developers in the United States, Germany, the United Kingdom, and elsewhere who supply sample libraries on CD-ROM for its digital samplers.

The majority of the companies dedicated to the supply of prefabricated sound patches for digital synthesizers, however, had extremely small operations and were obscure in origin. Indeed, one of the only ways to trace the general character and progress of this tiny, mail-order "industry" is through an examination of the expansion and diversity of classifieds and display advertising found in the musicians' press.[2] By 1986, for example, the section of *Keyboard*'s classifieds devoted to "software" filled almost three full pages and contained literally dozens of notices for patches—on data cassettes, cartridges, diskettes, and even printed sheets—for virtually every synthesizer available on the market, as well as prerecorded sounds for samplers and preset rhythm patterns for drum machines. Among the notices were the names of a handful of "companies" located, quite predictably, in the centers of pop music production, such as Deep Magic Music in New York City, or SoundCorp and K.M. Music in Los Angeles. A few had links to recording studios and/or large, urban retailers, such as Synthetic Productions and Patch/Works, both of whom had apparently gained the attention and support of Casio and whose patches were sold through Manny's Music Store in New York. Interestingly, however, the vast majority of the ads come from small, grassroots operations based in locations far from the centers of power in the music industry: for example, Patchman Music in Lakewood, Ohio; Patchworks in Roswell, Georgia; Mission Control Productions in Houston, Texas; and Synth Sounds in Auckland, New Zealand.

In addition to this ground swell of popular, small-time entrepreneurship, however, were a number of larger, more successful operations, which, by 1986, had begun to move out of the classifieds and to place display ads in the main body of the magazines. For some, such as Deep Magic Music and

MIDImouse Music, the simple, typeset, quarter-page (or less) display ads were little more than extensions of their own classifieds found in the same issue of the magazine. The ads of several other companies, however, such as Key Clique, Inc. (a clearinghouse/marketing outfit headed by programmer and Yamaha consultant Bo Tomlyn, selling his own work and that of a number of other programmers), could include elaborate graphics and lists of sounds that covered an entire magazine page. Still others, such as those for Symphony Series, Inc., included color photographs and sophisticated layouts that rivaled even those of the keyboard manufacturers.

By the end of 1988, however, this growing cottage industry apparently reached a kind of peak. Certainly, by this time, its existence had been legitimized by magazines such as *Keyboard*, which now included a separate category for "Sounds" in its advertising index, frequent reviews of sample and patch libraries, and a regular column and contest for patches submitted by readers. The brash, full-color ads now disappeared, and even the double-page spreads of apparently prosperous mail-order companies like Valhala looked drab, cluttered with their endless lists of sounds. A cover article appearing in *Keyboard* in January of 1989 (15 [1]: 66–77, 96–102) revealed much about the nature of this fledgling industry and its difficulties. One of its more significant observations was that the market for sound patches for a number of the most popular instruments had already become saturated. This fact had perhaps already become obvious even to the most casual reader: Classifieds proclaiming more than 3,000 sound patches for the Yamaha DX/TX series of synthesizers, 2,000 for Roland's D-50, 1,000 for Ensoniq's SQ-80, and 1,000 or more digital samples were appearing with increasing regularity. As competition within the cottage industry intensified, it seemed as if everyone was programming sounds for the same instruments.

The structural relationship underneath the sound production industry was, perhaps, more important than simple market saturation in the industry's difficulties, however. Third-party programmers could only ever hope to interest a fraction of synthesizer owners to buy their sounds; hence, their livelihood was ultimately dependent upon the success of any given synthesizer in the marketplace. In the volatile market of the mid- to late '80s, success became increasingly difficult to predict: "It's tougher now to target instruments that will sell enough to provide strong profit potential for programmers. As they see it, if you pour your time and resources into creating sounds for Synthesizer X, but the instrument bombs, the resulting lack of sales could wipe out your company" (*Keyboard* 15 [1], January 1989: 72). The structural relationship implied here is similar to that between computer software and hardware companies, but the problems are more pronounced in the synthesizer field because of the sheer number of competing keyboard "platforms" and the number of approaches to synthesis with which the entrepreneurial programmers must contend.

Much like the computer industry, though, if third-party programmers are dependent, in some way, upon the success of the manufacturers, then the opposite is also true. By the end of the decade, magazine reviews of new instruments placed as much emphasis on the quality of the presets and the potential for third-party support as on the hardware features themselves. This emphasis was made abundantly clear in one review of Yamaha's SY77, heralded as the successor to its popular DX line of synthesizers. Though the hardware and operating system enhancements were welcomed in the press, the preset sounds were disparaged:

This is where the SY77 falls short of its potential—Yamaha would do well to encourage third-party software. . . . Once programmers and third-party developers get a handle on the SY77's power (by reading the entire, comprehensive 255-page manual) we expect to hear some really dazzling sounds. Producers and keyboardists will find that sound libraries are a must because it takes so long to program "real" sounds.   (*EQ* 1 [3], July/August 1990: 77)

Here again, a third dependency, that of the user, is cited as a factor within the overall equation.

Another major problem for the sound "industry" is that there is no effective way of copy-protecting its products. In this sense, the programmers have fallen victim to the same local networks from which they sprang: Professional and amateur musicians alike trade sounds freely with one another, and local retailers have been known to give away entire libraries of sounds as an enticement to customers to purchase a big-ticket item such as a digital keyboard. Most of the third-party developers do not have the resources to pursue legal action against retailers (although a few have done so), let alone individual users (*Keyboard* 15 [1], January 1989: 69–71).

Despite these difficulties, the cottage industry that supplies sounds for today's synthesizers has apparently become a permanent part of the industry. Some manufacturers have developed on-going relationships with third-party developers, offering various forms of distribution and promotional support. For example, in 1991/92, when Korg re-launched its popular M1 synthesizer, it paid tribute to a number of its third-party developers by advertising a series of special discounts on their products with each purchase of a new instrument. Korg's telephone product support lines also offered information on third-party sounds and expansions. Indeed, the longevity of the Korg M1, which has become something of a phenomenon in a marketplace where new products were once introduced on a semi-annual basis, is no doubt based, in part, on the substantial support it has received from third-party interests. Sound patches numbering over 5,000, and additional samples and hardware expansions from more than a dozen major developers, have contributed to its success. Because of this enormous sound potential, the M1 has been described as a "chameleon," and musicians have embraced this aspect of the instrument.

At a somewhat different level, however, the trend among musicians toward the use of prefabricated sound programs must be seen within the context of the more general development of digital technologies throughout the 1980s. With the advent of inexpensive digital samplers during the early and mid-1980s and their increasing popularity among many musicians, most keyboard manufacturers turned their efforts toward creating methods of sound "synthesis" that actually used sampling in some capacity. Indeed, many new keyboards are little more than sample playback instruments. The DX7, which did not use sampling in any way, was one of the last true synthesizers to be developed for the commercial market during the 1980s. Until the present day, the quantity and quality of prerecorded samples supplied with digital instruments, or made available later on expansion cards or by other means, have become a matter of increasing importance to both the manufacturers and users.

Drum machines, which during the late 1970s had used various means of synthesizing drum sounds, now also employ samples of actual percussion instruments and often include a vast array of preset rhythm patterns (reflecting various styles of music) in their memory banks. These patterns can be freely combined as individual components within the rhythm tracks of a song. With the increasing use of digital sequencers (tape recorder-like programs or devices that record musical data, but not sounds), arrangements of hit songs can be marketed in the form of MIDI data that can then be manipulated or simply "orchestrated" and played back through virtually any synthesizer. This latter, emerging market, is quickly becoming an area of expansion and potential revitalization within the field of music publishing. Large concerns, such as Hal Leonard Publishing, a leader in music books, instruction manuals, and song sheets, have begun to develop a whole new genre of products, known within the industry as "songware," to exploit its potential. In virtually every area of digital musical instrument design, then, the coordinated supply of both hardware and software, in the form of prerecorded units of sound or music, has become an important facet of the industry overall.

Within this context, the growth of sound libraries and the cottage industry that produces them are a manifestation of two important aspects of digital musical instrument design. First, they are a sign of the essential nature of these new technologies: Digital synthesizers, samplers, drum machines, and sequencers are hybrid production/reproduction devices; that is, to "play" one of these instruments is also to "playback" pre-recorded sounds and sequences of sounds. In the overall history of the music industries, this aspect puts the digital instrument manufacturers in a position not unlike that of the gramophone industry at the turn of the century: Just as you could not sell gramophones without also producing and selling records, you cannot now sell digital musical instruments without also producing and selling prefabricated sounds.

Second, and partly as a result of this shift in the nature of the technology, the production and marketing of sound programs has extended capitalist relations deeper into musical production and, thus, signifies a new level of industrialization and commodification within the music industries as a whole. Not unlike record producers, sound designers and programmers must understand musical trends and fashions to create the kinds of sounds musicians will buy. Even hit record producers and engineers, such as Nile Rodgers and Bob Clearmountain, have been hired to create samples and sound programs by manufacturers and third-party developers. The nature of this second-order entrepreneurial activity is entirely in keeping with the organizational characteristics of the popular music industry since the mid-1950s, as described by Peterson and Berger (1971): Rapid changes in technology and market conditions have created a "turbulent" environment incompatible with traditional corporate forms of organization. Not unlike the record industry, the digital musical instrument industry has responded by shifting the burden of sound production to outside entrepreneurs and has concentrated its efforts on research and development, manufacturing, promotion, and distribution. Such strategies are also characteristic of David Harvey's (1989) description of the deepening of capitalist relations and recent modes of "flexible accumulation" in post-modern capitalist enterprise.

The Development of the MIDI Specification

The Musical Instrument Digital Interface (MIDI) is a hardware/software specification initially designed to connect commercial synthesizers together. It also allows digital musical instruments to be interfaced with computers. Introduced into the marketplace in 1983, the specification was initially criticized for its technical limitations, but, despite such criticism, the specification has become a de facto standard for digital instrument communications networks. The impact on the musical instrument industry and on musical production has been profound and lasting: The degree of instrument compatibility required by the MIDI specification has created a horizontal integration of the synthesizer market (Loy 1985: 20). The extension of digital control through MIDI to all aspects of sound creation, processing, sequencing, recording, and mixing has also altered the process of musical production for many musicians and called into question prior notions of musical skill (see Goodwin 1988).

In an essay entitled "The Coming of the Talkies: Invention, Innovation, and Diffusion" (1976), Douglas Gomery uses an economic theory of technological innovation to explain the process through which the Hollywood film industry converted to sound during the 1920s. This theory "posits that a product or process is introduced to increase profits in three systematic phases: invention, innovation, and diffusion" (ibid.: 193–94). This three-part framework is useful for separating different moments in the development of MIDI. The final stage of this process—that of diffusion—is especially important for understanding the social, organizational, and ideological conflicts that arose out of the effort to establish MIDI as an industry-wide standard. These conflicts went beyond the realm of simple profits and revolved around issues of democracy and the marketplace. They thus reflect a set of on-going concerns and confusions regarding the social role of technological innovation.

The technology of digital data transmission is not new, and, to a certain extent, MIDI is simply an adaptation of earlier concepts developed for interfacing computer terminals. For this reason, the first stage of technical development, the actual "invention" of digital interfaces, need not concern us here. The specific evolution of synthesizer interfacing—initially attempted in analog electronics during the 1970s—is perhaps more significant. Except for the evolution of an unofficial, one-volt-per-octave standard for pitch control on synthesizers, most strategies for interfacing keyboard instruments, sequencers, and drum machines were developed by individual manufacturers for their own products, with little concern about compatibility with the products of other companies.[3] Gareth Loy has described the period as one in which the synthesizer market was essentially "vertically integrated," a situation in which manufacturers could often count "on sales of one item of their product line carrying a package sale" (Loy 1985: 20). Users encountered considerable difficulties with the triggering of sounds and the synchronization of drum machines and sequencers whenever the products of two different manufacturers were connected together. In addition, the lack of standards increased consumer fears regarding product obsolescence (Anderton 1986: 1–13).

In part, these difficulties reflect the relative immaturity of the synthesizer industry during the 1970s. Bob Moog has described the problem of developing standards in a small, highly competitive, industry setting:

At the beginning, when the synthesizer industry was small and there were few competitors, all the manufacturers were developing products and concepts at a rapid rate. Their new developments were kept under tight wraps. . . . Now, whenever you discuss standards, you have to talk about future developments, and that means telling competitors what you have up your sleeve. . . . it's not easy to cooperate with a new company that's just stepped in and taken a bite out of your market.   (Moog 1983a: 58)

Before the introduction of MIDI, several manufacturers had developed their own digital systems for instrument (and, in some cases, computer/synthesizer) interfacing: for example, the Oberheim System, the Rhodes "Chroma" and the Alpha "Syntauri" (see Hammond 1983). These systems were proprietary, and none were intended for interfacing with instruments made by other manufacturers.

The "innovation" stage of musical instrument interfacing began in 1981. After a series of informal meetings between Dave Smith (then president of Sequential Circuits), Tom Oberheim (president of Oberheim Electronics), and representatives of the four major Japanese manufacturers—Roland, Yamaha, Korg, and Kawai—a formal proposal was made by Dave Smith and Chet Wood at the fall 1981 Audio Engineering Society convention held in New York City.[4] The proposal called for the creation of a "Universal Synthesizer Interface" (USI; Smith and Wood 1981). This action was followed by a meeting of major American and Japanese synthesizer manufacturers at the January 1982 National Association of Music Merchants (NAMM) convention in Anaheim, California, to discuss the possibilities for developing such a device. Differences among the participants arose around defining the optimum technical capabilities of the interface and, more importantly, the cost of its implementation. Most of the American companies, including Oberheim, opted out of further negotiations, and Sequential Circuits and the four Japanese companies were left actually to develop the technical specification. A working specification was developed in 1982, and the first MIDI-equipped instruments were introduced in the winter of 1983 by Sequential and Roland.[5] Because of continuing difficulties with technical incompatibilities, the final version of the interface—the "MIDI Specification 1.0"—was not agreed upon until August 1983.

There are a number of notable points concerning this stage of the development of MIDI. First, the "innovative" aspect of MIDI was that it was planned as a nonproprietary device (no one owns a patent for either the hardware or the software portions of MIDI) to be used on any digital instrument, regardless of manufacturer, thus setting a major precedent within the synthesizer industry. Second, the main source of conflict concerning the specification during the early stage of negotiations was over where the line between technical sophistication and cost of implementation would be drawn. Third, there existed no forum for the resolution of differences between the various parties; the lack of one would become a critical element during the next stage of MIDI's development.[6] Finally, the initial success of MIDI was apparently based, in large part, on the combined weight in the marketplace of a number of major companies working in consort. The combined influence of the Japanese companies is especially noteworthy in this regard.

Each of these points requires some further elaboration. The nonproprietary nature of MIDI should not be regarded as insignificant: Without the initial joint decision that no one should profit directly from the development of MIDI, the necessary trust, cooperation, and good will between the participating companies could not have been guaranteed. Patents have long been an accepted (and central) aspect of technological innovation because they allow individuals and corporations to control and profit from new inventions (Slack 1984: 95–137). Today, however, an important overriding motivation spurs the desire for cooperation: Recent technological change, especially within the audio, electronics, and computer industries, has been so rapid that voluntary technical standards have become more and more necessary, if only as a means of stabilizing the marketplace. As noted previously, prior to the introduction of MIDI, consumers were apparently becoming hesitant because of technical incompatibilities and obsolescence. Dave Smith has stated that, from the outset, the companies involved in MIDI's early development realized that an interface could help stimulate the market (personal interview, 1988). It is now generally recognized that MIDI has been a major contributing factor in the growth of digital musical instrument sales to their current billion dollar levels worldwide. Foregoing patent benefits and acceptance of increased competition as a result of the horizontal integration of the market would thus seem to have been more than offset by the advantages of increased consumption overall.

Although I do not wish to go into detail here concerning the debates over the technical limitations of MIDI, it is worth noting that much of the difficulty arose out of different intentions and expectations regarding the interface.[7] Electronic music historian Tom Rhea maintains that the initial idea of simply connecting keyboard instruments to one another was "mundane, predicated on equal temperament, and has shackled the development of wind and other continuous controllers" (personal interview, 1989). Others have criticized the limitations of the serial interface for highspeed transmission of digital information. In fairness to the developers of the specification, however, the synthesizer field has been dominated, almost from the beginning, by keyboard instruments. Even high-end systems such as the Synclavier and the Fairlight made use of standard key-

the new prophet $1995

Prophetic in more ways than one. Designed during the context of lowering prices and market expansion of the early 1980s, the Prophet-600 was Sequential Circuits' low-cost successor to its popular Prophet-5 polyphonic synthesizer. It was also the first synthesizer equipped with MIDI (Musical Instrument Digital Interface).

boards. It should therefore not be surprising that keyboards would be the main beneficiary of a commercial interface; furthermore, many of the uses to which MIDI has recently been put were simply not foreseen in 1983. For example, no one foresaw the current importance of SMPTE synchronization (the standard synchronization method used in film and television post-production and approved by the Society of Motion Picture and Television Engineers) in MIDI studios.

Of course, the main issue was never really one of foresight but, rather, one of cost:

From the equipment manufacturer's point of view, the hardware of a musical instrument interface should be as inexpensive as possible. In particular, the connectors should cost about the same as the phone plugs which are now universally used in our industry for audio signal interconnection.   (Moog 1983b: 19)

The attitude expressed in this statement indicates the severe economic limitations quite likely placed upon the development of the MIDI specification by the innovating manufacturers themselves. In the end, the MIDI interface added approximately twenty-five dollars to the price of a digital synthesizer (ibid.: 25).

The market context of this pricing strategy is often ignored in discussions of MIDI. At the time of its introduction, a number of manufacturers were consciously attempting to lower the prices of their products to develop a larger consumer base. A prime example of the period is the popular DX7, introduced by Yamaha in 1983 at a fraction of the cost of its earlier FM synthesizers. Bob Moog has described this general trend toward lowering the price of microprocessor-controlled synthesizers and samplers during the early 1980s as the "democratization" of the technology (Moog 1985: 42–46). Similarly, supporters of MIDI often labeled those in favor of a technically more sophisticated and, inevitably, more expensive interface as "elitist." Note how the particular notion of "democracy"—conflated with marketing strategies—is expressed in such statements.

Although the innovation stage of MIDI's development was achieved essentially through close, relatively informal cooperation between a handful of manufacturers, the diffusion of MIDI would require a more formal organization to disseminate technical information about MIDI, answer questions from instrument and software manufacturers concerning implementation, solve problems of incompatibility, continue the work of clarifying aspects of the specification that were still relatively undefined, and deal with problems encountered by users. As criticism of the interface mounted, the need for such an organization became even greater. To make matters worse, during the first year of MIDI, Yamaha accidentally misinterpreted part of the new specification, and soon rumors and accusations were heard among the competition concerning an alleged attempt by Yamaha to use its market strength to define unilaterally the development of MIDI (Milano 1984: 42–43).

It was at this particular, chaotic moment in the early "diffusion stage" of MIDI's development that the phenomenon of user groups and networks became significant. Before the industry could mobilize itself to deal in a coherent fashion with the technical problems encountered with implementing the interface, a "users' group" calling itself the International MIDI Association (IMA)—"dedicated to the growth, development, integrity, and promotion of the Musical Instrument Digital Interface (MIDI) and musical/computer interfacing" (IMA information brochure, 1.0)—was formed during the summer of 1983. Whereas the primary function of the IMA was to disseminate information about MIDI to users (including not only "end users" but also retailers, educators, software designers, and manufacturers), its founder, Roger Clay, had far more important plans for the organization. For the moment, however, I reserve my discussion of the IMA and the role Clay envisioned for the organization for Chapter 6, where I take up the phenomenon of user groups in greater detail.

Conclusion

What Bob Moog has referred to as the "democratization" of synthesizer technology (1985: 42) is a phenomenon based on at least three separate, though interrelated, trends in the electronic musical instrument industry. First, as microprocessor technology became faster and cheaper, it became possible for synthesizer manufacturers to make powerful systems at lower costs. The broadening of the so-called "price pyramid" allowed more musicians and amateurs to become involved with sound synthesis than ever before. Decreasing costs, however, was only the first step toward building a substantial consumer market for synthesizer technology.

The changing character of the instruments themselves also became a factor in the creation of a new kind of consumer. As microprocessors began to be used not only as audio control mechanisms but also for the digital generation of tones, synthesizer programming became increasingly complex. This complexity could easily have become a limiting factor for the potential market; but, with the simultaneous expansion of internal and external memory storage, synthesizers could function not only as instruments for the production of sounds but also for their *re*-production:

> Creating musically useful tone colors with digital synthesis algorithms poses some difficulties. . . . The DX7 appears to be popular not because it is easy to program but because it comes with a large number of good-sounding factory programs, and because there are several sound programmers who sell DX7 sounds by the cartridge. Most DX7 users never manage to master the programming aspect of their instruments. For musicians, the relative inaccessibility of the handles on the tone colors of digital synthesis instruments is a problem yet to be solved.   (ibid.: 44, 46)

Lacking adequate knowledge of the technical system, musicians increasingly found themselves drawn to prefabricated programs as a source of new sound material. As I have argued, however, this assertion is not simply a statement of fact; it also suggests a reconceptualization on the part of the industry of the musician as a particular type of consumer. Synthesizer manufacturers responded to this new vision of the musician-as-consumer by placing an increased emphasis on the availability of prefabricated sounds. As a result of the entrepreneurial initiative of third-party developers, a small, subindustry structure—a so-called "cottage industry"—evolved to meet the needs of this new market.

Finally, the introduction of the MIDI specification contributed to an increased compatibility between instruments by different manufacturers, thus stabilizing the marketplace and strengthening consumer confidence. In an industry driven by the need for continuous innovation, the importance of the kind of standardization offered by MIDI should not be underestimated. MIDI has helped overcome consumer hesitation based on immediate problems of incompatibility and the fear of technical obsolescence over time. By creating a standard protocol for communications not only between synthesizers but between synthesizers and computers as well, MIDI has become a vehicle for the growth of an entire generation of software products dedicated to music production. The context of falling prices and market expansion within the synthesizer industry was an important factor in the concept and design of MIDI; from the outset, market criteria (in the form of cost/performance measures) guided the development of MIDI, defining its form and its technical capabilities. Although various proposals have been made over the years for replacing MIDI with more powerful interfacing schemes, the manufacturers have made it clear that they will have no part in such deliberations; they realize that market perception of the stability of the MIDI specification is more important than its technical inadequacies.

These three developments have been important in the expansion of the market for digital instruments throughout the 1980s and '90s. None of these developments, alone or in consort, however, could have been sufficient to create the momentum necessary to achieve the kind of widespread acceptance that the new technologies have enjoyed during the past decade; various forms of communication have played an important promotional role vis-à-vis the electronic musical instrument industry. Musicians are a small and highly specialized group of consumers, and the musicians' press, in particular, has been a vital link between the industry and its market. As synthesizer technology has become integrated with the home computer, the types of association typical of computer culture—computer networks and so-called "user groups"—have been adopted by some musicians as well. Musicians' magazines, networks, and user groups foster a particular kind of group identity and a sense of "community," on the one hand, seemingly democratic and idealistic and, on the other, curiously bound to an identification with particular objects of consumption. The latter has helped bring these groups into even more direct contact with manufacturers and their marketing departments. Taken together, these forms of mediation have had a profound impact on how musicians perceive the new technologies, on how they learn to use them—both technically and in the kinds of pleasure they derive from their use—and, indeed, on how they define themselves and their collective goals as musicians. I now turn to this cluster of issues.

PART TWO

✳

MEDIATION: MUSICIANS'
MAGAZINES, NETWORKS,
AND USER GROUPS

✳

CHAPTER FIVE

Music Periodicals, the Instrument Industry, and the Musicians' Community

✳

With a view of promoting more general intelligence in musical matters—both theoretical, practical, and social—it has occurred that the periodical publication of a Journal for the Free Discussion of every matter of Musical interest, as well as for the exposition of Canadian Art, must prove acceptable to numerous musical devotees. . . . [The journal will contain printed music and] Selected Articles on the various branches of Music, Correspondence and Reviews of Music—the latter so arranged that parties purchasing Music may rely upon being able to select it, on reference to the Review, without any hesitation as to its merits or difficulties.
(*Canadian Musical Review* 1 [1], May 1, 1865: 1; reprinted in Kallmann et al. 1981: 742)

The *Canadian Musical Review* was the first Canadian periodical devoted exclusively to music and, from the outset, its "Prospectus" made clear its musical, social, and economic goals: to become a medium of communication on the dissemination and discussion of music, to create a sense of national identity through awareness of cultural production, and, not least, to provide an authoritative source of information for consumers of musical products. This latter goal was a prominent feature of even the first issue; advertisements selling musical instruments, practical instruction manuals, and mechanical music boxes filled its pages.

Early music periodicals like the *Canadian Musical Review* are often regarded by historians as important, though sometimes problematic, sources of information on the musical life of a society. They supply the historian with facts and insights into the music and society of the past, but they are also often regional, unsystematic, and lacking in historical perspective (Kallmann 1960: 195). Given that specialized periodicals have been an indispensable part of musical life since the eighteenth century, however, it is surprising that so little scholarship has been devoted to music magazines themselves as a specialized subgenre of the publishing industry. The role played by music periodicals in the formation and dissemination of musical ideas, aesthetics, and ideology, in the creation and maintenance of musical communities or "taste publics," and in the marketing, promotion, and sale of printed music and musical instruments has scarcely been acknowledged by traditional musicologists, let alone understood.[1]

By and large, popular music scholars have paid more attention to the music press and its relationship to the recording industry, but much of this work has been neither systematic nor self-reflective. Much of the scholarly work that does exist has focused almost exclusively on the role of the "charts" in the record industry trade magazines, such as *Billboard*, or on the role of mass-circulation consumer magazines, such as *Rolling Stone*, in the formation of rock music ideology.[2]

Dave Laing's account of the rise of punk music (1985) and Sarah Thornton's more recent exploration of dance club cultures (1994, 1996) are among the few studies of popular music that treat the music press as an integral part of musical/cultural processes. For Laing, punk "fanzines" were the print equivalent of independent record labels and needed to be understood in relation to discursive formations largely determined by institutions such as the record industry and the mainstream music press. Thornton offers an even more nuanced and layered analysis of the various roles played by both print and broadcast media in the formation of youth subcultures. Thornton finds no inherent opposition between media and subcultures. In her analysis, a variety of media, from word of mouth to street flyers, listings, and fanzines, to the music press and the national mass media, all contribute to the organization, construction, and development of dance subcultures and youth movements.

Laing's and Thornton's insights on the significance of the media and the music press within the wider discourse of music and culture must be complemented by an understanding of the role that music periodicals play at every level of music-making and in every sector of the music industry. In the present context, an understanding of how magazines organize the internal and external relations of the music instrument industry, influence technical innovation and diffusion, define the meaning of new technologies for the consumer, and affect the life of amateur and professional musicians is of paramount importance. Indeed, without the promotional and ideological support of the magazine industry, it is unlikely that digital music technologies would have had nearly the same impact and level of diffusion as they achieved since the early 1980s. Music periodicals, furthermore, provide their readership with a ready-made set of discourses for the framing and resolution of issues concerning technology and music—issues that are socially and culturally loaded.

In this chapter, I begin by outlining the historical background of the relationship between music instrument manufacturers and the music periodical publishing industry. To do so means focusing on what amounts to a very small, little-known, and highly specialized subset of the publishing industry as a whole. An understanding of the dynamics of this sector of the publishing industry is made even more difficult by the sheer number and variety of publications that have existed over the years and by the manner in which the contemporary music market has been divided up into more or less discrete functions and categories of interest. As this brief historical sketch will make clear, however, an increasing specialization within the field of music periodicals has taken place during the past century, and an understanding of this phenomenon and its relationship to the structure and economics of the publishing, recording, and musical instrument industries is essential to the analysis of present-day music periodical publishing.

An Historical Outline of Music Periodical Publishing

The formation of a market for specialized publications devoted to musical concerns may, in fact, predate the advent of periodical publishing itself by more than a century. The sixteenth century was witness to the rise of a growing emphasis on secular music, especially instrumental music, throughout western Europe; this shift was a broad-based cultural phenomenon occurring in both professional and amateur spheres of music. Donald Jay Grout notes that, in support of these developments, "a new kind of writing about music began to appear: 'how to do it' books, manuals of instruction for players and singers became important" (1960: 155). The first books of this type, written in the vernacular and focused on the practical concerns of singers and instrumentalists, began to appear from about 1511 onward. They differed markedly from earlier, Medieval treatises on music, most of which had been written in Latin for a relatively small number of scholars and music theorists (ibid.: 198). Printing music from movable type also dates from the beginning of the sixteenth century, and it is interesting to note that the publication of music collections—in the form of "partbooks" intended primarily for amateur performance and entertainment—runs parallel to the publication of these early "how to" books.

The early emergence of this market for specialized guides to music-making is thus related to a number of interrelated factors: the increasing emphasis on the development of musical instruments, a widening of the professional and amateur base of musicians, the rise of new, popular forms and styles of music, and improvements in print technology. Much later, during the eighteenth and nineteenth centuries, a similar set of factors would be important to the development of specialized music periodicals. In particular, the rise of the middle classes and the institution of the public concert, which provided a platform for middle-class musical tastes, and the expanding market for songs and piano music for entertainment in middle-class homes would stimulate the whole field of music criticism and create a need for announcements, advertisements, reviews, entertaining articles on music, and short works for amateur singers and pianists. William Weber has argued that, as the middle class became increasingly important—both socially and culturally—during the early nineteenth century, it was possible to discern the emergence of various "taste publics" in European musical life. He further argues that it was through their characteristic institutions, meeting places, and communications media that these taste publics became defined (1975: 10). The emergence of music periodicals, therefore, may have a particular significance in the rise of the middle class as a social/cultural formation during this period.

Articles about music appeared regularly in the newspapers of the European capitals and in general periodicals throughout the eighteenth century, but specialized publications devoted to musical matters began to appear from the early part of that century. The vast majority were short-lived; but in Germany especially periodicals flourished, and their pages were filled with articles and debates concerning new musical styles and the latest compositions by well-known composers. *Musica Critica*, published in Hamburg between 1722 and 1725, is thought to be the world's first music periodical. Others followed, of which Leipzig's *Allgemeine Musikalische Zeitung* (*General Music News*; 1798–1848) is among the best-known and longest-surviving periodicals.

Loesser regards the *Allgemeine Musikalische Zeitung* as the most important source of information on musical events in Germany during its fifty years of publication (1954: 131) and makes use of it in his account of the rise to dominance of the pianoforte in middle-class musical life. Of particular interest here are his remarks on the role of the *Zeitung* in the promotion of the instrument and its music in the home. In addition to advertisements, the magazine carried reviews of printed piano music assessing their entertainment value and relative difficulty for the amateur, primarily female, pianist (ibid.: 291). The prevalence of this type of content in music periodicals of the nineteenth century has already been noted in the quotation at the beginning of this chapter, but its presence in the *Zeitung* becomes particularly interesting in that the magazine was published by Germany's foremost sheet music publisher of the time, Breitkopf & Härtel (ibid.: 396). Even at this early date, then, the overlap between content and promotional material, so characteristic of present-day media culture (Wernick 1985), had already taken prototypical form in music periodicals.

In North America, periodical publishing got off to a rather slow and precarious start during the eighteenth century. From 1741, when the first political digests and general interest magazines were published in the United States, to the turn of the century, close to a hundred magazines were launched; few had circulation figures of any significance, and most lasted only a few issues (Mott 1957: 24). In any given year, no more than a handful of titles were published, so it is perhaps surprising to find that anyone would have even attempted to publish a music periodical. Nevertheless, in 1786, the *American Musical Magazine* began publishing in New Haven. It contained mostly printed music and lasted for twelve issues (ibid.: 29; Richardson 1931: 237–42).

Mott considers the magazine to have been a "novelty in the field" at the time of its publication, but it is interesting to note the context of this early attempt at music periodical publishing. Mott states that during the 1780s and '90s a number of attempts were made to reach specialized audiences that had been ignored. In particular, attention was given to the interests of women (1957: 64–67). Music, considered by many during the period as primarily a female pursuit, became regarded as an important means of gaining the attention of a female readership. General magazines of the period often carried short musical pieces, and, by the beginning of the nineteenth century, titles such as the *Ladies' Magazine and Musical Repository* and the *Ladies' and Gentlemen's Weekly Literary Museum and Musical Magazine* began to appear (ibid.: 172–73).

The connection between piano music and female readers continued throughout the early nineteenth century. In 1820 the *Euterpeiad, or Musical Intelligencer* was published in Boston by John R. Parker, a prominent piano manufacturer, importer, and music retailer. Loesser considers it the first true music magazine in America. After a shaky first year of publication, its publisher gave it the subtitle, *Ladies' Gazette*, and began to focus more attention on a female readership to keep it alive (Loesser 1954: 467–68). Similarly, in 1842–1843, a literary magazine entitled the *Boston Miscellany* was launched. Fearing that a purely literary magazine would not succeed, its editors decided that fashion, love stories, and music would attract a dependable readership of "factory girls" on which to "float" the more serious content of the magazine (Mott 1957: 719). In such instances, then, the stereotyping of gender (and class) roles in nineteenth-century magazines not only placed female cultural pursuits in an inferior position to those of their male counterparts but also put them in the service of male economic goals.

Gender stereotyping continues to be an essential characteristic of virtually all music industry markets, as contemporary magazine formats and ad campaigns attest. For example, in what has been described as an "historic" promotional drive, piano manufacturers and music retailers in selected regions of the United States recently launched a coordinated effort to encourage music in the home. The advertising component of the campaign included a series of television spots designed to air during programs watched by women in the twenty-five- to fifty-four-year-old age group (*The Music Trades* 139 [6], July 1991: 133–36). Although the digital musical instrument industry has attempted to lay claim to the home as the site of a new kind of musical production, then, other sectors of the industry still regard it as their traditional turf. It is not without significance that these territorial battles over the domestic market have taken place along gender lines.

In Canada, even prior to the advent of periodicals dedicated to musical concerns, magazines began to play yet another important cultural and commercial role in musical life from at least the 1830s onward. As in the United States, Canadian literary journals and general interest magazines such as *The Montreal Museum: or Journal of Literature and Arts* (1832–1833), *Le Fantasque* (1837–1845) and *Le Ménestrel* (1844–1845) of Québec City, and the *Anglo-American Magazine* (1852–1855) of Toronto had attempted to broaden their readership by regularly offering printed music supplements and, occasionally, articles or concert reviews as a part of their coverage of cultural events (Kallmann et al. 1981: 741–46). At the time, it was rare to find individual pieces of music on sale in music shops; most printed music was sold in books or in collections. It was only later, around 1850, that a publishing industry geared to individual song sheets began to emerge in Canada (Kallmann 1960: 113–15).

Kallmann's account suggests that, by publishing those two or three short musical pieces in each of their supplements, magazines provided a kind of direct distribution network where there had not previously been one and, in addition, may have helped stimulate the demand for popular songs, dances, and marches of the day. In this way, the musical offerings characteristic of early nineteenth-century magazines not only predated similar developments in the music publishing industry but may have acted as a catalyst to those developments as well.

It is intriguing that the short, sentimental song format often found in these magazines would, albeit with some alterations in style, eventually become *the* most characteristic commodity form during the height of the Tin Pan Alley era (roughly 1890–1930; see Loesser 1954: 545–49). Peterson and Berger have argued that the oligopolistic concentration of the Tin Pan Alley industry displaced the "communal" popular musics of the earlier broadside and ballad traditions (1972: 284–86). To argue this point would seem to ignore the role played by the nineteenth-century middle

Digital technology on the inside, traditional cabinetry on the outside. Samick's new line of
digital pianos for the home stresses traditional aesthetics while making use of leading-edge
technology. Drawing on a century-old connection between domestic objects and the sentimental attachments that they carry, the piano in this ad is depicted next to an antique sewing
machine.

classes in anticipating subsequent cultural forms and in establishing a market base—the home piano market—for such an industry. In this sense, the
music supplement of the nineteenth-century magazine trade could be regarded as a more likely ancestor to the popular song form than either the
early broadside or ballad.

In a certain sense, the market defined the nature of music periodicals
in even more significant ways throughout the nineteenth century. The
home environment—as the center of family life and the locus of individual consumption—specified the content of music magazines as they,
in turn, attempted to give value and meaning to that environment. In
a chapter entitled "Household Goods Are All Related" (1954: 560–64),
Arthur Loesser describes how the middle-class home became the site of a

diverse accumulation of durable commodities—an accumulation that necessitated its own peculiar organizational logic. In 1880, a new periodical
appeared called the *Musical and Sewing Machine Gazette*, making explicit a
connection between commodities that was by then firmly (if only tacitly)
established, not only in the homes of consumers but in many retail show-
rooms outside the major urban centers as well. The magazine attempted to
bring together news and features on the piano, organ, and sewing machine
trades. The publication did not last long (it soon changed its name and
became solely a music publication), but its focus was perhaps symptomatic of the times. Loesser cites other music magazines of the period that
carried ads for sewing machines and a range of other domestic products.
As the parlor piano became the symbol of domestic life, magazines helped
to ensure that it would also become associated with all those domestic objects that gave middle-class life its meaning: "The sentimental attachment
that the piano could arouse was bound up with the things with which
it lived" (ibid.: 563). Curiously, this particular "sentimental attachment"
has proved to be extraordinarily long-lived: In a recent advertisement for
its latest line of digital pianos for the "home owner of the '90s," Samick
Music Corporation stresses the "combination of leading-edge technology
with traditional cabinet design." The photo accompanying the text shows
a Samick piano in a middle-class living room containing, among other
things, an antique sewing machine (*Keyboard* 21 [8], August 1995: 122).

As the range and quantity of commodities increased during the latter
part of the nineteenth century and the early years of the twentieth, an
increasing specialization and a wider circulation became necessary components of music periodicals. In part, this development was also a response to the music instrument trade: The increasing production capacity
of the piano industry and the efficient distribution organization required
a national advertising strategy. Most of the periodicals mentioned so far
were very local in character—Boston, New York, Philadelphia, Toronto,
and Montréal each had their own music magazines. As already noted,
most publications were short-lived; but with wider distribution and more
secure advertising revenues, magazines took on a more national outlook,
and their lifespans tended to be much longer. This success was especially
evident in the United States, where a number of music periodicals founded
during the turn of the century are still published today.

These developments were by no means unique to the music periodical
industry. In his book *Magazines in the Twentieth Century* (1964), Theodore
Peterson describes the final decades of the nineteenth century as a "quiet
revolution" in the magazine industry in the United States: General-interest
magazines and a wide variety of specialized periodicals flourished during

this period, and the number of available titles increased by more than fourfold. Peterson cites a number of factors as contributing to this phenomenon, ranging from a general expansion in manufacturing and capital investment to technological advances in the publishing industry (especially the steam-driven press), to changes in U.S. postal rates and regulations that favored magazine circulation. The success of many late nineteenth-century music periodicals was simply part and parcel of these larger trends.

With the establishment of large-scale instrument manufacturing and distribution, the need for more specialized mediums of promotion and communication became evident within the industry itself. The latter decades of the century witnessed the founding of two important industry trade papers in the United States: first, the *Musical Merchandise Review* (1879), and then *The Music Trades* (1890). Over one hundred years later, both remain vital communications links for the U.S.-based industry. The *Canadian Music Trades Journal*, founded at the turn of the century, performed a similar role in the Canadian industry until the beginning of the Depression years (1900–1930).

The nature and purpose of this specialized medium of communication is equally significant. As John C. Freund, first editor of *The Music Trades*, put it in 1890:

The value of the trade papers, in any trade, depends upon the fact that by far the principal part of the product is disposed of through jobbers and dealers. By reaching the jobber and dealer all over the country, the trade paper provides the manufacturer with a far more valuable advertising medium for the disposal of his goods than any ordinary daily or weekly paper can possibly offer.

(*The Music Trades* 1 [2]; quoted in Majeski 1990: 30)

Indeed, according to Theodore Peterson, the single most important factor contributing to the rise of the modern magazine industry as a whole was the growth of advertising (1964: 18–43). As the quotation shows, advertising defined, in large part, the relationship between the manufacturing and retail sectors of the industry: To sell a product to the public, it was first necessary to sell it to the retailer. In both trade and consumer publishing, then, advertising "made the magazine a part of the system of marketing. . . . It transformed the publisher from dealer in editorial wares to dealer in consumer groups" (ibid.: 18).

Even a cursory glance at some of the trade magazines of the period reveals changes in the style and general level of prominence given to advertising. In the mid-nineteenth century, advertising, with its flowery, prose style, resembled formal announcements more than the advertising we know today. By the turn of the century, display ads, with their terse texts and more graphic appeal, were dominant. In what became the standard format of *The Music Trades*, at the turn of the century the front and back covers were given over to display ads (mostly those of the largest piano manufacturers), making them the most prominent public image of the journal. During the first decade of the century, the ads of instrument manufacturers were joined by those of the Victor Talking Machine Company (phonographs and gramophones were still sold in music shops at that time); one ad announced that, in support of its dealers, Victor's consumer advertising campaigns reached some 49 million people every month. (*The Music Trades* 31 [14], April 7, 1906: 46).

In the realm of consumer magazines, the latter part of the nineteenth century also gave rise to a number of music periodicals whose longevity was much greater than those of previous decades. In the United States, *The Etude*, *Musical America*, and *The Musical Courier* (formerly the *Musical and Sewing Machine Gazette* mentioned previously) were prominent titles; *Musical America*, founded in 1898, is still published today. In Canada, the periodical industry remained more precarious, in part because of an advertising base that lagged behind that of the United States, poor distribution, and competition from foreign publications (see Kallmann et al. 1981: 741); nevertheless, a number of magazines had substantial runs, including *Le Passe-Temps* (1895–1935, 1945–1949), which contained regular music supplements, and *Musical Canada* (1906–1933).

In these early modern magazines, advertising is often as much an indicator of a publisher's target audience as the magazine content itself. In *The Etude* of June, 1915 (vol. 33 [6]), for example, the most ubiquitous ads for products other than musical instruments, printed music, instruction manuals, and the like were for cold creams and facial powders; the back cover contained the only full-page, full-color ad in the entire magazine—an ad for Palmolive, the soap for the "modern woman." Although musical goods certainly made up the bulk of advertising revenue for magazines like *The Etude*, the prominence of these ads for other products indicate that gender continued to be an important factor in the construction of music magazine readership. For the advertisers, music-making in the home continued to be an important avenue for the promotion of an increasingly diverse set of feminine commodities.

Of course, magazines were not only a vehicle for advertising; other factors contributed to their growth and to their significance for their readership. In the consumer area, the spread of public education and increases in leisure time contributed to the increased circulation of magazines from the turn of the century onward (Peterson 1964: 47–49). Peterson argues that, despite their shortcomings, magazines in the United States provided an important forum for public debate and an inexpensive source of both education and entertainment (ibid.: 448–51).

Peterson further argues that the modern magazine, with its broad circulation patterns and its widely dispersed readership, interpreted issues and events within a national (i.e., U.S.) perspective, thus contributing to a sense of national community (ibid.: 449). This view was as evident for the trade magazines as it was for consumer periodicals, and it had a significant impact on the organization and functioning of industry. Initially, magazines such as *The Music Trades* saw their role as primarily a communications link between different sectors of the industry: "A trade paper has other values than as an advertising medium for the manufacturer. It is the mainstay of the industry it represents. It gives the members of that industry a machinery for inter-communication, which a hundred other publications could not begin to equal" (*The Music Trades* 1 [2], 1890; quoted in Majeski 1990: 30). It was not long, however, before *The Music Trades* began to play a more active role in the life of the industry. In 1900, the magazine was instrumental in establishing the groundwork for a piano dealers' association. Piano manufacturers had already established their own, exclusive organization three years earlier, but it was the trade magazine's lobby on behalf of the dealers that convinced manufacturers that two complementary associations could best represent the interests of the industry (ibid.: 57–58). In this way, *The Music Trades* hoped to establish a sense of community between various sectors within the industry and to help them begin to understand their relations and interests as part of an integrated whole.

Outside the trade publications, Peterson notes an increasing diversification and specialization in the development of the magazine industry during the twentieth century. The expansion in the market for this diverse range of consumer magazines is related to a number of factors, including increases in leisure time, education and the general level of economic prosperity (1964: 44–64). The first decades of the twentieth century and those following World War II were the two periods of greatest expansion. A number of successful music periodicals were even launched during the 1930s, an otherwise difficult time for the publishing industry.

The specific diversity, even within the already highly specialized music magazine sector of the industry, has been a response to a number of other factors. In particular, the diversity of music periodicals is apparently linked to the specialized needs and interests of professional and amateur musicians who play a wide variety of instruments, each fundamentally different in its construction and playing technique and used in very different institutional settings. This diversity is also linked to changes in the technologies of musical production and consumption and to changes in musical style. In almost every case, the various factors that contribute to the definition of a specific class of readership for specialized music publications also contributes to their differentiation as a market for specific musical products.

For example, virtually every musical instrument imaginable has had a specialized magazine or newsletter devoted to it during the twentieth century, and, to one degree or another, most contain advertising for a variety of products related only to the instrument in question. Not only the general popularity of a given instrument but also the relative stability of the institutional base for certain instruments may be a factor in the continued survival of a number of musicians' magazines founded at the turn of the century. These include *The Strad*, founded in the United Kingdom in 1890 for orchestral string players, and *Diapason*, a 1909 U.S. magazine for professional church organists. For some musical instruments, where markets were sufficiently large and sufficiently differentiated, more than one publication could be found even at early dates; for example, the *Organist* was founded even before *Diapason* (in 1896) and was designed primarily for amateur players of sacred music. As music became a more important part of the public school curriculum, magazines and newsletters were launched specifically for the needs of educators: for example, the *Music Educator's Journal* (U.S., 1914) and the *Canadian Federation of Music Teachers' Associations Newsletter* (formerly the *Canadian Music Teacher*, 1935).[3] Insofar as public schools have long been a major market for band instruments, it should be noted that even this category of publications owes its existence as much to the promotional needs of instrument manufacturers as to the educational needs of its institutional subscribers.

Phonographs, gramophones and radios (and later, even television sets) were initially sold through music dealers in many centers and were advertised through the music press (among other media). Soon, the industries manufacturing these sound reproduction technologies developed separate distribution and retail channels of their own, and, as demand for the technologies became sufficiently large, marketing warranted the publication of specialized periodicals as well: *The Gramophone*, founded in Britain in 1923, and *Radio* (now called *Audio*), launched in the United States in 1917, are especially noteworthy. In magazines of this type, music becomes primarily a pretext for showcasing technological products. Each successive change in audio technology—tape recording, LP's, stereo, and CD's—has brought about new titles in the field, and the audio magazine has become a marketing and promotional mainstay of both the electronics and the record industries. The importance given to the technical characteristics of music reproduction devices moves many such magazines to the category of hobbyist magazines, such as *Popular Electronics*, rather than to that of music magazines. Conflicts in content and outlook are evident in the most recent crop of specialized musicians' periodicals that attempt to combine these two magazine formats.

In an apparent acceleration and diversification of what William Weber described as the formation of "taste publics" during the nineteenth century, musicians and fans have increasingly turned to the magazine as a medium of communication on specific styles and genres of music. Some of the longest-standing, genre-oriented music periodicals have been devoted to the bourgeois concert hall tradition: For example, Britain's *The Musical Times* has been published continuously since 1844. In the twentieth century, various subgenres within this tradition have also been served: for example, *Opera News*, founded in the United States in 1936. The diversity of popular musics during the past century has spawned an equally diverse music press. Of the magazines founded during the early part of the century, *Down Beat* is among the best known and longest surviving. Founded in 1934 during the heyday of the Swing bands, it became known among touring jazz musicians as "The Musician's Bible" (*Down Beat* will be discussed in greater detail later). For their readers, periodicals of this type—whether designed primarily for professionals or consumers—help construct a coherent world of musical classifications and social "distinction" (Bourdieu 1984; Thornton 1994). For record companies and manufacturers of musical instruments, the exclusive focus of these periodicals has made them an indispensible means of accessing specialized markets for their products.

The character of the music periodical industry in the post–World War II era will be outlined later, but it is worth noting here that, in addition to the trade and commercial magazines, there are also several categories of periodicals—the professional and amateur music association newsletters, academic journals, and others—where advertising plays little or no significance in format or content. Indeed, there are a myriad of small and highly specialized professional and amateur associations whose existence is predicated on little more than the enthusiasm of their membership: amateur choral societies, obscure associations for the promotion of specific musical instruments (e.g., the American Banjo Fraternity), and ad hoc groups of fans for marginalized, subcultural musics. Many of these groups sponsor periodicals, fanzines, newsletters, and programs on community radio or other media whose editorial content and economic base can be quite different from the commercial media. As specialized as these groups and their characteristic communications media may be, they play an active role in helping musicians and audiences communicate with one another and in gaining a sense of shared interests and common goals. Perhaps more importantly, they contribute to notions of "community," cultural identity, and style that are, as often as not, defined in opposition to mainstream commercial music and media.

Contemporary Musicians' Magazines

Appearing among the successive waves of new technology and innovative musical styles transforming the worlds of music production, distribution, and consumption since the 1960s has been a striking number of new magazines to support the burgeoning markets that inevitably accompany such developments. Nowhere is this phenomenon more evident than with the newest group of magazines designed for pop music's vanguard—the popular musicians themselves. Even the titles of this recent crop of music periodicals—*Music Technology*, *Electronic Musician*, *Home & Studio Recording*, and *Music & Computers*—trumpet their commitment to new technology and to music production in the brave new world of the so-called "electronic cottage."

Of course, there is an easy explanation for the proliferation of such magazines: Despite heavy competition from the electronic media and the increasing use of the Internet and commercial communications networks, magazines remain one of the most economical means for advertisers to reach a specific market for their products (electronic or otherwise). This marketing aspect is especially true for the musicians' market, which is relatively small, highly specialized, and widely dispersed. Although these magazines are, at least in part, advertiser driven (indeed, this fact is central to much of what follows in this chapter), it also seems that the construction of a consumer market for new musical technology throughout the 1970s, '80s, and '90s has been extremely complex and perhaps unique in many ways. A number of economic, technical, and social/historical factors, although present throughout the post-war period, have become increasingly significant in the recent proliferation of musicians' magazines. These factors are not, furthermore, confined to any one industrial field but relate to a variety of changes occurring more or less simultaneously in the publishing, electronics, and music industries.

First, within the world of magazine publishing itself, business and special interest magazines in all fields have increased in both number and circulation. Peterson has noted that, although special interest magazines have existed at least since the turn of the century, advances in education, income, and leisure time during the '50s and early '60s led to a proliferation of new magazines of specialized appeal (1964: 363). Taft claims that this phenomenon has become increasingly important since the mid-'70s and that, whereas the idea of specialized publications itself is not new, the *degree* of specialization is (1982: 23). The trend in the magazine industry has been away from the earlier battle with television for mass-market advertising dollars and toward a reliance on more specific ad markets — "moving to a state of 'specialization within specialization' as the market becomes dissected into more minute elements" (ibid.: 17). The contemporary musicians' magazine is one such "specialization within a specialization" (ibid.: 278).

Evidence of this general trend can be found in data published by Statistics Canada (Ifedi 1990): During the mid-'80s, circulation figures for special interest magazines in Canada grew by 67 percent, while general interest periodicals declined by 3 percent. Statistics Canada reveals a compelling economic reason for the recent success of this category of periodicals: Because they rely more heavily on advertising, special interest periodicals, especially those containing business content and consumer information, are more profitable publishing enterprises than general interest magazines, with profits averaging as high as 9 percent compared to 5 percent average profits in the general interest area (ibid.; Desbarats 1991).

One of the largest areas of growth in the special interest category has been in business periodicals, including trade magazines and professional and technical magazines with controlled circulation, such as those directed to sound engineers, record producers, or club DJs. Although my main interest is in consumer magazines, it is perhaps worthwhile mentioning these publications, if only briefly. In the music periodical industry, the business and consumer areas are, in any case, often linked through ownership and editorial control. Industry has only recently realized the value of "business-to-business" advertising. Studies conducted during the mid-'80s showed that advertising could be more cost-effective when directed towards dealers, retailers, and other professionals as well as to end users, and this information has led some manufacturers to adopt a more integrated approach to advertising and promotion (Dougherty 1986). Such an approach is often encouraged by publishers; for example, Norris Publications, publishers of *Canadian Music Trade* (a musical instrument retailer magazine) and the consumer-oriented *Canadian Musician*, has for several years offered advertisers discounts when they place ads simultaneously in both magazines. The same studies revealed the success rates of various marketing strategies, such as reader service cards placed in business magazines; interestingly, service cards of this kind have now become a regular feature of a variety of consumer electronics publications as well, including magazines for musicians, hi-fi enthusiasts, and computer users. Publishers of business periodicals also offer additional services to industry: Some

Gear, gear, gear. Contemporary musicians' magazines promote an entire philosophy of music-making centered around the values of consumption. The emphasis on musicians' gear only came to the fore during the early 1970s, but, as this small selection of magazine covers illustrates, it is now a central part of the content of most musicians' magazines, even displacing photos of star performers as a means of gaining attention on news stands.

engage in mounting trade and consumer shows and other events; others publish annual industry directories—an increasingly important function in the fast-changing world of clubs, performance venues, recording studios, and video production.

Second, technological changes—in the form of computer-aided layout, in-house typesetting, data transmission, and other work—may have contributed to the increased viability of small-circulation, specialized publishing during the 1980s (Taft 1982: 342–43). Though such technical changes are certainly not as dramatic as the improvements in printing that gave rise to the mass-circulation magazine industry of the late nineteenth century, they have nevertheless become an important aid in overcoming the economic pressures of publishing. In this regard, it is interesting to note that the more successful musicians' magazines of the '80s have been absorbed by larger publishing interests and have been introduced to new state-of-the-art desktop production systems. They are also expected to share personnel and data banks with other group publications, thus reducing production costs and the size of their support staff.

A number of U.S. magazines devoted to hi-tech music-making have found it useful to maintain contact with industry professionals, contributors, and their more up-scale readership through a specialized music industry computer network called PAN (Performing Artists Network). As home computers and Internet access have become more popular, computer communications has become not only an important aid in magazine production but an alternative promotional and informational link with readers. By the mid-1990s, a number of magazines for musicians and audio engineers, such as *Keyboard, Mix*, and even *Guitar for the Practicing Musician*, had developed a presence on the World Wide Web.

A third factor contributing more directly to the recent increase in the number of musicians' magazines is related both to the promotional needs of industry and to changing modes of musical production. Since the growth of advertising in the early part of this century, magazine publishing has become part of the marketing system within contemporay capitalism (Peterson 1964: 18). To state the obvious, professional, semi-professional, and amateur musicians are one of the primary markets for musical instrument manufacturers. Other markets include the home market—often referred to as the "consumer" market—and the church and educational markets, each having their own dedicated publications. According to H. Stith Bennett, the market relationship between musicians and manufacturers has become even more salient since the rise of rock and other forms of popular music based around electronic instruments and sound recording: "Performers struggled against the disparity between their recorded sound and their live sound throughout the 1950s and 1960s, and slowly their frustrations were turned into a market by musical instrument manufacturers" (1983: 231). This factor has become increasingly significant with the use of samplers, sequencers, and special effects devices of all kinds in studio and stage production during the 1980s and '90s.

Advertising in musicians' magazines is just one among a number of strategies employed by the electronic instrument and sound reinforcement industry to reach this critical market. For instance, instrument manufacturers often sponsor artists, and in return their products are mentioned in tour brochures and album jackets. The album liner notes for a record by Suzanne Vega reveal, in minute detail, not only the brand of guitar, sampler, and other instruments she and her band use but also the brand of microphone, cymbals, and even her guitar strings. Since the early 1980s, music video has also been an asset to musical instrument promotion. As one industry spokesperson noted, with music video you can actually see, up close, the make and model of the instruments star performers play—something seldom possible in club and stadium concert situations. Increasingly, then, we learn not only *who* plays but also *what* they play as well.

Magazines still form the most direct link between instrument manufacturers and their market, however, and, interestingly, although musicians' magazines such as *Down Beat* have existed for many years, not until the early '70s did the attention on musicians' "gear" come to the fore. This spotlighting occurred most notably in magazines such as *Guitar Player* that had a large, youthful, pop/rock readership. This emphasis has only increased since the 1970s. For example, in *Down Beat*, small side-bars containing details of the instruments star performers play began to appear in artist interviews in 1979/80; by 1982 these inserts often contained photos and took up as much as an entire half page. During the late '80s, *Down Beat* also added a regular column on sound equipment and new products of interest. Similarly, in July of 1985, *Keyboard* announced a "new era" for the magazine; apparently in response to "reader demand," it planned to expand equipment reviews and coverage of technical applications.

By the 1990s, these features had become mainstays of the musicians' magazine industry. Information about the gear favored by star performers is now written directly into the articles themselves; in interviews, artists are regularly questioned about the equipment used in performances or on specific recordings. As a musician's "gear" has increasingly come to mean an entire studio full of equipment, magazines such as *Musician* have begun to carry regular features detailing the "home studios" of the rich and famous, including two-page, full-color photos. Equipment reviews have become so lengthy and detailed that they now virtually compete with artist interviews and other feature articles for magazine space.

A characteristic common to the majority of these magazines is that they contain *only* advertising directly aimed at musicians; that is, you find no ads for cigarettes, alcohol, and so on. This fact alone sets these magazines apart from large-circulation, general interest music periodicals such as *Rolling Stone* or *Spin*. In 1980, *Contemporary Keyboard* magazine stated openly in an editorial that it had "a policy of rejecting all ads that aren't music related" (vol. 6 [2]: 3). The same issue included, for the first time, an advertisers' index—another feature that has become characteristic of most musicians' magazines—thus assuring that accessing promotional information from advertisers was as easy for the readership as accessing the magazine's feature articles. In later issues, as if this practice had created some special form of intimacy between advertisers, music magazines, and their readers, a headline above the ad index read: "They're in *Keyboard* because they care about musicians."

A fourth element in the growth of musicians' magazines is related to recent shifts in the electronics industry and is as much technological as it is economic. Even though most musical instruments (beginning with the hammer piano in the early nineteenth century) are today manufactured using industrial processes, there is still a certain premium upon musical instruments that are hand made. There are still companies producing hand-crafted guitars and basses (even electric ones), and in the 1960s it was common for engineers to custom design and build mixing consoles for their own studio needs. Similarly, in the late '60s and early '70s, the synthesizer industry consisted of only a few small, privately owned companies; the instruments themselves bore the names of their inventors (e.g., the "Moog" and "Buchla" synthesizers).

Electronic instruments do not exactly lend themselves to small-scale production, however, and as the market expanded during the late 1970s and, more importantly, as the industry shifted to microprocessor-based technologies, a number of large Japanese corporations such as Casio, Roland, and Yamaha began to dominate the field. The Japanese corporations (especially Casio, which gears its products toward the amateur musician market) are closely linked to the manufacturers of integrated circuits and utilize modern production techniques. As outlined in Chapter 4, these companies pursued an aggressive marketing strategy during the early '80s that sought to bring the price of digital instruments down to levels accessible to the average musician/consumer (see Moog 1985: 42–44). These two elements—production capacity and marketing strategy—are clearly linked and, as Stuart Ewen (1976) has pointed out, have been an essential feature of capitalist production since the 1920s: With enhanced industrial production capacity, manufacturers increasingly need to be concerned about producing consumers as well as goods.

Here again, the need for musicians' magazines becomes evident for more than just advertising. The magazines promote a whole philosophy of music-making that is based around new technology and consumption. In the past, when a musician purchased a musical instrument it was usually with the assumption that the instrument would last for years, and often, musical instruments were handed down from one generation to the next. In our culture, however, technology is fundamentally linked with notions of progress and change, and, for the manufacturers of electronic musical instruments, it is important that musicians adopt these values, especially the need for renewed consumption of goods. Of course, such strategies have not gone unnoticed by musicians—the most prominent criticism of the new technology of the '80s, even among its advocates, was the excessive speed of technological change. It is precisely in the musicians' magazines, however, that these issues are most clearly raised and, to a certain extent, resolved.

In this sense, musicians' magazines are unique, at least those for hi-fi enthusiasts and computer users, because the relationship between musicians and their musical instruments is such a loaded symbolic terrain. Traditional values link musical instruments to romantic notions of authenticity and personal expression, and, for this reason, the role of new technology in popular music has become highly contested (see Frith 1986). Musicians' magazines play an important part in the redefinition of musical values, in renegotiating what William Leiss (1976) might call the "material-symbolic" status of musical instruments as objects of consumption and use.

Finally, a number of factors have been at work within the music industry of the late 1970s and early '80s that have had a powerful impact on the ways young musicians interact and pursue their career goals. These factors have, no doubt, also contributed to the increased popularity of musicians' magazines. Prior to this period, young musicians normally spent their early years learning songs from records, rehearsing with other like-minded musicians, and performing in small clubs. H. Stith Bennett has described this process as three separate though interdependent forms of interaction: a "musician-recording interaction," a "musician-musician interaction," and a "group-audience interaction" (1990: 232).

Since the late '70s, however, with the increased availability of inexpensive drum machines, synthesizers, and sequencers, young musicians have been able to work without certain band members or, in the case of songwriters, to produce fully arranged demo tapes without the aid of outside musical collaborators. Added to this enhanced technical capability and the possibility of autonomous musical creation was the negative impact disco had on the number of venues for live music performance in many urban centers during the late 1970s and early '80s. Interestingly, among the most significant new forms of popular music to emerge since the late '70s are hip-hop and rap music—musical forms based around DJ performers, phonograph turntables, studio sampling, and dance-club venues. Though live performance opportunities have been subject to a great deal of regional variation and have changed with time (by the end of the '80s, and with the rise of various forms of alternative music, there has been a resurgence of live music venues in many centers), clearly these factors have pressured many young musicians to develop their skills outside of group rehearsal and live performance contexts and to use demo tapes to gain exposure to record companies. Indeed, demo production has become the preferred method of introducing new talent to record companies. Bands now regularly produce demos even before playing in front of a live audience, and greater emphasis has been placed on demos of master quality. As one Artists & Repertoire representative put it, the 1980s became "the era of the competitive demo" (John Kolodner, in Kasha and Hirschhorn 1990: 267).

The new instruments and recording devices have also forced many musicians to rely more heavily on specialized musicians' magazines as sources of information due to difficulty in finding local musicians with adequate knowledge of the technologies or the techniques employed in their use. Indeed, during the mid-'80s—the most intense period of technological change in recent musical instrument design—it was often necessary for the magazine editors to seek out software developers and product specialists as authors of magazine articles on new products. In many cases, they were the only people who had adequate knowledge of all the available product features. This situation has become especially important for younger musicians, who find they can no longer rely entirely upon local networks of more experienced musicians for their apprenticeship training.

The music industry generally has become more complex throughout the 1980s; in addition to producing demo tapes, aspiring young musicians must now confront the problems of video production. Record deals with major recording companies are increasingly made at the international level, making decisions concerning repertoire, production, and management more critical, and the problems of exposure more difficult. If they decide to release their own recordings, musicians must choose between a variety of competing technical formats and distribution channels. The "how-to-make-it-in-the-music-business" type of book has long been a staple of the music publishing industry, and though such books continue to appear year after year, much of the information they contain quickly becomes outdated. The musicians' magazines have an obvious advantage in this respect in that they can provide more up-to-date informtion, and most of them devote regular features to changes within the industry, professional tips, career advice, and so on. Here again, much of this information is difficult, if not impossible, for musicians to obtain at the local level from their peers.

As I have attempted to demonstrate here, a number of factors occurring simultaneously across several different industries have contributed to the recent proliferation of musicians' magazines. Many professional, semiprofessional, and amateur musicians seem now to operate at increasing distances from one another and from their audiences, and they must thus often rely on other, more mediated forms of interaction. In this regard, musicians' magazines have come to play a role in supplying musicians with both essential information and, equally important, a sense of community—a community completely integrated, however, with their position as a market for musical instrument manufacturers.

To turn to the magazines themselves, the sheer number and apparent diversity of these publications and the manner in which musicians are divided, for marketing purposes, into discreet categories of interest are striking. The average news stand or musical instrument shop in Montréal, for example, carries magazines devoted to keyboard players, guitarists, drummers, sound engineers, and producers. In many cases, news stands carry more than one publication in several of these categories. For example, during the late 1980s and early '90s, there were four major publications focused primarily on synthesizer, sampler, and related technology alone—two published in the United States (*Keyboard* and *Electronic Musician*), one in Britain (*Music Technology*, which, until recently, also appeared in a somewhat different American edition with Canadians having the dubious honor of being able to obtain both editions), and one, a French-language publication with an English title (*Keyboards*), published in France.

At the 1990 summer trade show held by the National Association of Music Merchants (NAMM) in Chicago, over forty publications devoted to specialized sectors of the musical instrument trade were on display. Given the number of periodicals in the field and their relative degree of specialization, it is not surprising that their individual circulation figures are relatively small. The oldest among them, *Down Beat*, which used to think of itself as "The Musician's Bible," has been published continuously since the era of the swing bands (since July 1934). Until recently, its content was primarily oriented toward jazz musicians and fans. In 1972, a period when competition in the field was still relatively small, it had achieved an average circulation of over 90,000 copies per issue. By the late 1980s, competition had become considerably stiffer, and, even though editorial policies at *Down Beat* had changed to allow coverage of a broader range of musical styles, its circulation was still only 91,000 (the figure had risen to 96,000 by 1995). The list in table 1 (which is by no means comprehensive) reveals the more general pattern of expansion and increasing diversity in the market in recent decades.[4]

The impact of rock music on the music periodical industry (and, by extension, the musical instrument industry) is clear: The two magazines with the highest circulation figures are for guitarists (and there are several other guitar magazines in the field). Ever since the introduction of synthesizers, home recording equipment, and computers into popular music-making, an increase in the number of keyboard and high technology magazines is also evident, although this sector of the industry continues to be highly volatile. Still, when compared to the circulation figures of specialized hi-fi and computer magazines, which can be as high as several hundred thousand copies, the circulation of these musicians' magazines seems relatively limited. Only when you ignore the apparent diversity (or fragmentation) of the market and look at the field as a whole do the figures even begin to appear significant.

At the industry level, this surface diversity also masks what is, in actual fact, a very high degree of economic concentration; many of these pub-

TABLE I

Title & date of first publication	Circulation for the year	
	1989	1995
Guitar Player (1967)	132,000	144,000
Keyboard (1975)	65,000	69,000
(formerly *Contemporary Keyboard*)		
Musician (1976)	105,000	115,000
Modern Drummer (1977)	85,000	102,000
Canadian Musician (1979)	28,000	28,000
Music Technology (U.K. ed. 1981; U.S. ed. 1986)	50,000	(1993–94) 50,000
(formerly *Electronics and Music Maker*)	50,000	(defunct)
Stage & Studio (1980)	76,000	78,000
(formerly *Music & Sound Output*)		
Recording (U.K. ed. 1983; U.S. ed. 1987)	50,000	58,000
(formerly *Home & Studio Recording*)		
Guitar, for the Practicing Musician (1983)	153,000	170,000
Electronic Musician (1985)	65,000	62,000
Music, Computers & Software (1986)	56,000	(defunct)
Rhythm (U.K. ed. 1987; U.S. ed. 1988)	20,000	20,000
	40,000	NA
Modern Keyboard (1988)	65,000	65,000
EQ (1990)	—	37,000
Future Music (U.K., 1993)	—	NA
Music & Computers (1995)	—	NA

lications belong to "families" of musician-oriented magazines, which are published by the same interests. For example, Music Maker Publications, established in Britain during the early 1980s, publishes both books and magazines, the latter including *Music Technology, Guitarist, Rhythm, Home & Studio Recording, Home Keyboard Review*, and *Hip-Hop Connection*. During the late '80s, three of these titles also began appearing in separate U.S. editions, sharing about 25 percent of their content with their British counterparts. A similar concentration of ownership existed in the United States during the decade of the '80s with GPI Publications (publishers of *Guitar Player, Keyboard, Frets*, and various books and newsletters), Mix Publications (*Mix, Electronic Musician*, and the *Mix Bookshelf*—a distributor of books, videos, music software, and other products), and Billboard Publications (*Billboard* and, through its various divisions and subsidiaries, *Musician* magazine, books, and directories), among others.

The more successful among these enterprises became the object of takeovers by large corporate interests as the decade of the '80s drew to a close. The GPI group was acquired by Miller Freeman Publications, a California-based company founded at the turn of the century and publisher of trade magazines for the natural resources industries and specialized, high-technology areas of the medical, computer, and electronics fields. Miller Freeman also organizes trade shows and conferences and has continued to expand its operations in a number of fields, including the special interest music publishing sector, where it has added new titles such as *EQ*, *Bass Player* (both in 1990), and *Music & Computers* (1995) to its holdings. The company is owned by United News and Media (formerly United News-papers), a U.K. media conglomerate.

Similarly, Mix Publications was acquired during the late 1980s by ACT III Publishing, which also publishes magazines for the corporate video sector and for broadcast engineers. The company is part of a much larger media group with interests in film production, movie theaters, and television broadcasting. Mix Publications was subsequently purchased again, during the early 1990s, by Cardinal Business Media, publisher of technical books and magazines for specialized areas of the computer industries such as networking, imaging, and systems management. It also organizes trade shows and conferences for the computer industry. In a certain sense, these shifting alliances across the high-technology sectors of the specialized periodical publishing industries is a reflection of the broader trend toward transectorial innovation in the musical instrument industry. In the latter, instrument manufacturers have become increasingly dependent on personnel, hardware developments, and marketing strategies emanating from the electronics and computer industries.

It is difficult to gauge the effects of industrial conglomeration in the publishing industry. Although concentration of ownership has long been a concern in newspaper publishing, historians of the magazine industry have generally felt that the sheer number of titles, the relative fragmentation and complexity of the market, and other factors mitigate against the possible adverse effects of conglomeration. Others, however, have observed that such forces in one particular field of special interest magazines may result in a reduction in the number of available titles (see Taft 1982: 287). Something of this kind may have taken place in the field of musicians' magazines during the early 1990s. Faced with stiff competition from its rivals in the United States (and a general down turn in the synthesizer market), Music Maker Publications was forced to allow its U.S. edition of *Music Technology* to suspend independent operations and be absorbed by its more successful U.S. publication, *Home & Studio Recording*. In the fall of 1990, Music Maker also entered into an agreement in which Miller Freeman would take over the publication of *Rhythm* (U.S.), while continuing to share some of its editorial content with the U.K. edition.

The level of concentration within this specialized area of publishing may also affect relations between the publishers and the industry they serve, as well as having an impact on the general character of the magazines themselves. For example, in Canada, where the market is very small and already dominated by foreign publications, there are relatively few Canadian periodicals serving the popular music industry. As already mentioned, the Toronto-based Norris Publications publishes both *Canadian Musician* (a magazine that attempts to cross the boundary between a magazine aimed mainly at musicians and one aimed at a more general readership) and *Canadian Music Trade* (a business magazine distributed primarily to musical instrument retailers). Norris also launched a magazine for sound engineers in the fall of 1990 called *Professional Sound*. Perhaps even more significant than simple common ownership is that all three magazines share the same editorial and production staff. Norris also has interests in book publishing (music books and an industry directory) and artist management. In the Canadian situation, then, Norris Publications and its affiliates have become a singular, multifunction management, promotion, and information vehicle linking several sectors within the industry—from instrument manufacturers and distributors to retailers, artists, and consumers.

In contrast, most of the magazines published outside Canada have separate editorial boards and fewer direct links with the music manufacturing and retail industries. A large number of editors and contributors from the magazines have, nevertheless, on occasion or in regular featured articles, appeared in the pages of their so-called "sister" publications or in magazines by different (i.e., competing) publishers. Several current editors and other writers have also contributed to (or, in some cases, worked for) manufacturer-sponsored publications or user-group newsletters, written technical manuals, served as consultants for instrument manufacturers, or developed sound programs for new electronic musical instruments. One prominent writer claimed that he could never be accused of conflict of interest because he had worked, at one time or another, for just about everyone in the business; this action, apparently, was a guarantee that he was not beholden to anyone.

The net result of such economic and intellectual concentration is a certain homogeneity in general style, outlook, and approach between the various publications. This approach was neatly summed up in the editorial page of the recent inaugural issue of *Bass Player* magazine: "Our goal is simple: to provide electric and acoustic bassists with the information they need to become better players, more successful musicians, and more savvy consumers of equipment" (vol. 1 [1], Spring 1990: 4). *Canadian Musician* (perhaps because of its crossover orientation) put it somewhat differently: "We cover the People . . . the Business . . . the Products" (Promotional brochure, 1990). The elements are the same: star performers and musicianship, business and careers, and, above all, products. Indeed, the two former elements are ultimately collapsed into the latter: "In today's business, the musician's tools—from instruments to recording technology—can make or break a song. *Canadian Musician*'s regular product reports give detailed analysis of some of the latest technology—once again, by people using it on current projects" (ibid.).

It should perhaps be noted here, if only in passing, that this emphasis on new musical products has not been limited to the pop/rock sectors of the musical world alone; rather, it is apparently a widespread side-effect of the increased speed of technological innovation and high-intensity marketing strategies in the musical instrument industry of the 1980s. The *Computer Music Journal*, published by MIT Press, is one of the most prestigious forums of avant-garde electronic music; it publishes only the most specialized, learned articles on the mathematics, theories, techniques, and aesthetics of digital sound production. Because of the technical nature of the field, the journal has, since its inception in 1977, always included a short "Products of Interest" column and, from about 1979 onward, began to accept a limited number of advertisements from selected manufacturers. During its early years of publication, the products column and the ads combined seldom filled more than a couple of pages. Both sections expanded considerably during the 1980s, however. In 1985, Yamaha took out a two-page display ad at the back of the journal; by 1988, the ads and product reviews often exceeded thirty pages in length, constituting over one-third of the total content of the journal. Although the advertising content tends to be somewhat higher (amounting, on average, to 50 percent of the total magazine pages), these trends parallel, quite closely, similar developments in the popular musicians' magazines. Even the tone of the reviews sometimes approached that of the popular magazines, with expressions such as how much "bang for the buck" a particular product offered. There thus seems to be little difference between the avant-garde's fascination for technology and that of the pop musician.

What still distinguishes the academic computer music journal from the pop magazines, however, is the degree to which content can be separated from advertising messages. The articles and interviews found in most popular musicians' magazines heavily emphasize the equipment musicians use and, much like the ads that use star endorsements, an almost elementary process of transferral takes place where the attitudes and values attributed to the artist are transferred to the objects of consumption. In this regard, musicians are no different than any other fan; they are just as susceptible to the blandishments of the star system as anyone else. Again, whatever claims to integrity the avant-garde might have do not make them immune to this process. In an interview with Laurie Anderson, a photo caption reads: "Armed with a Roland D-50 and a challenging view of society, Anderson wails at the Brooklyn Academy of Music in 1988" (*Keyboard*, December 1989: 75). In this sense, contemporary musicians' magazines are prime examples of Andrew Wernick's description of media in a "promotional culture": "Thematically, ideologically and stylistically, the non-advertising content comes to be angled and coded in terms of the same economically functional categories as those which substructure the ads themselves" (1985: 14). Conversely, ads sometimes disguise themselves as interviews and product reviews and must be labeled, in small print, as advertisements by the magazine editors.

These observations suggest that any discursive analysis of musicians' magazines must avoid any strict, conventional categorizations or discursive typologies in favor of an analysis that seeks common procedures cutting across all boundaries and types (see Finlay-Pelinsky 1983). In the hi-tech magazines, both the advertisements and the feature articles emphasize various technical discourses, especially those concerned with power and control. Perhaps most interesting here, however, is the manner in which the discursive practices of "futurology" (ibid.: 18–22) come to serve these magazines in their attempts to stimulate the consumption of new technology. This discourse was especially prominent during the latter part of 1989 and the beginning of 1990 when many of the magazines attempted to sum up the technical achievements of the '80s and to assess the possibilities for the '90s. All seemed to agree that the pace of technical innovation had been too rapid during the 1980s, that a slow-down was welcome, and that musicians needed time to learn to use the instruments they already had. Then, as they turned to the '90s, all the ills of the past decade appeared to be magically resolved by the promise of new technologies of the future. This constant forward looking—this deferral of pleasure and satisfaction into the future—is what contributes to the sense of desire and need that is necessary to maximize the pace of technical innovation and profits.

Again, as discussed earlier, the area of musical instruments and audio devices is a highly contested territory, and not all musicians are readily inclined to rally behind the futurist call for newer, ever more powerful technologies. Not unlike the world of classical music where the fetish for old instruments places an excessive monetary and symbolic value on Stradivarius violins and the like, many pop musicians have a special reverence for guitars and amplifiers of a certain make, model, and year—for a particular Stratocaster or Les Paul guitar, for example, or for old tube amplifiers of the '60s. In the world of hi-tech, digital musical instruments, something similar exists in the romance with "warm" analog synthesizer sounds of the '70s. Andrew Goodwin has argued that to play an analog synth "is now a mark of authenticity, where it was once a sign of alienation" (1988:

45). *Keyboard* magazine has even dedicated a regular addition to their instructional columns entitled, "Vintage Synths."

There is something curious about these historical digressions within magazines that regularly publish buyer's guides with feature-by-feature comparisons of the latest and the "hottest" gear on the market. It seems to me that this interest in bestowing "vintage" status upon technically (but not musically) obsolete instruments of the past functions somewhat differently than it does in the case of other musical instruments. In effect, the magazines are saying to consumers, "Yes, you *can* buy that new synthesizer, sampler or drum machine because it *will* still be worth something several years from now." At least one reviewer has expressed exactly those sentiments: "I firmly believe this will be among the last generation of drum machines. . . . Certainly, I can see it being the kind of machine people will be desperate to get their hands on in 1995, or whenever nostalgia for good old 1989 becomes fashionable. We're talking investment opportunities here" (Nigel Lord, in *Rhythm* (U.K.) 5 [5], November 1989: 55). In this way, the discourse of "vintage" instruments is a strategic one; it helps counteract the fear among many consumers that their purchases will become obsolete and worthless.

As clear in the reviewer's comments, the fetish of older musical instruments is essentially a nostalgic one. "Vintage" instruments are understood to give the player a form of direct sonic (and sometimes iconic) access to the past and, thereby, an almost magical ability to evoke the power of some past music. In this sense, there is a curious kind of "fit" between technological "progress" in musical instruments and recording equipment in the post-war period and the dominant modes in which popular music is produced, distributed, and consumed. Nostalgia is coded into the lyrics of many pop songs—"Remember when . . . ," "She's gone," and so on—and into their structure in devices such as the fade-out. DJ patter and mainstream radio frame popular music in terms of the passage of time—"Contemporary Hits," "Golden Oldies," "Classic Rock"; and, among the various ways in which popular music functions for listeners is the manner in which it helps organize our sense of the present and the past, our notions of youth and adolescence (Frith 1987: 142–43). In the age of electronic reproduction, sounds themselves have become an increasingly important part of the way in which musical genres and the passage of time are coded. Musicians' magazines play a critical role in this process by helping musicians define the various relationships between sounds, musical styles, and the passage of time. The magazines help delineate those sounds that are truly "new"; those that through overuse have become merely stale; and those that have become the signs of a nostalgic past.[5]

Another issue already briefly discussed concerns how some musicians rely on magazines as a particular form of mediated interaction. In this regard, it is interesting to explore the manner in which the musicians' magazines construct their readers as both a kind of musical "community" and a market. They do this in a number of ways: First, many of the magazines hold yearly readers' polls. Polls are typically done in a "Vox-Pop" style, that is, readers are asked to choose among a select group of star performers for the best jazz or new age synthesist, rock guitarist, classical pianist, and so on. Such events offer the readers a chance to "vote" and thereby gain a sense of authority and competence in their ability to choose. In part the process reaffirms the choices they have already made when purchasing recordings. At the same time, the polling offers the magazine a chance to address the readers as a kind of pseudo "public" and to obtain information that can be useful in planning future interviews and articles. *Keyboard* magazine (then known as *Contemporary Keyboard*) made use of this technique during the mid-'70s, shortly after its first year of publication. By the early '80s, *Keyboard* was engaged in a different kind of polling, however, one more focused on probing the personal habits of this "body politic." Since that time, readers have been regularly asked to respond to questions concerning their age, sex, income, interest in the magazine, the kind of instruments they own, and, more importantly, how much money they are likely to spend on their *next* purchase and the kind of instrument it will be.

The shift to such information gathering is as significant for what it says about the changing function of the magazines themselves as for what it reveals about their readership. These surveys indicate a move away from a concern with the representation of a readership, a "public," and toward supplying marketing information to advertisers. The stated aim of the surveys is to "monitor current consumer trends, and to anticipate their future needs and buying habits," "to gather valid data on the technology-based music instrument market," and to provide advertisers with "unique insights" that will allow them "to better position their products and services in the mind of the consumer" (advertisers' report, *Trends in Technology II*, 1990: 3).

In a personal interview, one publisher of musicians' magazines responded with the following remark when I asked him whether their magazines were "advertiser-led": "We write for the readers, not for the industry . . . we're not advertiser led, nor product led. We are selling a readership to advertisers so our main aim is to develop and maintain a readership" (publisher, music books and periodicals, personal interview). For him, there was apparently no conflict whatsoever between writing *for* a readership and simultaneously selling it to advertisers. Other individuals involved in music periodical publishing have told me that conflicts often arise when manufacturers attempt to tie the amount of editorial content devoted to their products to the amount of advertising dollars spent in the magazine. All deny that their own magazines bow to such pressure, but many suggest that other, less scrupulous editors do.

For their part, some of the manufacturers seem to feel that the magazines do not cooperate enough with them in their marketing efforts. At the trade shows—those semi-annual rituals where the industry meets face to face—there have been incidents where manufacturers berated magazine editors for adopting a flippant or arrogant attitude toward reviewing their products. Ultimately, however, the industry knows it must accept bad reviews along with good ones; for, as Chapple and Garofalo have pointed out in their discussion of the record industry and the music press, what really matters is the implicit promise that the products will indeed be covered (1977: 165–66). Additionally, the greater credibility with their readership that the magazines gain through objectivity and honesty is then used by the manufacturers when they reproduce (with the permission of the magazines) the reviews of their products for distribution in musical instrument shops. The more "objective" the review, the more effective it can be as a promotional tool.

As for the community of readers themselves, the surveys reveal that they are largely young and male—as high as 98 percent of survey respondents in the magazines devoted to new technology—thus reflecting the more general male domination of popular music and, more specifically, the male orientation of technical culture. Editorials are all critical of this state of affairs and, thereby, attempt to absolve the magazines of any responsibility in the matter. Even a cursory look at the division of labor within the magazines, their editorial and advertising content, or the discourses and modes of address used in the construction and sharing of technical knowledge, however, reveals a definition of technology and musicianship that is highly gendered.

Indeed, the overriding characteristic of female involvement in the world of musicians' magazines is that of near-total abscence. As regards the division of labor in the magazines, the vast majority of the senior editors and the regular contributors are male. Women most often occupy positions as editorial assistants, designers on the production staff, marketing and sales reps, and so on—positions of low visibility (to the readership) and with little opportunity to speak publicly for themselves or their magazines. In popular musicians' magazines, then, males retain a monopoly on speech.

An absence of female performers in magazine content is also evident. By the end of 1995, after twenty years of publishing and a total of some

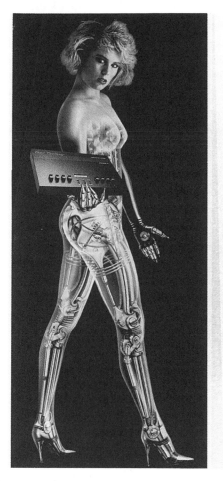

Woman as machine. Resonating with a cultural tradition that stretches back to the eighteenth century in European science and literature, this ad displays the problematic relationship between the male gaze and the desire for technical domination and control.

236 issues, *Keyboard* had devoted its cover story to only a handful of select, female artists: among them, Wendy Carlos (a transsexual, born Walter), Kate Bush, Laurie Anderson, and Tori Amos. The track record for the other magazines is generally no better, but the magazines with the highest commitment to new technology, such as *Electronic Musician* or *Home & Studio Recording*, avoid the issue entirely by not putting people on their covers at all. With technology receiving top billing instead, all social ills disappear into the glossy surface of the technical objects themselves. Magazine editors and marketing representatives for the manufacturers generally feel that photographs emphasizing "hardware" and copy dealing with tech-

nical specifications are gender-neutral. Of course, feminists have long held that, because women's access to technical training and discourse is limited, scientific and technical jargon often effectively alienate female readers (e.g., Lowe Benston 1988).

This "hardware strategy" can still often reveal a gender bias, however. For example, the cover photo on the October 1991 issue of *Electronic Musician* subtitled "Studio Toys" displayed a number of digital effects processors stacked one upon the other among a variety of children's toys, including a model sports car and a mechanical robot. Not surprisingly, Barbie dolls or other toys conventionally targeted to young girls were nowhere to be found. Although the musicians' magazines do not usually contain advertising for non-music related products, the conventions of commercial photography and graphic design ensure that music technology is, nevertheless, associated with a wide range of objects and commodities that are themselves highly gendered in character. Of course, not all manufacturers adhere to the hardware strategy in their advertising, and there are numerous examples where sexism in music periodical advertising is as obvious as in any other sector of the advertising world. The high technology periodicals, however, still tend to pride themselves on a notion that the advertising and editorial content in *their* magazines is not as blatantly sexist (a view occasionally challenged in letters from their own readers) as is often the case, for example, in guitar magazines, where guitar "heroes" are almost exclusively male and where ad photos depicting bikini-clad women lounging across stacks of amplifiers are not uncommon.

The advertising in high technology magazines can sometimes be more deeply disturbing, however, because of the cultural overtones occasionally brought into play by the gendering of technology. In an ad for a series of MIDI devices manufactured by Aphex Systems Ltd., a nude female figure—part human and part machine—is shown holding a device called the "Feel Factory." The ad copy stresses the need for making music "without having to think about the demands and limitations of machines" and the manner in which the Aphex devices put "the musician in command of the machine" (*Keyboard* 15 [6], June 1989: 76). This dynamic combination of motifs—the woman as machine, the need for human "feel," and the call for increased control over technology, overlaid with a distorted yet nonetheless seductive image of female sexuality—is reminiscent of Andreas Huyssen's analysis of the role of the female robot in Fritz Lang's famous film of the 1920s, *Metropolis* (Huyssen 1986: 65–81). Huyssen outlines the deep cultural resonance of the female/machine equation, and its problematic relationship to the male gaze and to the male need for domination and control, as symptomatic of a tradition that stretches back to the eighteenth century in European science, literature, and culture. This equation continues to find expression in contemporary culture, especially in film. For example, it is perhaps no accident that the most problematic figure that the character Deckard must deal with in the 1980s sci-fi film, *Blade Runner*, is the female android, Rachel. The existence of these gendered motifs in ads for electronic musical instruments, however, is all the more significant given a magazine readership that is primarily young, male, and technically oriented.

Equally important is the manner in which new technology and technical production activity is portrayed in its colonization of the private sphere. The home has been the traditional site of female music-making, but as the instrument manufacturers and the magazines have turned their attention toward building the "home studio," there has been a noticeable lack of female (or family) participation in this project. This deficiency is perhaps most graphically demonstrated in a series of ads appearing in a number of magazines in 1990 for Yamaha's "Personal Studio Series™" products. There are several advertisements for the series, all variations on the same theme: A young male, alone in an apartment, usually wearing headphones, is totally engrossed in a personal moment of creative inspiration. In one such ad, the musician is viewed from outside a window, it is almost dawn, and the city is quiet; the ad copy reads: "Don't eat. Don't drink. Don't sleep. Don't stop. . . . While the rest of the sane world sleeps, you're wide awake. Possessed by a need more instinctive than any other. The need to create music . . ." *Keyboard* 16 [12], December 1990: 96–97). The so-called "electronic cottage" has thus been located, or so it would seem, in a remarkably deserted terrain; furthermore, there is an emphasis in the advertisement on a notion of musical pleasure achieved through isolation and an almost ascetic devotion. The musicians' lifestyle is portrayed as virtually irreconcilable with the demands of conventional society, let alone family life. As Mavis Bayton (1990) has pointed out, such portrayals, by their very nature, exclude women from the community of popular musicians.[6]

On the rare occasion when the magazines have attempted to tackle the question of gender in the musicians' community, however, it is interesting to note that such questions are immediately linked to issues of marketing. A guest editorial written by Marsha Vdovin (marketing director for a software company) and published in *Electronic Musician* (November 1989: 130) raised the problem of how women have been "discouraged from technological paths." Typically, the most convincing argument she could muster for why women should be welcomed into the technological community was not that they stood to benefit individually or as a group from such participation; rather, "they represent a market of amazing potential," and marketing people should use tools such as advertising to "both *create* and tap into" this market (Vdovin's emphasis). Arguments concerning technology, economy, and social equity are not unique to questions of gender but, rather, have long been associated with discourses that center around notions of "democratization" and technology.

Musicians' magazines also attempt to create a sense of community by adopting terms and strategies that are characteristic of more traditional rituals of musician interaction. For example, regular articles dealing with musical technique in magazines such as *Keyboard* are titled "Private Lessons," invoking a traditional sense of musician apprenticeship. *Keyboard* also makes extensive use of musical notation in many of its articles and regularly carries transcriptions of popular songs and keyboard solos. In this way, the editors make certain assumptions about the musical training of their readers and place the magazine firmly within the range of activities—Bennett's "musician-recording" and "musician-musician interactions"—described earlier as typical among popular musicians. *Electronic Musician*, on the other hand, seldom uses traditional notation and, instead of transcriptions and lessons in musical technique, instructs its readers on how to build electronic devices and write computer software, thus reflecting its roots in the tradition of hobbyist magazines such as *Popular Electronics*. Such divergences in approach are not only significant in terms of the readership they attract but, more importantly, in how they define two very different kinds of activity as meaningful musical behavior.

Divergences of this kind are also evident in the editorial attitude taken toward the relationship between conventional musical skills and new technology. In response to the general uproar following the Milli Vanilli lip syncing scandal of 1990, one magazine editor espoused the virtues of live performance and "the level of human interaction that only real-time singing and playing can provide." He pleaded with his readers not to get "lost in the search for *perfection*. . . . Reach for your potential as a performer and do the best you can with the gear you've got" (Scott Wilkinson in *Home & Studio Recording*, July 1990: 76). A few months later, taking an opposing stance, *Electronic Musician* published a guest editorial that referred to performing musicians as mere "technicians" and decried the necessity of "spending several years learning (and maintaining) the specialized skills required to play a musical instrument." The solution to this dilemma was to be found in the search for new technology:

Manufacturers should make an effort to appeal to the composer in us all . . . there are those of us who are more interested in and able to work with the overall shape and feel of a composition than the details that comprise it. . . . Let's envision instruments and software aimed at the composer instead of the technician.

(Chris Meyer, *Electronic Musician*, 6 [9], September 1990: 114)

Interestingly, the editor's more moderate, conventional argument is stated as a personal opinion and appeals to the reader on the basis of traditional notions of musical skill. The radical, techno-utopian vision, on the other hand, adopts a mode of address that makes constant use of the third person pronouns "we" and "us" and explicitly calls for the increased production and consumption of goods. In this way, the author invites his readers to join this call for the development of new, innovative technologies, thereby contributing to both the formation of a market and the creation of communal ideals.

Sharing knowledge in less formalized settings than that of the private lesson is also typical of local communities of musicians. The conventional ritual where pop musicians share new "licks" they have learned is here reflected in the technical magazines' regular columns devoted to synthesizer sound "patches" submitted by readers. The prerequisite for participation in these mediated rituals is, of course, ownership of the synthesizers in question. Technology becomes, in this sense, the communal bond itself.

This idea—that technology has become the tie that binds—is the implicit, guiding assumption pervading much of the content of new musicians' magazines. Just as musicians have always identified themselves in terms of the instruments they play, the magazines now refer to this new community of musicians as "electronic musicians" or "recording musicians." Whereas subtle differences of class, taste, and musical style are conveyed by the appellation "violinist" as opposed to "fiddler," however, these new terms appeal to a kind of universality, that is, they make no claim to any stylistic or regional difference. This general attitude is perhaps most explicitly demonstrated in an advertisement that appeared in 1989 celebrating the success of the Korg M1 synthesizer:

In less than a year, the M1 has become more than the world's best-selling keyboard. It has become a form of communication. A universal tool allowing everyone in the creative process of music to exchange new sounds. Develop ideas. And collaborate on projects.
. . . [The M1 is] creating a worldwide network of professionals who are bringing about changes in music faster than ever before.
. . . And with the number of M1 products—and users—growing every day, you can imagine the potential of such a universal language.
Just think, then, how great your potential will be once you begin to speak it.
(Korg product ad, *Electronic Musician* 5 [6], 1989: 3)

Technology has thus replaced music in the old bourgeois myth of the "universal language." Technology has become transparent, "a form of communication," a "language" itself. If you learn to "speak" technology, that is, if you become a consumer of technological products, you are immediately admitted, or so it would seem, into that international fraternity of musicians—the "worldwide network of professionals." In a musical world where it has become difficult for the aspiring young musician to interact meaningfully with other musicians and audiences, where it has become difficult even to secure a gig at a local club, the myth of technology is, no doubt, a powerful force with which to contend.

Conclusion

The relationship between different sectors of the music industries and music periodical publishing has been well established for many years: in the nineteenth century, periodicals were not only the vehicles for music instrument advertising but, even more importantly, an ideal format for the dissemination of popular songs and sheet music for amateur pianists. Focused on the home as the locus of consumption, music periodicals played an important role in both the formation of musical taste and in reinforcing bourgeois family values. In particular, the magazines appear to have been a significant factor in the reproduction of gender roles in middle-class culture. The role of women as the center of family musical entertainment in the home during the nineteenth century stands in stark contrast to the recent, predominantly male preoccupation with the construction of the "home studio."

In the early twentieth century, with the advent of mechanical reproduction and the gradual waning of the parlor piano as the focal point of musical entertainment in the home, on the one hand, and the increasing circulation and specialization in magazine publishing, on the other, music periodicals began to take different forms. The sheet music supplement in general interest magazines quickly disappeared in favor of specialized magazines devoted to every imaginable musical instrument, to audio equipment and sound recordings, and to specific musical styles and tastes.

Above all, however, these changes must be understood in the context of the rise of modern advertising, the creation of a mass consumer culture, and the integration of magazines within the marketing apparatus of contemporary capitalist enterprise. In modern publishing, there is a constant tension between the role of magazines in servicing the interests and needs of a community of readers and their function in delivering that readership to advertisers.

In recent decades, such tensions have been most evident in that sector of the music periodical industry devoted to new technologies. The 1980s were witness to an enormous growth in the innovation, diffusion, and use of digital musical instruments in the production of popular music. This phenomenon was supported by the commercial magazines devoted to musicians and technicians. Indeed, without the simultaneous growth of the musicians' magazine industry, it is unlikely that this phenomenon would have achieved anywhere near the magnitude that it has today. By the late 1980s, the production of digital musical instruments had become a world-wide, billion-dollar industry.

In several of my discussions with the publishers and editors of these magazines, I found that they recognize the role they have played. They feel they have not only reflected the musical and technical trends manifest during this period but also feel they have helped establish those trends in the first place. When in July of 1988 *Electronic Musician* published a special issue on the past twenty years of achievements in musical electronics, one of those "achievements" included the launching of a newsletter called *Electronotes*. According to *Electronic Musician*, *Electronotes* had played a critical role in the development of electronic musical instruments during the 1970s. It is the combined influence of these two publications that is perhaps most significant however. Their influence is not unlike that of the early photography magazines described by Howard Becker (1982: 314–17); *Electronotes* belongs to that category of publications that grows out of the need for experimenters to communicate with one another in order to define the nature of new technical possibilities. Magazines such as *Electronic Musician*, on the other hand, appear at a later stage and are geared toward promotion and consumption; their main purpose is to help users *learn* the specific pleasures offered by the new technical medium. The publishers and editors realize the power they wield within the musical instrument industry: As one publisher put it, "the industry recognises that we are the link between them and their market" (personal interview).

As I have argued here, the growth of the digital instrument industry has taken place both within a high-intensity market context and when musicians have been compelled, for a variety of reasons, to operate at increasing distances from one another and from their audiences. In this sense, musicians' magazines have perhaps become a link not only between the musicians and the industry but, also, an essential mediating factor in "musician-musician interactions." This double mediation contributes to their simultaneous construction as both a community and a market.

Theodore Peterson has stated that the creation of a "cultural bond" and a sense of "national community" has been an important characteristic of magazine publishing in the United States throughout the twentieth century (1964: 449). The development of national magazine publishing itself complemented an expansion in the manufacturing and distribution of consumer goods that took place at the turn of the century. With increasing internationalization of commodity production, however, the logic of the "cultural bond" has perhaps changed: The sense of community takes place within specialized consumer groups whose frame of reference is less national than international, less bound to a shared "perspective" than to a bond with commodities themselves.

Musicians' magazines today play a critical role in the mediation of human needs through objects. New technology has been reified as the tie that binds a community of musicians together, while, at the same time, it is the object of consumption whose success in the marketplace is essential to the survival of the electronic instrument industry. In the final analysis, there is a double production going on: One industry produces technology, and the other produces consumers.

CHAPTER SIX

Communication Networks and User Groups
A Musical Democracy?

✳

> This, my friends, is power. The ability to learn about new uses of technology, and to discuss its implementation directly with the people responsible for that technology, is the power to directly participate in the evolution of technology. . . . It is happening on a daily basis over the computer Networks. . . . The buzzword is DAILY ACCESS.
> (Leopold 1987: 3)

As computers have been adopted as part of the technical means of production in music, communications networks typical of computer culture have also emerged within this specialized field. User groups, computer networks, "forums," "bulletin boards," "newsgroups" and Web sites have become an alternative means of communication for both individual musicians and for the music industry as a whole. Perhaps not surprisingly, some of the more idealistic discourses from computer culture have also manifested themselves within the musical community: in particular, as illustrated in the chapter's opening statement, the utopian belief in the essentially democratic, participatory nature of technologically mediated forms of communication. Of course, such idealism is not without its contradictions; indeed, although the various computer networks used by musicians may appear, on the surface, to be part of an egalitarian system, the manufacturers that use the networks have certain privileges and powers of access denied to normal members. They also make use of the networks for marketing purposes in much the same way that they use magazines and other media for marketing and promotional support.

These new forms of association and communication are certainly not without precedent in the world of music. For centuries, professional and amateur musicians have formed associations of one kind or another through which they organized their activities and advanced the practice of their art. Medieval music guilds, for example, formed a system of apprenticeship training, ensured continued employment, and were marked by exclusivity. In many ways, they were the ancestors of the modern musicians' unions with their extensive network of local administrations and their national and regional publications.

Besides the music guilds and unions (which, ultimately, are little different from those serving other skilled occupations), the more specialized interests of instrumentalists led them to form associations and societies for the promotion and development of even the most obscure musical instruments. Unlike the recent "user group" phenomenon, however, these societies have usually formed around a specific type of instrument (e.g., the violin, the guitar, or the clarinet) and not individual manufacturers; that is, to my knowledge there are no clarinet societies directly associated with Selmer or Yamaha, but there *are* synthesizer user groups associated with Roland, Ensoniq, and other manufacturers, not to mention user groups for individual products made by these corporations.

We need to look outside the history of music to find appropriate analogies for the phenomena currently manifest in the musicians' community. Several moments in the twentieth century have seen similar relations and associations resulting from the enthusiasm of individuals for the technology of modern communication. The amateur radio "hams" of the early twentieth century, the citizens band (CB) radio operators of the 1970s, and, most recently, the networks, bulletinboards, and user groups associated with computer culture are all, in different ways, examples of such patterns. To the outsider, these various movements have often appeared, as well as been portrayed by the mainstream media (at least, until the enormous media hype currently associated with the so-called Information Highway), as little more than "fads," the transient preoccupations of enthusiasts more interested in the act of communication than in its content. In contrast, to the insiders, the technology and the guarantee of popular access to it has just as often been associated with the most idealistic notions of community, democracy, and self-fulfillment.

In this chapter, I address the recent emergence of such networks in music in relation to the rise of technically oriented hobbyist groups such as ham radio operators during the early years of the twentieth century. Though there appears to be relatively little direct connection between these groups, there are interesting parallels to be made between them as regards the nature of their activities and their claims to a democratic political agenda. In the case of the music associations, which will be discussed in the latter part of the chapter, clearly there is a relationship between the new association and communication forms and the marketing activities of the instrument industry; the contradictions between the interests and goals of these two groups cannot be easily reconciled. The early days of the International MIDI Association, itself initially formed as a "user group" during the summer of 1983, demonstrate how quickly the rhetoric of democratic participation in the process of innovation became regarded as a threat to the electronic instrument industry.

"An Adventure into Space"—"Hams," "Hackers," and Other Users of Communication Media

Most histories of radio make at least passing reference to the young, amateur radio enthusiasts—"Marconi's youth" as Erik Barnouw referred to them (1966: 28)—who began operating in the midst of the early, chaotic days of the medium between the turn of the century and the beginning of World War I.[1] Although there appear to be few, precise accounts of who these enthusiasts were and there is some dispute as to their ultimate significance in the history and technical development of radio, there is one point on which most commentators agree: that the vast majority of these amateurs were males, mostly young, white, and middle class. Given the enthusiasm and background of these amateur experimentors, it is perhaps not surprising that many of them eventually filled key executive and managerial positions, not to mention the many positions as operators and engineers, in broadcast radio during the years following the war (Barnouw 1966: 28–31; Hornung 1940: 28–29).

The peculiar fascination that seemingly gripped these young men as they hovered over their home-made crystal radio sets and telegraph transmitters has been described with particular sensitivity by J. L. Hornung. He describes the amateur as a male between twelve and eighteen years of age who has spent hours and days building his own equipment, listening, learning, and tapping out messages in code, waiting for the day when he might hear his own call letters being sent by someone else—a moment "charged with emotion and exultation" (1940: 25–27). Perhaps this ecstasy, this "adventure" in communication across space, was what attracted so many young men to the medium of radio, even more so than the content of their "conversations" (Dunlap 1935: 162–65).

It was, in part, this enthusiasm that fueled what would eventually become "one of the largest independent non-commercial amateur fads" of the period (ibid.: 48). By 1917, (licensed) amateur transmitters numbered over 8,000, and receivers were estimated at 125,000 (Barnouw 1966: 55). The isolated activities of individuals seldom become "fads" without some help from mass media, however, and it should be noted that the popular science magazines and newspapers of the day, followed by amateur radio magazines, played an important role in popularizing radio as a hobbyists' medium (Harlow 1936: 468–69). It was the publishing industry that initially spread the word about the new-found pleasures of the medium to a wide audience and taught amateurs how to build their own sets.

With so many amateurs crowding the air waves, it soon became difficult to ensure uninterrupted communications between shipping vessels (one of the more "official" uses of the medium during its early days). The navy and other U.S. government bodies began to regard the amateur transmissions as "interference" in their own activities, and in 1912 the first radio licensing laws were passed in the United States. The law separated amateur, shipping, and military wave bands, thus forcing amateurs to develop new broadcasting techniques that made use of the so-called "short wave" frequencies.

What is perhaps most important for my purposes here is the manner in which these events contributed to the mythology of the amateur radio operators. During the years preceding the introduction of the 1912 licensing law, the press had valorized the radio amateurs as a group of independent, quasi-scientific experimenters whose lack of formal training in research was more than offset by their harmless obsession with radio technology and the complex phenomena of the air waves. At the same time, however, these amateur enthusiasts came to be regarded by the U.S. Navy as a nuisance—a group of clamorous and frivolous pranksters whose activities threatened both safety at sea and the legitimate operations of the military (Harlow 1936: 469–70).

This difference in "framing" the ham radio operators and their activities is curiously reminiscent of more recent shifts in the public image of computer "hackers." Regarded variously as technical genius, "nerd," and prankster (see Hayes 1990: 91–99), the hacker has become increasingly scrutinized by corporate, government, and military interests as a potential perpetrator of computer crime. Indeed, Andrew Ross has described what is undoubtedly an overreaction to the threat of computer viruses in the aftermath of Robert Morris's disruption of the Internet in 1988 as akin to a "moral panic" (1991: 107; see also, Hafner and Markoff 1991: 253–341). The on-going security problems of keeping corporate information from "outlaw" hackers on the Internet was again brought to public attention in early 1995 with the spectacular arrest (for the second time) of Kevin Mitnick for computer theft (*Newsweek* 145 [8], February 27, 1995: 32–33). Interestingly, Mitnick is also reported to be an accomplished ham radio prankster.

For their part, the amateurs (both the early radio hams and the computer hackers) have often defended their activities by invoking notions of democracy, personal freedom, and public access. In the early decades of the century, the radio hams saw fit to organize themselves, for technical and political reasons, into coherent national and international groups. Organizations such as the American Radio Relay League and the International Amateur Radio Union were formed, and, in 1915, the magazine *QST* became their official organ of communication (it is still being published, some eighty years later). In December of 1918, when the U.S. government held hearings on a proposal to allow a naval monopoly of the air waves following the war, the American Radio Relay League spoke for the interests of the amateurs (Barnouw 1966: 54–55).

By that time, the public image of the radio amateur had already begun to change again. As conscripts during the war, the former amateurs had proven to be useful to the military. The practical knowledge of the amateurs provided an invaluable resource for the development and maintenance of radio communications on the battlefield, and the amateurs returned home as heroes of the war effort. After the war, this new perception of the amateur was augmented with stories, published in popular magazines such as *Reader's Digest*, of a variety of emergency communications services being rendered to local communities by amateurs during times of natural disaster (Harlow 1936: 499–500). Additionally, organizations like the American Radio Relay League and other supporters began to stress how important amateur experimentation was for the technical development of radio, for research into areas such as short wave transmission, and as a training school for future industry leaders (see Hornung 1940: 28–35).[2]

Besides these supposed strategic, communal, and technical contributions, the activities of the amateurs became infused with a peculiar idealism. Hiram Percy Maxim, president of the American Radio Relay League, was quoted as once saying: "To me amateur radio has a more important destiny to fulfill than mere scientific attainment, and that destiny is the furtherance of world peace" (ibid.: 164). In the context of World War I and its aftermath, such appeals to "destiny" and the goal of "world peace" had, no doubt, a deep resonance for the public and for supporters of the amateur radio movement. It is precisely this fusion of arguments—one concerning quasi-scientific and technical pursuits, on the one hand, and another appealing to an idealistic social program, on the other—that apparently became typical of male, technical subcultures during the twentieth century.

To assess such idealistic claims and the more general "folklore" surrounding any given technical subculture, it once again becomes important to consider who the "amateurs" in question might be and precisely what constitutes the nature of their activities and exchanges. For example, in an article discussing the use of citizens band (CB) radio during the 1970s, Hershey and others argue that our image of the ham radio operator as someone concerned mainly with the technical aspects of transmission and reception and with the specialized codes and protocols of radio communications suggests that their "electronic neighborhood" is a relatively exclusive one (1978: 238–39). CB users, on the other hand, tend to have relatively little technical knowledge and are apparently more interested in communicating than in equipment or transmission range per se. The authors argue that the CB "neighborhood" is thus more "populist" in nature (ibid.).[3]

Any community of interest, however, requires at least a minimum degree of "commonality," and in the case of technologically based communications, that commonality, at least initially, boils down to possession of the technical equipment itself (ibid.: 238). Factors such as the relative cost of equipment, the level of knowledge required in its use, and modes of user interaction will, in part, determine the degree of exclusivity exhibited in any medium. Such factors need to be weighed against, for example, claims often made by enthusiasts on the "democratic" nature of the technology and the degree of "global" accessibility. Given consideration of these issues, the global territory potentially accessible via contemporary computer networks such as the World Wide Web is much more limited than its enthusiasts would have us believe; furthermore, although electronic communications may encourage the formation of communities of interest unencumbered by the constraints of time and space, some recent studies of computer networks show that, as the size of the social group grows, so does its instability. This growth places increasing demands on the capacity of individuals to maintain the network itself (Rice 1987).

A number of recent commentators have remarked on the make-up of computer subcultures and compared them to the folklore that has been generated about them. Dennis Hayes dismisses the popular mythology of the "outlaw" and the computer "terrorist" by arguing that hackers are "typically white, upper-middle-class adolescents" who generally lack political motivation despite their antibureaucratic posturing (1990: 92–93). Arguing against Hayes's assumptions, Andrew Ross is less ready to judge the political commitment of hackers as implied by their class status alone or by an overly simplistic interpretation of their activities (1991: 122). Ross makes a more revealing and potentially more important observation about hackers, however, when he argues that, despite the hackers' countercultural stance, there exists an underlying "fit" between the hacker's system of values and that of the entrepreneurial elements of computer culture:

The hacker cyberculture is not a dropout culture; its disaffiliation from a domestic parent culture is often manifest in activities that answer, directly or indirectly, to the legitimate needs of industrial R&D. For example, this hacker culture celebrates high productivity, maverick forms of creative work energy, and an obsessive identification with on-line endurance (and endorphin highs)—all qualities that are valorized by the entrepreneurial codes of silicon futurism.   (Ibid.: 121)

Ross's description of the adolescent computer hacker bears some resemblance to Hornung's valorization of the energy, freedom, and excitement that characterized the working habits of the early ham radio experimenters (1940: 30–32). Hornung referred to this "peculiar psychic or psychological phenomenon" as simply the "amateur spirit in research" but then went on to claim that this "spirit" was valued by many professional engineers of the day, that it was even largely responsible for "America's dominance in technological radio fields," and that its preservation was essential for "progress" (ibid.: 33). In this way, Ross, in a critical manner, and Hornung, in a more celebratory fashion, point to an essential continuity of values that inform male technical subcultures, regardless of their professional or political status.

Importantly this "folklore of technology" (Ross 1991) surrounding male subcultures—the stories of their obsessions, feats of accomplishment, and supposed transgressions, and their advocates' idealistic statements of purpose, values, and destiny—obscures female relationships to the same technology. Indeed, in the various accounts of the early radio enthusiasts cited here, women are not mentioned at all. Even Hornung's book (1940), which is ostensibly an introductory training manual for those interested in a career in radio, assumes that those wishing to enter the field will be exclusively male.[4]

Unlike commercial broadcast radio, which eventually superseded it, the early wireless was hardly a domestic instrument at all. Instead, it inhabited an entirely different set of spaces, separate and secluded from family life: "In attics, barns, garages, woodsheds, apparatus took shape. Because of the noise and other menaces and hazards, real or imagined, the activity was for a long time banned from living quarters" (Barnouw 1966: 28). This separation from the central spaces of family activity is perhaps typical of male hobbyist pursuits; similarly, the notion of the "home studio," so prevalent among popular musicians today, begs the question of how it and its activities are to find a place within the home.

The popular valorization of male hobbyist activities and the corresponding neglect of women's relationships to the technologies of communication is particularly disturbing since the activities engaged in by women, at least in some cases, may be more socially and economically significant than many of the isolated, technical preoccupations of male hobbyists. Although male users, from the early ham radio operators to the perpetrators of computer "viruses," have been variously portrayed as "pranksters," "mavericks," and "outlaws," there is little evidence that the majority of their "pranks" have been in any way damaging to commercial or government interests. Women's transgressions, on the other hand, often occur in the workplace and thus have a more direct impact on the operational efficiency of the organizations in which they work:

In the mainstream everyday life of office workers, mostly female, there is a widespread culture of unorganized sabotage that accounts for infinitely more computer downtime and information loss every year than is caused by destructive, "darkside" hacking by celebrity cybernetic intruders. . . . In many cases, a coherent networking culture exists among female console operators, where, among other things, tips about strategies for slowing down the temporality of the work regime are circulated. (Ross 1991: 123)

Both Ross (ibid.) and Hayes (1990: 95–96) agree that corporate managers recognize this widespread ability to tamper with data and programs, even within unskilled elements of the work force; however, executives are reluctant to publicize the extent to which their companies are vulnerable to this kind of activity, and much of it goes unreported.

It is perhaps no accident that the vast majority of the early radio enthusiasts were not only male, but male *teenagers*, and that their activities and modes of interaction took on such peculiar characteristics. Sherry Turkle has made an explicit link between male adolescent attitudes and a number of activities, including ham radio and computer hacking (see 1984: 207–11). Turkle has argued that the psychologically difficult time of adolescence, when social and sexual pressures are particularly acute, is when males are most likely to turn to the worlds of technology and formal systems as a means of overcoming their personal anxieties about social relationships (1988: 43–44). Her comments concerning the use of computers as a compromise solution to the "conflict between loneliness and fear of intimacy" seem especially appropriate when applied to the ham radio phenomenon: "In its activity and interactivity, it offers the illusion of companionship without the demands of friendship" (ibid.). The recent formation of so-called "user groups" around particular musical instruments bears a striking resemblance to these male adolescent subcultures; the deeper aspects of male psychology described by Turkle are no doubt a factor in the organization of activities surrounding musical technology as well.

Commodities, Users' Groups, and Computer Networks
in the World of Music

Clubs, users' groups, and newsletters have been common within the subcultures surrounding the various technologies described previously. They are certainly prevalent in the personal computer world since the mid-1970s, and, to a large extent, the recent proliferation of such groups around digital musical instruments has been directly patterned after similar groupings of computer "hackers": "Since music generation is rapidly becoming more computer intensive, there is a need for the same end-user support that has become common in the personal computer market: an INDEPENDENT user's news magazine" (*Transoniq Hacker* promotional brochure, emphasis in the original).

The *Transoniq Hacker*, initially formed to provide information to users of the Ensoniq Mirage sampler (and, later, all Ensoniq products), was founded in 1985 by Eric Geislinger, an engineer, and Jane Talisman, a music/synthesizer teacher. By the end of the decade, *Transoniq Hacker* had about 4,200 subscribers, many of whom were "hacker types who come from the technical end of the spectrum—engineers and tech types with musical interests" (Jane Talisman, personal interview). Talisman acknowledges computer and software users' groups as the model for *Transoniq Hacker* and feels that for musicians this type of group works best when organized around digital samplers rather than synthesizers: "Because of the disk operating system, people (especially hackers) will be developing new or improved uses of the technology and, as with computer users, they will be predisposed to network-type information sharing" (ibid.).

Talisman's technical rationale for the formation of user groups can only go so far in explaining the existence of so many groups of this nature, even around systems that are not disk-based. In fact, the desire to form such groups and networks might have relatively little to do with the unique capabilities of the individual instruments themselves. Possibly, one of the problems with synthesizers today is the degree to which they all seem to resemble one another, and only through marketing and promotion can they achieve any sense of identity at all.

This latter point bears some resemblance to arguments made by William Leiss in *The Limits to Satisfaction* (1976) concerning twentieth-century commodities more generally. Drawing on the work of Kelvin Lancaster, Leiss states that commodities have reached a level of complexity during the twentieth century that requires consumers no longer to judge them purely on their objective properties but also on the particular "characteristics" they embody. Advertising, socialization patterns, and interpersonal relations all play a role in determining the "imputed" characteristics of commodities:

> Imputed characteristics are those that people believe to be present in things; these beliefs arise out of the innumerable messages about things that each individual becomes acquainted with through advertising and the opinions of other consumers. . . . Commodities are not straight-forward "objects" but are rather progressively more unstable, temporary collections of objective and imputed characteristics—that is, highly complex material-symbolic entities. The disintegration of the characteristics of objects stands in reciprocal relation to the fragmentation of needs.
>
> (Leiss, 1976: 82)

If synthesizers and samplers are not merely musical instruments but are "material-symbolic entities," then clearly user groups and information networks are not simply a means of exchanging technical information; rather, they might be a means by which consumers develop alternative definitions of their needs and new forms of satisfaction from their relationships to commodities and other consumers.

Howard Becker's account of the early development of stereographic image technology during the nineteenth century (1982: 314–17) offers another perspective on the introduction of new technologies and the specific phenomenon of user groups (whether they be ham radio operators, computer hackers, or electronic musicians). Photographic experimenters needed to communicate with one another to define the nature of the new technical possibilities. Then, for consumers, it was necessary to *learn* the specific pleasures offered by the new medium: "In addition to learning to read the stereographic image, viewers must have learned a taste for its unique pleasures. The early appreciative articles dwell on these . . ." (ibid.: 317). Similarly, articles and product reviews in popular synthesizer magazines and user-group newsletters serve a dual function: They not only provide information about product innovations but also suggest specific applications from which new musical pleasures can be experienced. As new sounds, instruments, and techniques develop, new forms of pleasure thus develop in tandem with them—"unique pleasures" that are experienced individually but arrived at collectively.

To a certain extent, this communication and sharing of information can itself become part of the process of technical invention and innovation; for example, the role played by the *Transoniq Hacker* magazine in "uploading" user feedback to the Ensoniq Corporation. Talisman claims that the *Hacker* has managed to maintain its independent status while facilitating a system of two-way communication between manufacturer and users. Ensoniq technicians respond to user questions in the pages of the *Hacker*, and, partly as a result of this openness, Ensoniq has apparently acquired five or six times as much third-party software support for some of its products than have other manufacturers (Talisman, personal interview).

For Ensoniq, the user group is not simply a source of technical feedback, however; Ensoniq advertises the existence of the *Transoniq Hacker*, various other information networks, third-party software companies, and so on as part of its overall promotional strategy. In an ad entitled "Mirage Diner" (*Keyboard* 13 [1], January 1987: 111), Ensoniq lists both the *Transoniq Hacker* and the Performing Artists Network (described later) as among the basic advantages of owning Ensoniq equipment: Direct access to other users as sources of information is considered a fundamental enhancement to ownership. Ensoniq also buys issues of *Transoniq Hacker* and places them with the owner's manual and the other support information included with the sale of their instruments. In this way, user groups have become a factor in the promotional strategies of many hardware and software manufacturers currently involved in the production of musical technology.

This latter application for the users' group phenomenon became increasingly important to the larger manufacturers of samplers, synthesizers, and software during the 1980s; promoting users' group information support for new products became a common marketing tool. For example, Roland Corporation publishes a glossy, in-house magazine called *Roland Users Group*, complete with instrument "reviews" written by its own product specialists (of course, these pieces resemble television "info-mercials" more than objective assessments of the instrument's capabilities). Similarly, Yamaha published a newsletter for its "official" users' group entitled, *Aftertouch*, excerpts of which appeared regularly as news/ads in commercial magazines; and, Passport Designs (a software company) formed a user group called "Club Passport" whose membership fees included access to the Performing Artists Network (PAN), newsletters, and other benefits. The information that comes back to the corporations as a result of this increase in direct contact with consumers can be used for future design and/or marketing purposes. In this way, the musical instrument/user group phenomenon resembles Kevin Wilson's description of home networking as a means of enhanced, point-of-sale marketing strategies, or "transactional marketing" (1986: 28–33). It also indicates a fusing of the conventionally separate stages of design and marketing into a single, integrated process.

The exact nature of the manufacturer/user relationship via networking is not easy to define, however. In the promotional literature for the PAN network, a number of ways in which the network has been used for research and development, advance product announcements, user feedback, direct sale of synthesizer sounds via MIDI, and so on are described. Whether these incidents represent the power of consumers to participate directly in the evolution of technology or are simply good marketing strategies on the part of manufacturers is a matter of interpretation.

The membership of user groups and musical information networks also deserves a closer look. On the surface, the heterogeneous make-up of these groups appears to contribute to the general blurring of distinctions between musician and technician, amateur and professional, often noted as a typical result of innovation in musical technology. Any group based on the acquisition of technical knowledge and/or the capacity to consume will, however, inevitably generate its own set of distinctions. The evolution of the Pennsylvania-based PAN network is perhaps a case in point.

According to Perry Leopold, founder and director of PAN, the network began in 1981 and was originally a service to provide information (in the form of directories sent through the mail) concerning new performance venues, recording opportunities, and so on primarily to self-managed musicians. As the organization shifted its services to computer-based networking, however, the composition of its membership was radically altered; representatives of the record industry (such as CBS) joined the network, as did synthesizer manufacturers, professional musicians, and many others. As a result of the shift to computer-oriented services, the network became, in effect, more mainstream and professionalized. This change in general orientation was apparently quite inadvertent: "When I started out I never thought I'd be helping CBS to make money" (Leopold, personal interview, 1989).

The type of information carried by the network also changed in accordance with its user base. For a time the network was almost entirely oriented around information, education, and help for MIDI and synthesizer users (PAN is the on-line resource for the International MIDI Association and the MIDI Manufacturers Association). Later, when the mid-'80s technology explosion leveled off, the organization became less education oriented and returned to its original concept of connecting freelance composers and musicians with film producers, recording studios, and so on, but the emphasis was now fully on professionals.

By the mid-1990s, PAN was made up of approximately 3,000 members (25 percent of whom lived outside the United States) who represented virtually every facet of the music industry: well-known musicians (such as Herbie Hancock, Madonna, and Pete Townsend), soundtrack composers, recording studios, instrument manufacturers, computer programmers, accountants, tour managers, and technicians. PAN now screens prospective members and discourages "amateurs" from joining, in part because its new, up-scale clientele needs to be insulated from fan mail. In the process, young, entry-level musicians have been squeezed out: "A kind of class differentiation has developed . . . professionals and non-professionals don't mix" (ibid.). As with most forms of "class differentiation," PAN membership is marked, at least in part, by economic status: "We keep amateurs out by the price structure. This is not casual stuff" (Leopold, in *Musician* 190, August 1994: 64).

The professionalization of PAN and the employment of user groups in manipulative marketing strategies indicate that the diffusion of computer-based technologies and the formation of user networks do not necessarily lead toward greater levels of democratization (as many utopian accounts of the new technology would have us believe). Indeed, new technologies often present a variety of potential uses, but their introduction into existing social and economic structures can have a constraining effect upon them.

By the mid-1990s, with the increasing popularity of Internet access, PAN was not the only, nor even the principal, network forum for musician and music industry interaction; although, because of its relative exclusivity, it remained a viable entity. The wide range of activities characteristic of the Internet, however, makes it difficult to grasp, let alone assess, the overall impact it is presently having on musicians, their artistic practices, and their modes of expression and interaction. Musicians have used the Internet as an informal means of communicating and gathering information; independent record labels and even individual bands have used it as an alternative to mainstream channels of promotion and distribution; and manufacturers have set up Web sites to explore and exploit its marketing and promotional potential. It is impossible to examine all the ways in which the Internet is currently being used by musicians, but it may be useful briefly to outline a few areas that relate to the various issues discussed previously.

One of the most open and freewheeling areas of net culture is "Usenet." Usenet consists of a collection of special interest groups called "newsgroups," of which several thousand are broken down into a series of subject categories. Many music-related subtopics can be found in the "alternative" ⟨alt⟩ and "recreation" ⟨rec⟩ categories, including newsgroups devoted to various genres of pop and rock (e.g., ⟨alt.rave⟩, ⟨alt.music.alternative⟩ or ⟨alt.rock-n-roll.metal.heavy⟩), individual artists (e.g., ⟨alt.music.prince⟩ and ⟨rec.music.phish⟩), and so on. The newsgroup for synthesizer enthusiasts is ⟨rec.music.makers.synth⟩.

Newsgroups tend to be very informal. Individuals "post" messages that can be read by anyone visiting the newsgroup, and literally dozens and even hundreds of messages are posted every day in some of the more popular topic areas. Although individuals can engage in on-going "discussions," the potential for developing relationships or a sense of "community" is extremely limited. In the synthesizer newsgroup, the technology itself seems to constitute the main focus of identification. It is common, for example, to find messages extolling the virtues of a particular synthesizer or passionately defending it against detractors. Such messages convey a sense of the enormous personal investment *in* technology and the sense of power that can be derived *from* these "material-symbolic entities." Individuals looking for help with technical questions concerning MIDI, synthesizer programming, or simply looking for new sounds often post messages. As I argued in Chapter 5, the reliance on mediated forms of communication for obtaining such information reveals how difficult it is to find local musicians with adequate knowledge or expertise in new musical technology.

Perhaps the closest equivalent to a user group on the Internet is a "mailing list." Individuals "subscribe" to mailing lists, and messages posted on the list are automatically sent to all subscribers via e-mail. List membership tends to be much more stable than in a newsgroup, and, consequently, the topic area is often more focused. Whereas the *Transoniq Hacker* is the user group newsletter for users of *all* Ensoniq products, there are Internet mailing lists for each individual product manufactured by the company—not only synthesizers and samplers but even the DP/4, a signal processor released in the early '90s. As with user groups more generally, the mailing lists foster an almost exclusive identification with technology that has become increasingly narrow in its focus. The support for Ensoniq products among users and third-party developers is almost legendary within the industry, and it is perhaps not surprising that there is a Web site, located at ⟨http;//www.netaxs.com/˜mikeh/ensoniq.html⟩, that contains an extensive directory of Ensoniq Internet resources.

Despite these criticisms, the independent control and user orientation of newsgroups and mailing lists might suggest that they are fundamentally democratic in nature. In the areas of the Internet that are experiencing the greatest pressures toward commercialization, such as the World Wide Web, however, the contradictions between "democracy" and the marketing needs of industry are becoming increasingly evident. For example, the "home page" of The MIDI Farm, a Web site connecting users to a wealth of MIDI information and products, states that "our goal is to create a central location for all musicians, from the hobbiest [sic] to the pro, to gather and help each other and themselves. It is also a place for the manufacturers to contact you about new products and upcoming events" (⟨http://www.midifarm.com/midifarm/farminfo.html⟩).

Contemporary capitalism thus continues to exert its influence over even the most "democratic" media. This pressure need not be totally determining, however. Individuals can and do develop their own specific uses of technology and, in some instances, can even intervene in the development of new technologies, although such intervention is somewhat rare and haphazard. For a brief, chaotic moment in the early diffusion of MIDI, a call for direct and democratic user participation in the development of the technology was heard. The conditions that gave rise to that call and the manner in which it was ultimately contained offer an object lesson in the potential, and the limits, of user intervention.

Democracy and the International MIDI Association

The formation of the International MIDI Association (IMA) during the chaotic early months in the life of the MIDI specification gave the organization a potentially powerful role to play during this critical stage of the diffusion of the technology. Roger Clay, founder of the IMA, apparently had an innate sense of the importance of the moment and immediately began to formulate a game plan for how the user group might maximally input the decision-making process surrounding MIDI. Those plans included participation in the formalization of MIDI as an official technical standard (in preparation for which the IMA joined the American National Standards Association (ANSI) in 1984); the establishment of a network of local chapters of the IMA in major metropolitan areas; and the creation of an independent MIDI Research and Development Center "to continue research on instrument/computer interfacing technologies and designs, and to initiate MIDI software development in a cooperative, open environment" (*IMA Bulletin*, spec. ed., December 1983: 3).

In the midst of the fast-moving, highly competitive synthesizer industry of the early 1980s, there is something curiously idealistic and naive about the notion of a research facility—conceived as something partway between the commercial industry, academe, and a regulatory agency—where "cooperative" research could take place. Clay seems to have been possessed by a "zealous attitude towards the technical possibilities of MIDI" (Dave, a musician and early member of the IMA, personal interview, 1989), and he was convinced that the IMA had an important role to play not only in the development of MIDI but in the future of music as well:

Accurate information and helpful advice on products and resources are important to any creative process. In the new world of musical equipment/equipment interfacing (let's call this *musical cybernetics*) they become essential services.
The IMA is designed to provide you these services and offer assistance in

locating the resources you will need to creatively interact with the new artistic technologies.

At the same time, we believe that it is important to encourage humanistic approaches to our use of these devices; they are tools to use not gadgets to collect. . . . We at the IMA are working to insure that we move beyond the toy stage . . . and onto stages that will allow us to better realize our artistic potentials.

(*IMA Bulletin*, special edition, December 1983: 2; emphasis in the original)

The emphasis on the IMA as a disseminator of "information"—information essential to the discovery of the potential hidden within the machine—reinforces the arguments put forward by William Leiss concerning the complexity of commodities and the need for information that will release the power of their objective and "imputed" characteristics. Equally important are the values expressed in this early editorial statement from the *IMA Bulletin*—especially those concerning the "artistic" side of technology, the "humanistic approach," and the realization of "our artistic potentials." These ideals are not unlike those voiced by many people involved in the early stage of the introduction of personal computers, as described by Sherry Turkle: "people . . . whose work experiences prepared them to use the machines . . . and gave them a desire to exploit the machines' potential for creating worlds of transparency and intelligibility" (Turkle 1984: 171). Continuing, Turkle states that there was also a political agenda behind these notions of creativity:

There is something else notable about the introduction of personal computers: they came on the scene at a time of dashed hopes for making politics open and participatory. Personal computers were small, individually owned, and when linked through networks over telephone lines they could be used to bring people together. (Ibid.)

This latter point is clearly in keeping with Clay's vision of an IMA network and his politically idealistic notion of a "co-operative and open environment" for independent research.

A similar analysis of the "countercultural" roots of much of the enthusiasm for recent technologies is presented in the chapter entitled "Alternative Technology" in Jennifer Daryl Slack's book, *Communication Technologies and Society* (1984: 30–39). Slack argues that the fascination with technology and the "commitment to the equation of technological growth and social progress" place too great an emphasis on the uses of technology at the expense of an adequate analysis of the relations of production (ibid.: 38).

This would appear to have been the case with Roger Clay: His enthusiasm for the technical potential of MIDI may have prevented him from seeing that there could be no easy reconciliation of the needs and demands of "users," on the one hand, and the responsibility of the manufacturers to make a profit, on the other. The problem for the IMA was that it essentially had no political mandate: Some of the manufacturers cooperated with the IMA, others refused to acknowledge its existence, and many were hostile to the idea of being told by "users" how to conduct their business. Clay had proposed that a lab be set up to test products and ensure that implementation of MIDI was up to proper specifications. In the competitive and secretive synthesizer industry, few manufacturers were willing to release pre-production models of their equipment for such testing (Keith, a member of the IMA software group, personal interview, 1989).

At the January 1984 annual trade show of the National Association of Music Merchants, the synthesizer manufacturers created a Steering Committee of Manufacturers of MIDI Equipment, and, later in the same year, the MIDI Manufacturers' Association (MMA) was formed.[5] Membership in these organizations was restricted to manufacturers and representatives of the larger software houses. As a result, interested users began to feel even more alienated from the process of improving MIDI. As tensions between various factions increased, the tone of Roger Clay's editorials in the *IMA Bulletin* became more desperate and aggressive:

As Network Coordinator . . . I support and promote the MIDI Open-System Concept. . . .
Unfortunately, the actions from some isolated but potent members of the manufacturing community have been anything but nurturing. In fact, their actions on a couple of occasions has bordered on the out-and-out malicious. . . .
MIDI is supposed to belong to everyone (*non-proprietary!*), attempts by one manufacturer or a self proclaimed consortium to "control" the access to MIDI information, or to band together to exclude those who may wish to get involved if they are "not of the party" is counterproductive to the concept. . . .
Let me make it clear that while we are very interested in the developments of MIDI as a concept and an interface, we *are not* interested in joining in any manipulative politics! (*IMA Bulletin*, 1 [3], 1984: 2)

Clay continued to promote his version of the "Open-System Concept" and to work toward the development of new standards in conjunction with MIDI. During the summer of 1984, the IMA sponsored a conference for software developers—"MIDISOFT'84"—in San Francisco. The aim of the conference was to provide information about MIDI to software developers and end-users and, more importantly, to establish a "MIDI Software Standards Board." Clay had already realized that, as musical software for MIDI devices began to develop, there would soon be a real need for common file formats; in this area, as with many of Clay's ideas and instincts concerning MIDI, he was basically correct and far ahead of the rest of the industry in his thinking (Keith, personal interview, 1989).

The conference drew over two hundred participants, many drawn from the ranks of independent software developers. Only a handful of representatives from the manufacturing sector bothered to attend. The atmosphere at the conference, especially during the question and answer periods, appears to have been highly charged, and the general level of discussion, quite sophisticated. Participants criticized the technical limitations of MIDI and offered possible solutions, openly expressed anger and disappointment at the lack of manufacturer cooperation with independents, discussed the role of the IMA itself, and formed Special Interest Groups to work on various aspects of the MIDI specification with the intention of sharing their findings with the manufacturers.

Dr. Gareth Loy, software coordinator of the Computer Audio Research Laboratory at the University of California, San Diego, and one of the featured speakers at the MIDISOFT event, has described the sessions devoted to the establishment of a MIDI Software Standards Board as "open threshing sessions held in the style of a town meeting" (*IMA Bulletin*, 1 [5], 1984: 1). With regards to the MIDI phenomenon as a whole—including its technical, political, and economic aspects—Loy is an astute observer, participant, and commentator, and the precise choice of words used in this "Open Letter" to the IMA readership should not go unnoticed. Loy conjures up the image of the "town meeting," with all its attendant associations with the roots of democratic process in America. In so doing, he sums up the entire struggle of the conference participants (and by implication, the struggle of the IMA itself) to contribute to the development of something they believe in, despite the resistance of an industry seemingly bent on excluding them from that process. Even in the opening sentence of the "Letter," Loy is careful to establish himself as a legitimate spokesperson of the conference participants: "I have been asked by a unanimous floor vote of the participants of the MIDISOFT '84 Conference . . . to compose this letter which describes some important developments which transpired there, and to enlist your support and encouragement of these developments" (ibid.). He thus emphasizes the collective nature of the proceedings and their importance as a model for the development of "open, honest dialogue" concerning MIDI.

One limitation of most theories of technological innovation is that they often understand innovation as motivated only by the desire for increased profits. It seems important to me to understand the particular stage in the development of MIDI outlined above not only in terms of technology and economy but also in terms of power and democracy. In a series of essays published in *Democratic Theory: Essays in Retrieval* (1973), C. B. Macpherson describes two different ontological assumptions that underlie our liberal theories of democracy:

One of these is the liberal, individualist concept of man [woman] as essentially a consumer of utilities, an infinite desirer and infinite appropriator. This concept was fitting, even necessary, for the development of the capitalist market society, from the seventeenth century on: it antedates the introduction of democratic principles and institutions. . . . The other is the concept of man [woman] as an enjoyer and exerter of his uniquely human attributes or capacities, a view which began to challenge the market view in the mid-nineteenth century and soon became an integral part of the justifying theory of liberal democracy. (Macpherson 1973: 24)

The first concept supports those democratic theories that emphasize the freedom of individual choice and justify liberal democracy by claiming that it allows for the maximization of individual satisfactions, or "utilities," and that it does so equitably. The second downplays consumer satisfactions and emphasizes human attributes, such as creativity, as ends in themselves and justifies liberal democracy by claiming that it maximizes the freedom to use and develop one's innate capacities. The first claim is an economic one, intimately linked with the emergence of capitalist market society; the second, an ethical one, arising with nineteenth-century demands for the extension of democratic franchise. In actual fact, the two concepts are incompatible, and Western liberal democracy has been incapable of delivering the goods for either claim (ibid.: 4–12, 25–36).

Clearly, Bob Moog's notion of the "democratization" of digital synthesizer technology, discussed in Chapter 4, is related to the market society concept of democracy. It assumes that the cheaper technology becomes and the more available to the average consumer, the more democracy has succeeded in the equitable distribution of utilitarian satisfactions. In contrast, an ethical notion of democracy was clearly implied (though never explicitly made) in the early goals of the IMA. It placed a humanistic emphasis on the creative, "artistic potentials" of individuals and stressed the importance of the association as a facilitator of "open" dialogue in the development of technologies that could help release those potentials.

It is also important to note the contradictory role played by technology in these arguments. On the one hand, the companies involved in the innovation of MIDI feel that they have been vindicated against their critics by the fact that MIDI has been accepted in the marketplace. The MIDI specification may display a certain lack of technical excellence, but it has nevertheless proven itself to be useful by thousands of musicians. The success of the technology as a consumer product thus proves to be more important than its precise technical capabilities. The argument is a bogus one, of course, because consumers were never really given a choice between MIDI and some other interfacing scheme.

For those involved in the initial organization of the IMA, on the other hand, the contradiction was more profound: Because they regarded technology itself as a prerequisite to the enjoyment and development of human creativity, they were obviously more sensitive to the technical limitations of MIDI but nevertheless felt committed to promoting it as an idea. The often extravagant claims for the possibilities of "musical cybernetics" made by people like Roger Clay certainly contributed to the acceptance of MIDI in the marketplace. Ironically, such enthusiasm may have actually enhanced the position of the major manufacturers as the primary arbiters of the specification.

Once the manufacturers had established their own association (the MIDI Manufacturers Association, MMA) to guide the future development of MIDI, there was no longer a clear purpose for an organization such as the IMA. It has continued to exist, however (without the leadership of Roger Clay), as essentially the information service of the MMA; that is, it distributes information from the manufacturers to users but does not take an active role on behalf of users' interests. The organization continues to publish the *IMA Bulletin* but refuses to distribute any issues of the *Bulletin* that pre-date November 1984. According to some individuals within the IMA and MMA, the views expressed in these older issues were "almost slanderous and took a position not in keeping with current IMA philosophy" (Larry, current member of the IMA, personal interview, 1988). Although it may be difficult for an outsider to find anything particularly offensive in the early issues of the *Bulletin*, the industry, nevertheless, appears to be quite sensitive about this period of early dispute and would prefer to forget that it ever occurred. In an article published in *Keyboard* magazine in 1989, Bob Moog used the occasion of the sixth anniversary of the introduction of MIDI to "talk a little about the politics behind the MIDI specification" and described its history as "a story of remarkable collaboration of dozens of manufacturers across the electronic musical instrument spectrum" (Moog 1989: 117). The entire year or more leading up to the subordination of the IMA to the interests of the manufacturers' group is summed up as a period of "many informal meetings of both manufacturers and MIDI users (and a couple of organizational false starts)" (ibid.).

Perhaps Moog's rewriting of the social history of MIDI is relatively insignificant. Certainly, for some, the current interdependence of the MMA and IMA, with its explicit, hierarchical division of labor, "fulfills the original intent of the IMA but even better" (Dave, personal interview, 1989). For others, despite the present informality and relative openness of the structure of the MMA (it has about eighty members, including a large group of software manufacturers), there still exist influential power blocs within the organization: "Anyone can *propose* a change [to the MIDI spec], but implementation of the change is very political and is getting increasingly difficult to get major changes" (Bob, a MIDI hardware and software developer, personal interview, 1989). What no one seems able to predict is whether this supposed "remarkable collaboration" of manufacturers could actually effect an evolution out of MIDI and into a wholly new specification. For many in the industry, the answer is as clear now as it was during the early 1980s: "The only way to go would be to get the four or five big manufacturers together and make it a *de facto* standard" (Don, a synthesizer engineer, personal interview, 1988).

As far as industry standards are concerned, the problem of technical innovation in the synthesizer industry is not simply one of profits but also one of power: "This industry is so small that it's easily dominated and swayed by the people that own 30% of it" (Carmine Bonanno, in Milano 1984: 60). Although it should be noted that, since its introduction, many of the newer developments in MIDI (such as MIDI Time Code) have been proposed by software companies, such improvements must occur essentially within the framework of MIDI as it was originally formulated by the major manufacturers and, to be successful, must meet with their approval. In this respect, the manner in which the MMA operates is significantly different from the more formalized procedures of a professional society or standards organization.

In the fall of 1988, representatives of the MMA were invited by the Audio Engineering Society (AES) to discuss the possibility of formalizing MIDI for approval by the American National Standards Institute (ANSI). The process of ratifying a new standard is complex and involves the negotiations and approval of two separate committees, the S4 Committee and the subcommittee S4-1:

> The membership of S4 . . . is composed of organizations, both industry and professional. In addition, government agencies, consumer organizations and a few individuals of significant professional standing are members. . . . As a subcommittee, S4-1 may be composed of individuals rather than being restricted to organizations as is S4. In either case, a reasonable balance must be maintained within each membership, ensuring fair representation of all interests: producer, consumer (domestic and industrial), general interest and government. (Langdon et al. 1982: 230)

The MIDI group was "appalled by the ratification process" and felt that "it would set the MMA back five years" (Jeremy, a member of the MMA, personal interview, 1989). Significantly, what bothered the MMA representatives was not only the time-consuming nature of the process but also the number of organizations external to the synthesizer industry itself that would have to be consulted (ibid.).

Of course, as far as the manufacturers of MIDI are concerned, outside interference in technical matters is what they have been trying to avoid all along. For the MMA, there are no longer any significant political problems that confront the further development of the MIDI specification, only technical ones: "ANSI doesn't understand the excellence of the MMA technical group. . . . Overall competition disappears once the engineers start looking for solutions to bugs in implementation. . . . There's no dialog with the public, we just hack out problems" (ibid.).

Conclusion

The increasing emphasis on technology in music production has spawned new forms of association and communication that bear as much resemblance to groups such as the early ham radio operators and computer "hackers" as to any form of affiliation previously connected with music-making. What is particularly striking in all of these examples is the predominantly male, hobbyist orientation of these activities; the fascination with technology itself; and, perhaps most important, the idealistic, democratic, and utopian rhetorics that are often mobilized in support of such activities. In this regard, the "cultural bond" between users of new musical technologies may be even stronger than that associated with most present-day commodities seen as "material-symbolic entities," in part, because it is so loaded with both an appeal to personal and artistic potential, on the one hand, and an idealistic rhetoric of political democracy, on the other. Indeed, it is the conflation of these two sets of ideals that makes the allure of new technology so powerful. To a certain extent, musical instrument and software manufacturers recognize this fact and make use of it for their own marketing purposes, as is demonstrated in the following excerpt from an open letter addressed to users of a new type of MIDI software called MAX:

MAX challenges all notions about music and multi-media software. A world full of MAX products could change the entire music technology market . . . MAX gives all of us the power to redefine the role of computers in music and art. . . .
   Think of MAX as a chain letter. If each of you could turn ten other people onto MAX, our revolution would become a political movement to be reckoned with.
(MAX Development Package, 1990)

In contrast to the blandishments of marketing directors, however, clearly the formation of a "user group" such as the International MIDI Association can be motivated by a genuine desire on the part of independent developers and end-users for greater participation in the process of technological innovation. In this way, the user group and computer network phenomenon can, indeed, have important political implications. For C. B. Macpherson, the realization of the political aspirations of groups such as the IMA ultimately depends upon the evolution of our notions of democracy, in particular, upon resolving the contradiction between economic and ethical views of the democratic process. Macpherson further argues that twentieth-century developments in technology are certainly one of the focal points where such a resolution must take place (1973: 36–38).

Macpherson, I think, places too much emphasis on technology as a prerequisite for the realization of democratic aims, arguing that technology increases the general level of productivity and frees society from the need for compulsive labor. As a result, he finds it conceivable that the market concept of human essence could potentially be discarded, thus enabling society to concentrate more exclusively on the development of human capacities (ibid.). Macpherson consequently falls prey to a kind of technological utopian vision; furthermore, he appears to adopt, uncritically, the nineteenth-century humanistic vision of democracy as a stop-gap strategy by the bourgeoisie to distract attention from their own capital accumulation, which, in the face of demands from the working class, could no longer be justified by the older democratic ideology.

This contradiction in the work of Macpherson is indicative of the ongoing confusions in our society about the relationships between technology, individual creativity, and social and political processes. Given the close relationship (both real and imagined) between musical instruments and notions of personal creativity and expression in music, it is not surprising that individual musicians should wish to become involved in the development of new technologies such as MIDI. Most interesting is that such a desire should also become linked to a collective call for democratic access to the process of technical innovation. Significantly, the confusions that resulted from this conflation of aims and motives tended to disguise the actual political nature of the challenge in the IMA's conflict with the larger forces at play in the capitalist marketplace.

For the moment, the most likely outcome of rapid technological development is that consumption will be made even more attractive through the creation of new desires, thus reinforcing the image of human essence as one of infinite consumption. This latter possibility appears predominant in the world of digital musical technologies, for, although it is always possible in a capitalist market society that new technologies will be invented outside the immediate pressures of the marketplace, the innovation and diffusion of technology can only be justified on the basis of potential marketability. The continuous flow of capital that is required to bring any technology to its full development requires that many technologies be released in stages, each time submitting them to the vagaries of the marketplace. In part, this requirement accounts for why the ultimate test of a product in the synthesizer or music software industry today is not its technical excellence but its market success.

PART THREE

✳

CONSUMPTION/USE:
TECHNOLOGY AND MUSICAL
PRACTICE

✳

CHAPTER SEVEN

Music/Technology/Practice
Musical Knowledge in Action

✳

I am reminded that the transition from acoustic instruments to digital ones, *mutatis mutandis*, has not included a corresponding transition from acoustic to digital music. . . . What has necessarily been a search for a new instrument should now mandate a search for a new music *endemic* to its nature. That is: *computer* music. Here I conceptually implicate *piano* music and *orchestral* music, for instance, with respect to their accumulated *sensibilities* (but not their materials).
(Gaburo 1985: 43; emphasis in the original)

The search for a new music and the technical means with which to express that music has preoccupied various quarters of the musical avant-garde ever since the dawn of modernism. Indeed, for many composers, true "progress" in the one area—"music"—could not take place without a parallel "progress" in the other. For example, writing in 1911 and calling for a new system of harmony based on microtonal intervals, Ferruccio Busoni described the need for new instruments of production as both "important and imperious"; questions of musical notation were, by comparison, of only secondary importance (reprint 1967: 14–15). Realizing that his program for musical change would remain only a dream without new instruments, Busoni took great encouragement in the news from America of the invention of the Dynamophone, an electronic instrument for the production of "scientifically perfect music" (invented by Thaddeus Cahill, ca. 1906). Interestingly, he had never seen nor heard the instrument but had simply read about it in a magazine article (ibid.). Following in Busoni's footsteps, Edgard Varèse's life-long search for "an entirely new medium of expression: a sound-*producing* machine" (Varèse 1967: 196–201) has become legend in the history of electronic music, and his notion of "the liberation of sound" has assumed the status of a guiding ideology for avant-garde composers of electronic and computer music alike (Russcol 1972).

For the avant-garde, however, the question of how new musical instruments could become a truly vital part of musical practice, how they should be put into the service of musical form, was not simply one of means and ends. For Kenneth Gaburo, quoted previously, the idea of using computers to pursue musical ideas based on principles derived from acoustic instruments is to "trivialize" the domain of digital music (1985: 41). Here again, Gaburo is only repeating what was one of the more rigid propositions of avant-garde electronic music during the 1950s. Under the burden of such beliefs, even the modernist "revolution" in musical language launched by composer Arnold Schoenberg—and valorized by Theodor Adorno (1973) as the negation of both the tonal system of music and the social order to which it belonged—became regarded as "impure" by composers such as Karlheinz Stockhausen. The system was impure because of the "fundamental contradiction" that supposedly existed between the twelve-tone system of composition and the harmonic structure of traditional musical instrument sounds. The turn to technical production in the German school of *electronische musik* was an explicit attempt to eliminate such contradictions by submitting both musical and sonic material to the dictates of a single, unifying compositional logic (Eimert 1958; Stockhausen 1961; Théberge 1987: 77–117).

Most interesting in these statements of aesthetic purpose, however, is the underlying assumption of an essential identity between musical form and its means of expression. A similar kind of "theorizing" takes place, albeit only rarely betraying a similar degree of essentialism, among pop fans and critics when they make the familiar observation that rock, or heavy metal, is *guitar* music. Such observations are usually based on the immediate identification of timbral elements that define the genre in some significant way, such as the sound of a distorted electric guitar: "Anytime this sound is musically dominant, the song is arguably either metal or hard rock; any performance that lacks it cannot be included in the genre" (Walser 1993: 41). For many fans, it is the predominance of not only the sound but also the image of the guitar—a "real" instrument—that sets rock off from pop, with its "unnatural" synthesizers and drum machines (Frith 1986: 268). Such statements beg the question of the nature of the relationship between musical instrument, sound, and idea. They also demand a more thorough consideration of a complex set of issues ranging from the intimate, physical relationship between performers and their instruments (and, not incidentally, the social relations between performers, composers, and engineers as well), to the role of instruments in the definition of musical genres and in musical change, and to broader theoretical issues concerning technology as a "means" of production versus technology as a "mode" of production (Blacking 1977).

Although I do not intend to debate the validity of the avant-garde preoccupations outlined above, it is worth underlining one fundamental flaw in their arguments, if only as a way of introducing a number of broader issues concerning technology and musical practice. The concept of an "*electronic* music" or a "*computer* music," as espoused by Gaburo and others, is based on a musical and an historical error that seeks, in typically modernist fashion, to divide these musics from all previous or contemporaneous musical forms, thus making claim to an unprecedented uniqueness and originality. Although Gaburo may be right in pointing to a repertoire of music that can be considered "pianistic" or "orchestral" in nature, the piano and orchestral literature are not as exclusive with respect to one another, or to music as a whole, as he suggests.

For example, throughout the nineteenth century, orchestral music was typically composed at the piano, and piano transcriptions of orchestral works were prepared, as a matter of course, for study *and* performance without any sense of either medium being "trivialized" in the process. It is furthermore not uncommon for innovative performers to adopt playing techniques or sounds derived from instruments other than their own. When these innovations in performance style are recognized by audiences and other musicians, they then become part of what may well be described as the "accumulated sensibilities" of the instrument. Finally, although there are certainly fundamental differences between electronic or digital technologies and acoustic instruments, such differences do not inevitably separate them from the broader continuum of musical expression; only the crudest technological determinism could support the argument that musicians approach these new technologies without bringing with them at least some of their own "accumulated sensibilities" with regards to music-making.

What *is* important to determine, however, is precisely the manner in which *selected* characteristics—physical, acoustic, stylistic, or aesthetic—which constitute the total "accumulated sensibilities" of a piano, a guitar, an orchestra, or even a computer, interact with a variety of musical and extra-musical factors to create innovations in musical form. I stress the word "selected" here because it is primarily through their *use* that technologies become musical instruments, not through their form. Perhaps one of the best examples of what I am suggesting here is Robert Walser's perceptive account of the various timbral innovations and playing techniques exploited by heavy metal players—their specific uses of distortion and sustain resulting from signal compression, power chords, and resultant tones, their use of modality, and their cultivation of virtuosity. Such techniques have redefined the guitar as a musical instrument (1993: 42–

51). In this sense, musical instruments are not "completed" at the stage of design and manufacture, but, rather, they are "made-over" by musicians in the process of making music.

Indeed, the processes of "making" the one and, then, the other are intimately tied, but not entirely in the ways suggested by Gaburo and others of the avant-garde. For Gaburo, a new kind of music will be created out of the various "interactions" between composer and machine (1985: 41–42). Such an attitude assumes, however, that the machine is already fully constituted, endowed with a "nature" that is already more-or-less complete and given. What I want to suggest here is that the machine, too, is, in a sense, "created" by the user in the act of making music. In the context of this book, where the notion of musicians as "consumers of technology" has been suggested, the ability of the consumer to define, at least partially, the meaning and use of technology is an essential assumption and theoretical point of departure.

In this chapter, I explore a wide range of issues related to music and technology that will serve to highlight certain continuities and discontinuities in musical practice that have occurred with the adoption of digital musical instruments during the 1980s. The focus, then, is not so much on technology per se as on "technique," understood in its broadest possible sense. I refer to the notion of technique not simply in the limited sense commonly employed in music (e.g., performance or compositional technique) but in its full sense as the organization of means—material and social—employed for musical ends.

I also want to use the term "technology" in a number of different ways. First, in keeping with the notion of "technique" used here, the symphony orchestra or the recording studio—each with its own characteristic hierarchies, hiring practices, conventions, and patterns of work—is considered a form of "social technology" (Frederickson 1989: 194–97). Social technologies are distinct from, though they may be related to, specific "machine technologies" (ibid.). Second, I examine certain "technologies of music"; that is, "technologies" in the form of discourses, institutions, and practices—aesthetic, scientific, pedagogical, legal, or economic—that "produce" representations of music that have concrete ideological or material effects on music-making.[1] I continue, however, to use the more common expression, "musical technology," to refer to musical instruments, recording devices, and so on. In this sense, copyright law might be considered as a particular "technology of music": a set of principles and legal instruments that define "music" in specific ways, assign authorship, and parcel out legal and economic rights. In its day-to-day operations, this legal "technology" can have a profound impact not only on the profits of individuals and large corporations but also on defining the limits of legitimate musical/creative activity.

It follows, then, that this brief examination of "musical practice," and its further development in the following chapters, will necessarily be diverse in its approach, using theories and observations derived from a variety of sources and disciplines, including musicians' accounts of their work, music theory, ethnomusicology, sociology, and law.

Instruments and the Body in Musical Knowledge and Practice

In the curriculum of the conservatory or the university music program, the study of the techniques of instrumental performance are kept separate from the study of theory, composition, and, to a lesser extent, even history. In this way, the tools and the practice *of* music are thought of as distinct from the discourses of knowledge *about* music. We are thus presented with two systems of "logic": One concerned with the practical—a world of skill, dexterity, immediacy, expressive action, style, and subjectivity— and the other, with knowledge—analytic, methodical, detached, formal, structured, and objective (cf., Bourdieu 1990). To a large degree, this separation is an expression of a more fundamental division in Western culture between the body and the mind (McClary 1991: 23–25, 53–54, 136–39).

Of course, these divisions are in many ways artificial but, nonetheless, deeply rooted in the history of Western art, music, and thought.[2] Indeed, long philosophical tradition has debated the status of music as a "language," an argument essentially idealist in character and neglecting the social and corporeal aspects of music-making. As Bourdieu has pointed out, aesthetic theories from the time of Kant have been based on a notion of purity of form as the primary source of pleasure—a "pleasure totally purified of all sensuous or sensible interest" (1984: 493). Even in the comparatively recent work of philosophers such as Susanne Langer is distrust in the special qualities that the performer brings to music. Though Langer states that the performer plays an integral part in the expression of music, she sees the performer's role as one of delineating the deep, formal structure of the music. If the performer plays in a passionate manner, the performance becomes a mere "symptom of emotion" rather than a clear articulation of expressive form (Langer 1953: 145). For Langer, emotion in music must be *"formalized*, and the subject-matter 'distanced'"* (1969: 222; emphasis in the original).

Music theory and analysis, though certainly the domains of a more narrowly specialized group of musical thinkers than that of philosophy, have, especially since the beginning of the nineteenth century, adopted an outlook remarkably similar to that of the aestheticians. Indeed, the reduction of theory and analysis to the task of explicating musical form could be considered the necessary technical support structure (a "technology") of idealist musical aesthetics (see Kerman 1985: 64–85). By the turn of the century, Schenker's methods of musical analysis could not only dispense with the performance of music but even the surface details of the score itself. In the twentieth century, music analysis has increasingly turned to abstract, mathematical models of explication (ibid.: 90–112; Dunsby and Whittall 1988). For Foucault, the genesis of such a complex "technology" is always a response to an "urgent need" and thus has a certain "strategic function" (1980b: 195). In the case of the nineteenth-century development of positivist musicology and music theory/analysis, Kerman has suggested that the preoccupations of these disciplines masked the nationalist, religious, and class interests of the European middle and upper classes (1985: 31–36).

If the musical (and social) context of these theoretical and philosophical attitudes is the bourgeois concert tradition of notated art music, then it is not surprising that the popular musics of the West, and indeed the musics of much of the non-Western world, were for a long time considered to have no bona fide music theory of their own (Feld 1982: 163–65). This assumption is far from the truth, although it may be difficult in many of these musics to separate theory or aesthetics from the specific contexts and practices of music performance. In a very real sense, the ideational aspects of these musics are intimately bound to the very processes of music-making, to the instruments employed, and to the characteristic verbal constructs— often oblique and metaphoric in nature—used to describe musical activity (ibid.; and Feld 1981).

The field of ethnomusicology, its theories and methods, may be useful here in offering a model of how concepts and practices are intertwined in meaningful ways in music-making. For example, in the theoretical research model put forward in *The Anthropology of Music*, Alan P. Merriam distinguishes between three analytic levels: the conceptualization of music (concepts and values concerning what music is and should be); behavior in relation to music (physical behavior, both in producing and responding to sound, as well as social and verbal behavior); and music sound itself (1964: 32–36). Interestingly, in his elaboration of the basic model, Merriam begins with sound, the third level of analysis, and works backward to the level of musical concepts. Music sound in this context is understood to have structure, and may be part of a system, but it is inseparable from the human behavior that produces it. This model of music-making, furthermore, is dynamic; the third and first levels form a feedback loop that represents the learning process of the musician and the non-musician alike (ibid.).

I am, however, also uncomfortable with various aspects of Merriam's model. In particular, there is an implied one-way linearity (or circularity) in the model that suggests that changes in one area—concept, behavior, or sound—lead unproblematically to changes in the other areas. More importantly, there is a sense that this "feedback loop" operates in the manner of a relatively closed circuit; that is, the mutual influences and interdependence between musical behavior and other types of social and cultural behavior are difficult to discern within the model. Merriam's concept of the role of music *in* culture thus appears to stem from a functionalist outlook (ibid.: 47).[3]

Having stated these reservations, however, I still think Merriam's formulation of music-making as a integrated process has distinct advantages over the way in which music is dealt with in traditional music theory and in musicology, and I will make use of his model, at least implicitly, in much of what follows. In addition to his tripartite model, Merriam describes six areas of inquiry for the in-depth study of music in culture (ibid.: 44–48), several of which are of immediate interest to the study at hand. The most relevant is what he refers to as "musical material culture," essentially the study of musical instruments, their recognized taxonomy, physical characteristics, techniques of performance, symbolic value, distribution, and the economics of their production (ibid.: 45). Again, however, I see these areas of inquiry to be interrelated to a degree not entirely evidenced in Merriam's work. For example, as I have argued earlier, the successful production and marketing of new musical instruments cannot be entirely separated from the training of musicians, which is treated as a separate area of inquiry in Merriam's scheme.

Turning now to the role of musical instruments in the formulation of musical concepts and practices, it is instructive to consider one of the most fundamental problems of music theory: the structuring of pitch materials in the form of modes, scales, and tuning systems. Questions of pitch, and especially tuning, are commonly considered to be among the more abstract areas of music theory, but, although the pitch systems of the West have often been represented in the most mathematical and/or metaphysical of terms (e.g., in the language of ratios or in appeals to "the music of the spheres"), the origin and the significance of most scales and tuning systems are usually found in musical practice, not in abstract science. This fact is well understood in a number of recent anthropological studies of musical cultures where there appears, on the surface at least, to be relatively little in the way of formalized music "theory."

For example, Hugo Zemp's (1979) account of the panpipe music of the 'Are'are people reveals a subtle differentiation of pitch relations—differences in the "interval" between two tones—which are systematically linked to the characteristics of the various panpipes in use, to specific performance practices, to the melodic figures and polyphonic organization of the music, and even to the spatial configuration of musicians playing in ensembles. All of this is described by the *'Are'are* through an extensive vocabulary that makes frequent use of visual metaphors of distance and movement. The musical concepts of the *'Are'are* and the tuning of their panpipes are thus closely interwoven into the context of musical practice and constitute a kind of "system," but one not easily recognized as such through simple observation or by analysis of the music or the instruments themselves.

According to these insights, it could be argued that, virtually anywhere that drums, pipes, or stringed instruments are found, there will also exist a clearly defined "logic of practice" (Bourdieu 1990), which, even if it only takes the form of distinguishing between different types and sizes of instruments, nevertheless constitutes a kind of musical "theory":[4]

Partial as these native theories are, . . . they demonstrate how terminology and technical theory may well develop where there is an object or instrument on which an otherwise abstract system can be observed in visible operation; the growth of musical theory and of scale-systems also is connected with observations on musical instruments, not on the singing voice or on acoustic phenomena in the abstract.
(George Herzog, in Zemp 1979: 34)

In sharp contrast to these practically based notions of pitch relations, however, scientists and theorists of music in the West have come to study the sounds produced by various instruments quite differently from the manner in which performers might approach the same (or similar) objects. For example, at least since the time of Pythagoras in the sixth century B.C., a great many theorists in the West have developed (or justified) their ideas on musical scales and tuning by observing the vibratory characteristics of a string instrument known as the "monochord"; following Pythagoras, the vibrations are usually classified according to the mathematical ratio of the string lengths that produce them. What is interesting about this practice, for my purposes here, is that the monochord is seldom considered to have been a significant instrument of musical performance per se. Although the vibrations of the monochord are essentially no different than those produced by any stringed instrument, the monochord only found a very limited use in musical practice during the Middle Ages, primarily as a pedagogical aid in the training of singers and, occasionally, in ensemble music (Sachs 1940: 268–71). Indeed, despite its importance among music theorists, the instrument existed almost entirely outside any significant tradition of musical performance. The monochord was thus a very peculiar form of technology—an instrument of science, not music—and knowledge derived from it was, from the outset, rational, objectified knowledge.

Whereas scientific knowledge of the physical characteristics of sound has certainly played an important role in the development of Western concepts of tuning, scales, and harmony, it was far from being the deciding factor in the adoption of our modern system of twelve-note, equal-temperament tuning. Other factors of a more practical and musical nature were also influential, including the limitations of the human hand, the problems in instrument design, the system of music notation, and the evolving taste among musicians and audiences for music in a modulatory, harmonic style (Partch 1974: 407–19; Weber 1958b: 97–103).

The development of keyboard instruments, however—first the organ, then the clavier instruments, and finally the hammer piano—was of the utmost importance in all these matters because of the extended note range of the instruments, the fixed nature of their tuning, and their widespread use in both polyphonic and chordal music. Interestingly, these developments, being of interest to both musicians and theorists, occurred both inside and outside the mainstream of musical practice and, for this reason, tended to have a quasi-scientific character. Max Weber has argued that the objective, rational approach taken toward experimentation with keyboard instruments, especially from the sixteenth century onward, became a model of experimental method that would only later be adopted in science (1958a: 141–42). For Weber, then, instrument design in the West has, at least since the Renaissance, exhibited a marked tendency toward rationalization.

Unlike the monochord, however, the central role of keyboard instruments in musical practice ensured that modifications in the mechanics and tuning of keyboards would proceed, at least in part, in response to the requirements of science, aesthetics, *and* musical performance. The size of the human hand, the need for a common practice among musicians, habit, and training, all contributed to the continued dominance of the twelve-notes-to-the-octave limitation on tuning and to the traditional seven-white-five-black configuration of the keyboard (Partch 1974: 408). Even today, with few exceptions, these factors continue to exert a considerable pressure toward conformity on the designers and marketers of new musical instruments.

Because of the increasingly widespread use of keyboard instruments in both professional and amateur music-making during the eighteenth and nineteenth centuries, significant modifications in keyboard design were almost guaranteed to make substantial contributions to the evolution of musical style. The adoption of a fully chromatic, equally tempered scale in keyboard instruments during the eighteenth century contributed to the realization of complex modulations and chromaticism in European art music and, in turn, placed greater demands on all musical instruments. For example, improvements in the technical design of woodwind and brass instruments—specifically, the addition of key mechanisms and valves during the nineteenth century—were a direct response to the increasing demands of chromaticism in orchestral and chamber music of the same period (Carse 1964: 200–219). Clearly, musical instruments take part in a dynamic interplay with musical concepts at the most fundamental level. Material culture and abstract systems of musical thought and organization thus form a dialectical relationship of the utmost importance in music-making.

Ultimately, however, musical instruments, scales, and tuning systems are only the material and conceptual infrastructure onto which musical style is built. They may, in part, determine *what* sounds are played, but they have much less influence on *how* they are played. Indeed, the manner in which you play an instrument can transform both the instrument itself and the nature of the musical sounds produced. You need only compare, for example, the characteristic body postures, hand positions, and bowing styles of the orchestral violin player to those of the folk fiddler to realize that there is more to the difference between "classical" music and "folk" music than just the relative complexity of musical form. The folk fiddler neither holds, plays, nor even tunes the instrument in the same manner as the orchestral player. Indeed, as their names imply, there is a sense in which the "violin" and the "fiddle" can hardly be considered the same musical instrument, although, in virtually all respects, they are physically identical.[5] For all their superior training, the violinist can seldom match the sense of style that any fiddler acquires intuitively through direct musical experience. Even when the violinist is able to imitate the techniques of the fiddler, it will sound "wrong" to their ears, and they will tend to adapt the music to their familiar playing technique (Thede 1967: 14).

In a certain sense, the physical attitudes taken toward a musical instrument, like those toward the body and the material world more generally and the intuitive sense of style developed only through living in a particular musical culture, are elements of what Bourdieu refers to as the *habitus* of a given social group or class—"the system of structured, structuring dispositions, the *habitus*, which is constituted in practice and is always oriented towards practical functions" (1990: 52). What most trained musicians do to acquire and maintain instrumental technique has little to do with the *habitus*; even in the most refined expressions of the awareness of bodily balances and movement, the activities of the professional musician are concerned with a conscious disciplining of the body (cf., Menuhin et al. 1976: 14–85). For Bourdieu, the *habitus* is precisely that which does not pass through discourse and consciousness but is learned through imitation, or, rather, "a practical *mimesis* (or mimeticism) which implies an overall relation of identification and has nothing in common with an *imi-*

tation that would presuppose a conscious effort to reproduce a gesture, an utterance or an object explicitly constituted as a model" (1990: 73). In music, then, the *habitus* takes the form of that unconscious yet fully structured system of sounds, gestures, meanings, and conventions that we commonly refer to as "style."

For my purposes here, the most important issue concerning musical style is that, for musicians, style is something that is primarily felt; it is an awareness that is as much physical as it is cognitive. Nowhere is this fact more evident than in improvised and semi-notated forms of music, where a sense of the relevant musical traditions and conventions are passed on not through discourse but through practice. In his discussion of jazz improvisation, Howard Becker (in terms reminiscent of Bourdieu) observed that "conventions become embodied in physical routines, so that artists literally feel what is right for them to do. . . . They experience editorial choices as acts rather than choices" (1982: 203–4). Similarly, David Sudnow has described the technique of jazz improvisation as "the knowing ways of the jazz body" (1978: xiii). Fluent improvisational technique, because it must answer to the needs of performance in "real time," demands that the body become accustomed to routines, not simply as a form of acquired technique but as elements of musical style:

Only after years of play do beginners attain that sort of full-fledged competence at place finding that the jazz pianist's left hand displays in chord execution. . . . Through repeated work in chord grabbing, an alignment of the field relative to the body's distancing potentials begins to take place, and this alignment process varies in delicacy and need in accordance with the form of the music. The rock-and-roll pianist's capacities for lookless left-hand reaching differ from the baroque specialist's, and these both from the stride-style jazz pianist's. Every musical style as the creation of human bodies entails correspondingly constituted tactile facilities for its performers. (Sudnow 1978: 13)

Similar observations could be made about virtually any group of instrumentalists. For example, drummers know that to move between playing the steady beat of rock to the shifting accents of reggae or to the melodic and polyrhythmic style of jazz requires not simply a knowledge of relevant rhythmic patterns and phrases but a realignment of the body and its balances—a complete re-"patterning" of the coordination of the limbs. Style, then, for the musician, is something that is acquired only through an extended *process* of learning through practice.

Style, thus acquired, is not necessarily as rigid, as mechanical, or as unchanging a thing as one might suspect, at least not for the improvising musician; style becomes a physical resource through which variations—and indeed innovations—are created. Sudnow relates how, after a lengthy period of playing jazz piano in a relatively spatial and tactile manner—

a manner governed by visual and conceptual schemata and supported by a certain physical dexterity—he began consciously to "aim" for particular sounds, not simply "places" on the keyboard (ibid.: 37). The capacity to hear, in advance of an action, is a subtle (and essential) aspect of a performing musician's creative ability: "It is one thing to recognize familiar sounds you are making and another to be able to aim for particular sounds to happen. A different sort of directionality of purpose and potential for action is involved in each case" (ibid. 38). What is essential in Sudnow's account is that this inner hearing is related to action in a temporal way; he describes this momentary pre-hearing of a note-to-note course of action as the "emergence of a melodic intentionality" that had been dormant in his playing prior to that time (ibid.: 41–42).

I will return to this notion of inner hearing and intentionality in music in the following chapters, but for the moment, note that accounts such as Sudnow's may go a long way in explaining the particular attachment so many musicians have to specific instruments, the importance they place on the acquisition of skills of execution, and, consequently, the threat felt by some when confronted with new technology. When drummers, for example, approach digital drum machines for the first time, it is not primarily an unfamiliarity with the functioning of the device that is the source of a certain discomfort; it is, in part, the apparent loss of that entire "field" of physical/spatial/aural potential, so intimately tied to their sense of musical style and purpose, that is perhaps most disquieting. Adopting new instruments, new sounds, or a new style of playing is thus a very gradual process for most musicians, as attested to even by jazz trumpeter Miles Davis, a musician whose long career was defined by change: "When I started playing against that new rhythm—synthesizers and guitars and all that new stuff—first I had to get used to it. At first there was no feeling. . . . You don't hear the sound at first. It takes time. When you do hear the new sound, its like rush, but a slow rush" (Davis 1989: 323).

At the risk of belaboring the obvious, it should nevertheless be noted that "the sound" that Davis refers to in this instance is not the same notion of "the sound" with which much of this book is concerned—"sound" as an isolated object of reproduction and exchange; rather, as with Sudnow, "the sound" Davis is trying to hear is that inner projection of a musical action. For the improvising musician, new musical contexts require new ways of feeling and an attentiveness to hearing/playing new patterns of sound.

A musical style is thus always *learned*, to paraphrase Leonard Meyer, even by the musicians who "invent" it (Feld 1988: 76). In this sense, musicians are little different from other listeners (i.e., audiences): The codes, habits, and strategies of a given style or genre of music are intuitively felt by listeners as a set of implied relationships and expectations that are "empirically real, but . . . necessarily general, vague, and physical" (ibid.). For the listener (and here I again include musicians), the problem of translating these vague feelings into more concrete terms usually involves language and is thus always an active and on-going interpretive process—a process that is, like music itself, both subjective and socially interactive, composed of a set of "interpretive moves that metaphorically locate, categorize, associate, reflect on, or evaluate music experience" (Feld 1984: 16). Like musicians, listeners learn to *anticipate* certain features and patterns within a given style and, even when this sense of anticipation is not as precise nor as specific as the "aiming" process of the improvising musician, it is nevertheless essential to the formation of the listener's sense of stylistic "boundaries" (ibid.: 11). More than a simple matter of recognition, the perception of boundaries or "frames" becomes part of that other musical practice—consumption, where issues of "value," "identity," and "coherence" are instantly, and simultaneously, felt and reflected upon.

Thus far, I have used the terms style and genre almost interchangeably, but the two concepts are not equivalent. Franco Fabbri has offered a definition of genre as "a set of musical events (real or possible) whose course is governed by a definite set of socially accepted rules" (1982: 52). His definition is rather broad but contains the possibility of defining "sub-sets" or "subgenres." For Fabbri, style or musical form is but one factor defining the character of a given genre of music; other factors, including various semiotic, behavioral, social, ideological, and economic "rules," as well as the structure of the musical community itself, combine to identify a particular genre (ibid.: 54–60). Though much of the present discussion centers around the use of musical instruments in stylistic, temporally based expressions of musical sound and form, musical instruments, the sounds produced on them, and elements of style or form are never, in themselves, sufficient to define a genre (ibid.: 55). Understood in this way, it is clear that individuals can adopt unique approaches to playing their instruments or idiosyncratic ways of dealing with musical sound and syntax while remaining within the confines of a given genre. The distinction between sound, style, and genre will become important in the following chapters, especially when dealing with the problem of technical reproduction and musical genre.

Putting aside, for the moment, the problem of musical genre, let us take up again the fact that musical performance, and perhaps especially improvisation, is bound to a set of acquired physical and aural techniques and capacities that are oriented toward action within a particular temporal flow—a flow that places present and future into a relationship of intimate proximity (hence, as noted above, the importance of anticipation, even among listeners). The same temporal relationship also characterizes the actions of musicians when they perform together, and, as Bourdieu has pointed out, this temporal dimension—the implied "presence in the future"—may indeed be essential to all forms of practical "logic." Bourdieu offers sport as an example of its operation:

A player who is involved and caught up in the game adjusts not to what he sees but to what he fore-sees, sees in advance in the directly perceived present; he passes the ball not to the spot where his team-mate is but to the spot he will reach—before his opponent—a moment later, anticipating the anticipations of the others and . . . seeking to confound them.   (Bourdieu 1990: 81)

Bourdieu's description of this play of anticipations is remarkably similar to Alfred Schutz's account of the social structure—"the structure of the mutual tuning-in relationship" (1964: 162)—that is characteristic of any musical performance by two or more individuals:

Either [performer] has to foresee by listening to the Other, by protentions and anticipations, any turn the Other's interpretation may take and has to be prepared at any time to be leader or follower. Both share not only the inner *durée* in which the content of the music played actualizes itself; each, simultaneously, shares in vivid present the Other's stream of consciousness in immediacy. This is possible because making music together occurs in a true face-to-face relationship—inasmuch as the participants are sharing not only a section of time but also a sector of space.   (Schutz 1964: 176)

Even when a musical event is not, in itself, communal in structure, it could be argued that the collective experience of playing and listening together still informs the subjective, temporal impulses of the practicing musician:

Every once in a while the time would get into the fingers as I sat . . . setting a beat first by getting my shoulders going around a little, while I tapped my foot and snapped my fingers before play; counting off the time with a care I had never taken before, a care for the jazz to be played, a care for the others with whom I would have been coordinating my moves, for that bass player and drummer who were never around . . . a care for the new listener I had become myself and for the one who had been missing, ready to hear that song, that jazz, to tap his fingers to it.   (Sudnow 1978: 115)

This inner feeling for the imagined presence of the other that Sudnow describes is derived, in part, from the same phenomenological experience of musical time that, for Schutz, constitutes the "social relationship" between composer, performer, and listener. This relationship is present regardless of whether that experience is mediated by mechanical devices, such as recordings. Schutz argues that, from a communication point of view, the experience of listening to music is qualitatively different from, for example, reading a book. The experience of music requires what Schutz refers to as a "coperformance" that must, of necessity, occur within a shared temporal domain constituted by the moment-to-moment flow of the music itself, quite apart from whether this "coperformance" takes place in a genuine face-to-face relationship (1964: 169–75). For Schutz, then, we are always "making music together" (the title of his essay).

In this sense, the experience of musician and listener have much in common: The *feel* of musical time—whether conceived of primarily in terms of rhythmic patterning or, more broadly, in terms of Schutz's inner experience of *durée* (the concept itself derived from Bergson)—is shared by musician and audience. Schutz goes further, however; he argues that, although the musician's performance requires that their sense of time be geared toward the "outer world," that of the listener remains "merely an internal activity" (ibid.: 175). I agree with Schutz that the musician's mental and physical attitudes may well be directed toward a specific kind of action that requires a direct awareness of the temporal flow of note-to-note configurations and musician-musician interactions, resulting in what Bourdieu refers to as a feeling of "urgency" that is a property of all practice (1990: 82); however, his characterization of the listener's experience as "merely internal" is, I think, biased by his implicit adoption of a model of audience dispositions drawn from the contemplative mode of listening typical of nineteenth-century concert hall tradition. Similarly, Bourdieu's analogy of the scientist as a "spectator" at some sporting or dramatic event also depends heavily on a rigid distinction between "actor" and "spectator" that may not be in keeping with various forms of popular production and consumption.

Without collapsing the very real distinctions that exist between musicians and audiences (and here the notion of "urgency" may well be an important issue), note that the reception of popular music, especially popular forms oriented toward dance, is far from the passive activity that most cultural critics have taken it to be. The relationship between music and dance has long been lost within the tradition of European art music; even by the eighteenth century, so-called "dance suites" had already become autonomous and highly stylized forms of instrumental music. It is thus not surprising that Schutz should turn to the more abstract (even reified) notion of *durée* rather than to rhythm in his discussion of the essential experience of musical time.

Much popular music of the twentieth century, on the other hand, especially those forms based on African-American sources, has never made as complete a break with dance. As a result, there exists a different level of participation in the consumption of popular music through dance that mitigates against the distanced logics of reception and objectification suggested by both Schutz and Bourdieu. Indeed, ethnomusicologist John

Blacking (1971) has argued that, in the West, we have confused specific musical skills (e.g., the ability to perform on an instrument or to compose music) with musicality; he maintains that any true theory of "musical competence" must be based instead on the more general ability to *listen* in a creative or structured manner. He goes on to suggest that in some African cultures communal dancing is the first stage in the acquisition of a more specific set of musical skills related to performance (ibid.: 24–25).

In dance, the body both responds to the shaping influence of rhythmic sound and makes use of it—channels it toward another kind of expressive action that is at once related to, but different from, musical performance. The active and potentially creative nature of these practices poses problems for conventional notions of "consumption." Critical theory of the past has too often dismissed dance as a form of meaningless abandon or, worse, as in the case of Adorno's account of the "jitterbug" craze of the 1930s and '40s, as a set of mere "socially conditioned reflexes"—false consciousness in its most frenzied and hysterical form (1941: 45–48). More recently, pop culture theorists have tried to recoup dance as a meaningful process of self-realization through the body (e.g., Chambers 1985) and have placed considerable emphasis on the importance of dance in the gendered expression of self-control, pleasure, and sensuality (McRobbie 1984). Whereas males have made use of musical instruments in public displays of physical control and technical mastery (e.g., the electric guitar), women have had fewer outlets for similar forms of public expression. Dance has become one of those outlets.

The relationship between popular music and dance can also be seen in the manner in which the latter feeds back into musical production practices. Much like Sudnow's statement concerning the way in which the musical tempo would "get into the fingers" as he prepared to play, dance music can inform the subjective impulses of popular musicians even as they engage in the relatively detached and analytic practices of electronic production, as when programming a drum machine. It is important to note, however, that these basic impulses are also mediated, complemented, and even guided by other kinds of (consumer) knowledge derived from specialized magazines, industry tip sheets, and the like. This feedback— of consumption into production—is, then, both conceptual and physical in nature, both fully intentional but also intuitively felt. A history of personal and collective consumption can thus form not only an awareness of the general outlines of musical style but even the precise "feel" for the details of musical form. Not surprisingly, it has been in the various genres of contemporary dance music that new technologies have been most fully utilized. In dance music, the physical relationship between sound and the audience is more direct, less mediated by other kinds of physical gestures related to instrumental performance and/or the spectacle of live concerts (cf., Langlois 1992). In this sense, new technologies have not so much been an influence *on* dance music as they have become utilized *within* the already existing cultural context of dance—a context with its own needs, aesthetics, production practices, and modes of listening (Harley 1993: 223).

From the foregoing discussion it is clear that how you learn to make and listen to music cannot be explained solely by the direct physical or cognitive relationship between you and your chosen instrument. Indeed, although Sudnow's perceptive and poetic account of learning to play jazz piano may be revealing, it also portrays the learning process as essentially a personal (even solitary) journey toward both the acquisition of skill and the realization of individual potential. Similarly, when addressing the creative role of new technology in music, music theorists (such as Kenneth Gaburo quoted at the beginning of this chapter) often assume that the most important issues revolve around the problems of human/machine "interaction" (cf., Truax 1976). In either case, the focus is almost exclusively on the individual whereas, as important as the phenomenological and communicative relationship between individuals and musical instruments may be, other problems of a more collective or social nature are equally significant.

Among those problems are the conventional sociological issues related to race, class, and gender. If learning is, indeed, a *social* process, then the factors influential in determining not only *who* has access to musical knowledge and skill, in the first place, but *how* that knowledge is transmitted need to be addressed. For example, throughout most of their history, keyboard instruments have generally been the province of the middle and upper classes. Compared to other musical instruments, they are relatively expensive, they need to be kept indoors, they must be regularly tuned and serviced by trained technicians, and playing even a simple accompaniment on them might demand considerably more study than is required on an instrument such as the guitar. Not surprisingly, then, the piano was one of the last musical instruments to be mastered by black performers in America and incorporated into African-American musics (L. Jones 1963: 90). The early blues and boogie woogie pianists played in an extremely percussive style, and at least one historian has suggested that this style may not have been simply the result of musical predilection. In his book *The Jazz Scene*, E. J. Hobsbawm has stated that most of the boogie woogie pianists were "limited" at best, and, even among the most expressive players, some were "technically downright bad" (1989: 120).[6] Whether you accept Hobsbawm's harsh (and perhaps inaccurate) assessment of the technical achievement of the early jazz pianists or not, clearly access to particular instruments as well as training will have an impact on any given social group's approach to music.

Sociologists have paid some attention to popular music as an occupation and to the role of the musicians' community in the formation of particular social attitudes. As a rule, popular musicians have relatively little formal training (Denisoff and Bridges 1982) and develop their skills and knowledge of musical conventions by pursuing casual and semi-formal relationships with other, often more experienced, musicians. These local musical cultures tend to be exclusive in character, in part because of the social stigma attached to being a popular musician. In his participant observation study of dance musicians in the late 1940s, Howard Becker has described how popular musicians often develop an attitude, a style of dress, and a specialized vocabulary that sets them apart from the rest of society. Conventional society regards the lifestyle of the dance musician as "deviant," and, in response, musicians further isolate themselves from social norms through their attitudes and behavior and thus become "outsiders" (Becker 1963: 79–100).

The local network acts as a kind of support group and can be important both in the type of music played by musicians and on the career development of individual performers. In some cases, the spiral of social isolation and self-imposed segregation can result in self-conscious innovations in musical style and the creation of "avant-garde" movements within popular music; as a group of musicians struggles to define musical values and to maintain notions of artistic integrity, they resist interference from outside and may attempt to push even further the boundaries of both social and musical convention. Regardless of the degree to which the artist rejects social and musical norms or simply becomes a "commercial" musician, success as a performer often depends on the ability to maintain ties within the network of "interlocking cliques" where jobs are allocated and skills adjudicated (ibid.: 103–14).

One of the more immediate consequences of pursuing a career in an occupation defined as "deviant" is that it places pressures on the family life of the individual. In Becker's account, parents discourage their children from pursuing careers that are both financially insecure and socially unconventional; and when the musician marries, the pressure for maintaining a steady income and a stable home life is intensified (ibid.: 114–19).

What is striking here is how Becker assumes that the dance musician is male; his entire description of the deviant group mentality, the control of work opportunities by cliques, and the pressures of family life ignores how each of these factors makes it extremely difficult for women to enter the culture of the popular musician. Adopting a "deviant" lifestyle is always more socially damning for women than for men. Historically, men have tended to exclude women from the workplace, and this exclusion has been true in virtually every genre of music, from the concert hall to the recording studio. Finally, the pressures of family life, especially about raising children, are that much greater for women.

In more recent forms of popular music, such as rock, the male domination of musical performance and studio recording appears to be equally problematic. Mavis Bayton (1990) has described some of the difficulties encountered by women seeking to enter the world of rock. These problems include not only the issues of deviant lifestyle versus family commitment already described but, also, the very relationship of women to music, instruments, and amplification. Bayton argues that, unlike young male musicians, women are less likely to be proficient on their instruments when they enter a band, or, because of the limited number of females who play rock instruments (especially bass guitar and drums), women often end up playing an instrument other than the one on which they are most familiar. Many female players also have backgrounds in classical, notated music, which can be an impediment to learning songs from records and to adopting rock instruments and playing techniques.[7] Finally, women often feel that it is more difficult for them than for males to become comfortable with both the ancillary technology of rock (amplifiers, mixing consoles, and the like) and the specialized technical terms and abbreviated slang employed in its use (Bayton 1990: 238–43, 248–49). As regards the latter point, even though the home has become the site of music production through the development of inexpensive home recording equipment, the market for that equipment is still largely male, as high as 94 percent according to an AMC survey (1988).

The problems cited by Bayton, however, extend beyond simply deciding to adopt a certain instrument and becoming comfortable with amplification and recording technology. *How* one plays an instrument is influenced by social stereotypes, teachers (formal and informal), and a variety of other factors. For example, Charlotte Ackerley has described how female guitarists have been systematically discouraged from playing lead guitar. With the exception of only a handful of artists, such as Bonnie Raitt, one of the few female artists in the country/blues tradition who can boast a career as both a singer and a lead guitarist, most women learn to play rhythm guitar or accompaniment-type patterns (1978: 260).

Clearly, then, musical practice, even at the most fundamental level of the relationship between musicians and their instruments, cannot be separated from either the specific contexts of musical style and genre or larger issues of race, class, and gender. In this way, the constitution of individuals as social subjects has at least as large an impact on their relationship to musical technology as the form of the technology itself, an issue almost completely ignored by theorists like Gaburo and others in their attempt to construct an unproblematic relationship between humans and machines.

For the moment, I leave these initial observations concerning musicians and their instruments to be elaborated upon in the following chapters. I do not, however, want to abandon them entirely in the current discussion, for in turning to the twin problems of musical notation and sound recording, it will be useful to explore the various ways in which notions of musical style, knowledge, and performance can be embodied, implicitly, in the structure of musical technologies.

The Role of Notation in Western Musical Practice

It is not possible in the present context to detail the gradual but profound changes in musical culture that attended the development of musical notation, a process that required several centuries to come to full fruition; nor is it possible to describe fully the equally momentous changes in musical production and consumption that have occurred since the introduction of sound recording technology. I will address here, however, a number of specific issues concerning musical notation as they relate to composition and performance, to the organization of musical labor, and to matters of economy. These issues will be taken up again in subsequent chapters and discussed in relation to the uses of sound recording and digital instrument technologies in contemporary music-making.

Although musical notation and sound recording are, in most respects, fundamentally different from one another—both technically and with regards to their modes of production, distribution, and consumption—there are, nevertheless, ways in which notation has prepared the social, cultural, and economic ground for sound reproduction. Both notation and sound recording were initially conceived of as primarily mnemonic or reproductive technologies, but each has, in its own manner, become *productive*; that is, each has become a vehicle for the planning and creation of musical works. Finally, recent computer-based programs, such as sequencers, exhibit characteristics related to both notation and sound recording. I wish to proceed, then, with an eye toward such continuities as well as the discontinuities between these technologies.

The development of a refined notational system in Europe during the Middle Ages constituted Western music's first real break with a mode of musical production based essentially in performance and oral tradition.

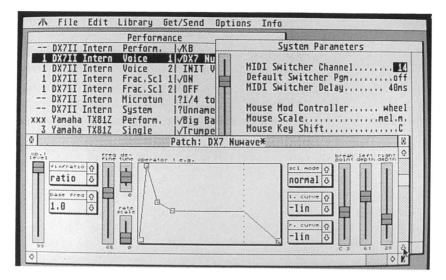

Representing synthetic sound. Synthesizer programmers have long employed a set of graphical conventions for the representation of synthesizer parameters. Analogous to a kind of notation or tablature system, computer programs such as Dr. T's X-Or (pictured here) have adopted these conventions and offer users a variety of possibilities for the abstract calculation and manipulation of synthetic sound.

The significance of notation—both theoretical and practical—in Western music should not be understated: Music historians have generally regarded the invention of staff notation as an event of momentous import—an event as important to music as the invention of writing in language. Although histories that deal specifically with the development of notation have often taken a technical/musical approach to their subject (e.g., Rastall 1983), it should be stressed that this history is as much social as it is musical.

Introduced initially as a simple mnemonic aid in the performance of monastic chant, early notations based on the system of *neumes* (from about the ninth century or earlier) were relatively imprecise and left considerable latitude in interpretation to performers (Grout 1960: 39, 55–56). According to Max Weber, "This circumstance favored flexibility of official musical patterns with respect to the musical needs of ordinary practice and favored the penetration of popular tonal traditions into musical development" (1958b: 86). The innovation of early staff notation by Guido d'Arezzo (ca. 995–1050) was one attempt to remedy this "un-orderliness" in liturgical music and, implicitly, a means of suppressing secular influences on sacred tradition (ibid.).

The power in notation was not wielded unilaterally for long, however, and, ultimately, notation became one of the means by which musicians would break with liturgical and other musical traditions. By the fourteenth century, French composers of the *ars nova* were achieving new levels of rhythmic subtlety through the adoption of duple time division (itself derived from secular sources) and the invention and exploitation of new rhythmic and formal complexities in musical notation: new time signatures, colored notes, dots, stems, and flags (Grout 1960: 106–16, 127–28; Rastall 1983: 61–78). By the end of the century, an extreme form of "mannered" notation—where the visual impact of the score was as important as the intended sounds—had come into use in certain types of music (Rastall 1983: 79–96).

What is most interesting in the history of these various notational innovations is the manner in which Western art music began to evolve as a specifically notated art form from about the fourteenth century onward. The increasing trend toward polyphonic vocal music during the latter part of the Middle Ages undoubtedly created the need for greater precision in notation, but by the fourteenth century *composition*—as a form of musical activity separate and distinct from performance—had begun to emerge. The role of notation prior to this time had been primarily descriptive, that is, an attempt to accurately record the essentials of an oral tradition. It now became prescriptive—a set of more-or-less clearly defined instructions written by one individual to be executed by another.

This activity was, from the outset, characterized by a relationship to time that was different from performance; with notation, not only was the musical work preserved in a concrete form, but musical time itself was represented in a spatialized pattern. The "urgency," anticipation, and shared sense of time characteristic of performance was replaced (for the composer at least) by a detached set of quasi-mathematical calculations and operations executed with little reference to "real-time" modes of action. In this sense, the characteristic compositions of the extreme notational art forms of the period—isorhythmic motets and, later, mensuration canons —display a rationalization and objectification of temporal (and tonal) relations more closely related to the "logic" of science than that of practice. The representation and manipulation of temporal, dynamic, and tonal relations in recent digital technologies, such as sequencers and drum machines, have much in common with notation and extends the possibilities of rational control even further.

It should be noted, however, that not all systems of notation allow for the same degree of rationalization and large-scale planning. From at least the late fifteenth century onward, various types of "tablature" were developed to meet the needs of the growing number of amateur instrumentalists.[8] These included tablature systems for keyboard instruments, the lute, guitar, and a variety of other instruments (see Rastall 1983: 143–71). Although they gradually fell into disuse in art music after the seventeenth century, various kinds of tablature are still in widespread use in popular music today.[9]

Tablature systems sometimes share characteristics with conventional staff notation (especially with respect to rhythm), but they are otherwise unique to the type of instrument in question; tablatures are designed to indicate the position of the fingers on the keyboard, fretboard, or other sound-producing mechanism rather than the actual sounding pitches. Indeed, the use of nonstandard tunings on string instruments often makes it difficult to determine, in advance, what the sounding pitches will be. Because of their close relationship to the physical layout of the instrument itself and the mechanics of performance technique, tablatures are relatively easy to learn. The performer's ability to use tablature as an abstract means of musical organization or as a tool of analysis, however, is extremely limited. Synthesizer patch diagrams, used to record the technical parameters utilized in the production of individual sounds, and graphic pattern displays in sequencers and drum machines are perhaps analogous to tablature both in the possibilities they offer to popular musicians who do not read notation and in their inherent limitations.

Historically, however, only through the development of the more abstract conventions of staff notation, not tablature, would composition evolve into an art form based on the detailed calculation of technical means and the coordination of many-voiced musical ensembles. The evolution of a "social technology" to realize the work plan embodied in the musical score would eventually culminate, in the eighteenth and nineteenth centuries, with the development of the symphony orchestra, with its balanced, specialized sectional divisions and its highly trained personnel all under the musical/administrative control of the conductor. Before this event could happen another musical role had to be invented: Whereas a certain anonymity had accompanied compositional activities prior to the fourteenth century, after that point individual musicians began to achieve public recognition in their new-found role as *composers*, eventually setting themselves apart as "artists" and "geniuses" from the rest of the musical world.

If the advent of complex, multi-voiced music organized through notational art can be regarded as a critical step in the creation of the role of the composer in Western music, it can also be described as the first step toward the devaluation of the performer as well. With increasing precision in notation, the composer began to take exclusive responsibility for more and more of the significant detail of music. Indeed, from the standpoint of contemporary musicology, theory, and analysis, the score defines what is, and is not, significant in Western art music. Michael Chanan has argued that with notation, the subtle uses of vocal or instrumental timbre and rhythmic and tonal inflection, which are part of the essential, expressive domain of performers, "cease to carry structural significance in the music because structural significance is granted only by what the notation renders articulate" (1981: 236).

At first, this change took place only slowly: From the fourteenth to the seventeenth centuries, much musical detail in certain types of music was left to the discretion of the performer, who interpreted the score according to generally understood conventions. Even after 1600, when much that had previously been left to convention became specified in notation, the ability to improvise or to realize a figured bass line was expected of any soloist or accompanist. Again, the parallel between this seventeenth-century practice and the uses of "chord charts" in popular music during the twentieth century is striking (Rastall 1983: 204–6). By the beginning of the nineteenth century, most of the areas in which the performer had formerly made direct contributions to the structure of a work had been eliminated. Accompaniments were written out in detail, and cadenzas and other improvisational episodes in musical works likewise became the responsibility of the composer rather than the performer. Musical notation alone, of course, could not exact compliance from musicians; as is still true today, it was the task of the various social institutions concerned with music education, professional training, and criticism both to define and delimit the role of the performer in relation to the score. "The classical artist operates within a social organization of professional certification, excellence, and competitiveness . . . his circumstances placing extraordinary demands upon a faithfulness to the score, where what 'faithfulness' and 'the score' mean is defined by that social organization" (Sudnow 1978: 53).

The growing importance of the score as the authoritative source of meaning in music provoked an opposing reaction among a group of performers (or, rather, performer/composers) and their followers during the romantic period. Richard Sennett has argued that the task of the nineteenth-century virtuoso was to distract attention away from the musical text and draw it, instead, toward themselves as performers, as individuals possessing extraordinary powers (1977: 198–201). Practical knowledge was thus transformed into technical mastery. The art of the virtuoso was an art of immediacy, personality, shock, and stimulation (ibid.). It was, in short, everything that notation (and conventional performance) was not. It operated, in part, because of a complementary self-disciplining of the audience to a position of silence, also an "invention" of the nineteenth century (ibid.: 205–7). By virtue of the emphasis placed on individual personality, it established, in prototypical form, the basic character of the star system in Western music (Attali 1985: 138–44). The legacy of nineteenth-century romanticism is thus two opposing schools of genius: One focused on the composer as master of the "language" of music, and the other on the virtuoso, the performer who exhibits extraordinary physical powers.

Between the sixteenth and the nineteenth centuries, the score gradually became the vehicle for an economic and moral ownership right that ultimately granted status to the composer as the individual creator of the musical work. According to Jacques Attali, music publishers were the first to attempt to exploit copyright as a means of bringing about a capitalist organization of musical production and thereby enhancing their own economic control over it:

> This valorization of music took place in opposition to the entire feudal system, in which the work, the absolute property of the lord, had no autonomous existence. It was constructed on the basis of the concrete existence, in an object (the score) and its usage (the representation), of a possible commercial valorization. Music, then, did not emerge as a commodity until merchants, acting in the name of musicians, gained the power to control its production and sell its usage. . . . In the beginning, the purpose of copyright was not to defend artists' rights, but rather to serve as a tool of capitalism in its fight against feudalism. (Attali 1985: 51–52)

Within the early capitalist organization of musical production, the reproduced score was thus considered a separate entity from both the original manuscript created by the composer and its eventual performance.

Composers themselves, however, had few legal rights, but as the feudal system continued to break down and composers began to work outside the confines of court life, they, too, began to wrest control of the score away from, first, the lord, and, then, the music publishers:

> Little by little, as they dissociated themselves from the courts, musicians obtained part ownership of their labor; in other words, they succeeded in separating ownership of the work from the object manufactured by the publisher—even though they sold the right to publish it, they retained ownership of it and control over its usage. (Ibid.: 53)

In this way, the simultaneous ideological and economic valorization of the score—as definitive artistic statement, on the one hand, and object of exchange, on the other—became the source of both the composer's musical status and socioeconomic independence.

It is important to note again the reduced importance of performance within this evolving "technology" of legal rights and economic entitlement. Performers were given no special rights or privileges with regards to the sounds they made, to their improvisations, or to their specific interpretations of the musical score. For the purposes of copyright, performance was regarded as little more than a generator of income for those who could claim ownership of the score and its reproduction. Granted, such performer-oriented issues would only come to the fore when a means for the mechanical reproduction of sound became possible, but, still, the interests of performers have not, to this day, been well served by copyright law. Janet Mosher (1989) has suggested that twentieth-century forms of experimental music that rely less on the details of a given score and more on the interpretive and improvisational characteristics of individual performances pose problems for conventional copyright law. The law remains committed, she argues, to a strategy of fixed forms and cannot accommodate the open-ended structures of these more recent categories of artistic work.

Mosher's argument is primarily concerned with various forms of experimental art music where graphic scores and other types of nonspecific notation are employed. Twentieth-century popular music, especially jazz, however, presents an even more salient example of the problem of performance versus copyright, which is perhaps analogous to the situation prior to the nineteenth century when all performers were expected to improvise. For the jazz musician, the melodies and harmonies of a song are only the bare-bones framework within which a musical process—the improvisation—evolves. In this sense, the song "chart," the score in its most elementary form, is simply the pretext for a different kind of music-making; yet, under the law, the composer of that song has more rights and protections than does the performer, even when the performance has been recorded.

As already suggested, one reason for the decreasing use of improvisation skills in Western art music is the increasing use of notation in musical training. In the West, formalized musical training has, until quite recently, been associated with either relatively exclusive social groups (in the Middle Ages, the church or the municipal guilds) or with the aristocratic and the middle and upper classes (those who could both afford a formal education or private instruction and had the leisure time to enjoy it). Whereas formalized training in Western art music may include instruction in a range of skills, including *solfège*, vocal or instrumental technique, music theory, history, and composition, it is characterized above all by the need to acquire skill in music "literacy," that is, the ability to read and interpret musical notation and to gain, thereby, an introduction to the repertoire of so-called "great music." As with musical style discussed previously, you never simply learn to play a musical instrument; in the process, you also assimilate both a repertoire and a set of musical/aesthetic values.

Learning to play a musical instrument through the mediation of the notated score changes the nature of the learning process itself. Sudnow's account of learning to play jazz piano emphasizes the physical/spatial aspects of execution as well as a certain aural and rhythmic intentionality that relates directly to the music to be played. In the technical training of performers in musical traditions dependent on notation, the acquisition of performance skill is standardized in the form of the *étude*. Although the piano *études* of composers such as Chopin and Liszt could sometimes achieve great musical and poetic depth, the vast majority are tedious and banal, giving only the impression of skill and often responding to little more than an "interest in the simple athletics of piano playing" (Loesser 1954: 254–56). Musical skill is thus transformed into mere "technique," a purely physical phenomenon scarcely requiring, at least in the case of the piano, any aural capacity at all.

Musical literacy has never been equally distributed across social classes, however, and, even within the privileged classes, it has not been equally distributed across lines of gender. In nineteenth-century Europe, whether taught primarily through private lessons or at one of the private or state-run music academies, professional-level music training was reserved almost exclusively for men. Though an ability to sing or to play music was considered a desirable part of any cultured woman's upbringing, women were actively discouraged from pursuing professional careers, and their training was limited to "a smattering of knowledge . . . only sufficient for the domestic drawing-room at best" (Rieger 1985: 142–43). In particular, the study of music theory or composition was considered completely unnecessary for women (ibid.: 141); furthermore, certain instruments tended to be reserved for males (most orchestral instruments, including both strings and winds) and were considered unfit, within the standards of middle-class propriety, for females. Women were primarily limited to singing, playing the piano, and, to a lesser extent, the harp or the guitar (Koza 1991: 107–8). At the same time, the status of "amateur" music-making in the home became denigrated during the nineteenth century, unlike the eighteenth century when upper- and middle-class males themselves had engaged more readily in amateur musical activities (ibid.: 112–13; Rieger 1985: 143).

Feminist writers have rightly described this situation as an example of male domination in music and the systematic repression of female creativity (ibid.; McClary 1991). The fact that the majority of women were not allowed to participate in the full range and extent of musical practice (either as performers, composers, or teachers) has a particular importance for the study at hand. Although the role of nineteenth-century women as amateur musicians in the home cast them as musically "inferior" to the public, male professional, it also placed them in a position of dependency upon those same professionals: The female amateur became the musical "consumer" par excellence. Many composers, publishers, and piano manufacturers dedicated themselves to exploiting female amateurs as a market.

They began creating a technically and aesthetically suitable repertoire, thus simultaneously responding to and creating the conditions for a specifically defined "feminine" taste in music. In a certain sense, then, the character of female musical practice in the home has traditionally been defined along the same lines as conventional notions of consumption: as essentially lacking in creativity (and therefore "passive" in the eyes of male sociologists) and rooted in the aesthetics of fashion.

Western middle-class values of musical literacy and educational methods organized around notated music have been adopted in most public school systems throughout Europe, North America, and, indeed, many non-Western countries as well. In this way, Western notation has become the dominant system of notating music throughout the world, although that dominance is certainly on the wane (Bennett 1983: 224–25). It has had an impact on genres of music quite removed from the tradition of Western art music. Christopher Small has argued that, in education, the reliance on the notated score places the student in the position of receiving a product rather than engaging in a creative process (1980: 30–31). He further argues that the producer-consumer relationship characteristic of modern society and the notion that knowledge exists essentially outside and independent of the individual foster a consumer mentality within the entire educational enterprise (ibid.: 182). Though Small does not unduly emphasize the role played by musical notation, clearly it has become an important component in a complex set of objects, rules, and procedures—an "educational technology"—which, taken together, "serve to confirm the pupils as consumers of knowledge" (ibid.: 185).

Conclusion

The relationship between musical instruments and the entire process of music-making as analyzed by Merriam—including the conceptualization of music, musical behavior, and sound—is extremely complex and, indeed, can only be separated in theory; that is, through an application of the "logic" of science, not that of practice. For the performing musician, as I have argued in this chapter, both the relationship to musical instruments and the musical process itself are completely fused so as virtually to defy analysis: While learning to play a musical instrument, the musician develops a sense of style that is intuitive, a sense that is felt as much as consciously understood. Sudnow's reflections on playing jazz piano reveal the degree to which performance practice is dependent upon more than the acquisition of simple "technique" (in the limited sense of physical dexterity); it relies, rather, on a type of listening that involves a "directionality of purpose" derived primarily (although, as I have argued, not exclusively) through practice.

Musical skills, attitudes, and a sense of style are not acquired in a vacuum, however. Notably, the social networks of popular musicians, by their very nature, have tended to exclude women. With regards to new technology, this isolation makes for a form of double exclusion. As noted in Part II of this book, musicians' magazines, user groups, and networks are overwhelmingly male in their orientation, and, with the male domination of popular musical practice overall, it thus becomes difficult for women to gain access to either technical knowledge or practical skill.

The gradual development of a sophisticated form of musical notation in the West made possible the conceptualization and rational planning of large-scale musical works. Only through notation could "composition," as a distinct form of activity entirely different and separate from performance practice, exist. As I have argued, however, not all forms of notation (for example, instrument tablature) necessarily lead to the same levels of rationalization. Only through the evolution of a complex social technology—in the form of an educational system, a trained and disciplined orchestral ensemble, and a legal system of rights and entitlements—did notation come to play the role that it has in Western musical culture.

Notation, and the music publishing industry that became associated with it, dominated both art and popular music during the nineteenth and early twentieth centuries. With the advent of technical reproduction of sound, however, a new relationship between technology, musical practice, and the capitalist organization of production began to evolve. Musical "sound," as the product of both the unique contribution of the performer and a technological process, has become a focal point of this development. It is to musical "sound," as a conceptual category, a concrete entity, and a commodity, that I now turn.

CHAPTER EIGHT

The New "Sound" of Music
Technology and Changing Concepts of Music

✳

> I've been getting into sounds lately . . . realizing that if something has an interesting enough sound, you don't have to play as much on the instrument. If you get a keyboard that has an interesting sound, you don't have to play a lot of notes on it. The *sound* takes over. . . . They're part of the composition, even though I think a lot of people . . . might see it as being kind of superfluous to the essence of the music. But in this music I think it's really important.
> (Marcus Miller, in Milkowski 1987: 22)

The use of synthesizers and other digital musical instruments has had a profound impact on musicians and their conceptualization of musical practice. With the expansion of sonic technologies, the musician is able to engage with the micro-phenomena of musical sound itself, and such an engagement often forces a reassessment of the role of more traditional categories of musical practice. For example, a concentration on the "right" sounds for a given musical context can shift the musician's attention away from other, more familiar levels of musical form, such as melody, rhythm, and harmony. In this sense, Marcus Miller's reflection on musical "sounds," quoted previously, clearly constitutes a kind of "theoretical activity"; a kind of "tactical device" that draws "attention [his own and his listeners'] towards selected aspects of the music-making process" (Blum 1975: 217).

Implicit in Miller's statement is an attitude toward production and consumption quite different from traditional attitudes toward skill and the inherent sound capabilities of musical instruments. The contrast between Miller's statement and the attitudes expressed in Sudnow's work quoted in the previous chapter could not be greater. In the past, you certainly might have purchased an instrument for its particular sound qualities, but your own approach to playing could be as important a factor in such a decision as the inherent quality of the instrument itself. The various means by which musicians have coaxed new and unorthodox sounds from an instrument such as the electric guitar—the "bottle neck" slide technique, B. B. King's sustained vibrato and trill, Stanley Jordan's right hand finger-tapping (more akin to piano technique than conventional guitar playing), Jimi Hendrix's use of feedback, and other techniques—demonstrate that traditional instrument technologies can sometimes be little more than a field of possibility within which the innovative musician chooses to operate. The particular "sound" produced in such instances is as intimately tied to personal style and technique as it is to the characteristics of the instrument's sound-producing mechanism.

Ironically, despite the enormous variations in sound generation possible with modern programmable synthesizers, many musicians seem increasingly concerned with whether the instruments they purchase *already* possess "an interesting sound" or, similarly, with whether the instrument gives the owner access to a desirable range of easily obtainable sound programs: "When I buy a sampler, I think in terms of libraries, rather than capabilities. I rely heavily on available sounds, and get variety by layering timbres, EQing them, and finally adding effects during mixdown" (Michael Josephs, TV composer, in *Keyboard* 15 [6], June 1989: 23). Clearly, the emphasis here is on the acquisition and technical modification of pre-existing sounds rather than on their direct production through performance, recording, and/or original programming. Unlike other musicians, synthesizer players are rarely spoken of in terms of their playing technique at all.[1]

There are a variety of reasons for this apparent opposition between "sound" and performance skill, consumption, and production; but what interests me most is precisely how a particular interest in musical sound has been represented and theorized, even by its advocates, in terms of such binary oppositions in the first place. Many of the controversies surrounding new musical technology can be traced to a long tradition of rigid dichotomies, such as instrumental sound versus the "language" of music, and sound reproduction versus "live" musical performance. Attitudes toward new technology have become imbricated with these arguments in a fundamental way, and, as a result, the place of synthesis within the larger history of musical and cultural change is often misunderstood.

In this chapter, I explore some of these oppositions as a means of understanding what, to many musicians, is at stake in the adoption of new technologies. The conflicts that arise between musicians result from different value systems and different conventions and priorities operating in different genres of music. The relationship of sound to various musical genres is important, and, in this regard, note that Miller does not speak of all music but of jazz music and, in particular, small-group improvisation.

Alan Durant has argued that many of the fears concerning new technology and the perceived loss of human input into music-making can be attributed to a clash of values surrounding different genres of music and their associated conventions (1984: 227).

One way to approach the problem of technologically reproduced sounds in music production is to examine the speech of musicians and audiences themselves and the manner in which they portray their activities and their responses to musical sound. In musicians' language, in particular, is a wealth of concepts, slang, and metaphor that describe the qualities of musical sounds and their importance in the musical texture. Through an examination of the characteristic words and phrases used by musicians who use new technologies, I will demonstrate how the concept of musical sound has become increasingly associated with the technology of sound recording in the late twentieth century.

In addition to linking specific instruments and sounds with particular genres of music, I explore the contemporary idea of a unique and identifiable "sound," which has evolved since the rise of various media of electronic and mechanical reproduction: radio, television, sound film, and phonograph recording. In particular, I examine how "sound," as a conceptual category, has become separated (quite wrongly I think) from the "language" of music as represented in the notated score. At issue here is not simply music, however, but a complex set of social and legal conflicts that seek to maintain a particular order of status and economic reward for those engaged in the production of music.

Instruments, Sound, and the Language of Music

Many cultures do not recognize a clear distinction between musical instruments, sounds, and musical theory, often making it difficult for outside observers to understand native musical concepts and practices. The problem is further compounded in cultures where there exists little difference between playing music and dancing to it, or a clear division between spoken and sung speech. Some traditional African languages, for example, do not even have a precise word for "music," as such. In East Africa, the word *ngoma* stands for "drum," but it also refers to the integration of music, dance, and drama; where a generic term for "music" exists in Africa, it has often been adapted from European languages (see Bebey 1975: 12, 119–24; and Wallis and Malm 1984: 31–32).

In the West, the scientific development of physics and acoustics and, equally important, the development of a precise form of musical notation have led to a series of distinctions that separate, conceptually if not always practically, sound from music and performance from composition. One of the legacies of the eighteenth and nineteenth centuries was the growing separation between the score, as musical text, and performance, as mere execution and virtuosic display. The apparent division between composition, conceived of as an analytic activity, and performance, as an activity based in skill, expression, and shock, has been one of the most enduring characteristics of Western musical culture. This complementary division of specialized musical activity also articulates a hierarchy of distinction: Despite the public enthusiasm for the virtuoso performer, it was the score that constituted the "immortal" and more valued artistic statement (at least until the advent of sound recording, which gave performers a measure of immortality as well). In the more extreme forms of this discursive polarity, the actual physical sound of music, as produced by musical instruments, is considered to be little more than an unfortunate though necessary medium for the presentation of the "pure" structure of the music manifest in the score.

This distinction in music has been rallied time and again by composers, from Beethoven to Charles Ives to Milton Babbitt, whenever their music has been declared (often by inadequate performers) "unplayable":

Some of the songs in this book, particularly among the later ones, cannot be sung, and if they could, perhaps might prefer, if they had a say, to remain as they are; that is, "in the leaf" . . . a song has a *few* rights, the same as other ordinary citizens. . . . Should it not be free at times from the dominion of the thorax, the diaphragm, the ear, and other points of interest? . . . In short, must a song always be a song?
(Ives 1961: 130–31)

Ives's passionate individualism was as much a mark of his alienation from the (largely conservative) musical culture of his time as a personal character trait. What is striking in this passage, however, is how, "music" is taken to exist as an ideal, separate from any possible manifestation in sound. The (notated) song is anthropomorphized, given an existence and a will of its own, afforded "rights" and prerogatives. This appeal to a kind of democratic spirit should not be ignored. Certainly, in a culture that lacked musical notation, such a statement would be impossible. Much of the work of John Cage and, in electro-acoustic music, that of Pierre Schaeffer and other composers of *musique concrète* are part of the twentieth-century avant-garde's self-conscious response to the on-going musical dilemmas posed by such conceptual dichotomies.

The problem goes beyond one of simple distrust between composers and performers; for, despite the efforts of the avant-garde, the fundamental opposition between formal structure and its expression in sound—inherent in the representation of music through notation—continues to be a basic tenet of Western musical aesthetics. Perhaps one of the most virulent demonstrations of this opposition can be found in Theodor Adorno's polemic against the music of the early modernist, Igor Stravinsky. Adorno argued that Stravinsky's exploitation of instrumental techniques in his compositions was motivated by nothing more than the desire for "effect" and that his heightened sensitivity to instrumental color overpowered his music, resulting in a "fetishism of the means":

The means in the most literal sense—namely the instrument—is hypostatized: it takes precedence over the music. The composition expresses only one fundamental concern: to find the sounds which will best suit its particular nature and result in the most overwhelming effect. There is no longer any interest in instrumental values per se which will . . . serve the clarification of continuity or the revelation of purely musical structures. . . . The intensification of "effect" had always been associated with the progressive differentiation of musical means for the sake of expression. . . . The goal of musical effects is no longer stimulation . . . in the emancipation from the meaning of the whole, the effects assume a physically material character.   (Adorno 1973: 172–73)

Adorno's argument was clearly influenced by his desire to connect particular tendencies, which he perceived within modernism and manifested in the music of various composers from Wagner to Stravinsky, to his analysis of capitalism and the "culture industry." The adaptation of Marx's theory of commodity fetishism, and the concern for the manner in which the "progressive differentiation" of means and the pursuit of "effects" obscures musical (i.e., social) structure, are all consistent with his more general social critique. Although I do not wish to debate the overall validity of Adorno's critique here, it seems appropriate in the present context to point out the entirely conventional (even conservative) nature of the musical assumptions upon which Adorno bases his broader analysis: It valorizes the unity of musical structure above all else and demands that all coloristic and expressive tendencies be sublimated to the force of compositional logic, to "purely musical structures."[2]

Curiously, the language Adorno uses to describe the compositional tendencies in Stravinsky's music—the concern for choosing the right sounds for a given context, the progressive differentiation of musical timbre, and the way sounds assume an independent, physical, and material character—could be equally associated with digital synthesis and sampling in popular music during the 1980s. Indeed, among critics of the new technologies, the basic opposition between the apparent fetishism of "sound" and the demands of compositional structure are virtually the same: "A lot of the technology has made it so easy for facile writers and inconsequential writers to play with the sound, rather than write a great piece of music, that it's tended to water down a good deal of substance in composition" (Billy Joel, in *Keyboard* 16 [1], January 1990: 54).

Although there are certainly valid distinctions to be made between "songs" and their realization in sound, for much popular music such distinctions have become increasingly difficult to make. Indeed, musicians today (as well as critics and audiences) often speak of having a unique and personal "sound" in the same manner in which another generation of musicians might have spoken of having developed a particular "style" of playing or composing. The term "sound" has taken on a peculiar material character that cannot be separated either from the "music" or, more importantly, from the sound recording as the dominant medium of reproduction. With regards to the latter, the idea of a "sound" appears to be a particularly contemporary concept that could hardly have been maintained in an era that did not possess mechanical or electronic means of reproduction. Indeed, such a concept could not have been viable, for example, during the period of Tin Pan Alley popular music (roughly 1890 to 1930) when sheet music dominated the production and consumption of popular songs. Even when songs were "plugged" on the radio, they were seldom associated with particular artists to the same degree that they are today, and, in any event, once purchased in the form of sheet music, the ultimate act of consumption/reproduction lay, quite literally, in the hands of the consumer.

Mike Hobart (1981) has argued that there were four distinct forms of "capital" during the early part of the twentieth century—publishing, touring, broadcasting, and sound recording—each exerting its own pressures and priorities upon the character of music and its production and reproduction. It was not in the interest of the publisher, for example, to promote among performers a unique approach to sound or to foster the display of virtuosity and improvisational skill, for neither would be reproducible by amateur pianists in the home. The opposite was true, however, for the other media where the essential commodity was the star performers themselves. Hobart's historical observations and, at a more theoretical level, the recent analyses of sociologist Bernard Miège (1982, 1986) concerning the various forms of capital operating within cultural industries and the potential conflicts between them indicate that the capitalist organization of culture is not as unified in its structure or purpose as Adorno would have us believe.

In the case of sound recording, the essential identity of the individual performer as manifest in sound was made clear almost from the outset: The first great star of the recording medium, Enrico Caruso, impressed himself upon the public as much by the force of his unique voice (as conveyed by the gramophone recording) as by the repertoire that he sang. During the 1930s especially, radio and Hollywood sound film played an even larger role in establishing the equation between individual performers and their equally individual sounds, as revealed by technology. Simon Frith has argued that during this period the rise of "crooning," as a distinct style of vocal production, was dependent upon microphones and electronic amplification (1986: 263); furthermore, from at least the early 1930s onward, a preoccupation with sound quality itself became an important issue among record enthusiasts. Read and Welch (1976) have described how, with the advent of the microphone and electrical methods of recording during the mid-1920s, notions of "high fidelity" and sonic "realism" slowly came into being. For the first time, it became apparent that the recording engineer had a powerful influence on the ways in which the public heard music.

By the 1950s, independent record companies were making a mark on the industry not only with the new styles of music that they promoted—for example, rhythm and blues and rock and roll—but also with their basic approach to the recording medium:

Tommy [Dowd] did revolutionary things with how he would mike the bass and drums. Nobody used to mike drums in those days [the 1950s] . . . later on he started using multiple miking. We learned all the advantages of remixing and sweetening.
. . . Back in those days we had a thing called the Atlantic sound. I would describe our sound best as clean funk. We had a very strong bass line, a lot of bottom, a lot of bass drum. We had a very good midrange, and I always fought for treble in the remix. It's amazing how, to this day, people are careless about getting the top end in the proper perspective.   (Jerry Wexler, in Fox 1986: 146)

By finding what they considered to be "the proper perspective," engineers and producers thus created a new aesthetic of "sound."

Although it is difficult to locate the beginnings of a public awareness of this phenomenon with any degree of accuracy, clearly by the early 1960s the notion of a "sound" was part of the vocabulary of popular culture. Phil Spector was perhaps the first pop producer to be recognized as having his own unique sound—"Spector Sound" (also known in more general terms as the "wall of sound")—and a variety of recording studios and musical genres soon were identified as the promoters and/or possessors of a particular "sound": for example, the "Nashville Sound" and, somewhat later, the "Motown Sound." The concept also gained some currency in Hollywood film of the same period. In *Two Weeks in Another Town* (1962), Edward G. Robinson admonishes his younger colleague, Kirk Douglas (both playing the role of film directors), to follow his lead and dub his film in order to create the "Krueger Sound." Here, a particular approach to sound—achieved through the kinds of technical enhancement only available through post-dubbing—is juxtaposed with the "realism" of direct sound and defines the director's sense of personal style and integrity.

My emphasis on the idea of a distinct and recognizable "sound" is important, because the expression gives semantic weight to a change that was much more fundamental in nature. At one level, the term "sound," like "groove" and "beat," "refers to an intuitive sense of style as process" (Feld 1988: 74). Unlike the expression "groove," however, which both Charles Keil and Steven Feld (1994) have so thoroughly explored in all its subtle and contradictory meanings—from the "feelingful participation" of making and listening to music to the mediation and commodification of "grooves" in the form of sound recordings—the term "sound" seems at once more limited and more directly related to the changing technologies of musical production. This relationship explains its common usage in combination with the names of record producers, record companies, and urban centers of record production. For ethnomusicologist John Blacking (1977), any true transformation in the production of music must be recognized by musicians and listeners alike. The notion of a "sound" as an identifying feature by which musicians, record companies, critics, and listeners categorize the music they make, promote, and listen to is one indication that such a transformation was already well under way by the 1960s. It should be made clear, however, especially for this period in the development of sound technology, that the concept of "sound" was not simply a "technical" phenomenon in the limited sense of the term; recording technology must be understood as a complete "system" of production involving the organization of musical, social, and technical means.

This perspective has been well illustrated by William Ivey (1982) in his discussion of the development of the "Nashville Sound" between 1957 and 1971 (the label itself appears to have gained widespread currency around 1963). Ivey describes the rise of the Nashville Sound, first, as a particular response to the pressures of the marketplace, that is, in response to the need to create a "permanent niche within the larger popular music spectrum of the United States"; and second, as a specific outgrowth of the industry's drive to increase the availability of country music on commercial radio (ibid.: 131–32). In technical and musicological terms, the Nashville Sound was the result of several factors: an emphasis on a unique instrumentation consisting of small ensembles of primarily fretted stringed instruments; a distinctive approach to arrangements (often created on the spot) that allowed for a relatively sparse instrumental sound that was subordinate to the sound of the lead vocal; the use of a nonstandard notation that allowed non-readers to draw on their skill and sense of musical tradition in providing semi-improvised accompaniments; and an approach to recording that emphasized sonic clarity over the "wall of sound" techniques then prominent in popular music (ibid.: 133–37).

Ivey's analysis is interesting in the attention given to the interlocking skills of sound engineers, producers, arrangers, and, above all, a network of studio musicians, examined within the overall commercial contexts of record production and radio airplay.[3] The "music," as such, cannot be easily separated from these contexts and the attendant mode of studio production. Equally interesting is the fact that, though Ivey emphasizes the role of these specialized, local networks of individuals, he later argues that the Nashville Sound quickly became so familiar and repetitive that, by 1975, "a performer could cut a record in Los Angeles, New York, or London and have it emerge in perfect emulation of the Nashville Sound" (ibid.: 138).

The fact that one could record in the Nashville style (or just about any other style) almost anywhere in the Western world was a sign that, by the mid-'70s, the recording studio apparatus had become a widespread phenomenon. Both the technology and the social organization of the system had evolved to where the multitrack studio, as a mode of production, had become an important factor in the internationalization of musical sounds and styles. As local networks of session musicians became less of a determining factor in the constitution of musical "sound," star performers could choose to record wherever the technical or financial advantages seemed to be greatest.

In Canada, in part because of the establishment of broadcast quotas for Canadian content in 1970, studios began to acquire the latest and most complex equipment to meet the demand for domestic recordings. In addition, certain tax advantages helped attract foreign recording artists to Canada, especially in the pop field. During this period, for example, André Perry's Le Studio, first located in Montréal and, after 1974, in Morin Heights, Québec, became one of the most sought-after recording facilities in the world, producing approximately seventy-five gold or platinum hits by Canadian and international stars by the mid-1980s; in 1985–1986, the studio's recording and post-production work generated some $2.8 million in total revenues (*The Montreal Gazette*, August 2, 1986: C1). Prior to this time, Québec would never have been considered a production center for styles of music destined for the international market.

Of course, the success of Le Studio was built not on country music but on mainstream pop and rock music, two genres of music that, during the 1960s and '70s, had perhaps become more fully integrated with the technology of sound reproduction than any prior style of music. Edward R. Kealy has argued that, except for the drums, most rock instruments were already electrified during this period and made use of electronic signal processing to one degree or another (even in live performance). As a result, it became increasingly difficult to draw a line between the musical instrument and the recording apparatus in rock music (1982: 106–7). With the rise of sophisticated synthesizers, samplers, and drum machines during the late 1970s and early '80s, it could be argued that this trend toward the fusion of instrument and recording device had become complete:

Electronic music making today is a main stream activity and few popular music recordings are made that do not use synthesis or sampling in some capacity. In fact this may well be the last issue [April 1988] in which it is possible to see any dividing line between electronic music and the recording process.

(K. Spencer-Allen, in *Studio Sound*, 30 [4], April 1988)

One reason for this fusion of technologies is simply economic; it is much cheaper to use synthesizers and samplers in the studio, especially for certain productions such as advertising and low-budget film scoring, than it is to hire even a small ensemble of players. As sampling techniques became more sophisticated and more convincing in their ability to replicate instrument sounds, it became difficult to resist the economic imperatives of the music business. Certainly there has been, from the outset, much concern expressed over the loss of jobs among session musicians (see Doerschuk 1983), but much of the protest has come from the ranks of orchestral string players and others who, as Faulkner's study of Hollywood musicians revealed during the 1960s, have traditionally been among the most alienated members of the pop/rock studio community (1971: 156–60; 190).

Another reason for the increasing use of studio technology has to do with the increasing concern in the music industry with creating new and unique "sounds" with which to sell new artists and define particular genres of music. The ability of digital instruments to both create new timbres and to reproduce older ones has made them an indispensable tool. In the age of electronic reproduction, with recordings and radio disseminating and reinforcing "sound" as an identifying mark of contemporary music-making, individual "sounds" have come to carry the same commercial and aesthetic weight as the melody or the lyric in pop songs. Canadian singer-songwriter, Jane Siberry

works with her keyboard player Anne Bourne in generating sounds she thinks will tweak the listener's mind. "We always try to get things that become hooks themselves. . . . As soon as you hear that sound you think of that song. You have to use everything that way, creating hooks on every level."

(*Music Technology* 2 [11], June 1988: 32)

Once associated with the song in this way, however, the "sound hook" begins to exert a force of its own, virtually demanding that any "authentic" rendition of the song be performed with the same or an equivalent sound. The dominance of the recording medium in popular music culture has placed considerable pressure on performing local musicians to match the sound of hit songs in their live performances or, for an original pop or rock act, to reproduce the sound of their own recordings while on tour (Bennett 1983, 1990). Digital technology has been a powerful tool in this regard, and even guitar-based rock groups have turned to synthesizers and samplers for reproducing studio arrangements of their songs that could not otherwise be played live without a large number of backing musicians. When the Rolling Stones embarked on their "Steel Wheels" tour in 1989, they hired the services of two keyboard players, Matt Clifford and Chuck Leavell, to help perform and reproduce the sound of songs they had recorded as much as twenty-five years earlier:

Chuck is working mainly as part of the rhythm section, and I supply the melodic lines and the orchestration. . . .

I spend a large part of my time being a horn section. . . .

In terms of synthesis, what I'm doing is largely imitative. As far as sampling is concerned, I do a few acoustic guitar parts. For example, I play a 12-string guitar sound on "One Hit to the Body." . . . I also supply the cello for "Ruby Tuesday," and things like recorders and strings.

I'm putting what was there on the recordings into the live performance, rather than adding outlandish electronic noises. People tend to forget the lovely arrangements, which are very much a part of the Stones sound, especially in the early days . . . and that's the sort of sound that I can put back in.

(Matt Clifford, in *Music Technology* 4 [6], February 1990: 40–41)

The grammatical anomaly present in this last statement (that these sounds from the "early days" "*are* very much a part of the Stones sound") is perhaps significant. Once established, it is difficult for even the originators of a given "sound" to change it; the nostalgia for "Golden Oldies" in pop culture demands "authentic" reproduction. The search for authenticity can reach absurd proportions: Clifford describes in detail how, for one song, he re-created the sound of a Mellotron, a keyboard instrument introduced in the 1960s that used pre-recorded sounds on loops of magnetic tape much like a sampler uses digital recordings today. The process became what I would call a form of "second-order simulation," where a digital device was called upon to simulate the sound of an analog device reproducing the sound of an acoustic instrument.

Perhaps nowhere, however, has the link between "sound" and musical genre been so intensely formed as in rap and various forms of dance music since the 1980s (e.g., house, techno, hardcore, industrial, acid, and rave, among others). In the high-fashion world of the dance club, dance styles, fashion statements, musical genres and subgenres abound, and new sounds and rhythms (often created with little more than a sampler and a drum machine) play a large role in defining the unique sound of each new genre or subgenre, before it exceeds its brief half-life in the seasonal upheavals that seem to characterize the highly volatile club scene.

One particular drum machine, Roland's TR-808 (released in 1980), has been singled out for its contribution to the sound and style of rap music as it moved from its early stages as street and club music, during the 1970s, to mainstream prominence in the '80s:

Drum machines—the easiest and cheapest source of drum sounds—were the seminal rap axe. By general consensus, the Roland TR-808 was the instrument of choice, mainly because of its bass drum. "The 808 is great because of the bass drum," Kurtis Blow reports. "You can detune it and get this low-frequency hum. It's a car speaker destroyer. That's what we try to do as rap producers—break car speakers and house speakers and boom boxes. And the 808 does it. It's African music!" (*Keyboard* 14 [11], November 1988: 34)

The relationship between a Japanese-manufactured drum machine and "African music" may seem, on the surface, somewhat tenuous; but this statement draws on what has virtually become a part of pop common sense during the past two decades—the idea that dance music with a heavy bass sound is an expression of African-American cultural identity (cf., Brophy 1991).

Elaborating on this commonsense proposition, Tricia Rose has argued that rap producers have consciously transformed technology and used it to express a black cultural identity in sound:

Using the machines in ways that have not been intended, by pushing on established boundaries of music engineering, rap producers have developed an art out of recording with the sound meters well into the distortion zone. When necessary, they deliberately *work in the red*. . . . If a sampler must be detuned in order to produce a sought-after low-frequency hum, then the sampler is detuned. . . . The decisions they have made and the directions their creative impulses have taken echo Afrodiasporic musical priorities. Rap production resonates with black cultural priorities in the age of digital reproduction.
(Rose 1994: 75, emphasis in the original)

Interestingly, the continued popularity of the 808 bass sound in not only rap but in other styles of music led Roland, when it developed a new line of digital drum machines in the late 1980s, to make available a set of digital samples of the original 808 sounds. Another instance of "second-order simulation," the 808 sounds were simply added to the newer instruments' sound data. Some rap producers say that they appreciate having access to these sounds but complain that the samples are "too clean"; rap "cultural priorities" demand that they work at making them "dirty" like the 808 originals. Manufacturers have their own *economic* priorities, however, and the digital "repackaging" of musical style has gone one step further. Roland, and other companies such as Casio, have included the sound of turntable "scratching" in their drum machines and synthesizers to facilitate the *simulation* of a rap "sound" without recourse to its specific techniques or content.[4]

Quite apart from the sound capabilities of drum machines such as the TR-808, the characteristics of the instrument's operating system also appears to have had a direct influence on the musical style of rap during this period. Tom Silverman of Tommy Boy Records has stated that "the 808 forced you to program in a hiphop style. . . . You couldn't program in real time . . . you had to drop the beats into a certain framework. Everything sounded ultra-mechanical. That's partly how the hiphop sound originated" (ibid.).[5]

Musical style can be influenced by, among other things, both the characteristics of musical instruments as well as the particular ways in which they are played in a given genre of music. Because of a combination of factors—such as the novelty and unfamiliar nature of digital technology, the inherent limitations of the technology at various stages of its development during the 1970s and '80s (later drum machine designs did allow for "real time" programming), and the relative lack of technical and/or musical training among some users—digital musical instruments have had a more determining influence on sound-making activity throughout the 1980s than they might otherwise have had. In addition, the vast array of sounds produced by these instruments has had a more general and subtle influence on pop musicians and their approach to music-making, partly because of the unique, pre-formed character of the sounds themselves: "Sounds really make you play a certain way. If you have a little, dry, ticky-type sound, you might not take the soaring solo that you would with a different sound. . . . I really think that sounds inspire you" (Starr Parodi, in *Music Technology* 4 [6], February 1990: 66).

There is a striking difference in approach between Sudnow's account of "aiming" for particular sounds and that of *responding* to them in the manner suggested here by Parodi. Parodi's comment seems to support Marcus Miller's view that, "if you get a keyboard that has an interesting sound, you don't have to play a lot of notes on it. The *sound* takes over." Sudnow's practice suggests a form of subjective, internal listening that precedes and guides the act of sound-making, whereas this more recent form of practice suggests the opposite: an external form of listening where the objective character of the pre-existing sound strongly influences the manner in which it should be played.

The subtle impact of this influence has been felt by many musicians, and in some cases they feel they have to work against it to get back to some other "essence" of music. Composer/performance artist Laurie Anderson, for example, claims that when she writes music she usually calls up a standard piano "patch" on her synthesizers rather than allow "sounds" to distract her:

I just don't want to be too distracted by color. When I decided to write the songs on *Strange Angels*, I thought, "Well, if I just sit down at a piano and play them and sing them, then they'll work." I decided to take that approach rather than immediately getting distracted—"Oh, I have this great Akai sample that I just have to use, and even though it doesn't have too much to do with what I think the tempo of the song is, we'll, uh, work around that."

Writing with piano sounds makes me pay closer attention to the real structure of the song. It strips the song down to the most plain kind of version.

(*Keyboard* 15 [12], December 1989: 78)

The idea that piano sounds themselves are somehow "neutral" is curious. Ethnomusicologist John Blacking has argued that the physical experience of playing an instrument (and not just the sounds that it produces) can have a strong influence on the character and conceptualization of music, and that we can gain different insights into musical structures when we know that, say, Hector Berlioz composed at the guitar and Beethoven at the piano (1973: 12–21, 109–12). The apparent neutrality of the piano sound is perhaps the result of, on the one hand, its long-standing cultural heritage, its basic familiarity, and its acceptance as a tool of composition and, on the other hand, the physical/structural "fit" between bodily gesture and the resulting sound.

The more or less direct relationship between physical gesture and sound that is characteristic of most traditional musical instruments is completely severed with electronic devices. For example, despite its conventional appearance, the keyboard of a synthesizer or sampler is an "interface," little more than an elaborate switching device; thus, the relationship between gesture and resulting sound (i.e., the manner and the degree to which a sound responds to the body through touch, breath, etc.) becomes entirely arbitrary, something to be rationally planned for as part of the overall characteristics of the sound program. The technical separation of the physical interface from the sound-producing mechanism in electronic instruments may account, in part, for the apparent autonomy and uncommon power that "sounds" have in determining how you play them.

This relationship between the "sounds" produced by new technology and sources of musical "inspiration" has become pervasive and now extends beyond the use of prefabricated sounds in drum machines, synthesizers, and samplers. Complex special effects, such as multiple delays, phasing, and gating available in digital signal processors and applied to virtually any acoustic or electronic sound, have been cited as offering new ideas to musicians who regularly use these technologies in musical production: "Just listening to one of these effects immediately gives you compositional ideas . . . you only conceive of it because they occur and you notice them" (William Goldstein, in Karlin and Wright 1990: 411). Again, the prior existence of the sound effect is a key factor; these effects are "discovered," almost as if by accident, as much as created by the individual user. Decisions made by engineering teams at the early design stages of a processing device can thus have a profound impact not only on the ability to make use of the device but also on musical/compositional practices and concepts.

I believe this general phenomenon has had a significant influence on the character of popular music production since the 1980s. In effect, musical production has become closely allied to a form of *consumer* practice, where the process of selecting the "right" pre-fabricated sounds and effects for a given musical context has become as important as "making" music in the first place. Musicians are not simply consumers of new technologies, rather their entire approach to music-making has been transformed so that consumption—the exercise of taste and choice—has become implicated in their musical practices at the most fundamental level. In a somewhat different context, Ross Harley has described this event as an inversion of the conventional production/consumption hierarchy: "Electronic recording establishes a listener who is characterized by an apparatus that precedes him/her" (1993: 214).

It is here that the market context of digital instrument manufacturing, including the "software" side of the industry, has had a direct influence on musical practice and the status of the musician as a consumer. The past decade has witnessed the growth of so-called "sound libraries" for digital synthesizers, samplers, and drum machines; each instrument comes with a collection (often numbering in the hundreds) of relatively standard instrument sounds—pianos, basses, saxophones, drums, brass, and strings—in its memory banks. For most models, additional sounds can be obtained on cartridges, cards, diskettes, or CD-ROMS and added to this basic repertoire. The sounds are usually tailored for specific musical genres, and a small cottage industry has developed to maintain a steady supply of new sounds to keep up with changing tastes and musical styles.

In part because of this proliferation of sonic material, high-tech musical production not only involves choosing the right sounds for a given musical context but also requires layering and combining several pre-fabricated (or pre-recorded) sounds to achieve new instrumental effects. As in other areas of consumer culture, *more* is always better, and musicians' magazines during the late '80s and early '90s were filled with descriptions of recording sessions where, for example, a rap artist layered several sounds from different drum machines or from sampled records to create a single instrumental part:

Drum programming in rap is incredibly complex. These kids will have six tracks of drum programs, all at the same time. This is where sampling gets kind of crazy. You may get a kid who puts a kick from one record on one track, a kick from another record on another track, a Linn kick on a third track, and a TR-808 kick on a fourth —all to make one kick!   (Bill Stephney, *Keyboard* 14 [11], November 1988: 36)

The world in a box. Fusing discourses of exoticism, authenticity, and unlimited access, this ad for E-mu's Proteus/3 World stresses the diversity of world music culture at the same time that it delivers it as "raw material" for personal creative work.

The potential for layering sounds is inherent in multitrack recording and has long been used for doubling, and thereby reinforcing, vocal or instrumental sounds; but seldom has it been used to the degree or in the particular manner made possible by sampling.

Such practices are based on the assumption of a virtually unlimited access to sound material; therefore, along with the standard repertoire of Western orchestral and pop sounds, it has now become commonplace for digital instruments to include a set of musical instrument and percussion sounds from different parts of the world. Often labeled generically as "ethnic" sounds, these diverse instrument sounds provide exotic timbres to be used freely, in virtually any context, in combination with the more familiar, "naturalized" instrument sounds of the West.[6] The ubiquitous sound of the shakuhachi (a Japanese bamboo flute, popularized as part of the E-mu Emulator II sample library) in television advertising, films, and popular music during the 1980s demonstrates the shifting musical contexts wherein the sampled sounds of non-Western instruments can be found. It goes without saying that few of these contexts, or the manner in which the sounds are played, are associated with the traditions and musical/stylistic traits appropriate to the instruments. During the early 1990s, building on the international popularity of world beat music, E-mu released an addition to their Proteus series of sample playback modules, subtitled "World," containing the sounds of close to two hundred different traditional instruments: various African and Asian drums, an Australian Aboriginal didjeridu, Indonesian gamelan, and the like. By the mid-1990s, numerous CD-ROMs containing samples of "ethnic" or "world" instrument sounds, rhythmic phrases, and excerpts of musical performances were widely available.

Of concern to me here is not the issue of simple economic exploitation; as with musicians in the West, it is difficult to determine what would constitute "adequate" compensation for the individual musicians who have been recorded for the purposes of compiling sample libraries. Nor is my interest a moral concern for the "purity" of the musical traditions of the world, although it must be noted that most of these sample libraries are made up of primarily traditional instrument sounds and phrases, not the sounds and rhythms of contemporary, non-Western urban pop. To condense the riches of world musical culture to a mere set of isolated sounds must certainly be regarded as reductivist in the extreme; but I agree with Andrew Goodwin and Joe Gore that an understanding of the increasing globalization of the music industries requires acknowledgment both of the specificity of music as a cultural activity and of the global discourses with which various musics become associated (1990: 75–76).

What is important about these vast collections of sounds and excerpts of sampled performances—from Africa, Japan, Korea, Java, South American, the Middle East, and India—is that they have been promoted, almost exclusively, as a kind of "sonic tourism" for musicians in the industrialized world (ibid.; Mitchell 1993). In this way, they simultaneously fuse discourses of the exotic with those of "tradition" and "authenticity":

. . . authentic African sounds created for the serious World Music and Film Composer. This disc is part travelogue and part history lesson in the rich tradition of African Music. . . . Many of these sounds were sampled in actual African villages and have been used on several major motion picture soundtracks. Take a trip to Africa with Roland!   (Roland CD-ROM Catalog, 1994)

Not unlike the ways in which perceptions of African pop music in the West have been mediated by the tastes and sensibilities of French record producers and French audiences (Frith 1989: 171), musicians' notions of the sound and performance traditions of world cultures are now being filtered through the marketing departments of American, Japanese, and European instrument manufacturers and a small group of largely anonymous, independent sound developers. Presented with sound fragments from an increasingly diverse collection of musical cultures, the musician in the industrialized world is invited to adopt the position of "musical *flaneur*"— a uniquely privileged position with respect to the music of other cultures (Mitchell 1993).

New musical technologies have thus become an important factor in the internationalization of musical sound—what, in a somewhat different context, Wallis and Malm have referred to as "transculturation" (1984: 269–311). More to the point, sample libraries are one of the most salient examples of what Steven Feld has described as the movement from "schizophonia"—the splitting of sound away from the maker of the sound (Schafer 1977: 90)—to "schismogenesis"—the patterns of progressive cultural diversification and escalating interactivity and interdependence that have become characteristic of the international economic and cultural order (Keil and Feld 1994: 257–74). Contemporary music-making demands that any musical sound be as available as any other; technological reproduction guarantees availability and, in so doing, contributes to the increasing commodification and industrialization of world musical culture. Although musicians (and audiences) in the West have attained an unprecedented, technically mediated access to the musical sounds and traditions of the world, marketing discourse continues to construct and maintain that world as distant, exotic, and "other." In this way, the discourses of imperialism and ethnocentric ways of understanding the world are perpetuated (Goodwin and Gore 1990: 76–77).

Of course, digital musical instruments, especially samplers, not only make use of instrumental sounds but of *any* sound that can be recorded. For instance, drum machines often include a number of sound effects— breaking glass, gun shots, screeching tires—as part of their memory banks. In this sense, the commodification of sound is perhaps only the logical extension of the modernist desire to use all possible sound phenomena in musical composition. First proposed by the Italian futurist, Luigi Russolo, the idea of technical control and regulation of natural sounds for musical purposes was championed in the early twentieth century by composer Edgard Varèse and later realized by members of the *musique concrète* school of tape composition in France of the 1950s. Their musical techniques and aesthetic can be understood as an almost literal expression of the modern scientific philosophy of "domination of nature" (Leiss 1972). The subjection of the entire natural world to the order of production, which is characteristic of modern instrumental reason, thus found its expression in modernist music (Théberge 1987).

In some ways, popular uses of samplers today exhibit a certain continuity with these modernist ideals and may exemplify the absorption of modernism into popular culture, cited by many as a characteristic of the post-modern era. Certainly, since the early 1980s, groups like the The Art of Noise have taken up modernist techniques and processed them through a pop aesthetic. The group took its name from the title of Russolo's manifesto of 1913, and its music has even been described as something approaching *musique concrète* with a beat. A major component of the modernist aesthetic of *musique concrète* composers such as Pierre Schaeffer, however, was the manipulation of natural sound to render it abstract: Schaeffer's notion of the *objet sonore* is a conceptual, technical, and quasi-scientific program for the objectification of sound materials to render them more useful as abstract elements of art.

Much pop music, on the other hand, has retained the sense of identity that sounds carry with them — their ability to act as a kind of referent for the object that is the source of the sound — thus leading to an aesthetic fundamentally based in collage and ironic juxtaposition. Furthermore, the tendency in pop to draw its sound materials from other media texts represents a predilection for what is already cultural over that which is "natural." In this regard, recent technologies not only change our relationship to the world but also to the past, to our sense of social and cultural history.

During the 1980s, many pop musicians used samplers to collage together bits and pieces of rock, soul, and funk records from the 1960s and '70s. This practice was especially common in hip-hop and various dance genres. Some of the samples were recognizable, but others were not: samples of single drum sounds that could then be programmed into new rhythmic patterns or entire segments of a rhythmic groove (the "beats" or "breaks"), electric basses, guitars, or James Brown's vocal pyrotechnics. Pop acts like M/A/R/R/S, Bomb The Bass, and others leaned toward the recognizable, adding snatches of cartoon music, radio broadcasts, classical music recordings, and the like. Canadian John Oswald's "Plunderphonics" recordings used entire pop songs (referring to them as "macrosamples") and subjected them to various treatments and manipulations, although mass recognition of the quoted material was essential. Strangely, the most technically innovative forms of pop music in the 1980s were obsessed with self-referentiality, with the reproduction of pop culture's past (Goodwin 1988; Beadle 1993).

I do not want to overemphasize the supposed "post-modern" character of these practices. In music genres such as rap, the intent and effect of sampling can be quite different:

> Sampling in rap is a process of cultural literacy and intertextual reference. Sampled guitar and bass lines from soul and funk precursors are often recognizable or have familiar resonances. . . . These samples are highlighted, functioning as a challenge to know these sounds, to make connections between the lyrical and musical texts. It affirms black musical history and locates these "past" sounds in the "present."
>
> (Rose 1994: 89)

Similar practices in Caribbean music have been interpreted by Dick Hebdige as a form of paying homage or tribute (1987: 14). In the case of rap, however, it seems that there is also a kind of ritual transferral of power operating (which is not fetishism in any way but quite positive in character), where a person takes technical control of sounds that have, in the past, exerted a certain powerful effect on the individual or on the community. Again, these practices are not confined to musical materials alone: Rappers have sampled voice recordings of past black leaders, such as Martin Luther King and Malcolm X, and mixed them in with their rhythmic "grooves." By attempting in this way to make a connection with a past from which they have been physically, and most often violently severed, rappers use sampling as a form of "dialogue" with the past:

> Latifah strategically samples the legendary Malcolm X phrase: "There are going to be some changes made here" throughout "Ladies First." . . . Latifah calls on Malcolm as a part of a collective African-American historical memory and recontextualizes him not only as a voice in support of contemporary struggles in South Africa but also as a voice in support of the imminent changes regarding the degraded status of black women and specifically black women rappers. "Ladies First" is a cumulative product that, as Lipsitz might say, "enters a dialogue already in progress." (Rose 1994: 165–66)

In rap, sampling practices can thus become a form of political action and empowerment.

At a somewhat different technical and cultural level, however, what is essential about sampling practices in virtually every genre where they are employed is that, first, they operate entirely within the realm of electronic reproducibility (these are not "cover" versions of a song, or fragments of a song, but uses of the actual recordings themselves). Second, they reflect a particular type of memory and subjectivity—a form of "technological imagination" (Huyssen 1986: 9–10)—that is the result of experiencing technology and everyday life within the matrix of mass media and consumer culture. In this sense, sampling practices must also be understood within the broader context of dominant modes of music consumption within a mass media environment.

Jonathan Crane (1986) has singled out Top 40 radio for its particular, "post-modern" configuration of media texts: through constant repetition, Top 40 radio ensures that our listening experience takes place in a state of constant recontextualization, fostering a sense of "interpretive instability," multiple readings, and an endless awareness of the present (listening to tapes on a "Walkman" can have similar effects). Crane argues that, despite the media rhetoric of "Golden Oldies," the airing of past hits ultimately makes us even more aware of our affective place in the present. Even recent covers of old pop hits do not place us in the past, but rather, "they operate by pretending to mimic older material while technologically recontextualizing the past in the present" (ibid.: 68).

Sampling from old records and media texts, Top 40 radio formats, covers, and even CD-reissues of old classical, jazz, and pop recordings during the '80s are all different facets of an overall sonic environment that emphasizes the present while giving an unprecedented access to the music of the past. The obsessive concentration on the present has been cited by Jameson (1984) as the hallmark of a schizophrenic subjectivity—a form of subjectivity that he, and others such as Crane and Harvey, take to be emblematic of the post-modern experience.

Although I do not necessarily come to this particular conclusion regarding contemporary subjectivity, clearly technology has had a powerful influence on both popular musicians and the listener. In its most extreme forms, the pop song of many samples becomes akin to a "container" within which a large number of references to other music and sounds of the past and present are made. The musical "work" opens up, loses its autonomy and its "aura," its distance, its unapproachability, its uniqueness (Benjamin 1969), and becomes, in a sense, invaded by the music of the past and present and the sounds of everyday life. When confronted with such a work, the listener is immediately struck by a feeling of a fluctuating, multiple temporality; a difference in the perceived relationship between past and present; the nature of one's own subject position as a listener; and the apparent dispersal of the unified subject, or persona, of the composer/songwriter embodied in the work itself (see Cone 1974). The artistic practices of collage, assemblage, and montage used in popular music virtually destroy the organic integrity of "the work" (i.e., the "song"), and are not unlike the strategies of various avant-garde movements described by Andreas Huyssen (1986: 9–15). These practices bear the mark of a "technological imagination"; they are the result of the transformation of everyday life by the technologies of mass production and reproduction.

To the extent that digital musical instruments and recording devices are no longer *separate* technologies—indeed, for all intents and purposes a sampler *is* a recording device (Oswald 1986)[7]—sound *re*production has become a central element of musical practice. This fact, among others cited previously, has changed the most fundamental relationships between popular musicians and the sounds they make and the music they listen to, on the one hand, and their experience of popular culture, on the other.

This shift in musicians' sensibilities toward "sound," however, can be clarified by examining, in greater detail, the musical concepts employed by musicians in their day-to-day activities in the sound studio. Indeed, further evidence of the fusion of musical practice with electronic technologies of production/reproduction can be found in the language musicians characteristically use to describe the sounds they make. There has always been a great variety of specialized terms and slang associated with popular music, but what often goes unrecognized is the degree to which they function as meaningful "style statements":

> Linguistic shorthands like the terms "groove," "sound," or "beat," significantly code an unspecifiable but ordered sense of something . . . that is sustained in a distinctive, regular and attractive way, working to draw a listener in. Terms like these say that the perception of style is empirically real, but that it is also necessarily general, vague, and physical. (Feld 1988: 76)

As Feld suggests, speech about music is always metaphoric and somewhat vague in nature, but, I believe, it can also be quite precise and systematic.

In fact, musicians and studio engineers have developed a virtual "theory" of sound through the deployment of metaphoric expressions and binary oppositions that, first, define their experience of sound in meaningful ways and, second, help organize their sound-making activities. For example, studio devices such as dynamic expanders are commonly referred to as "gates"; the term offers a precise visual metaphor for the opening and closing of the signal path. Similarly, loud, aggressive drum sounds are often referred to as "rude"; an instrument sound or a music mix that puts great emphasis on the low-frequency, bass register is "heavy." A synthesizer "pad" is a sustained sound (a string, brass, or even a piano sound) often used for soft, background accompaniments. The original attack portion of the sound is slowed down (i.e., "softened"), and its natural sustain is "looped" and/or "chorused" to expand artificially the durational and spatial characteristics of the sound (the "chorusing" technique will be described in greater detail later).

Perhaps more significant is the vast array of paired terms, such as fat/thin, warm/cold, wet/dry, clean/dirty, organic/processed, that are used to describe fundamental aesthetic values through which sounds in a given context are assessed and, ultimately, judged to be acceptable or not. Significantly, the majority of these metaphors are physical in character, linking the experience of musical sound directly to bodily sensations. There is, furthermore, often a curious reversal of the conventional social expectations concerning the value relationships attributed to any given pair of terms. For example, a "fat" synthesizer sound is considerably more desirable than a "thin" one; and whereas sound engineers typically prefer "clean" recordings to "dirty" ones, rock guitarists often go to great lengths to "dirty-up" their sounds (i.e., find ways to create large amounts of mid-range distortion). Sociologically, such reversals of conventional meaning could be regarded as one way in which pop musicians affirm (if only to themselves) their position as "outsiders" to mainstream culture.

Most interesting is the manner in which these terms articulate certain value positions vis-à-vis music itself, not only among musicians but also within popular culture at large. As Andrew Goodwin (1988: 41–42) has demonstrated, some of these distinctions can be quite complex and subject to change and revision over time. Goodwin discusses how the warm/cold distinction was mobilized during the 1980s as a value statement about analog (warm and human sounding) versus digital (cold and inhuman) sounds. This distinction applied equally to recordings, LPs versus CDs, and to synthesizers. What Goodwin finds curious in this situation is that, during the 1970s, analog synthesizers were labeled as "cold" and "inhuman" by rock musicians and fans of the day; by the 1980s, however, a new generation of musicians and listeners were regarding analog synthesizers as the very sign of human "feel" and "authentic" expression (ibid.). Indeed, I argue that such attitudes have undergone a further, even more subtle change in recent years: Although the warm/cold distinction still operates, the gradual acceptance of digital synthesizers during the past decade has brought an appreciation for their increasing ability to mimic the "warmth" of analog instruments while, at the same time, offering the clarity of digital textures. The term "icy" has actually taken on positive connotations when used to describe a certain type of sound quality only available on digital instruments.

Following the research model of ethnomusicology advocated by Merriam (1964), it is important to observe how musical sound, concept, and behavior are linked in significant ways in musical practice. How do differential metaphors such as warm/cold or fat/thin, influence the activities of musicians engaged in the production of music? The search for a "fat" sound, for example, has long been a preoccupation among popular musicians who use synthesizers. The origins and precise meanings of the term are obscure, but it appears to have been a part of the musicians' and engineers' vocabulary at least since the mid-1970s (if not earlier) when synthesizers came into widespread use in popular music. Because of its popular origins and its slang character, it is not a generally accepted term (or even necessarily a sonic goal) among most university-based composers of electronic music. In pop music, the term is most closely associated with the desire to create a sound with the acoustic complexity and richness of a large ensemble playing together: "Most groups can't get (or can't afford to get) enough performers to get a really fat sound, and this means that they have to rely on a synthesizer player to fill in a wide variety of sounds, that otherwise would not be possible" (Marty Golden, in *Music Market Canada* 1 [9], October 1977: 8). Although this commentator implies that the term "fat" describes an attempt to create the effect of a diverse range of instruments, it is most often employed in a more precise fashion to describe the sound of several instruments of the same type playing together: for example, as with a string or brass section of a symphony orchestra or a choir of voices. When several instruments play together in unison, tiny discrepancies in timing, loudness, and intonation and, to a lesser extent, differences in the arrival time of the sounds at the listener's ears create an acoustic effect that is subtle yet vibrant and seems to account, in large part, for the unique impression that ensemble playing has upon the listener.

An attempt by sound engineers to give more fullness to the sound of a single voice or instrument led, by the late 1960s, to the development of various types of delay units, which could duplicate a sound at an interval of a few milliseconds. When mixed with the original sound, the delayed signals gave the impression of multiple parts playing in unison. Although this "doubling" effect, which can also be described as a "spreading out" of the sound in the temporal domain, could be useful in certain recording situations, it was too simple and regular to give the impression of a true ensemble. Gradually, a more sophisticated device, known as a "chorus," was developed. The name describes the intended effect, but the device is used on a wide range of instruments—guitars, electric pianos, string synthesizers, and so on—not just voices. In a "chorus" device, various controls are added that allow delay times to be modulated and/or fed back into the unit in a regular or random fashion to create a more complex sound. In some chorus units, the amplitude (loudness) and/or pitch of the signal can be modulated in the same way. Later, stereo chorus devices were developed that added a spatial, left-right "spread" to the delayed sounds, enhancing the overall effect even more.

A "fat" sound, then, can be defined as a sound that is the result of this "spreading out" or expansion of the audio signal in one or more domains: temporal, spatial, amplitude, and/or frequency. As electronic technology has become increasingly integrated with popular music production, there appears to have been an evolving, dialectical relationship between the concepts of musical sound and the various possibilities offered by the technology. The transformation of these musical concepts or statements of aesthetic value into material form (i.e., sound) has become entirely dependent upon electronic technology and on sound re-production as the primary medium and context of music-making. This dependency has had an impact on both the behavior of musicians and on the development of new technologies.

In the case of synthesizers, for example, observers have suggested that a predilection for "fat" sounds may have come about because of the limitations of early synthesizer technology rather than from its more "positive" attributes (e.g., see Kaplan 1989: 612–14). Analog oscillators had an inherent tendency to drift out of tune, and musicians soon discovered that the combined sound of two or more slightly out of tune oscillators actually had a fullness and a slightly animated, beating quality that was more interesting than the sound of a single oscillator. Musicians began to *purposefully* de-tune the oscillators on their synthesizers as a means of enhancing this effect and thereby "fattening up" the sound.

Initially, the greater stability of digital oscillators appeared to be a positive advancement over analog designs, but it was soon found that they did not meet the sonic expectations of musicians; digital synthesizers, for a variety of reasons, sounded "thin" to the ears of analog synthesizer enthusiasts. Keyboard manufacturers subsequently developed a variety of techniques to add calculated, "random" fluctuations to the output of the oscillators and to give musicians more precise control over oscillator (de)tuning (ibid.: 613). Ironically, the ultimate test of the new digital technology was not whether it offered substantial improvements over older designs but whether it could successfully imitate the technical inadequacies (and the "sound") of the previous technology. For musicians, a practice that had once been spontaneous and intuitive, involving little more than the twist of a knob while playing, now became the object of rational calculation: The *precise* de-tuning of the oscillators (calculated in hundreths of a semitone) had to be determined in advance, programmed, and stored as part of the synthesizer sound "patch."

Equally important, the "chorus-like" effect produced in this manner is no longer seen as a separate operation applied *to* a sound, rather, the effect becomes an inherent characteristic *of* the sound itself. This movement has become increasingly prevalent in the design and use of synthesizers throughout the 1980s. "Effects" such as delays, flangers, reverbs, and the like have become thought of as inherent properties of a sound, and virtually all contemporary keyboards now contain sophisticated digital effects units built directly into the instrument. Guitar players also process their guitar sounds through an array of footpedals and special effects devices. With samplers, and sample-based instruments such as drum machines, there has been a trend toward recording effects or natural acoustic ambience as part of the basic sampled sound; here again, the character of the sampler as a recording/reproduction device allows for this option where conventional synthesizers do not:

I couldn't imagine that any kind of synthetic reproduction would be able to give you the type of nuance that you get out of a sample. . . . You see, with samples, not only are you getting the sound of the instrument, you're getting the ability to capture the instrument in different types of air spaces. For example, we have both dry and ambient room sound percussion noises, and dry and ambient wind. Even with the classical guitar, different types of environments make a big difference.
(Frank Zappa, in *Keyboard* 13 [2], February 1987: 61)

The multitude of variables associated with recording or sampling acoustic sounds, programming synthesizers and drum machines, and taking special effects into consideration as part of the basic characteristics of a sound has led to an increasing complexity in the programming structure of digital musical instruments. This complexity requires, on the part of the user, a substantial amount of technical and theoretical knowledge that is quite different from the types of knowledge associated with conventional musical language and performance practice. A consideration of the synthesizer "patch" diagram as an indicator of increasing abstraction in the design and use of synthesizers will illustrate this change in knowledge requirements.

The term "patch" is derived from the old system of modular, analog synthesizers of the 1960s and '70s, where individual oscillators, envelope generators, and other devices were "patched" together with an audio cable to create a particular flow of audio and control signals; the configuration of this flow and the settings on the individual devices created the sound the musician was after. Although it certainly helped to have a good knowledge of the theory of sound synthesis, many musicians and engineers were able to program analog synthesizers, at least at a basic, practical level, through an intuitive process aided by the similarity between the design of synthesizers and other, more familiar audio components.

Because the early synthesizers had no microprocessors or RAM where these configurations could be stored, "patch diagrams" were developed to record and remember specific patches. The patch diagram was not unlike a form of tablature; the diagram was little more than a template of the physical layout of the synthesizer's front panel, its knobs, settings, and connections via the patch cords. In the same way a guitarist can read tablature without having a thorough knowledge of music theory simply by following the tablature like a road map to the fingerboard of the guitar, any individual could reconstruct a synthesizer patch by following the diagram; no theoretical knowledge of synthesis or even the functioning of the specific devices themselves was required.

With digital synthesizers and samplers, however, the various devices and functions of synthesis are merely *represented* in computer hardware and software, and the musician has no direct access to the various "modules" at all. Similar to the organ-like keyboard itself, the front panel of a digital synthesizer is an "interface" that acts as a new kind of mediation between the user and the object. As Dick Hebdige has noted in regards to the transition from the motorcycle to the motorscooter: "The 'sheathing' of machine parts placed the user in a new relationship to the object—one which was more remote and less 'physical'" (1981: 51). Whereas Hebdige argues that this change led, in the case of the motor scooter, to a relationship of "ease" with regards to the mechanical nature of the machine, in the case of the synthesizer it has led to one based on near-total abstraction.

Because microprocessors can only deal effectively with numbers (i.e., quantified data), a typical "patch chart" for a digital synthesizer or sampler consists of little more than a large table of numbers that again, *represent* various synthesizer parameters and states. Interpreting these tables requires a much greater knowledge of both the internal architecture of the synthesizer in question and a more general understanding of the theory of the synthesis model that it employs. This knowledge is by its very nature more abstract, formal, and quasi-mathematical than the "practical logics" (Bourdieu 1990)—visual, aural, tactile—formerly associated with analog synthesis and with music-making more generally.

The level of complexity and abstraction inherent in this new relationship between musicians and their chosen instruments of musical production is generally accepted to be one reason for the rise of an industry dedicated to marketing pre-fabricated sound programs created by specialists and sound-editing software for computers.[8] Software, at least, gives the musician a graphic, visual representation of the data required in sound programming. Here again, this situation merely reinforces the position of the musician as a "consumer" of new technologies. As Peter Lyman has pointed out in his discussion of computer word processing:

A computer is both a machine and a social relation. Computer "hardware" can only be used with computer "software," and software is essentially a technical culture which defines the practical techniques necessary to operate the machine, as well as an implicit theory of knowledge (information theory or cybernetics) and implicit social relationships as well (the consumer as "user," the computer as provider, and others). One must be an expert to consume the hardware without the software; few experts could do so. (1984: 76–77)

Conclusion

Ever since the development of notation in Western art music, musical sound has become a problematic entity, a necessary though sometimes unwanted distraction from the perfect order embodied in the musical score.

In popular music, the ultimate reproducibility of sound through synthesis and sampling has likewise become regarded as problematic, again with regards to the structure of music but also in relation to the values of musical performance.

Such dichotomies are misleading, however, because the reproduction of sound has actually made it a more vital component in the recognition of musical genres; indeed, in the age of electronic reproduction, the achievement of a unique "sound" has become one of the means through which new musical genres are created in the first place. The importance of sound has been evident in the recording studio, especially since the rise of digital musical instruments. Digital instruments have become the means for both the production of new sounds and for the reproduction of old ones—the perfect vehicle for a music industry based simultaneously in fashion and nostalgia. As musicians have developed an aesthetics of "sound," a set of techniques and a vocabulary to describe them have evolved as well. Interestingly, even musicians who reject digital technology use the same vocabulary of fat and thin, warm and cold, to describe the characteristics of microphones and various analog recording devices, thus betraying their preoccupation with technologically reproduced sound (see Jackson 1992: 28).

Most important for the present argument is the manner in which many musicians have come to rely on outside sources for not only the sounds but also, with samplers and drum machines, the rhythmic grooves and even the melodic and harmonic phrases that they use in musical production. On the one hand, this phenomenon is related to the difficulty in acquiring the knowledge and skills required to program new sounds and, on the other, by an aesthetic that demands that all sounds (and sequences of sounds)—domestic and foreign, musical and natural—be made available for musical purposes. In this regard, making music with new technology has indeed become a process of simultaneous production and consumption.

CHAPTER NINE

"Live" and Recorded
MIDI Sequencing, the Home Studio, and Copyright

✳

> During the Digicon digital arts conference in Vancouver in Aug. '83, Ralph Dyck ended his demonstration of an IBM-PC equipped with a MIDI interface by playing a disk of a MIDIed [Oscar] Peterson electronic piano performance. . . . Dyck fed that data into a Roland electronic piano on the stage, and we all heard Peterson play "live." It seemed that the essence of Peterson's performance was captured more convincingly in that MIDI data stream than it would have been in a normal audio recording.
> (Moog 1985: 48)

One myth of the "digital revolution" in music recording has been that the attendant increase in audio "fidelity" has somehow brought the listener "closer" to the original moment of performance; listening to a CD is, supposedly, like "being there." With sequencing (the recording of MIDI data), however, something quite different has occurred. On the one hand, certain uses of sequencing have been associated with the most rigid, mechanical, and inhuman-sounding performances, and, on the other, the distinction between "live" and "recorded" seems to have completely dissolved. Indeed, with regard to the latter, apparently for some listeners MIDI sequencing virtually returns the "aura" (Benjamin 1969) of live musical performance to the medium of digital reproduction.

At one level, these attitudes are little more than the most recent expression of the same contradictory feelings of shock and fascination that greeted the mechanical reproduction of music on the phonograph and the player piano at the turn of the century. At a deeper level, however, the particular notion of "live" performance referred to in the chapter opening, together with a whole series of controversies surrounding the changing status of the "live" in popular music during the past decade, have been the signs of a more fundamental shift in musical production brought on by recent uses of electronic and digital technologies. Here again, to paraphrase

Craig H. Roell's observations on the debates that raged over music and machines at the turn of the century (1989: 31), the digitization of music is essentially a story of values, not inventions.

In this chapter, I look more closely at multitrack recording in popular music, giving special attention to the use of computers and MIDI technology within the multitrack studio environment. In many ways, the developments that will be discussed here are closely related to the issues of "sound" discussed in the previous chapter; however, what interests me most in the present context is not only how the "sound" of musical instruments has become the object of rational calculation and commercial interest but, also, how the "feel" of a "live" musical performance has become the object of a similar kind of rationality.

I also consider the rise of the "home studio" as a particular outgrowth of the "democratization" of musical technology. The home studio has become both the site of significant musical activity at every level, from professional to amateur music-making, and the focal point of the consumer market for electronic musical instrument suppliers. Despite the utopian rhetoric found in many magazine articles and in advertising, however, this broad-based activity has not necessarily led to a breaking down of barriers between amateur and professional; indeed, as the home has increasingly become a technically viable site of production, conflicts between the professional and the amateur worlds of music-making have come to the fore. The rise of the home studio also represents a shift in values concerning the organization of domestic space, an issue that has considerable implications for gender and family life.

Finally, I discuss a number of issues related to musical copyright that tie together some of the concerns found in both the previous chapter and the present one. These issues touch upon the problematic status of sound recordings (as opposed to musical scores) as objects in copyright law, the increasing commodification of "sounds" and the desire for legal protections from sampling and other digital technologies, and the problems of defining musical *processes*—such as certain styles of composition and performance—as meaningful forms of musical practice.

Multitrack Sound Recording as a Medium of "Composition"

During the 1960s the production of popular music was completely transformed by the establishment of multitrack tape recording as the norm in studio production. Multitrack technology allowed for the sound of individual instruments to be recorded separately from one another in a process known as "overdubbing." Later, the various lines of music (the recorded "tracks") could be combined, electronically enhanced, and balanced during the "mixdown" session. As a result, the process of group performance and the social/musical exchange between musicians became rationalized and fragmented—both spatially and temporally—and control over the overall musical texture was increasingly given to the sound engineer and producer (Théberge 1989). Pop songs were no longer simply composed, performed, and then recorded. More and more, the studio became a compositional tool in its own right.

This situation was certainly not the case prior to the introduction of the tape medium in sound recording. In the early days of recording, "the accent was on the performance and the recording was a more or less perfect transmitter of that" (Eno 1983: 56). With multitrack recording, however, individual performances became less important than the manipulation of individual strands of recorded sound material. With multitrack technology,

two things happened: you got an additive approach to recording, the idea that composition is the process of adding more . . . ; it also gave rise to . . . in-studio composition, where you no longer come to the studio with a conception of the finished piece. Instead, you come with actually rather a bare skeleton of the piece, or perhaps with nothing at all. . . . Once you become familiar with studio facilities . . . you can begin to compose in relation to those facilities. You can begin to think in terms of putting something on, putting something else on, trying this on top of it, and so on, then taking some of the original things off, or taking a mixture of things off, and seeing what you're left with—actually constructing a piece in the studio. (Ibid.: 57)

Eno's description is interesting in that it defines this new form of "composition" as essentially a process of layering (an "additive approach"). The tendency for synthesizer players to layer sounds is not simply a matter of searching for a "fat" sound but, rather, has been a fundamental part of a technique and aesthetic of pop music production since the 1960s.

More importantly, however, Eno's comments point out the degree to which the technology of sound recording has become *productive*, not simply reproductive. H. Stith Bennett has likened sound recording to a form of musical "notation" for pop musicians who, for the most part, do not read conventional scores. Sound recording allows the musicians to distance themselves from the act of performance and to create "impossible music," that is, music that could not otherwise be conceived or performed. For Bennett, the creation of "impossible music" is one of the signs of a musical practice that has been influenced by the creative possibilities and pressures of a notational system (1983: 228–30). He cites guitarist Les Paul, who created a number of unperformable experiments (and hit records) using overdubbing and speed changes during the early 1950s, as the first historical sign of such a development (ibid.: 230–31).[1]

In fact, although I agree with the general outlines of Bennett's thesis, the idea of layering sounds and individual performances as a specific compositional process has little to do with traditional composition using notational means.[2] Indeed, the move toward such layering techniques appears to have historical precedents that antedate multitrack recording by many years. For example, on a "one-man band" recording released in 1941, jazz reed player Sidney Bechet is said to have overdubbed (through a process of sound-on-sound recording not unlike that used in Les Paul's own early experiments) the saxophones, clarinet, bass, drum, and piano parts of the music.[3] Earlier still, between 1917 and 1927, composer Igor Stravinsky created a series of pianola transcriptions of his orchestral music, several of which were written as four-hand piano scores; he performed each of the parts in synchronization with himself on previously recorded rolls (Craft 1957: 35). The idea of overdubbing separate performances by a single (or multiple) individual(s) is thus rooted in the technology of mechanical reproduction itself. Once a sound is made repeatable through mechanical reproduction, it lends itself to being experimentally combined with other sounds in an empirical manner that is not possible, at least not in the same way, through notation. This inherent possibility of reproductive technologies could not be fully exploited (for technical as well as aesthetic reasons) until the second half of the twentieth century.

The multitrack tape recorder was not simply a new device for the recording or layering of sound, or even for the composition of music; it was part of a larger "social technology" (Frederickson 1989) and, as such, played a role in the entire reorganization of production in popular music. In the studio, the architecture of the recording space was redesigned to allow for greater separation and control over reverberant sound. Sound engineers developed novel microphone, signal processing, and mixing techniques and became full-fledged members of the musical process (Kealy 1974, 1979); performers had to adapt to the conditions of temporal and spatial separation; and, at a level beyond the studio itself, entrepreneurial producers became increasingly responsible for musical production within the overall economic organization of the record industry (Peterson and Berger 1971). Initially, then, the prerogative of "composing" with the new medium was not given equally to all who participated in the multitrack enterprise; it was the producer, more than anyone else, whose judgment prevailed within the studio environment. Indeed, it is the producer who is valorized in modern copyright law. As far as mechanical rights to the recording are concerned, it is the producer (or the record company) who holds all rights of reproduction.

Antoine Hennion has described the role of the producer as that of an "intermediary" between the recording artist and the marketplace. Although producers are often not musicians or engineers by training, Hennion stresses that their role is never passive:

Intermediaries are not passive functionaries administering laws (musical, economic, or cultural). They produce the worlds that they want to make work for them. They force, tear out, knit together; they have tools and techniques for isolating, measuring, testing. Nothing is given in advance for them.

(Hennion 1989: 402)

In Hennion's view (not unlike those of Eno and Bennett), the studio becomes the "laboratory" of the producer; a site where experiments—a trial-and-error process of tests, operations, and evaluations—in sound take place. The insulated studio acoustics, the isolation of the musicians from one another in the studio, and the separation of their sounds on multi-track tape must necessarily be correlated with the insulation/isolation of the studio from the outside world:

The isolation of people is as important as the physical isolation: in this vision we are not confronted with an acoustic problem but with the plans from an idealized microcosm of creation . . .
. . . Having thus separated off, isolated, and emptied of its natural content a volume whose boundaries become the limits of an artificial universe, what needs to be brought in so that our creatures have some chance of making their way?

(Ibid.: 408)

It is perhaps no accident, then, that during the 1970s recording facilities like Le Studio in Morin Heights, Québec, sought the refuge of isolated rural settings for their musical "experiments." The rise of the "home studio" during the 1980s must be seen as part of this general trend. In the case of the home studio, the privacy of domestic space becomes the ideal site of musical expression and inspiration rather than the more public realms of night club and stage.

As intermediary, and despite the ill-defined nature of their skills, much rests on the shoulders of the producer:

these "magicians" who turn up with their hands in their pockets, without well-defined skills, but whose flair and impressions are the key to success. It is a matter of showing that no one operates within a more realistic network than theirs, that no one operates so material a construction of the act of listening, that no one acts less at a distance. (Ibid.: 402)

In essence, their authority is based on the assumption that they will deliver hits because they listen with the ears of the consumer. The success of producers is thus dependent on their ability to completely identify with the public: "A song-object is not produced first and consumed later; rather a *simultaneous production-consumption* process takes place first inside the studio, and the impact on those present must be repeated later on outside the studio" (Hennion 1990: 203, emphasis in the original).

In a certain sense, this process of listening puts the producer in the same position as the consumer:

> The producer is not a calculator. His knowledge of the pop music scene and his experience of the public are of value only when he has integrated them within an "immediate" sensitivity: only then do they mutely guarantee the genuineness of his taste. . . . He can forget the criteria that he has interiorized and allow himself to give in to his feelings, to react to what he perceives as purely physical sensations.
>
> (Ibid.: 201)

Hennion's observations suggest that Blacking's (1971) theory of musical competence—defined as a form of structured listening—is central to the production of popular music. It is not musical "skill," in the traditional sense of the term, that defines the role of producers; rather, it is their ability to listen, to feel what is "right" for the given musical context that is their focus in the studio.

In part because of the increasing importance of producers in the recording of popular music, there has been a tendency throughout the 1970s and '80s for producers to become as well known as the stars they record. This fame has been noteworthy throughout mainstream pop but especially in early disco and in many subsequent genres of dance music. During the 1970s, for example, producers such as Giorgio Moroder and Freddie Perren became well known for their work with disco artists Donna Summer and Gloria Gaynor. In the 1980s and '90s an increasing number of producers, representing a much wider range of mainstream musical genres, became known to the public: for example, Brian Eno, Quincy Jones, Nile Rodgers, and, among Canadians with international reputations, David Foster and Daniel Lanois.

If the producer as consumer represents the "dictatorship of the public" in studio production, then it should come as no surprise that musicians and engineers, in some genres of music, have long attempted to reassert control over the production process. It is not that these studio collaborators are not equally concerned with success in the marketplace but simply that their values and their definition of success may be different from the producer's. In large part, it was a desire for greater control and artistic freedom that led to the early artist-owned studios of the 1970s; and this step was the first and perhaps the most decisive one toward the idea of the "home studio" of the '80s.

Edward R. Kealy (1974, 1979, 1982) has described in detail the changing patterns of collaboration that came about in the recording of rock music between 1965 and 1975. According to Kealy, an "art mode" of production

Budget multitracking for the home studio. In an effort to simplify multitracking and make it more affordable for the amateur and semi-professional markets, Tascam introduced the Portastudio concept. Combining inexpensive cassette technology with an integrated mixing console, the idea was copied by a number of other manufacturers during the 1980s.

evolved during this period where the recording artists themselves were responsible for aesthetic decision-making in the studio. They relied heavily on the technical expertise and growing artistic contributions of recording engineers, with whom they had developed an understanding relationship. Often, successful artists invested tens of thousands of dollars to construct their own studios where they could experiment freely without the pressures of paying for studio time at hourly rates.

As musicians became more comfortable with the studio apparatus, they acquired new forms of knowledge and new concepts of musical "sound" that were quite unlike traditional forms of knowledge and practice associated with musical theory, performance, and composition. To work creatively in the studio, musicians and engineers had to acquire both a basic theoretical and a practical knowledge of acoustics, microphone characteristics, electronic signal processing, and a variety of other technical processes. In Bourdieu's terms, the changes in the physical and temporal relationship to the production of musical sound inherent in these activities results in a kind of objectification that is entirely different in character from the "urgency" of conventional performance practice. There is a kind of "disincarnation" of musical production and a subjection of recorded sound to rational processes that is not unlike what stems from the use of notation in the production of musical scores (1990: 73). In part because of this objectivist position, pop musicians have increasingly taken on the more detached, evaluative role of the producer in assessing the commercial potential of their material. By the 1980s, it was not uncommon to find, on record liner notes, artists listed as producers on their own albums; the songwriter-producer had arrived.

Because of their own need to become familiar with the disciplines necessary to work in the multitrack studio, because of the growing, do-it-yourself, independent recording movement of the '70s, and because of the image of star performers with unconstrained access to these powerful technologies of creation, semi-professional and amateur musicians began to look for ways in which they, too, could construct their own studios. At about the same time that professional formats were expanding from 8-, to 16-, to 24-track capability during the late 1960s and early '70s, consumer multitrack recorders began to appear on the market. At first, this technology took the form of modifications to existing tape decks, but by 1972, the first 4-track tape recorder expressly designed for amateur and semi-professional use (the TEAC 3340) had been introduced.

According to Steve Jones, as the enthusiasm for the new consumer technology grew, so did the industry, and in 1977 the first Multi-track Expo was held in Los Angeles with workshops dedicated to "The Musician's Home Studio" (1992: 139). Suddenly, as Jones puts it, the meaning of "paying your dues" in the music business took on a new meaning among pop musicians; instead of struggling with a band year after year, performing in bars and night clubs, the purchase of suitable recording equipment seemed a more viable route to a successful career in pop music. "Paying your dues" now meant making payments on your gear (ibid.: 140). The impetus behind this movement became even stronger during the early 1980s with the arrival of inexpensive cassette multitrack recorder/mixers and MIDI, on the one hand, and fluctuations in the availability of public venues for live performance, on the other.[4]

Most interesting about this development is that the acquisition of new knowledge and skills, the acceptance of new definitions of what it means to be a "musician," and the mobilization of the domestic space as a production environment all take place simultaneously. This phenomenon is underscored by the emergence of what has been referred to as the "hyphenated musician": the singer-songwriter-producer-engineer-musician-sound designer. The assumption that a single person can perform each of these roles equally well is particularly striking. In the professional studio, music production had always been a *collective* project. For the producer to perform well in the studio, it was necessary to have a team of skilled collaborators—recording artists, session musicians, and recording engineers—to do much of the "work" associated with musical production. Even in artist-owned studios, "one-man band" recordings such as those occasionally released during the early 1970s by artists such as Stevie Wonder were extremely rare, and even these recordings usually involved the cooperation of at least a few technical assistants. The particular notion of independent, solitary production in the home studio, however, is related not only to the rise of consumer multitrack equipment but also to the availability of (and reliance on) digital synthesizers, sequencers, and drum machines. Only with the aid of these technologies was it possible for an individual to perform all the roles necessary to make a successful recording.

From Multitrack Tape to MIDI Sequencing

Sequencers allow musicians to store, manipulate, and reproduce digital information relating to performance gestures, such as playing notes on a keyboard instrument or drum pad, without referring to the actual sounds produced by the instrument at the time of recording. Like a musical score, sequencers store information such as pitches, note durations, dynamics, and so on, but they can record the information in "real time" much like a tape recorder; unlike a tape recorder, however, they do not store sounds. The playing mechanism of a digital instrument (most often an organ-type keyboard) is simply an "interface" that supplies MIDI data to the sound-producing hardware; as such, it is completely separate from the sound synthesis or sampling capabilities of the instrument and can be used to input data to a sequencer. Sequencers are in a variety of forms: as a basic component within drum machines and many synthesizer keyboards, as stand-alone hardware devices, and in computer software form with elaborate, graphical representations of the MIDI data.

To a certain extent, MIDI sequencers reproduce the divisions defined in traditional musical notation and extend them further. Not only is the "language" of music kept separate from its manifestation in sound but so are performance gestures. This reproduction (and extension) of a conceptual and practical distinction in Western musical thought has been evident from the first applications of computer technology in music synthesis. Beginning in the late 1950s, for example, Max Mathews developed a series of computer programs (MUSIC 4 and MUSIC 5 being the most sophisticated and best known) at Bell Telephone Laboratories that used two different kinds of input data based on an analogy between the "score" (note data) and the "orchestra" (function data for sound synthesis).[5]

Because sequencers can store performances themselves (or simulations of them) and reproduce them electronically, they have often been compared to the early player piano whose rolls stored the physical gestures of a pianist's performance so that they could later be reproduced mechanically on a similarly equipped piano. The piano lent itself to this type of treatment because of the basic mechanical nature of its design, but with synthesis and sampling, virtually any instrument sound can become the object of the MIDI sequencing process:

I used to write arrangements with different players in mind. In the past few months I've been able to go into the studio alone or with one other musician. . . . Sometimes I can do the whole thing myself—all the synthesizers, rhythms, drum machines, bass and guitar.
There's nothing like actually playing the parts, but it seems like programming and sequencing are really taking over.
(Arthur Wright, in *Mix* 9 [2], February 1985: 74)

After performance gesture has been separated, conceptually and practically, from sound and defined as simple information, the necessary data can be input in any number of ways provided it can be recognized by the sound-generating hardware. The earliest sequencers of popular music production were developed for use with analog synthesizers during the early 1970s; they were monophonic (much like the instruments they were designed to control) and could store only a limited number of notes. One of the first polyphonic digital sequencers introduced into the commercial market, the Roland MC-8 (introduced in 1977), was based on a design by a Vancouver musician, Ralph Dyck. Involved in a variety of musical projects, including film, record, and jingle production, Dyck wanted to be able to control his analog synthesizers with more precision than was possible with a conventional, organ-type keyboard. His prototype sequencer used a numeric key pad (like that found on a calculator) to enter data controlling the various synthesizer components.[6] As a result, precise data on every aspect of the sound could be entered in "steps" rather than as part of an integral performance. Although Dyck's initial design was monophonic, he developed a method for synchronization with multitrack tape. Roland improved the basic design for commercial release, making the sequencer polyphonic (i.e., it could play several virtual "tracks" of information) and giving it 16k of RAM so that the instrument could store over five thousand notes (Vail 1990; Anderton 1988: 45–46).

The two essential features of the MC-8 were its numerical, step-entry mode of programming and its multichannel capability. The latter feature placed sequencing firmly within the dominant modes of recording studio production practices. The step-entry mode of operation is significant, however, for both its immediate and its more long-term influence. In the short term, step-entry programming led to the same kind of mechanical precision noted for the TR-808 drum machine and hip-hop music. Much of the music associated with electronic technology during the late '70s and early '80s—mostly the dance music of producers such as Giorgio Moroder or the electro-pop styles of bands such as Devo and Human League—had a similar rhythmic insistence, an almost robotic feel of hyper-precision stemming from the extensive use of synthesizers and sequencers. Once again, the peculiarities and limitations of a particular technology seemingly contributed, in a positive way, to the aesthetic predilections of an entire genre of music.

In a curious kind of reversal, the type of precision available with the definition of a musical note as a set of independent, stepped data has become the source of a new rationalization of performance practice. By the mid-1980s, many drum machines and sequencers allowed data to be entered in "real time," thus preserving the "feel"—what ethnomusicologist Charles Keil refers to as the "participatory discrepancies" (Keil and Feld 1994: 96–108)—of a live performance. Although sequencers have often been used to create a more "precise" performance—through resolving discrepancies to the beat through a process known as "quantization"—there has been a simultaneous attempt to use them as a means of actually quantifying "feel":

When I was producing, I would endeavor to pick the take with the best feel. . . . On each take the notes played were essentially the same; yet there were differences between takes—differences in the *feel* the players gave the music.

In the control booth, trying to get the feel I wanted, I used to tell my artists that there was no "feel" button on the console. But in a way, now there is. Thanks to computer-aided music, we have been able to explore and quantify these effects a bit more precisely than in the past. (Stewart 1987: 58)

Continuing, Stewart attempts to define various subjective rhythmic terms such as "groove," "heavy," and "driving" in terms of millisecond delays or anticipations in the relationship between beats in a drum pattern. Charles Keil is interested in the measurement of "feel" as a means of "proving" that such discrepancies exist and that they are significant aspects of musical style as realized through performance (Keil and Feld 1994: 154–55). The aim of pop producers such as Stewart, however, is more instrumental in character: Such knowledge can be used to establish the basis for "predictable effects that you can use with predictable results" (Stewart 1987: 60). In recent years, the manufacturers of drum machines have attempted to introduce design modifications that will facilitate the programming of virtually every nuance of drum technique, including not only variations in the rhythmic placement of individual beats but in their pitch and timbral shading as well. Several sophisticated sequencer programs (e.g., "Cubase," by the German software company Steinberg) now can extract the "groove" from a MIDI performance and store it as a kind of template for later analysis and/or use with other instrumental parts in a musical texture or in completely different musical contexts.

The quantification of performance variables does not end with rhythm alone; within the MIDI specification, a numerical value is assigned to each aspect of a note—its pitch, its precise location in time, its duration, its loudness (a function of on-set velocity), and several continuous variables such as key pressure, pitch bend, and so on. With regards to dynamics, traditional notation can only indicate about eight discrete levels of loudness (from *ppp* to *fff*); the precise loudness of any given note within a musical passage is determined by the performer within this relative framework and in keeping with the style of music in question. Individual notes may be somewhat louder or softer (intentionally or within an overall scheme of accents and phrasing) without disrupting the overall sense of a single dynamic level. With MIDI, however, it becomes possible (even necessary) to specify the precise dynamic level within a range of 128 values (the maximum number of values available given the size of a MIDI byte) to achieve subtle nuances of musical performance. Even when a performance is recorded into a sequencer in "real time" from a velocity-sensitive keyboard, any editing required in the material takes place along this same scale of numerical values.

The tendency towards a rational, calculated approach to the nuances of performance as represented in the MIDI data stream is, in part, a result of the quantitative nature of the data itself. In this way, MIDI can be understood as an extension of the shifting complexities of traditional musical notation and the general, historical trend toward greater notational specificity. Whereas traditional notation uses a cluster of symbols indicating pitch, duration, dynamics, and articulation around each individual note, however, the data contained in the MIDI sequencer is often presented to the user in the form of separate lists of numbers or in the form of graphical representations, limited to one or more of the characteristics of the note at any given time. The various elements of gesture and performance thus undergo a fragmentation far greater than that associated with conventional notation.[7]

Of course, introducing performance nuances through the manipulation of several streams of digital data for each note can be extremely complex and time consuming, leading to a search for more efficient ways of dealing with the numerical data. One solution offered by software programmers has been to supply editing features that randomize the data within boundaries that can be set by the user. For example, for data that has been entered in step mode, or where timing values have been auto-corrected through a process called "quantization," the timing of a note can be randomized by extremely small amounts (as small as a 1/1920th note on some sequencers) to give the impression of a less machine-like performance. This practice is often referred to as "humanizing" the data.

What is interesting here is how the "human" has been defined, primarily within technical culture, as "random" in the first place. Certainly, human beings do not perform music with the same precision as a machine, but the nuances of performance cannot be reduced to simple randomness; they are as much intentional as they are random, as much the result of phrasing and the dynamic flow of the music as performed in "real time" as the result of error or human frailty. Both these elements—phrasing and dynamic flow—place individual notes within a performance or interpretive *context*, a meta-level of organization and intentionality beyond that of the isolated, individual sound—what Sudnow might refer to as "aiming" for the sounds within a particular course of action. The idea of "humanizing" musical data through the use of random deviation is derived from the "implicit theory of knowledge"—statistical and information oriented—that guides software design within computer culture (Lyman 1984: 76). As such, it might offer an efficient means for producing a particular result but has relatively little to do with traditional forms of musical knowledge or performance practice per se.

Although these techniques have apparently been adopted by many musicians who use sequencers or drum machines on a regular basis, at least some have recognized a certain irony in the calculated application of randomizing techniques for achieving the spontaneous "feel" of live performance:

It is possible to program a considerable degree of feel into these machines [Roland's R8 and R5 drum machines], but you're going to have to get to know them inside out if that feel is to be recognized as *human*. Myself, I can't help feeling there is a basic paradox involved in the premeditated insertion of random elements into a rhythm. (Nigel Lord, in *Rhythm* 5 [5], November 1989: 57)

Indeed, although various forms of randomness, probability, and chance operations have been a feature of avant-garde composition at least since the experiments of John Cage, Iannis Xenakis, and others during the 1950s (and have been especially prominent in academic electronic music), pop musicians have been rather reluctant to pursue the path of random genera-

The multitrack studio as metaphor. Steinberg's recent release, Cubase VST (virtual studio technology), pushes the idea of the multitrack studio in software form to its limit. VST integrates multitrack MIDI sequencing with digital audio recording, automated mixing, and signal processing in a single computer program. The on-screen interface mimics the layout of tape recorder transport controls, mixer faders, and racks of external processors.

tion or manipulation of musical material, made possible, for example, by the use of so-called "algorithmic" composition programs.[8] Most appear to be "put off by the complexity of the process and unconvinced by the randomness of the product" (Carter Scholz, in *Keyboard* 15 [6], June 1989: 12). This fact has been something of a disappointment to those who felt that the new technologies would lead to radical musical and stylistic change:

One of the things that's been a disappointment to me personally is that there seems to be a relatively small community of people who are interested in taking this stuff further than traditionally composed domains. It seems like most of our customers are doing some kind of pop music or soundtrack work. . . . they try to do something that sounds like what they're used to listening to, instead of taking one of the multiple infinities of paradigms that MIDI provides you and doing something new. I think because of that, it's harder and harder for a software company to justify pushing the limits in terms of algorithmic composition and whatnot.
(Emile Tobenfeld, in *Keyboard* 19 [2], February 1993: 83–84)

Such discontent stems, in part, from a modernist ideology that assumes that, once the avant-garde (aesthetic or technical) has led the way, the popular masses will follow. In fact, the uses of technology in popular culture have followed their own form of logic. Because multitrack recording had become the dominant process for producing popular music from the 1960s onward, the designers of software-based sequencers have, since the mid-1980s, used the multitrack tape recorder both as a model of composition and as the prime metaphor for the sequencer program's user interface.[9] Today, most computer sequencers are based on the same idea of linear tracks and layers as the multitrack tape recorder. On-screen, there are even "buttons" corresponding to tape recorder functions such as play, rewind, and fast forward, even though there is no physical tape or transport mechanism to control.

The adoption of the multitrack metaphor has been regarded by some as a simple expedient—little more than a marketing decision calculated to overcome the inhibitions of musicians concerning the use of computers. Such an attitude disregards, as I have argued previously, the degree to which successive layering in multitracking has become a true mode of composition among popular musicians. This fact is not without its consequences: For example, because a computer screen can only display a limited amount of information at any given moment, most sequencers allow the user to gain detailed access to the note information contained on only one track at a time. In this way, precise editing as previously described can be performed *within* a given track, but gaining access to the same information *across* tracks is usually more difficult to achieve. This situation is quite different from that encountered in a full musical score, where each individual part is arranged vertically on the page and detailed comparisons between each part can be readily made.[10] The sequencer "windows" that appear on the computer screen—as the basic units of electronic text—thus have very different implications for compositional method than does the page of a score—as the basic unit of printed musical text (cf., Lyman 1984: 79). The sequencer can draw the user's attention to selected aspects of the music-making process that are microscopic in their level of detail, but it does so in a fragmented and disjointed way.

In a curious fashion, then, the temporal and spatial separation between performers in the multitrack studio is reproduced in the separation of information on individual tracks on the sequencer. This fragmentation of the ensemble information is further paralleled, and extended, by the fragmentation of each individual note into separate MIDI parameters. In this way, the organization of data in the MIDI sequencer reinforces a method where the recording and editing of material takes place as a series of successive passes, each largely independent of the other.

The adoption of the multitrack metaphor as the basis for the user interface in software sequencers may have some unexpected social consequences as well. As in other areas of technology and music described in this book, the market for computer music software has been predominantly male — over 93 percent in a 1994 survey. This figure may seem surprising given that a significant number of the computer users surveyed were female, that the majority were well educated, and that 80 percent of those who used music software were keyboard players, a class of instruments conventionally associated with female music-making in the home. A plausible explanation for this discrepancy is not a lack of experience with musical instruments or computers per se, but, rather, an unfamiliarity with the basic concepts and techniques of multitrack recording. By reproducing the multitrack tape recorder in software form, programmers may thus have reproduced the social inequalities associated with access to this older form of technology as well (cf., Bayton 1990).

MIDI sequencing also has impacted production methods more directly related to the computer itself as a form of technology. Unlike the multitrack tape recorder, which is a linear medium, computers allow for random access of material stored in memory, thus facilitating the block, "cut and paste" style of editing familiar to word-processing and other kinds of computer applications. During the 1970s, the practice of creating separate mixes of a song for radio or dance club use had already become commonplace; multitrack tape made this process possible by making the music available in the form of raw, unmixed tracks. With computer sequencing, however, and the use of sampling or digital audio recording programs to reproduce parts of vocal and acoustic instrument tracks, cut and paste operations can be performed so as not only to remix a song but to create entirely different arrangements of the song material. In this way, a three-minute song can easily be transformed into an extended version (with a duration of two or more times that of the original) for dance clubs and other purposes.

Although such practices fit clearly within the economic imperatives of the industry — that is, the profit potential of every song must be exploited to its fullest (Tankel 1990) — they also have a subtle influence on the status of the song as an "authoritative" artistic statement (cf., Lyman 1984: 78). The infinite maleability of the sequenced data mitigates against the idea of a single, finished product; indeed, many musicians complain that in the studio it is difficult to know when to stop working and rearranging the sequenced material. Unlike a performance that has been committed to multitrack tape and is therefore relatively fixed in character, sequencing allows for continuous modification and reorchestration of the basic tracks even after they have been "recorded."

At another level, this maleability lends a spontaneous character to the sequenced material that has, in part, led to blurring the distinction between what is "live" and "recorded" in studio production. The conceptual shift that has occurred is subtle, at times only half conscious, but is manifest in the speech of musicians who engage in MIDI sequencing. My first encounter with this phenomenon occurred during an on-site observation of a recording session where a number of young musicians were recording a demo tape. The musicians had brought to the studio a set of sequenced tracks on diskette, which were loaded into a computer and used to trigger a combination of sounds from their own synthesizers and the studio's sampler. The computer was then synchronized to a multitrack tape recorder, where vocals and guitar tracks were to be recorded.

During playback after one of the initial takes, the engineer said to the group: "Listen . . . there's a problem in one of the live tracks that we've got to fix." The taped and sequenced tracks were played back again, and everyone in the room listened intently for the mistake; several of the musicians offered suggestions on what to do. The engineer repeated, this time in a somewhat frustrated tone of voice: "No, no, listen again to the live tracks." During the discussions following the third playback, it became clear to me that, when the engineer spoke of the "live" tracks, he was actually referring to the sequenced material; the musicians, on the other hand, had instinctively listened to the vocal and guitar tracks (i.e., the tracks that had been performed "live" at the session). This confusion continued for several minutes until each party realized they were not in fact listening to the same things.

For the engineer, the sequenced tracks were "live," first because the computer was, in effect, "playing" the MIDI instruments in "real time" while the other tracks were simply being "reproduced" on the tape recorder. Second, the sequenced tracks, stored in RAM, were still in a relatively volatile state and could be manipulated at will. For example, throughout the session a variety of adjustments were made to the drum tracks, and several snare drum samples were tried out at different times in an effort to maintain both the right "feel" and "sound" as each new track was added to the basic texture. By comparison, the "recorded" tracks (the vocals and guitar tracks) seemed fixed and unchangeable. Finally, in mixdown, the MIDI instruments were again "played" by the computer and recorded directly to the stereo master without the slight noise and sonic degradation unavoidably introduced into a second-generation analog recording (as occurred with the vocals and guitars, which were mixed from the multitrack deck to the master). Sequenced tracks thus *sound* like they are being played "live" rather than being mixed from tape.

Since my initial observations at this recording session, I have encountered numerous instances, in magazines and in the everyday speech of musicians, of this same typification of sequenced versus recorded sounds. Some, as in the case of Bob Moog quoted at the beginning of this chapter, date back to the early days of MIDI and computer sequencing. For example:

On a recent production the multitrack contained only two vocal tracks and a sync code, whilst the desk had a further 22 channels of "live" sound from the assorted keyboards, samplers, drums and effects. The only people involved in the production were a singer/songwriter and the programmer.
(Roger Jackson, in *Studio Sound* 28 [8], August 1986: 20)

Musically speaking, the use of the term "live" in such instances is of fundamental import because it reflects a new perception of the role of technology in musical practice and a redefinition of the distinctions between production and reproduction.

In broader cultural terms, the significance of this peculiar reversal of linguistic expectations should not be underestimated. Throughout the 1970s and '80s, popular electronic musicians suffered the abuse of unions, critics, and other, more conventional musicians and fans who opposed the increasing use of new technology in both studio production and in live performance. Even more important, the Milli Vanilli lip-synching scandal of 1990 must be seen as the culmination of nearly a decade of concern over the status and legitimacy of live performance in an era of sequencers, samplers, and backing tapes. For the critics, the problem was not simply that musicians were trying to sound like their recordings when performing on stage (a longtime preoccupation among pop musicians) but that concerts had indeed *become* recordings (Handelman 1990: 15).[11] Given this concern, the use of the term "live" to refer to sounds produced by machines should perhaps be regarded as strategic — as an appropriation of the very qualities that critics had denied were possible in machine music.

Home, Sweet Home in the Studio

From the late 1960s onward, as the multitrack recording studio became increasingly used not only for recording music but also as a tool in its very conception and construction, the costs of producing an album quickly skyrocketed. It became obvious that one of the advantages of recording at home, rather than at a commercial studio, was the ability to experiment and create while relatively unfettered by the constraints of time and money. For some musicians, simply recording over and over in a relaxed atmosphere until they got the right "take" was well worth the cost of setting up a private studio. Home studios began to appear during the 1970s, first in the homes of star performers who could afford a wide range of quality equipment to rival that of the commercial studios and, later, in the homes of semi-professional and even amateur musicians as inexpensive, consumer multitrack equipment became available and easier to use.[12]

Semi-professional and amateur studios did not function as autonomous production centers where a finished product could be turned out for commercial release. The number of available tracks, the quality of the equipment (including not only the tape decks but also the microphones, mixing console, and external signal processors), and the character of the recording environment itself left much to be desired. For most musicians, the home studio was a place to experiment with musical ideas that would only later be realized, if finances permitted, in a more professional recording facility.

There have, of course, been notable exceptions to this rule: Much of the punk and early new wave music of the late 1970s, and many of the so-called "alternative" bands of the early '90s as well, made use of consumer recording equipment as the vehicle for a do-it-yourself industry of "lo-fi," independent record production. On rare occasions, even big-name performers released recordings produced on low-cost equipment, when they felt that the recordings captured the raw spontaneity of a particular performance in a way that could not be reproduced in a commercial studio. Bruce Springsteen's album *Nebraska*, released in 1982 (CBS Records TCX 38358), was produced initially on a 4-track cassette. Any apparent losses in sound quality were more than made up for by the cachet of "authenticity" that the recordings carried with them. Despite such exceptions, the majority of home studios were never used to produce more than the roughest of demo tapes.

With MIDI sequencing, however, the nature of the home studio began to change. Because sequencers only record MIDI data, there is no loss of audio fidelity when the sequence is reproduced on a synthesizer or sampler. In genres of music that rely heavily on electronically generated sounds, a great deal of pre-production sequencing in the home studio (no matter how modest the quality of the synthesizer set-up) became possible. You could then simply carry the work on diskette to a more professional facility where "finishing" work could be performed in a reasonably short amount of time.

What was significant about this shift in the nature of home recording was the evolution toward a greater integration of the home and the professional studio. Some magazines began to refer to this possibility as the "Mothership Scenario" (here again, the future-oriented and gendered character of this expression should not be ignored). Within this scenario, the professional studios, forced by competition to invest heavily in the latest, most expensive equipment, had become the "motherships"; and the low-cost home studios, where every creative whim could be pursued free from time and financial constraints, had become the "satellites" (Gary Helmers, editorial in *Home & Studio Recording* 1 [2], November 1987: 2). Indeed, to a large degree, much of this vision had come true: During the late 1980s many professional studios began to construct special, small recording rooms to accommodate such projects at a reasonable cost to the home producer. Often, the spatial configuration of these MIDI studios was the reverse of earlier recording studio designs. In the MIDI studio, the control room, where much of the work of electronically orchestrating and mixing the sequences was done, was often larger than the room used to record vocals or extra instruments (cf., S. Jones 1992: 157–58).

Although this ideal of the fully integrated home and professional studios still possesses a considerable amount of popular appeal, clearly the relationship between these two levels of production is no longer as amicable as was originally thought. As home studios became increasingly sophisticated (and commercially oriented in their operations), they became regarded as competitors rather than clients in the professional studio scene. The 24-track studio—the backbone of the recording industry during the 1970s and early '80s—has become an endangered species, squeezed, on one side, by the high-end digital studios and, on the other, by the low-end home recording phenomenon (Daley 1990).

Nowhere has this squeeze been more acutely felt than in some of the largest recording centers such as New York and Los Angeles. In Los Angeles, the problem became so pronounced that an organization known as the Hollywood Association of Recording Professionals (HARP) was formed during the late '80s to challenge the right of home recordists to take on commercial work. They based their claim against the home studios on the fact that they often existed in residentially zoned neighborhoods, paid no commercial taxes, violated building codes, and so on (*Mix*, November 1989: 19–24; *Music Technology*, December 1989: 58–62). By 1992, it was reported that over thirty home studios had been shut down for violations of one kind or another. The real issue, however, was the increasing sound quality (often rivaling that of commercial operations) of the products offered by the home studios. This result was a direct consequence of the proliferation of inexpensive digital technology; without the range of sounds and recording flexibility offered by digital synthesizers and MIDI sequencers, few home studios would have ever been able to compete in the first place.

With the advent of the home multitrack studio, the idea of "paying your dues" in the music industry fundamentally changed, and with the rise of MIDI technology during the mid-1980s, the cost of membership in the world of popular music increased considerably. Many young musicians were no longer content with owning a keyboard and a tape recorder; a home studio was not complete without several synthesizers, signal processors, a mixer, digital recorder, and computer. As the home studio became an important new market for the manufacturers of microprocessor-based technologies, there was an increasing pressure on musicians to surround themselves with an ever-expanding array of consumer goods. It was perhaps inevitable that many musicians would turn to commercial work to finance the acquisition of even more equipment.

Often ignored in this scenario of the home studio is the manner in which the domestic space has been transformed into a production environment. Musicians' magazines often use clichés such as the arrival of the "information age" and Alvin Toffler's (1980) notion of the "electronic cottage" to explain the existence of the home studio. It seems to me that there is something else quite striking about this particular manifestation of contemporary music-making that is very different from previous uses of music technology in the home; that is, the degree to which the home studio is an isolated form of activity, separate from family life in almost every way.

The home studio is, above all, a private space. Studios tend to be located in bedrooms, dens, or basement rec rooms, far from the main traffic of everyday life. Magazines have offered feature articles on headphones suitable for the demands of working and mixing in the home or the apartment: "Today, the home recordist utilizes headphones as an instrument of isolation. Few apartment dwellers can blast drum machines or sampled industrial noise into the wee hours. Headphones allow the home recordist the luxury of laying tracks at any time without risking eviction" (Michael Molenda in *Electronic Musician* 8 [2], February 1992: 57). The home studio is thus, by design, a private space within a private dwelling.

The significance of this private act of music-making can perhaps be further understood through a comparison (a comparison that, granted, requires a certain license but is nevertheless revealing). The parlor piano of a century ago was important as a piece of home furnishing; but the tangle of wires, racks, and devices typical of the home studio (far more obtrusive than any hi-fi setup) could hardly be designed for any room that might be visited by strangers. More important, the location of the piano in the main living rooms of the house or apartment made it a center of family life and entertainment in the home.

The incompatibility of these two modes of domestic production/consumption was apparent to me in a discussion I had with a young musician. He was telling me about his studio, which was located in the basement of his parents' home. He had often wished he could make use of the family piano (which, significantly enough, was only played by his mother) in his recording sessions but found it virtually impossible to set up his equipment and make a quiet recording because of the location of the piano in a busy part of the house. As a result, he had no alternative but to use commercially produced piano samples in his recording projects. Even where both these technologies exist within close proximity to one another, the nature of their conventional location and usage in the home precludes any easy reconciliation between them at the level of their social/musical function.

Copyright

Much like the legal instruments used by HARP against home recordists, copyright has become a powerful tool used by well-known artists, and the music industry itself, to inhibit certain applications of new technology that threaten their traditional sources of income. With this issue, I hope to demonstrate again that institutional pressures can have a direct and profound impact not only on specific musical practices but on the very concept of what music is and can be. Both Canadian and American copyright legislation originate in British Common Law. As a result, certain fundamental principles are common to copyright law in each of these countries, but there are significant differences as well, especially as regards recent amendments and revisions to the law.

Drafted in 1921 and enacted into law in 1924, the Copyright Act established performing rights—perhaps the most significant form of income-generating right—for musical works in Canada. Similar rights had been enacted in U.S. law as early as 1897 but had little practical effect until well after the revisions implemented in the U.S. Copyright Act of 1909. Although government studies and discussions concerning copyright revision have been on-going in both countries since the mid-1950s, legislation remained substantially unchanged until the 1970s in the United States (when a copyright in sound recordings was introduced), and even later in Canada (not until 1988 did the Canadian Parliament pass Bill C-60, the first of a series of promised amendment packages).

The influence of British law on the original Canadian act of 1924 was not without its pitfalls; for example, the definition of a "musical work" contained in the act—which restricts music to "any combination of melody and harmony, or either of them, printed, reduced to writing, or otherwise graphically produced or reproduced"—is unnecessarily limiting both with respect to its exclusion of rhythm, timbre, and other essential elements of music and to the requirement of fixation in the form of a musical score

(Mosher 1989). The definition itself was drawn from a previous British law that had already been abandoned by Britain in 1911 (ibid.: 69). From the outset, then, the Canadian Copyright Act was not only derivative but also out of date.

Music is the only type of artistic work to be specifically defined by the Copyright Act; other types of artistic work are described through examples and illustrations, which allows for greater flexibility in the application of the law. With regard to music, this definition leaves copyright overly committed to a "strategy of forms" (ibid.). Even with the 1988 amendments to the act, parts of the original definitions remain intact, and the graphical fixation requirement was used as a kind of legal red herring as recently as 1990 by cable television networks to stall tariff payments to music copyright owners (*Probe*, April 1991).

The Copyright Act of 1924 also recognized a copyright in sound recordings, piano rolls, and other mechanical devices "as if such contrivances were musical, literary or dramatic works." Again, the wording of this section was almost identical to that of the British act. Similar legislation regarding sound recordings was not enacted in the United States until 1971, and broader protections for a wide range of technologies were introduced in the U.S. Copyright Act of 1976. This recognition poses a number of problems, however: First, the law makes a conceptual distinction between mechanical reproductions themselves and the underlying musical (or other) work contained therein. As musicians have come to rely on technology as an integral part of their musical practice, such distinctions have become increasingly problematic.

Second, copyright in mechanical reproductions was vested in the owner of the original plate or, in more recent terminology, the "producer." In both Canada and the United States, this entity is usually held to be the record company, but, depending on contractual agreements, it may also be the artists themselves or an independent producer. In either case, there is a fundamental problem in the manner in which the claim of authorship is made. For musical works, artists are conceived of as individuals, and their claims are based on having made the works (they may assign their economic rights to another party, but the actual claim of authorship is relatively straightforward). For a sound recording (a work resulting from a collective process), the contractual agreement between the producer or record company, on the one hand, and the musicians, arrangers, and engineers, on the other, sets one party off as employer/copyright owner and the other as employee/wage laborer. In cases of sampling, the compatibility of interests between these two parties, or a lack thereof, has a direct bearing on the degree of protection offered to musicians (Desjardins 1990: 140–41).

Third, all copyrights are not created equal, and, although the original Canadian Copyright Act appears to give sound recordings equal status with other works of art, the possibility of exercising performance rights in sound recordings (often referred to as "neighboring rights") was never taken seriously in Canada until 1968. By that time, the issue of neighboring rights was firmly on the international agenda; a number of countries, including Britain, had long been collecting performance and broadcast fees for recordings and had already formulated a set of international agreements—the Rome Convention of 1961. In Canada, where 90 percent of the records manufactured during this period were of foreign origin, it was feared that substantial royalties would soon be pouring out of the country. On the recommendations of a report by the Economic Council,[13] the government amended the Copyright Act in 1971 to restrict the copyright in sound recordings to a simple reproduction right, thus preventing the exploitation of sound recordings as generators of income from performances and broadcasts and, in the process, creating a legal imbalance in the quality of protection afforded two forms of music media—print and recording. The copyright in sound recordings first introduced by amendment in the United States during the same year was limited, from the outset, to rights of reproduction and did not include any right of performance. Music publishing thus continues to be valorized over sound recording in the copyright law of both countries (and in many others as well), despite the fact that its role in musical culture has been drastically reduced since the rise of the record industry (see Fabbri 1991: 110). Furthermore, the legal treatment of sound recordings in the amendment created a basic inconsistency in Canadian copyright law, since other forms of mechanically reproduced work, such as film, continued to enjoy a full regime of protections.

The introduction of digital technologies in music production during the past decade has resulted in the development of new kinds of creative activity that have, on the one hand, exacerbated already existing problems in the conceptualization of music as a form of artistic expression and, on the other, demanded that even further distinctions be made in copyright legislation. Here again, technical possibilities are closely linked to economic opportunities. For example, prior to the introduction of digital synthesizers and samplers, no real market existed for individual sounds, but now that there is such a market, issues of economic and artistic rights have come to the fore.[14] As regards these problems, Canada, with its lack of neighboring rights legislation, has more in common with United States than British law.

Throughout these debates there have been a number of recurring issues that touch on basic problems in the conceptualization of music as form, expression, and sound. For example, under the present law a musician's sound can in no way be considered equivalent to a musical "work"; and as mentioned above, musicians seldom own the copyright in their recorded performances because of the contractual agreements made with producers and record companies. The appropriateness of granting copyright protection to musicians' sounds and the question of actual ownership have thus raised copyright discussions.

Even if Canada and the United States were to bring neighboring rights in musicians' performances into legislation, it is doubtful whether they could be used to protect musicians from certain uses of sampling. Samplers allow you to make digital recordings of acoustic sounds or pre-recorded sounds, manipulate them in various ways, and then play them from a keyboard, a computer, or other device. Typically, only a few milliseconds of sound might be recorded and, once incorporated into the rhythm, melody, or harmony of a musical work, the precise origins of the sound may be difficult to identify. Proof of ownership and violation of the neighboring right would thus, in many cases, become almost impossible. In conventional cases of infringement of musical works, it has often been the role of the so-called "expert witness" to establish whether copying has taken place (Der Manuelian 1988). For sampling, however, where the recording process is so complex and the possibilities for manipulation so great, musician Frank Zappa has suggested that computer analysis may be the only means of establishing similarity between a sound and its copy (Torchia 1987). Even when ownership can be established, the duration of most samples raises the question of whether the actual amount of material copied is substantial enough to support a claim of infringement.

Similar problems exist with synthesizer programs. The U.S. Copyright Office has recently made provisions for accepting patch diagrams as an adequate means for copyrighting synthesizer sound programs. Because it is possible, in theory, for almost anyone to stumble upon the same set of parameters for any given synthesizer sound, conclusive proof of infringement may only be possible when programmers intentionally place bugs or other "mistakes" in the originals, which then turn up in the copies, a strategy that has already been used by some synth programmers for a number of years (see Tomlyn 1986). In such contexts, ownership becomes defined in negative terms rather than positive attributes. Since computer software packages designed for editing synthesizer sounds often contain utilities that allow for the random generation of new sounds, the concept of "originality" in this domain can sometimes appear virtually meaningless.

In sampling, however, the critical questions are not merely technical ones concerning the identity or originality of a sound; indeed, in many cases, well-known performers have been sampled precisely because their sounds are so unique and recognizable. In infringement cases involving musical works it has always been necessary to prove "substantial similarity"—usually taken to mean a certain quantitative or qualitative amount of musical material—between an original and a copy. When using a recognizable sample, however, no matter how brief (for example, the use of less than a second of James Brown's scream in the middle of a rap record), quantitative criteria become more or less irrelevant. McGraw (1989: 161–65) refers to the concept of "fragmented literal similarity," perhaps one of the most succinct descriptions, legal or otherwise, of this use of sampling technology, in describing instances where similarity is both evident and intended. When recognition is intended, the most relevant question becomes the degree to which unauthorized appropriation constitutes improper use; and to date, there have been no cases that firmly establish either the boundaries of "fair use" or the monetary value of a sampled fragment of sound.

In most discussions, the tendency has been to give vocalists a special status denied instrumental performers. Because the human voice has such immediately recognizable tonal qualities, it has often been regarded as the carrier of individuality, personality, and identity. Vocalists are thus considered by many as having a special moral right in their sounds that instrumentalists do not enjoy to nearly the same extent (Porcello 1991: 77–78). To consider the voice in such existential terms rather than legal ones risks mistaking mere physical attribute for artistic creativity. In this regard it is significant that the main arguments for protecting musicians from unauthorized digital sampling has not been in terms of copyright (which protects only specific artistic creations) but in relation to common law rights of publicity. These laws guarantee individuals the right to exploit their personality, image, or name for commercial purposes (as in product endorsements by entertainers and sports figures), and a number of American states and several Canadian provinces permit such exclusive marketing rights (McGiverin 1987; Desjardins 1990). This line of argument clearly places the issue of sound rights outside the realm of creativity per se and into the sphere of notoriety and entrepreneurship.

The problem for instrumentalists is that they are recognized as much by their phrasing as by their sound (McGiverin 1987: 1740)—a quality seldom captured by the brevity of most sampling techniques. The distinction is not a trivial one, because it really concerns how the law should define value in the recording of musical performances. Some argue that the creation of new, interesting sounds, such as Phil Collins's trademark snare drum sound, has become so important in the music business today that individual sounds should be protected under copyright law (e.g., McGiverin

1987). Others argue that the individual object is less important than the musical context in which it is placed (Keyt 1988).

What may appear to be simply a difference of aesthetics could have important implications. It seems to me that the debate over the uses and abuses of sampling has created an inflated value in sounds as objects of exchange and has obscured other, equally essential aspects of performance. Digital sequencers allow musicians to record virtually every nuance of their performances on digital keyboards, drum machines, and other devices without actually recording the sounds produced on the specific instruments themselves. MIDI data generated by the performance can then be edited, arranged, and reorchestrated at a later time. The underlying character of a performance can thus be fixed in a technical form without any reference to sound at all.

A market for popular songs, arranged and performed by session musicians and stored in the form of digital sequences, has already begun to develop. Performances stored in sound recordings can be translated into digital data as well, and it has become quite commonplace for remix engineers to use recorded performances in conjunction with sequencers to trigger synthesized or sampled sounds. In this way, the style and phrasing (the sense of timing and the "feel" of a live drum track, for example) can be retained, while the sounds are changed so that they bear little, if any, resemblance to the original recording. Again, even if Canadian and American law supported neighboring rights in performances, these two uses of sequenced data pose significant problems. Conventional neighboring rights are conceived of in terms of recorded sounds, and the protection of performance gestures that have been translated into digital form might require yet another layer of definition. Even after this definition was in place, the burden of proving ownership, originality, the act of copying, and improper use in cases of infringement would indeed be formidable.

In another sense, these new technical capabilities pose a dilemma that remains far beyond the horizon of most present-day copyright concerns: a problem of the conception of music as a set of fixed forms—scores, recorded sounds, or even digital sequences—rather than as a specific kind of creative activity with its own particular modes of expression. If music was understood in this latter way, copyright legislators might become less concerned with concepts of originality and ownership of cultural goods and develop a more flexible attitude toward different kinds of musical activity—including not only composition but also performance, digital sampling, and sound recording—and the various relationships between creation, convention, and norm.

Conclusion

The need for reevaluating music—as concept, as form, and as performance practice—in the antiquated categories and strategies of copyright law is the direct outcome of a century of changes in the technologies of sound reproduction and their use by both musicians and consumers. The fact that this reevaluation is long overdue is testimony to the enduring character of various musical institutions and their involvement with the centers of economic and political power.

In musical practice, the changes wrought by the employment of new technologies have been swift and far reaching. In the multitrack studio, ensemble musical performance has become simulated through layering and synchronizing a series of independently recorded tracks. The process, detached and objective in character, has as much to do with composition as it does with any traditional form of musical performance. Musicians are encouraged to adopt an evaluative position vis-à-vis their work that is akin to that of the producer; a position where, as Hennion (1990) suggests, consumption and taste play a significant role.

By adopting the multitrack metaphor as part of its operational characteristics, MIDI sequencing has extended the idea of recording, layering, and mixing, but added a new level of rationalization to the overall process of recording. Musicians who use sequencing are drawn to a level of detailed calculation never before realized in musical composition; ironically, this attention is focused on creating the "feel" of a "live" performance. In the process, however, the very notion of what is "live" in music becomes increasingly problematic:

> You get so many sounds out of the keyboards now it's incredible, and you want to use all those sounds. You can layer things now, and it still sounds live. I do stuff now in my home studio, and you can't tell it's not live. I can take a sampled drum track and quantize it so you can't tell it's not a live drummer.
>
> (Art Neville, in Jackson 1992: 29)

The "live" has become little more than a "sound" produced and consumed in private. The domestic space has become one of the primary sites of these new technological practices—a private and increasingly isolated site of musical production and consumption.

Given the profound nature of some of these changes in musical practice, it is not surprising that copyright law has been overly focused on spectacular cases of sampling. It has done so, however, at the expense of a more thorough-going analysis of the nature of musical practice and its commitments to specific forms of musical reproduction.

CHAPTER TEN

Conclusion

Toward a New Model of Musical Production and Consumption

✳

It is . . . so easy to write songs now, you know, with sequencers and various programs—
any idiot can put together an acceptable set of chords and a decent drum beat, 'cause you
can buy them off the shelf.
(Brian Eno, *Musician* 204, November 1995: 34)

A new kind of consumer practice now lies at the very heart of music production in the digital studio. This practice changes, in a fundamental way, the very nature of contemporary music-making. Such a development is certainly not without its positive effects, for it potentially opens the doors of creative activity in music to a wider range of individuals: "What has become interesting is the idea that artists are people who specialize in judgement rather than skill. And this of course, reopens the question of who can use that job description" (Brian Eno, *Mix* 16 [6], 1992: 30). Indeed, it could be argued that with the introduction of digital technologies and their attendant uses, the distinction between production and consumption has become increasingly blurred and, to a certain degree, meaningless.

As I have attempted to demonstrate throughout this book, however, this development has taken place within a cultural formation that is complex—composed of a diverse set of institutions, pressures, mediations, and individual interests. The imbrication of production and consumption, at every level of the cultural formation, has resulted in a curious mixture of creative energy, economic opportunity, and associational complexity, on the one hand, and an assortment of musical, technical, and economic dependencies, on the other.

The interweaving of production and consumption within the synthesizer industry is a result, in part, of the shift to microprocessor-based technology during the 1970s and '80s. These forces exerted themselves in a variety of ways. In the design of the instruments themselves, many manufacturers have adopted a product development strategy that uses a combination of custom chip design and standard microprocessor components. In itself, this choice hardly seems unique; all industries consume (raw materials, parts, and components from outside suppliers, labor power, etc.) as much as they produce, and by the turn of the century, an entire sector of the piano trade had been built around the ready availability of prefabricated parts from a growing piano supply industry. What is different about the digital musical instrument industry is the degree to which technical innovation within the field has become dependent upon the general level of sophistication and the market success of technologies originating within the computer industry. Developments in the industrial sector are, furthermore, strongly dependent upon the particular characteristics of the musicians' market. The strategy of continuous innovation has created the need for continuous consumption. This strategy, in turn, has placed considerable pressure on the manufacturers to emphasize market criteria even at the initial stages of instrument design; the limitations of MIDI as a technical specification are the outcome of such pressures and criteria.

As a result of the increased complexity of the new instruments and because of their reproductive capabilities, a small cottage industry dedicated to supplying new sounds for digital instruments has evolved. This industry has created the basis for an entire set of dependencies: On the one hand, musicians have come to rely on manufacturers and third-party suppliers for new and interesting sounds; and, on the other, the cottage industry has become dependent on decisions made by the larger manufacturers, on the general success of their instruments in the marketplace, and on their promotional and distributional resources.

The musicians' magazine industry is an equally complex cultural formation. Magazines have played a key role in the division of musicians into discrete market segments. Specialization allows them to act as a more efficient promotional vehicle for advertisers and, increasingly, as a source of marketing information as well; furthermore, they have begun to act as a surrogate "community" for some musicians, adopting the conventional rituals of musicians' interaction and offering a dubious form of career exposure.

Musicians' magazines have played an important role not only in promoting the new technologies but in creating a climate wherein the values of consumption could flourish. Linked to the creation of this general climate is the simultaneous valorization of "progress" in musical instrument design. Finally, the mobilization of the home as a site of production was encouraged by the magazines; the specific contours of this phenomenon, in terms of gender and family interaction, stand in marked contrast to earlier constructions of home music-making in the music press.

User groups and computer networks have also been an important factor in the growth and dissemination of technical knowledge among some musicians. Groups of synthesizer enthusiasts display a certain continuity with the (largely male) radio hobbyists of the early twentieth century and with the more recent forms of association that have become characteristic of computer culture. In particular, they demonstrate an intense interest in technology for its own sake and, above all, a democratic idealism expressed as self-realization through technology. In the early days of the International MIDI Association, this combination of characteristics proved to be disastrous in the face of pressure from the musical instrument industry. Equally important, these groups have fostered an even more highly intensified form of identification between individuals and the objects of consumption—and the manufacturers that produce them—than has the musicians' press.

With the introduction of electronic and digital technologies, musicians have had to rethink their musical practices. In the recording studio they have adopted a somewhat distanced and objectified view of sound-making (the view of the producer), and with MIDI, an even more rationalized and calculated form of control over sound production has developed. These shifts in musical practice have been marked by an expanding set of sophisticated techniques and an emerging vocabulary (albeit vague and metaphoric in nature) that directs the attention of the musician and the listener to selected aspects of the music-making process. In this context, the redefinition of familiar terms such as "sound" and "live" mark a significant change in the conceptualization of musical practice in relation to sound recording as the dominant mode of production in contemporary musical culture.

At the same time, musicians have found themselves increasingly drawn toward a particular mode of consumption in order to supply themselves with not only instruments and recording devices but with the very sounds they need to produce music. This consumer behavior has manifested itself along several different dimensions. First, there has been an expansion in the range of technology deemed necessary for contemporary amateur and semi-professional practice. Many musicians no longer find it adequate to simply own a guitar or a keyboard and an amplifier. The average home studio is filled with musical gear, often including multiple synthesizers, samplers, and/or drum machines; microphones, mixing console, and monitoring equipment; racks of signal processors and tape decks; and a computer and peripheral hardware and software. Even a modest studio can cost thousands of dollars.

Second, a new temporal dimension has been added to the musicians' purchasing patterns. Whereas a musical instrument was once understood to last for years, the increasing pace of technical innovations within the microprocessor-based musical instrument industry since the 1980s suggests that an investment in high technology will likely become obsolete within one or two brief product cycles. Despite the "vintage" status conferred upon a small number of electronic instruments, the increased frequency of instrument purchases is attested to by the large used instrument market for keyboards, signal processors, and the like.

Third, there now exists what might be understood as an increase in the depth of the music market. The buying and selling of prefabricated sounds, preset rhythm patterns, and even entire popular songs in the form of MIDI sequences for digital instruments has become a new area of the market that exists somewhere below the level of the instrument itself, in essence forming a new sublevel of cultural commodification. These three dimensions — the increased number and diversity of products, the frequency of purchase, and the increasing depth of commodity relations — characterize the pattern of consumption among many musicians since the early 1980s. As I have argued throughout this book, however, the significance of this pattern does not lie simply in the fact that musicians appear to consume more now than in the past, but rather in that a pattern of consumption has become an integral aspect of their musical production practices. A more fundamental shift in the conceptualization of music-making overall has thus occurred.

Within the musical instrument industry during the early 1990s, attention shifted, to some degree, away from sampling and synthesis toward the new possibilities offered by digital audio recording. There are at least two reasons for this redirection: First, the pace of both the introduction and the acceptance of innovations within the synthesizer market slowed. Even the latest synthesis techniques, such as physical modeling, failed to capture the imagination of consumers in the way that both FM synthesis and sampling did in the 1980s. Second, the introduction of inexpensive digital audio recorders in the form of both modular multitrack tape systems and computer-based, hard disk recording systems expanded the market for these devices beyond the realm of the high-end professional studios. Because recording devices can attract a much broader spectrum of potential consumers within the musicians' market than can keyboard instruments, investment in this area of technology has intensified.

Certainly, there can be no clear division between these technologies and those described throughout this book. Modular multitracks are, in many ways, simply an extension of the home studio phenomenon; and hard disk recording systems have been fully integrated by a number of software manufacturers into their sequencer programs, allowing for the simultaneous editing and synchronization of MIDI and digital audio data.[1] At a deeper level, the minute editing capability of digital audio systems on computers is not unlike the kind of sound manipulating possibilities offered by samplers and synthesizers: "Workstations mimic synthesis because the cut-and-paste editing occurs at such a minute level that it is transformed into a generative operation independent of its source" (Kahn 1990: 75).

What interests me here is how these developments both sum up some of the main issues addressed throughout this book and extend them even further. Two events, in particular, that occurred during the summer of 1992—the introduction of a new product by the Alesis Corporation and the demise of a company known as New England Digital—appeared to be important signs of these new trends in the marketplace: The former seemed like an indication of things to come, and the latter, a sign of the end of an era. More importantly, these events struck me as being symptomatic of the entire process of innovations in music technology during the past two decades. Both events were greeted in the trade and consumer press with a certain surprise, or even dismay:

I'm not sure whether this is a review of a product or a phenomenon, as no device in the recent history of professional audio has created such controversy, speculation and conjecture as the Alesis ADAT. . . . The long-awaited system uses a modular approach to digital multitrack recording, at a price that's comparable to the least expensive pro analog decks available.
The repercussions are far-reaching indeed.
(George Peterson in *Mix* 16 [10], October 1992: 180)

New England Digital is out of business. The New Hampshire-based company, whose Synclavier systems defined current trends in digital hard-disk recording, ceased to exist on July 1, 1992. . . . [Robert L. Doerschuk]
"The 300 people who use the Synclavier every day, and the other 700 people who own one, are basically fucked and far from home."
[Shelton Leigh Palmer quoted by Doerschuk]
(*Keyboard* 18 [10], October 1992: 40–41)

In certain respects, it could be argued that these two events were precipitated by the development of MIDI during the 1980s. On the one hand, the Alesis Corporation owes its very existence to MIDI and microprocessors. Founded in 1985, it established itself as a bold, market-driven company that rode the crest of the MIDI wave with a series of innovative, low-cost products—drum machines, MIDI sequencers, and digital reverbs—aimed at the broadest possible market of professional and amateur musicians. By 1989, Alesis had become one of the top twenty musical instrument suppliers in the United States.[2] Their decision to develop the ADAT was both consistent with their previous successes in the marketplace and a gamble, since it brought them into a new area of technology (multitrack digital audio) and, equally important, into potential conflict with a group of already well-established competitors.

New England Digital (NED), on the other hand, was founded during the early 1970s by composer Jon Appleton and engineers Sydney Alonso and Cameron Jones. In this regard, the company was an outgrowth of the kind of collaboration between academic composers and entrepreneurial engineers that was typical of the early years of electronic synthesizer development during the 1960s and '70s. NED produced the first fully digital synthesizer, the Synclavier, in 1976 and went on to become a leader in audio, film, and video post-production systems. Unlike Alesis, however, NED's product development strategy was aimed resolutely at the "high-end" user. Early systems were priced at approximately $50,000, and by the late '80s, a fully equipped post-production system could cost close to $500,000. NED thus represented the opposite pole of the music instrument and audio industry market, one populated exclusively by superstar recording artists (e.g., Sting, Frank Zappa, and Stevie Wonder), professional studios, and Hollywood post-production facilities. In fact, because of the costs involved, the Synclavier was never even sold through music retailers; it was only available through a small network of company sales representatives and independent dealers.

With the introduction of inexpensive digital synthesizers, samplers, and MIDI sequencers during the mid-1980s and, more recently, with the advent of PC-based digital recording and editing systems, the capabilities (if not the sound quality and integration) of the Synclavier could be achieved at a fraction of the cost. Incapable of producing (or unwilling to produce) product innovations for the mass market, it was perhaps inevitable that NED would eventually succumb to the market forces unleashed by MIDI and microprocessor technology, as did its early competitor in the high-end digital synthesizer market, the Fairlight company of Australia. Indeed, with the closure of NED in July of 1992, it could be argued that there no longer exists a "high-end" in digital synthesizer technology; MIDI technology and the "democratic" consumer marketing strategy that it represents is triumphant.

The company has since been revived but is little more than a shadow of its former self. Perhaps not surprisingly, its once coveted sound library, formerly available only to Synclavier owners, has now been released as a series of CD-ROMs in formats for Akai, Roland, and other popular samplers and is distributed by third-party interests. In a sense, the Synclavier has been relegated to the status of a "vintage" synth—little more than a set of "sounds" from a unique instrument of the past that has failed to survive the periodic, volatile upheavals of the keyboard marketplace.

It is precisely this kind of volatility in the electronic instrument and audio industries that made the introduction of the Alesis ADAT appear to have such far-reaching implications. The ADAT was the first concrete realization of what many in the music instrument industry had long been predicting as the coming "revolution" in consumer hardware for musicians in the 1990s. It seemed poised to do for the world of digital audio what the introduction of low-cost microprocessor technology and MIDI had done for the world of synthesizers during the 1980s.

Alesis was certainly not unaware of such predictions within the industry, and it helped fuel those very sentiments by promoting the ADAT as more than just a digital tape recorder. Indeed, everything about the ADAT appeared to have been planned so that it became something of a "phenomenon" in the minds of consumers and industry observers alike, even before it achieved concrete form as a product. To achieve a status of product-as-phenomenon, Alesis drew on all the marketing strategies and promotional rhetorics commonly utilized within the electronics industries throughout the 1980s.

First, the ADAT was announced with great fanfare in January of 1991 at the National Association of Music Merchants (NAMM) winter trade show held in Anaheim, California, the largest industry gathering of its kind in North America. Although the device itself was not scheduled for release until December of 1991, advertisements and product brochures touting the capabilities of the new recorder began to appear almost immediately. When December had passed and even the winter and spring months of 1992 and the ADAT was still not ready for commercial release, local retailers (in Montréal and elsewhere) began to speak of the ADAT as little more than "vaporware." Although such talk had the potential for seriously damaging the reputation of Alesis in the marketplace, clearly the "controversy, speculation, and conjecture" caused by both the pre-release publicity and the subsequent design and manufacturing delays had created an undeniable "buzz" within the industry.

When the ADAT was finally ready for release, advance units were sent to reviewers and testers in what must have been one of the most coordinated promotional efforts seen within the industry in recent years. In the fall of 1992, virtually every special interest magazine devoted to producers, recording engineers, and so-called "electronic musicians" carried detailed reviews of the ADAT. In Britain, *Music Technology* and *Recording Musician* (September issues) and, in North America, *Electronic Musician* and *Mix*

(October issues) and *Keyboard* (November issue) carried feature articles proclaiming the ADAT as an almost unqualified success. Alesis's strategy of advance promotion and the (only partially planned) long delays in releasing the device had paid off: The majority of the reviews were not merely generous in their praise of the ADAT, they were positively, and somewhat uncharacteristically, effusive. One magazine editor even felt it necessary to offer a mock apology for the unabashed enthusiasm of the review.

The design and pricing of the ADAT left no doubt in anyone's mind about the market for whom this product had been created. Modular in concept, the basic system begins with an 8-track configuration and is expandable up to an unheard-of 128-track capability simply by adding additional units and external controllers. The formidable task of synchronizing the machines is made possible through Alesis's innovations in microprocessor chip design. It is clearly the basic 8-track system, however, that positions this product for the semi-professional and amateur home recording market. Alesis had played no small part in the construction of the idea of the home studio as a viable production environment, with its line of digital reverbs and MIDI products during the late 1980s, and, significantly, the ADAT is fully compatible with MIDI synchronization standards (a feature seldom found on professional multitracks). Even the tape format chosen for the ADAT seemed geared to the home rather than for the professional recording studio. Instead of the standard reel-to-reel tape format familiar to studio recording, Alesis chose the most ubiquitous home entertainment technology of the '80s—the VHS cassette—as its entry vehicle into the arena of digital recording. Unlike other digital tape mediums already in use, VHS has the distinct advantage of being universally available, thus supporting Alesis's worldwide marketing aspirations for the ADAT.

The promise of the ADAT extends beyond the home as well. Because of its modular design, ADAT-equipped home studios are potentially compatible with more elaborate professional studios (possessing multiple ADATs) to a degree never before attainable, and it is this potential that had the music press proclaiming the ADAT as "a major recording revolution in the making" (*Mix* 16 [10], October 1992: 185). For its part, Alesis began coining new slogans to promote the ideal of total compatibility and expandability: "8 Tracks to Megatracks" became a registered trademark of the corporation. In addition, in a move quite familiar within the computer and electronic musical instrument industries during the past decade, Alesis announced, in a second wave of ads launched simultaneously with the appearance of ADAT reviews in major publications, the establishment of a company-sponsored "user group" known as the ADAT Worldwide Network™, ostensibly formed to facilitate communication between ADAT owners as well as to foster direct contact with Alesis's marketing department: "Imagine a network of ADAT users from bands, composers and project studios to professional studios, video editing suites and broadcast production studios. All recording master quality tracks with full compatibility and no barriers between their creative disciplines" (Alesis product ad, *Mix* 16 [10], October 1992: 6–7). The idea of "no barriers" between low- and high-end users reflects the same utopian rhetoric—a rhetoric that assumes "democratization" of the marketplace—that has been typical of consumer culture throughout the twentieth century. The particular conflation of simple technical compatibility with social equality and a unified artistic aesthetic, however, has been a peculiar articulation of this rhetoric within the computer and electronic musical instrument industries during the past decade.

Certainly no single product could hope to fulfill the promises that have been made on behalf of the ADAT since it was first launched. At first glance, the ADAT simply looks like one more incompatible format within an audio industry already fraught with incompatible formats, sampling frequencies, digital communications protocols, and the like. In a bid to re-create the enormous success of MIDI as a de facto standard within the synthesizer industry during the 1980s, however, Alesis has entered into licensing agreements with Fostex, Panasonic, Digidesign, and other leading manufacturers of consumer and professional recording equipment in the hope of establishing the ADAT technology as an industry standard (Tascam, the manufacturer of a competing modular, digital multitrack format has made similar licensing agreements with Sony). The tradeoff in the early '90s was as clear as with MIDI a decade earlier: Risk greater competition in the hope of stabilizing the marketplace and stimulating consumer confidence. As before, the gamble has paid off; by the end of 1995, Alesis had reportedly sold over 70,000 units worldwide and was poised to launch the second generation of ADAT technology.

What about the musician in this grandiose scenario? The reality for most popular musicians in the 1990s is that a successful career in the music business is as elusive as ever (if not more so). Advances in technology have not made access to recording industry executives any easier; indeed, it has made the former luxury of producing a competitive, professional-sounding demo tape a necessity. The Alesis ADAT and the various hard disk recording systems currently available are contributing, in their own way, to the growth of such expectations and to the further transformation of the home into a production environment. These new devices, especially the computer-based recording systems, have once again placed microprocessor technologies at the center of contemporary music-making, escalating demands on musicians to attain the knowledge and skill required to operate them. A serious conversation between musicians in the '90s is as likely to be concerned with the problems of optimizing hard drive and CPU performance as with adjusting the action on an electric guitar.

The demise of the Synclavier and the rise of digital multitrack recording for the home studio are logical outcomes of the various forces at play within the music industries since the late 1970s. Beyond the confines of the music instrument and audio industries, the music periodicals, and the musicians' community, however, the developments within this cultural formation may be part of a much larger change in the nature of cultural production and consumption in the late twentieth century that is perhaps, in structural terms, similar to what occurred nearly a century ago. In this regard, Craig H. Roell's (1989) interpretation of the changes within the piano industry at the turn of the century (in particular, the rise of the automatic player piano) as part of larger pressures within capitalism toward the creation of a broad-based consumer culture is perhaps key. Among those pressures was the development of powerful new technologies of mechanical reproduction: not only the player piano but, more characteristically, the phonograph and the cinema.

In contrast to the cultural values of the previous Victorian era, with its "producer ethic"—its notions of creativity and personal achievement—the consumer culture associated with the new technologies was characterized by its apparent "passivity"—its emphasis on effortless recreation, leisure, and instant gratification (ibid.: 156–59). Of course, much recent scholarship has attempted to overcome the legacy of early twentieth-century theories of "passive" consumption; within Roell's overall discussion, production and consumption are described in terms of a shift in cultural *values* rather than evaluated as to their actual character. What I want to argue here, however, is that in the late twentieth century, electronic and digital technologies have become associated with a new kind of consumer practice that is quite different from both those associated with the piano during the nineteenth century and those connected with mechanical reproduction during the early part of the twentieth.

The contours of such an emerging pattern of consumption (I hesitate to call it an "ethic") can be observed in a number of areas in popular culture, but especially in popular music. For example, the kind of consumer practice within musical production that I have described appears to have been complemented by a new kind of active engagement with recorded material on the part of consumers, thus constituting a kind of production practice within consumption. At the most general level, such a complementarity of practices can be discerned in the way in which consumers have used cassette technology during the past two decades: "Sounds are selected, sampled, folded in and cut up by both the producers (DJs, rap crews, dub masters, recording engineers) and the consumers (we put together our personal play lists, skip some tracks, repeat others, turn up the volume to block out the external soundtrack or flip between the two)" (Chambers 1990: 2). Interestingly, the roles and responses of the various industry players have been similar in this instance to those described throughout this book. On the one hand, the introduction of cassette tape recorders during the 1960s made it possible for consumers to create their own listening programs in the first place. Once established as a consumer practice, hardware manufacturers had a field day making it as easy as possible for consumers to indulge in their preferences: Dual cassette decks with automatic dubbing facilities now dominate the marketplace. For their part, the record industry responded with outrage and demanded compensation for their supposed losses due to home taping. For the record industry, the issues surrounding home taping (often conflated with those of cassette piracy) were simply the flip side of the sampling controversy writ large. Indeed, the financial stakes were perhaps much greater in the world of distribution and consumption (piracy and home taping) than they ever were in the smaller world of production (studio sampling).[3]

A more recent, and perhaps more intriguing, instance of change in production and consumption can be found in *Karaoke,* a practice originating in Japan but increasingly popular in the West during the late 1980s and early '90s, where consumers are invited not only to sing along with their favorite songs but actually to take on the role of lead vocalist, performing with pre-recorded arrangements of popular hits.[4] In a panel discussion at the conference of the International Association for the Study of Popular Music held in Berlin in 1991, Japanese scholar Toru Mitsui described this practice as a form of "participatory consumption" and argued that it should be regarded as significantly different from older patterns of consumption with which we have become accustomed. Similarly, ethnomusicologist Charles Keil has suggested that we need to consider this novel form of "mediated-and-live" performance as a kind of "humanizing or, better still, personalization of mechanical processes" (Keil 1984: 94).

In fact, the idea of "participatory consumption" could describe a wide range of similar activities, such as DJ "talkover" in reggae "dub" music (Hebdige 1987); the mixing and "scratch" practices of hip-hop, rap, and dance music (Langlois 1992); the use of various cassette distribution/exchange networks (Erlhoff 1984; Pareles 1987) that have become common in popular music during the past two decades; and the more recent uses of the Internet as an alternative forum for the distribution and discussion of music. It is perhaps ironic that, at a time when professional singers have been accused of using electronic technology to foist lip-synched performances upon an unsuspecting public, an increasing number of that same public, at home, in dance clubs, in *Karaoke* bars, or on the Internet, have been using technology as a means of reclaiming their own "voices."

Elsewhere, manufacturers such as Roland and software developers such as Passport Designs have been developing MIDI technologies for the home computer market in the hope of tapping the amateur musical interests of computer owners. By creating standardized hardware and software formats that allow for both the playback and manipulation of songs in the form of pre-recorded MIDI sequencer files (some music publishers have used the term "songware" to describe the new format), these technologies grant the listener an unprecedented ability to control their listening experiences and to rearrange popular songs to suit their own tastes. In effect, the listener is invited to act as producer/engineer, to experiment in arranging and re-recording material that is familiar, pre-formed, and yet still in a malleable state.

Similarly, recent music releases on CD-ROM and CD-I (Compact Disc Interactive), by artists such as David Bowie, Peter Gabriel, and Todd Rundgren, offer consumers an expanded set of options for not only accessing certain types of material (text, sound, or image) but, in some instances, for shaping and rearranging that material as well.[5] Certainly, for the industry at least, many of these new releases are intended simply as novel ways for fans to "interact" with pop stars, hence the emphasis on biographical material, baby pictures, and the like. At least one of these projects, however—Todd Rundgren's CD-I version of *No World Order*—allows users to manipulate and reassemble various components of the musical recordings themselves. In this way, not only are notions of "passive" consumption called into question but, also, the integrity of the musical work and claims of authorship and originality—key components of the star system itself.

On the one hand, such strategies, if successful, would go a long way toward realizing the dreams of unconventional creative artists such as Glenn Gould, who, during the 1960s, advocated the development of technologies that would give the listener greater editorial decision-making power over their listening experience (Gould 1966: 59–60). Interestingly, Gould used expressions not unlike Mitsui's to describe the new consumer with editorial prerogatives: the "participant listener" (ibid.) or the "listener-consumer-participant" (ibid.: 61). Gould's call for a new technology gave concrete form to similar (though more abstract) concerns voiced by theorists during the same period. For example, Roland Barthes lamented a form of "musica practica" that had virtually disappeared at the end of the bourgeois period ("Who plays the piano today?"), the remnants of which can only be found today in the intimate relationship between popular music and amateur guitar playing (Barthes 1977: 149–50). He wished for a renewed form of musical practice that would invite textual collaboration: "Not to give to hear but to give to write" (ibid.: 153).

On the other hand, however, such possibilities can be limited by the available technology and, more importantly, by the manufacturers' own perception of the needs and interests of this new class of consumers. Here again is a parallel with nineteenth-century salon music and the manner in which publishers consciously created a music for the home and the technical competence of its players. Indeed, although the new technologies increase the level of freedom and creativity afforded the listener, the consumer relationship may simply shift to another level of practice, as occurred with digital synthesizers and prefabricated sounds. The industry creates its consumers and their needs as much as it responds to them.

Outside of music, consumers have adopted a wide assortment of electronic and digital devices during the 1980s and '90s, ranging from home VCRs to CD-ROMs and computer games. On the surface, the various uses of these devices would seem to challenge conventional notions of "passive" consumption and, in many cases, an emphasis has been placed (for marketing purposes) on the "interactive" character of the new technologies. Indeed, the term "interactive" has become one of the most hyped buzzwords of the personal computer industry. The specific meaning of "interaction" promoted in these instances is significant, however. It speaks of an idealized form of "interaction" between subject and object (i.e., user and machine) and ignores the more problematic relationship between individuals as consumers and the industry as supplier of the new technologies. Whether the demands placed on the consumer to "interact" with the objects of consumption result in a form of self-realization or simply in more consumption is still an open question. Each of these new technologies incorporates the same ambiguities of empowerment and dependency, creative potential and formal constraints, that lead to renewed levels of consumption.

The changes in the relationship between production and consumption that I have described throughout this book can perhaps be seen as part of a broader cultural phenomenon occurring in a range of other media as well. Significantly, virtually all these new forms of cultural activity operate within the bounds of technical reproduction; that is, the reproduction and manipulation of prefabricated elements is a central component of the consumer practice associated with these devices (audio reproduction for digital musical instruments; and audio, visual, and textual reproduction for interactive computer technologies). Also, these practices tend to foster an intimate relationship between user and machine; "interaction" is, in this sense, as much a technically conceived and managed task as it is a social relationship.

There is still, nevertheless, something quite unique in how these new consumer practices have been articulated within the sphere of music production in the late twentieth century. By becoming "consumers of technology," many musicians have been able to take advantage of the enormous productive potential of new digital technologies. At the same time, however, they have witnessed the incursion of capitalist relations upon their creative practices at the most fundamental level and found it necessary to adopt increasingly mediated forms of communication with one another. Within the high-intensity context of technical innovation and capitalist marketing, this tension—between the desire to create, communicate, and consume—has become increasingly problematic, especially for young, amateur musicians and aspiring semi-professionals:

I could not believe how many possibilities these instruments offered me—particularly the computer and software combination. My only *real* problem was coming to terms with the continuing march of technology. A couple of great drum machines were released. . . . Samplers, too, improved dramatically and came down in price. I salivated in shops and wondered how I was going to manage without them. (Kofi Busia, in *Electronic Musician* 4 [7], July 1988: 24)

Indeed, as the technologies of electronic and digital reproduction have increasingly become the central mode of production, distribution, and consumption in popular music, learning "to manage," both with and without new technology, has become one of the essential ways in which many contemporary musicians learn to define themselves, their relations with others, and the "sound" of their music.

Notes

✳

1. Introduction (pp. 1–13)

1. Throughout this book I use the term "technology" in its broadest sense: that is, not simply to refer to machines but, more importantly, as in the case of the term "technique," to indicate the training and discipline of labor and the organization of means.

2. Among those who have adopted a conventional musicological approach to the history of electronic music one might include: Appleton and Perera 1975, Russcol 1972, Schrader 1982, and Schwartz 1975. Georgina Born's *Rationalizing Culture: IRCAM, Boulez, and the Institutionalization of the Musical Avant-Garde* (1995) takes a more sophisticated, theoretical, and anthropological approach and is perhaps the first major study to break with the musicological tradition and its uncritical valorization of the avant-garde.

3. Authors who have taken a more open attitude toward popular uses of electronics in music include: Darter and Armbruster 1984, Mackay 1981, and Holmes 1985. Georgina Born describes some of the prevalent attitudes toward popular music and its technology among the institutionalized composers of the avant-garde (1995: 279–307).

4. Among the more significant contributions to an understanding of the popular music industries are: Chapple and Garofalo 1977, Denisoff 1975, Frith 1981, Hirsch 1969, Peterson and Berger 1971, and Wallis and Malm 1984, 1988.

5. Chambers (1985) and Hebdige (1987), for example, have offered detailed accounts of the uses of sound recording technology in reggae and hip-hop music. Thoughtful articles on the relationship between technology, rock notions of "authenticity," and the aesthetics of pop can be found in Frith 1986, and Goodwin 1988. Durant's comments on MIDI and digital technology (1990) offer both an account of contemporary uses of technology and a perceptive analysis of the aesthetic and ideological issues that accompanied the introduction of technical innovations in pop music during the 1980s.

6. The notion of a "formation" has actually come to be used in both a broader and a more diverse fashion in the later writings of Williams himself (1989) and, more frequently, by other cultural theorists such as Stuart Hall and Lawrence Grossberg. For example, the term "social formation" has been used to describe a wide range of complex, structured relationships and practices—social, political, cultural, and economic—within the social order at a given moment in history. In part, this expanded use of the term may be the result of individuals working within

the field of cultural studies during the 1970s and '80s and their attempts to integrate certain aspects of Marxist, structuralist, and poststructuralist thought into their work; see, for example, Stuart Hall (1980, 1985, 1992).

2. The Industrial Context of a "Revolution" in Marketing and Design (pp. 17–40)

1. A basic source on the history of the orchestra and the development of orchestration during this period is Carse 1964: 22–85. See also Grout 1960: 250–61; and Sachs 1940: 297–304.

2. The expansion of music retailing took place relatively quickly. In London, for example, there were only about twelve shops selling music in 1750, but by 1824 there were 150 (Weber 1977).

3. The connection between pianos and sewing machines was not simply one of analogous financing: Both were major commodity purchases primarily intended for female use in the home. Companies were formed to manufacture both devices; they were often sold in the same retail outlets; and they were advertised and written about in the same specialized magazines, such as the *Musical and Sewing Machine Gazette* (Loesser 1954: 560–64).

4. Figures for instrument sales in the United States during the 1980s are derived from statistical data and estimates compiled by the American Music Conference (AMC), a nonprofit association funded in large part by the musical instrument industry. Figures for the '90s are taken from similar estimates compiled by the National Association of Music Merchants (NAMM), which has recently taken over this task from the AMC (see the *Music USA* listings in "Directories, Statistics, and Other Sources" in the Bibliography).

5. A summary of the MIAC statistics were published in the *Canadian Music Trade* 12, no. 4 (July 1990). The sales figure reflects the *wholesale* value of MIAC member sales only; that is, approximately 80 percent of the wholesale value of the total industry. If adjusted to reflect retail sales levels, the per-capita Canadian market would appear to be slightly greater than that of the United States.

3. Invention and Innovation in Electronic Instrument Design (pp. 41–71)

1. Except where otherwise indicated, historical details concerning the instruments and manufacturers discussed in this chapter are taken from a number of sources including Anderton 1988, Appleton and Perera 1975, Darter and Armbruster 1984, Davies 1984, Holmes 1985, Schrader 1982, Majeski 1990, and Vail 1993, among others. The specific focus and interpretation of these events, however, are primarily my own.

2. A similar example of introducing innovations in an area dominated by skilled individuals can be found in the Dvorak typewriter keyboard—a keyboard whose configuration is more efficient than the standard QWERTY layout—as described by Rogers (1983: 9–10). Rogers argues that not only the vested interests of manufacturers but also those of typing teachers and typists themselves have prevented the superior keyboard from being adopted ever since it was invented in 1932.

3. Some of the other instruments built by Le Caine were also available commercially in some form, though Young does not always mention this fact, leading the reader to believe (perhaps falsely) that each of the devices built by Le Caine was unique in some way. This observation lends further support to Wright's criticism (1990: 166) that Young's biography does not adequately situate Le Caine's work in

context with commercially developed instruments of the same period. Such omissions can only serve to reinforce the book's apparent hagiographic tendencies.

4. An analog synthesizer creates sounds through the generation, modification, and control of electrical voltages; sounds represented in electrical form are quantified on a continuous scale of voltages, and the resulting audio waveforms can be sent directly to tape recorders or amplifiers. Digital synthesizers, on the other hand, represent sound phenomena through numbers only; quantification is done on a scale of discrete steps, and the resulting calculations must be submitted to a process known as digital-to-analog conversion before being recorded or amplified via loudspeakers. Digital synthesizers offer greater precision in the generation and control of synthesized sounds, and, after initial designs have been incorporated into hardware and software form, they can be mass produced at lower prices than analog equipment.

5. Not surprisingly, a certain residual resentment has colored many of the conventional avant-garde histories of electronic music as a result of this shift in manufacturing priority. Schrader, for example, devotes only about three pages (half of them taken up with photos of various instruments) to the entire development of voltage-controlled keyboard synthesizers during the 1970s and ends his brief account with a lament for the lack of manufacturing support given to modular studio systems (1982: 138–41). Ironically, as Schrader himself admits, only a handful of institutions were ever able to afford electronic music studios during the 1950s and '60s; the vast majority of colleges and universities in North America established programs in electronic music during the '70s when voltage-controlled instruments became cheaper and easier to use. In many cases, they equipped themselves with the same inexpensive keyboard instruments used in the popular field—a phenomenon that became even more prevalent during the 1980s.

6. Moog later founded another company where he engaged in the custom design of electronic equipment and eventually joined Kurzweil Music Systems, during the 1980s, as vice president of new product research. Tracing the migrations of the various inventors and designers from the early period of synthesizer development to the present day would constitute a major study in its own right.

7. Piatier also uses the term "transectorial migration" but does so to refer to the movement of technologies rather than of individuals; in this sense, his use of the term is virtually synonymous with the notion of transectorial innovation itself. Although my adoption of the idea of "migration" here may be different from Piatier's, it is, I think, entirely in keeping with the general outlines of his argument.

8. The capabilities of other digital components can have a similar impact on instrument design: For example, Will Eggleston of Lexicon has related how, when the PCM70 digital signal processor was being developed during the mid-1980s, the device had to be redesigned to take advantage of denser and cheaper RAM chips that were then becoming available (Anderton 1988: 94–95). With the advent of digital sampling and drum machines and synthesizers based on sample playback designs, the cost/density ratio of memory chips (whether in the form of RAM or ROM) became an important factor in the overall capacity of an instrument to store and reproduce musical sounds.

9. The information presented here and elsewhere in this book concerning the Ensoniq Corporation was obtained from a variety of sources, including interviews conducted on-site at Ensoniq's headquarters, company brochures and product literature, and articles found in various trade magazines and newspapers; of the latter, see Poe 1988 and McBride 1988.

10. To a certain extent, these issues are not addressed in Wasserman's model because they do not fit well within the particular case study—the development of

loaded circuits in early long-distance telephone transmission—on which the model is based. Wasserman does mention, in passing, more recent work that takes into account the potential "loop" between production and design stages (1985: 9–10, and footnote 12, p. 132).

11. For practical reasons, I have provided relatively little information on developments in Japan. It seems worth mentioning, however, that the present dominance of Japanese firms, not only within the electronic musical instrument industry but within the electronics and microprocessor industries more generally, is, in part, the result of large-scale investment and planning at the state level over a number of years (see Japanese sources in the Bibliography under "Directories, Statistics, and Other Sources"). Such investment has placed Japan in a privileged position in high-technology development and may even be a factor contributing to the phenomenon of transectorial innovation. For an informative look at the design philosophy of a number of Japanese synthesizer manufacturers, see Doerschuk 1985.

4. Consumption and "Democratization" (pp. 72–90)

1. In part because of the controversies that raged during the mid-'80s concerning digital sampling and its supposed negative impact on musicians' employment, and because of the high-profile nature of McGill University as an institution within the Montréal music community, the Faculty of Music came under immediate attack from the Guilde des musiciens du Québec (union local of the American Federation of Musicians) for its involvement in the sampling business. Interestingly, in its defense, Joel Wapnick, co-producer of McGill University Master Samples (MUMS), portrayed the sample library as serving an "anti-elitist function" and argued for its role in the "democratization" of music (*The McGill Reporter*, May 30, 1989: 3).

2. There are no independent statistics or sales data available on the sound supply industry, and the companies involved in this enterprise tend to be rather protective of any information concerning their operations. Even if sales data were available, however, it would not likely be very accurate in an area of the industry so dependent upon mail-order sales. For example, the American Music Conference has, since 1987, compiled annual statistics on the retail sale of music software for computers; the reliability of these figures has been questioned by some within the industry precisely because they do not include mail-order sales, which constitute a significant part of the total computer software market.

3. How this unofficial standard came into existence is somewhat unclear. In an article published in *Keyboard* magazine, Bob Moog has simply stated that it exists "probably because one volt per octave is such a nice round number" (Moog 1983a: 58).

4. According to Dave Smith, the original idea for the interface may have been initiated by Roland Corporation's Ikaturo Kakehashi; Smith is nevertheless credited with much of the effort in actually bringing the specification to fruition. Roland Corporation continued to play a large role in its technical development, however, and in coordinating the contributions from the other Japanese companies (Milano 1984: 43–44).

5. To avoid possible legal charges of "restraint of trade" in the United States, MIDI remains a "specification" and not a formal "standard"; the word "universal" was dropped from the original name of the device for similar reasons.

6. There does seem to have been some precedent for communications between the Japanese companies that did not exist in the United States, where secrecy and competition were more the rule (Milano, 1984: 48).

7. A comprehensive (and largely unbiased) assessment of the technical advantages and limitations of MIDI can be found in Loy 1985. For a general account

of the early debates surrounding the introduction of MIDI, see the series of interviews conducted by Milano 1984. A focused criticism of some of the technical limitations inherent in the specification are detailed in Moore 1988.

5. Music Periodicals, the Instrument Industry, and the Musicians' Community (pp. 93–130)

1. Among those whose work acknowledges periodicals as an important facet of Western musical culture are Loesser 1954; Weber 1975, 1977; Kerman 1985; and, more recently, Koza 1991.

2. For a critique of the uses of the music press in histories of popular music, see Thornton 1990.

3. Another important characteristic of the early music periodicals in both Canada and the United States was their relationship to music education. Mott describes the launching of a Boston periodical, the *Musical Magazine* (1839–1842), as responding, in part, to the introduction of music into public schools (1957: 435). Similarly, Kallmann cites the music journals as "an important aid to musical education" in Canada throughout the nineteenth century (1960: 193). Addressed to amateurs and students rather than to professional musicians, the music magazines promoted the bourgeois values of "art music" and led movements for the reform of church music and Canadian school curricula. At the same time, the magazines' commercial role in the promotion and sale of salon music and other light musical forms belied these loftier goals (Ibid.: 193–94). Values and responsibilities to community life, so vaunted by the music magazines, were thus always at least partially compromised by the commercial context within which the magazines operated.

4. In addition to the consumer magazines listed in the table, there are a number of periodicals directed to sound engineers and producers, such as *db*, which began publishing in 1967, *Recording Engineer/Producer*, 1970, *Mix*, 1977, and *Pro Sound News*, 1978, whose circulation is generally smaller than those in the table—ranging from approximately 10,000 to 40,000 copies. Many of these magazines belong more to the category of business publications: Their circulations are mostly controlled (that is, distributed often free of charge directly to professionals in the field), and their main revenue comes from advertising. Because of their limited commercial distribution, I have not included them in the table.

Circulation figures are rounded to the nearest 1,000. They are taken primarily from *The Standard Periodical Directory* and *Ulrich's International Periodicals Directory*. Although figures in the two directories are supposed to be from audited sources, there can be considerable variation between them for individual titles. There may be a number of reasons for such discrepancies, such as the precise timing of the survey, but the figures quoted here are, to my knowledge, accurate. Wherever possible, figures were checked against audited statements (ABC or BPA) that were made available to me by the publishers themselves.

5. The role played by the magazines in defining sounds takes various forms. For example, in addition to the "Vintage Synths" column, *Keyboard* has devoted an entire issue to a nostalgic look at the Hammond B3 Organ (17 [11], November 1991). It also regularly reviews sound libraries with a view toward their suitability for various contemporary styles of music. In 1995, it ran a feature article entitled "20 Sounds That Must Die" (21 [10], October: 65–74) that described a series of synthesizer, drum machine, and sampler sounds that have become overused clichés in the entertainment industries.

6. Similar processes to those described here have certainly not gone unnoticed by scholars of popular culture, especially in recent years. For example, Dick Hebdige's article entitled "Object as Image: The Italian Scooter Cycle" (1981) reveals

the adaptations in design and marketing that transformed the motorcycle from a highly male-oriented form of transportation/recreation into the more feminized motor scooter. On the home front, Spigel's (1988) and Altman's (1989) work concerning the installation of the television in American homes during the 1950s, Keightley's (1994) exploration of the male-dominated hi-fi craze of the same period, and Haddon's (1988) reflections on the more recent development of the market for personal computers all offer important insights into the discourses of gender and domesticity that accompany the introduction of new technologies for the home.

6. Communication Networks and User Groups (pp. 131–53)

1. Among the histories of radio that refer to the early ham radio phenomenon, see Barnouw 1966: 28–38; Dunlap 1935: 159–66; and Harlow 1936: 467–500.

2. In contrast to the claims of the ham radio operators, those who had an interest in downplaying the contributions of the amateurs (e.g., Marconi himself) continued to argue that their technical and scientific contributions were greatly exaggerated (see Dunlap 1935: 164–66).

3. CB communications bear certain similarities to at least some of the typical interactions of the early ham radio enthusiasts and also to the various "bullet-inboards" and other communications forums commonly found on computer networks. Among other characteristics, Hershey and others describe CB communication as nonprivate, participatory, anonymous, affective, and concerned with defining the boundaries of a community of interest (ibid.: 239); each of these characteristics could be equally applied to ham radio transmissions and to various computer-based network communications. Their study also shows that, despite the media image of the CB user as a maverick truck driver out to circumvent police radar traps, only a small percentage of CB communications actually have such "instrumental" purposes (ibid.: 246). The authors classify the vast majority of communications studied as "expressive"—concerned with the maintenance of a network of friendships and social relations—thus supporting their hypothesis that CB radio is primarily an "affective" medium of communication (ibid.: 247).

4. This neglect stands in marked contrast to the prevalence of both men *and* women in most accounts of audiences for the medium of broadcast radio. During the early 1920s, broadcast radio became regarded as a domestic medium of entertainment for the entire family in a way that short wave radio had never been. The radio receiver, like the pianola and the phonograph before it, was given a central place in the parlor of almost every home. Some manufacturers even marketed what might be considered an early prototype of the present-day "home entertainment center" in the form of an upright piano with built-in radio and phonograph player.

5. The MIDI Manufacturers' Association in conjunction with the Japan MIDI Standards Committee (JMSC) jointly oversee changes in the MIDI specification.

7. Music/Technology/Practice (pp. 157–85)

1. By adopting this expression, I take as my point of departure the work of Michel Foucault, who has developed the notion of a "technology" of sex (1980a: 90, 119), and that of Teresa de Lauretis (1987), who has put forward a complementary concept: the "technology of gender." In certain respects, Lawrence Grossberg's notion of a rock and roll "apparatus" (1984: 236–40)—itself derived from Foucault (1980b: 194–98)—might be an even more appropriate concept than "technology"; but Grossberg has tended to describe the "apparatus" as a "machine" (1984: 237), and, although the two concepts may or may not be interchangeable (they may

only be the result of differences in English translation), my preference for the term "technology" over "apparatus" seems justifiable given the context of this study. To continue to use the term "technology" also affords a certain degree of linguistic ambiguity that allows for slipping from one use of the term to another.

2. These divisions between musical logic and practice are not necessarily oppositional; rather, they are complementary. Interestingly, Walser argues that when heavy metal guitar players turn to classical music as a model of virtuosity, they also tend to adopt its repertoire and its modes of theorization (1993: 57–107).

3. For a more elaborate assessment of Merriam's model, see the journal article by Timothy Rice (1987) and the various responses appearing in the same issue.

4. I use the word "theory" in this instance in a looser, more general fashion than does Bourdieu, where the term is more often reserved for forms of objectified knowledge.

5. For a perceptive discussion of such differences see Marion Thede's (1967) brief account of her own transformation from "violinist" to "fiddler."

6. Ragtime preceded boogie woogie as the first Negro music to make extensive use of the piano, but many historians of jazz regard its pianistic style (introduced by a handful of musically educated players) and its composed forms as the least-typical expression of Afro-American musical traditions (see Jones 1963: 90; and Hobsbawm 1989: 119).

7. Bayton (1990) describes the transition from classical keyboard to the synthesizer in terms not unlike those used by Thede in her description of violin versus fiddle playing (1967).

8. Tablature systems are probably as old as the most rudimentary forms of musical notation: According to Rastall, examples of keyboard tablature date back as far as the Middle Ages. Though they are most often associated with music of the sixteenth and seventeenth centuries, the use of a variety of tablature systems in popular music of the twentieth century is a testimony to their continued viability as a form of notation for specific musical instruments.

9. Guitar magazines regularly feature solos transcribed into tablature. The wide range of special playing techniques characteristic of contemporary popular guitar styles has created the need for an expanded set of notational symbols. Tablature thus continues to evolve as a system of notation. For an example of these new symbols and their meaning, see the tablature chart reproduced in Walser 1993: 91.

8. The New "Sound" of Music (pp. 186–213)

1. One exception to this rule is keyboard player Jan Hammer who is highly regarded for his ability to imitate guitar sounds and playing styles on the synthesizer. Not surprisingly, this ability is based as much on Hammer's feel for guitar voicings, fingering conventions, and pitch-bending techniques as it is on his knowledge of synthesizers (see *Keyboard* 11 [9], July 1985: 38–39).

2. Adorno's comments concerning Schoenberg's experiments in orchestration are revealing. Initially Schoenberg's music shows a tendency to explore instrumental timbre as an independent compositional element; once he adopts the twelve-tone system of composition, however, timbre returns to its subordinate role of illuminating musical structure (1973: 87–89).

3. In his analysis of the role of craftsmanship among studio musicians, Ivey draws directly on the work of Peterson and White (1979). Their work addresses many of the concerns laid out by Howard Becker (1963, 1974, 1982) and, along with Faulkner's study of session musicians in the Hollywood film industry (1971) and Kealy's initial research on the role of sound engineers in rock (1974, 1979), constitutes a defining moment in the sociology of pop music production in Ameri-

can scholarship. Peterson (1982) describes this focus on occupational careers as one strain of thought among several that emerged, by the late 1970s, as a coherent approach, which he refers to as the "production of culture perspective." Janet Wolff (1981: 31–32) has described some of the ideological, historical, and contextual limitations inherent in this dominant school of American empirical sociology.

4. At the consumer end of the market spectrum, Radio Shack, riding on the popularity of rap acts among pre-teens in the late '80s, introduced a small, portable, children's keyboard called "Rap-Master" that included preset rhythm patterns, an electronic "scratch platter," a built-in microphone, and sound effects processor for $129.95. Not only rap "sounds" but all of rap style and fashion were similarly packaged; for an additional $19.95, one could obtain a rap "lyric book," instructional cassette, and a pair of sunglasses.

5. Similar observations have been made concerning the influence of early sequencers on the rigid, mechanical aesthetic associated with much electro-pop and new wave music during the late 1970s.

6. Ironically, although the dominant manufacturers of synthesizers are Japanese, the standard repertoire of sound programs are of Western origin; with few exceptions, instruments associated with Oriental cultures are labeled as "ethnic" in drum machine, synthesizer, and sampler libraries.

7. The more advanced samplers introduced at the end of the 1980s, such as the Akai S1100, could even function as the "front end" of a full digital recording system. The ability of an instrument to function in this way had been a feature of "high-end" systems such as the Synclavier for a number of years; in the case of the average professional sampler, however, the limitations of the technology did not allow for such flexibility until the late 1980s and early '90s.

8. It is interesting to note that the problem of specifying sounds through an abstract process of defining "functions" in numerical form has plagued computer synthesis from the outset. Even among university researchers who attempted to use early computer synthesis programs, such as those developed by Max Mathews at Bell Labs, there was a need to have at hand a relatively predictable set of known sounds with which to compose. For this purpose, "instrument catalogs" were developed for the MUSIC 5 program (see Truax 1976). These sound archives could be thought of as precursors to the commercial sound "libraries" common today. Not unlike pop musicians who state that sounds can sometimes influence how they play music, there has been some concern that the instrument catalogs of MUSIC 5 could potentially influence the compositional logics of those who used the program (ibid.).

9. "Live" and Recorded (pp. 214–41)

1. Les Paul is credited with having invented the 8-track tape recorder (one was made for him during the 1950s by the Ampex corporation); for details concerning his early experiments with sound-on-sound techniques and multitracking, see Sievert 1978.

2. It should be noted that Bennett uses the term "notation" in a very broad, almost metaphorical style; musical sound itself and words used to describe music are all considered forms of "notation" within his typology of "sound-noticing" systems.

3. The recording in question was of the song "The Sheik of Araby," and was originally released by RCA Victor (VIC 27485). The song has recently been re-released on an album entitled *The Legendary Sidney Bechet*, Bluebird records #6590-1-RB, 1988. I want to thank Keir Keightley for bringing this recording to my attention.

4. It is extremely difficult to find any reliable data on the availability of performance venues (especially small ones), and, in addition, there appears to be a considerable amount of regional variation. A recent article in the *Montreal Gazette* described the closure of two of the city's venues as a reorganization of the local music scene and suggested that it has become increasingly difficult to stage live music without the economic support of corporate sponsors (playing pre-recorded music, it would appear, is cheaper and more profitable than live music). This argument supports observations made by Will Straw and Jody Berland (buttressed by information derived from Statistics Canada) that live performance is seldom a profitable enterprise. Even in the world of stadium rock, the profitability of large-scale concert touring has become dependent on the converging interests (and economic investments) of venue owners, major league sports enterprises, and large corporations (1992: 909).

5. For a detailed discussion of a derivative of these programs (MUSIC 4BF) and the division of tasks that follows from the score/orchestra analogy, see Howe 1975: 175–248.

6. The origins of the MC-8 design—in Dyck's own technical experiments and production practices—is perhaps another example of how the functional source of technical innovation can come from users rather than from the industry.

7. This fragmentation of performance data runs parallel to a similar kind of fragmentation characteristic of the models of sound generation that have dominated digital synthesis from its earliest days; only recently have some members of the academic computer synthesis community begun to address the problem of constructing more complex models that allow for various kinds of interrelations between sound parameters (Truax 1991: 30).

8. Algorithmic programs use computational logic (e.g., the use of "Markov chains" to define transitions from one state to another) to define a set of compositional "rules" that can automate certain aspects of composition and sound production; users experiment or "interact" with the output of such programs to compose music. Several programs of this type were released commercially during the mid-1980s but had only limited success among popular musicians. Detailed articles describing these programs have appeared in *Electronic Musician* 3 (8), August 1987: 36–52; *Computer Music Journal* 11 (4), winter 1987: 13–29; and *Keyboard* 16 (10), October 1990: 55–63.

9. With some sequencers, a looping process similar to that used in drum machines is used instead of the multitrack metaphor. The two compositional processes are not mutually exclusive, however, and many programs allow for a combination of looped and linear recording techniques.

10. To carry the analogy further, editing a sequence is like trying to edit the individual instrumental parts of a symphony without having access to the conductor's score.

11. For a perceptive analysis of the relationship between sound recording and the representation of "live" events, see Wurtzler 1992.

12. The creation of a market for semi-professional recording equipment for the home was perhaps not unlike the creation of a market for home computers during the 1980s; regarding the latter, see Haddon 1988.

13. Subsequent government studies criticized the report for placing economic issues rather than creative rights at the center of copyright policy. The recommendations, however, should perhaps be understood in the context of other nationalist policy initiatives of the same period, such as the Canadian Content regulations that set quotas for Canadian material broadcast on radio and television. In this sense, the Economic Council Report could be interpreted as placing copyright within the purview of broader issues of cultural policy rather than in the narrow,

legal focus of individual property rights. Other countries have developed a similar point of view (see Wallis and Malm 1984, chapter 6).

14. Perhaps precisely because such a large gap presently exists between new technology, musical practices, and market conditions, on the one hand, and Canadian and American law, on the other, a considerable body of comment and opinion has already appeared in recent years, both in the popular and industry press (e.g., Barry 1987; Bateman 1988; Christgau 1986; Considine 1990; DeCurtis 1986; Dupler 1986; Giffen 1985; Oswald 1986, 1988; Pareles 1986; Ressner 1990; Rosenbluth 1989; Tomlyn 1986; Torchia 1987) and in the pages of respected law journals as well (Desjardins 1990; Keyt 1988; McGiverin 1987; McGraw 1989; Mosher 1989). For a more detailed discussion of some of the issues presented here on copyright, see my own essay and those of a number of other authors in Frith 1993.

10. Conclusion (pp. 242–55)

1. To a certain degree, modular digital multitracks such as the Alesis ADAT and the Tascam DA-88 can be regarded as parts of a larger digital recording "system" for the home and the professional studio that links hard disk recording with tape. The huge demands placed on hard drive capacity by audio recording requires that sound files be regularly backed up on some other medium to allow for subsequent recording. Manufacturers of multitrack hard disk recording systems, such as Digidesign, have introduced interfaces that allow for the direct digital transfer of sound files from computers to digital tape recorders such as the ADAT.

2. For a discussion of Alesis's market philosophy and strategic planning, see "Newsmaker: Alesis' Russell Palmer," *Musical Merchandise Review* 149 (7), July 1990: 46–51.

3. For an informative account of the impact of cassette technology throughout the world and the particular problems of so-called "cassette piracy," see Manuel 1993; and Wallis and Malm 1984.

4. Technically, *Karaoke* resembles the decades-old "Music-Minus-One" recordings—a series of recorded arrangements of popular jazz standards where one instrumental part was left out so that the amateur or student instrumentalist could play along. As a pedagogical tool for aspiring young musicians, the intent of the recordings is, however, quite different from *Karaoke*, where the end product is envisioned, from the outset, as a performance that includes a combination of recorded and live elements.

5. See Alan di Perna's article in *Musician* 188, June 1994: 56–63.

Background Sources

✳

Personal interviews and conversations (by telephone and in person)

Musical Instrument Industry

Dave Smith, former President, Sequential Circuits, 21 Nov. 1988.

Marty Frafu, Engineer, Roland (USA) Corporation, 1 Feb. 1989.

Bill Southworth, President, Southworth Music Systems, 3 April 1989.

Jeff Rona, President, MIDI Manufacturers' Association (MMA), 6 April 1989.

Jim Cooper, President, J.L. Cooper Electronics, 18 April 1989.

Karen Pultz, Sales Representative, Korg (Canada), 6 May 1990.

Glenn MacGregor, National Sales Manager, Electronic Musical Instrument Division, Casio (Canada), 6 May 1990.

Lorne Weiner, Sales Representative, Tartini Musical Imports, Richmond Hill, Ontario, 6 May 1990.

Harry Tonogai, National Manager, Advertising and Public Relations, Yamaha (Canada), 7 May 1990.

Al Kowalenko, Executive Secretary and Manager, Music Industries Association of Canada (MIAC), 7 May 1990.

Frank Foster, Director of Specialty Markets, Atari Computers, 17 June 1990.

Mikel Estrin, International Sales Manager, Passport Designs, 17 June 1990.

Thomas A. Sheehan, General Manager, Yamaha Communication Center, New York, 2 Nov. 1990.

Jerry Kovarsky, Director of Marketing, Ensoniq Corporation, 8–9 Nov. 1990.

Albert Charpentier, Vice President of Engineering and Co-Founder, Ensoniq Corp., 8 Nov. 1990.

Bob Yannis, Senior Design Engineer and Co-Founder, Ensoniq Corp., 8 Nov. 1990.

Gary Trapuzzano, Director of Engineering, Ensoniq Corp., 8 Nov. 1990.

Bill Motley, Head of Software Development, Ensoniq Corp., 9 Nov. 1990.

Steve Cascia, Director of Customer Service, Ensoniq Corp., 9 Nov. 1990.

Steve Alexander, Ontario Regional Manager, Roland (Canada) Corporation, 9 May 1991.

Robert Currie, Project Engineer, Digidesign, 18 Oct. 1991.

Magazines, User Groups, and Computer Networks

Lachlan Westfall, President, International MIDI Association (IMA), 21 Nov. 1988.

Jim Aiken, Associate Editor, *Keyboard* magazine, 1 Feb. 1989.

Vanessa Else, former Senior Editor, *Electronic Musician*, October 1989.

Perry Leopold, Director, Performing Artists Network (PAN), 3 April 1989.

Jane Talisman, Editor, *Transoniq Hacker*, 5 April 1989.

Kevin Laubach, Programmer, Digital Music Service (former software editorial consultant for the *IMA Bulletin*), 18 April 1989.

Doug Provisor, Keyboards Manager, The Guitar Center (former technical editor for the *IMA Bulletin*), 18 April 1989.

Terry Day, President, Music Maker Publications (*Music Technology, Home & Studio Recording, Rhythm*, and others), 8 Nov. 1989.

David Henman, Editor, *Canadian Music Trades, Canadian Musician*, 6 May 1990.

Charles C. Baake, Senior Vice President, Miller Freeman Publications; Group Publisher, The GPI Group (*Guitar Player, Keyboard*, and others), 17 June 1990.

Steve Wigginton, Director of Circulation, ACT III Publishing (*Electronic Musician, Mix*, and others), 17 June 1990.

Robert Brodie, Manager of User Group Services, Atari Computers, 17 June 1990.

Bob O'Donnell, Editor, *Electronic Musician* (former editor, *Music Technology*, U.S. edition), 18 June 1990.

Steve Oppenheimer, Associate Editor, *Electronic Musician*, 18 June 1990.

John Maher, Publisher, *Down Beat*, 18 June 1990.

Frank Alkyer, Editorial Director, *Down Beat, Music Inc.*, *Up Beat Daily*, 18 June 1990.

Craig Anderton, Freelance Columnist for numerous magazines and user group newsletters (founding editor, *Electronic Musician*), 11 July 1990.

Domenic Milano, Editor, *Keyboard*, 19 July 1990.

Scott Wilkinson, Editor-in-Chief, *Home & Studio Recording* (former editor, *Music Technology*), 25 October 1990.

Atari Users Group, Ottawa, October/November 1990.

Musicians, Recording Engineers, and Researchers

Bruce Pennycook, Composer and Associate Professor, Computer Music, McGill University, Montréal, 15 and 22 Nov. 1988.

Gareth Loy, Software Coordinator, Computer Audio Research Laboratory, University of California, San Diego, 28 Nov. 1988.

Tom Rhea, Musician and Professor, History of Electronic Music, Berklee College of Music, Boston, 9 Feb. 1989.

Callum MacLean, Recording Engineer, Tower Studios, 28 Oct. 1989 and 9 Nov. 1989.

Fish Turn Human, Band, Newcastle, Scotland, 28 Oct. 1989.

Dave Garrett, Recording Engineer, Tower Studios, Glasgow, 4 Nov. 1989.

Another Bendy Window, Band, Edinburg and Glasgow, 4 Nov. 1989.

Eyes of Rita, Band, Glasgow, 9 Nov. 1989.

Midnight Crisis, Band, Glasgow, 5 Nov. and 14 Nov. 1989.

Craig Tannock, Producer/Manager/Owner, Tower Studios, Glasgow, 16 Nov. 1989.

Kevin Key, Recording Engineer, Ça Va Studios, Glasgow, 10 Nov. 1989.

Helen Clark, Chief Administrator, Ça Va Studios, Glasgow, 10 Nov. 1989.

Anna McGarrigle, Singer and Instrumentalist, Kate & Anna McGarrigle,

numerous conversations during the recording of an album, winter/spring
1990.

Pierre Marchand, Record Producer and Sound Engineer, former keyboardist for
the Luba band, 30 Jan. 1990.

Pierre Gauthier, Freelance Musician and Arranger, Montréal, several
conversations, winter 1990.

Diane LeBoeuf, Freelance Sound Engineer/Mixer, Montréal, several
conversations, winter 1990.

Ed Eagan, Musician and Sound Engineer, Twelfth Root Studios, Ottawa,
6 March 1990.

Jim Burgess, Musician and MIDI Specialist, Owner of Saved by Technology,
Toronto, 7 May 1990.

Tony McAnany, Musician, Coordinator of Special Projects (Sounds/Videos),
Ensoniq Corporation, 9 Nov. 1990.

Michael Nicoletti, Recording Engineer and Yamaha Professional Audio
Representative, NYC, 1/2 Nov. 1990.

Ed Wilson, Musician and MIDI Specialist, Saved by Technology, Toronto,
7 Feb. 1991.

John Oswald, Musician/Electro-Acoustic Composer, Toronto, 8 Feb. 1991.

Owen Clark, Music Consultant, Clark Productions, Winnipeg, 10 May 1991.

Tim Brady, Composer/Electric Guitarist, Montréal, 10 May 1991.

Clive Perry, Sound Engineer/Sound Designer for Film and TV, Regional
Representative for Digidesign products, Winnipeg, 10/15 May 1991.

Bibliography

✳

Primary References

Ackerley, Charlotte. 1978. "Women and Guitar." In *The Guitar Player Book*, edited by Jim Ferguson. New York: Grove Press, 259–61.

Adorno, Theodor W. 1941. "On Popular Music." *Studies in Philosophy and Social Sciences* 9: 17–48.

———. 1973. *Philosophy of Modern Music*. Translated by Anne G. Mitchell and Wesley V. Blomster. New York: Seabury.

Allen, Richard. 1990. "Made in Canada: The Markets, The Manufacturers, The Merchandise." *Canadian Music Trades* 12 (1), Dec./Jan.: 22–38.

Altman, Karen E. 1989. "Television as Gendered Technology: Advertising the American Television Set." *Journal of Popular Film and Television* 17 (2), summer: 46–56.

Anderton, Craig. 1986. *MIDI for Musicians*. New York: Amsco.

———. 1988. "20 Great Achievements in 20 Years of Musical Electronics 1968–1988." *Electronic Musician* 4 (7), July: 28–97.

Appadurai, Arjun. 1986. "Introduction: Commodities and the Politics of Value." In *The Social Life of Things: Commodities in Cultural Perspective*, edited by Arjun Appadurai. Cambridge: Cambridge University Press, 3–63.

Appleton, Jon, and Ronald Perera, eds. 1975. *The Development and Practice of Electronic Music*. Englewood Cliffs, N.J.: Prentice-Hall.

Attali, Jacques. 1985. *Noise: The Political Economy of Music*. Translated by Brian Massumi. Minneapolis: University of Minnesota Press.

Baba, Yasunori. 1989. "The Dynamics of Continuous Innovation in Scale-Intensive Industries." *Strategic Management Journal* 10: 89–100.

Barnouw, Erik. 1966. *A Tower in Babel: A History of Broadcasting in the United States*. Vol. 1, *To 1933*. New York: Oxford University.

Barry, Henry V. 1987. "Legal Aspects of Digital Sound Sampling." *Recording Engineer/Producer* 18 (4), April: 60–67.

Barthes, Roland. 1977. *Image-Music-Text*. Translated by Stephen Heath. New York: Hill and Wang.

Bateman, Jeff. 1988. "Sampling: Sin or Musical Godsend?" *Music Scene* 363, Sept./Oct.: 14–15.

Bayton, Mavis. 1990. "How Women Become Musicians." In *On Record: Rock, Pop, & the Written Word*, edited by Simon Frith and Andrew Goodwin. New York: Pantheon, 238–57.

Beadle, Jeremy J. 1993. *Will Pop Eat Itself?: Pop Music in the Soundbite Era*. London: Faber and Faber.

Bebey, Francis. 1975. *African Music: A People's Art*. Translated by Josephine Bennett. New York: Lawrence Hill & Co.

Becker, Howard. 1963. *Outsiders: Studies in the Sociology of Deviance*. New York: Free Press.

———. 1974. "Art as Collective Action." *American Sociological Review* 39 (6), December: 767–76.

———. 1982. *Art Worlds*. Berkeley: University of California Press.

Benjamin, Walter. 1969. "The Work of Art in the Age of Mechanical Reproduction." In *Illuminations*, translated by H. Zohn. New York: Schocken, 217–51.

Bennett, H. Stith. 1983. "Notation and identity in contemporary popular music." *Popular Music* 3: 215–34.

———. 1990. "The Realities of Practice." In *On Record: Rock, Pop, and the Written Word*, edited by Simon Frith and Andrew Goodwin. New York: Pantheon, 221–37.

Blacking, John. 1971. "Towards a Theory of Musical Competence." In *Man: Anthropological Essays Presented to O. F. Raum*, edited by E. J. De Jager. Cape Town: C. Struik, 19–34.

———. 1973. *How Musical is Man?* Seattle: University of Washington Press.

———. 1977. "Some Problems of Theory and Method in the Study of Musical Change." *Yearbook of the International Folk Music Council* 9: 1–26.

Blum, Stephen. 1975. "Towards a Social History of Musicological Technique." *Ethnomusicology* 19 (2): 207–31.

Born, Georgina. 1995. *Rationalizing Culture: IRCAM, Boulez, and the Institutionalization of the Musical Avant-Garde*. Berkeley: University of California Press.

Bourdieu, Pierre. 1984. *Distinction: A Social Critique of the Judgement of Taste*, translated by Richard Nice. Cambridge, Mass.: Harvard University Press.

———. 1990. *The Logic of Practice*, translated by Richard Nice. Stanford, Cal.: Stanford University Press.

Brophy, Philip. 1991. "The Architecsonic Object: Stereo Sound, Cinema & *Colors*." In *Culture, Technology & Creativity*, edited by Philip Hayward. London: John Libbey & Co., 91–110.

Burgess, Robert G. 1984. *In the Field: An Introduction to Field Research*. London: Allen & Unwin.

Busoni, Ferruccio. 1967. "Sketch of a New Esthetic of Music." Excerpt reprinted in *Contemporary Composers on Contemporary Music*, edited by E. Schwartz and B. Childs. New York: Da Capo, 4–16.

Carse, Adam. 1964. *The History of Orchestration*. New York: Dover.

Chambers, Iain. 1985. *Urban Rhythms: Pop Music and Popular Culture*. London: MacMillan.

———. 1990. "A Miniature History of the Walkman." *New Formations* 1, summer: 1–4.

Chanan, Michael. 1981. "The trajectory of Western music or, as Mahler said, the music is not in the notes." *Media, Culture and Society* 3: 219–42.

Chapple, Steve & Reebee Garofalo. 1977. *Rock 'n' Roll is Here to Pay*. Chicago: Nelson-Hall.

Christgau, Robert. 1986. "Down By Law." *Village Voice* 31 (12), March 25: 39–40, 42.

Cone, Edward T. 1974. *The Composer's Voice*. Berkeley: University of California Press.

Considine, J. D. 1990. "Larcenous Art?" *Rolling Stone* 580, June 14: 107–8.

Craft, Robert. 1957. "The composer and the phonograph." *High Fidelity* 7 (6), June: 34–35, 99–100.

Crane, Jonathan. 1986. "Mainstream Music and the Masses." *Journal of Communication Inquiry* 10 (3): 66–70.

Daley, Dan. 1990. "How Will the Wolf Survive?: Changing Times for the Small Studio." *Mix* 14 (10), October: 113–16.

Darter, Tom, and Greg Armbruster, eds. 1984. *The Art of Electronic Music*. New York: William Morrow.

Davidow, William H. 1986. *Marketing High Technology: An Insider's View*. London: Free Press.

Davies, Hugh. 1984. "Electronic instruments" and various other entries on specific instruments and manufacturers. In *The New Grove Dictionary of Musical Instruments*, edited by Stanley Sadie. Vol. 3. London: Macmillan.

Davis, Miles (with Quincy Troupe). 1989. *Miles: The Autobiography*. New York: Simon and Schuster.

DeCurtis, Anthony. 1986. "Who Owns A Sound?" *Rolling Stone* 488, Dec. 4: 13.

de Lauretis, Teresa. 1987. "The Technology of Gender." In *Technologies of Gender: Essays on Theory, Film, and Fiction*. Bloomington: Indiana University Press, 1–30.

Deming, W. Edwards. 1981. "What Top Management Must Do." *Business Week* 2697, July 20: 19–21.

Deming, W. Edwards, and Christopher S. Gray. 1981. "Japan: Quality Control and Innovation." *Business Week* 2697, July 20: 18–44.

Denisoff, R. Serge. 1975. *Solid Gold*. New Brunswick, N.J.: Transaction Books.

Denisoff, R. Serge, and John Bridges. 1982. "Popular Music: Who Are the Recording Artists?" *Journal of Communication*, winter: 132–42.

Der Manuelian, Michael. 1988. "The Role Of The Expert Witness In Music Copyright Infringement Cases." *Fordham Law Review* 57 (1): 127–47.

Desbarats, Peter. 1991. "The Special Role of Magazines in the History of Canadian Mass Media and National Development." In *Communications in Canadian Society*, edited by Benjamin D. Singer. Scarborough: Nelson Canada, 50–66.

Desjardins, Michel. 1990. "Digital Sound Sampling And Copyright In Canada." *Canadian Patent Reporter* 33 C.P.R. (3d): 129–57.

Doerschuk, Bob. 1983. "The Great Synthesizer Debate." *Keyboard* 9 (12), December: 38–62.

———. 1985. "Many Mountains, Many Peaks: Encounters With the Driving Forces in Japan's Synthesizer Industry." *Keyboard* 11 (8), August: 48–58.

Dougherty, Philip H. 1986. "Trade ads aid sales study says." *New York Times*, October 16: D22.

Dunlap, Orrin E., Jr. 1935. *The Story of Radio*. New York: Dial Press.

Dunsby, Jonathan, and Arnold Whittall. 1988. *Music Analysis in Theory and Practice*. Boston: Faber.

Dupler, Steven. 1986. "Digital Sampling: Is It Theft?" *Billboard* 98 (31), Aug. 2: 1, 74.

Durant, Alan. 1984. *Conditions of Music*. Albany: State University of New York Press.

———. 1990. "A New Day for Music? Digital technologies in contemporary music-making." In *Culture, Technology & Creativity*, edited by Philip Hayward. London: John Libbey & Co., 175–96.

Eimert, Herbert. 1958. "What is Electronic Music?" *Die Reihe* 1: 1–10.

Ellul, Jacques. 1967. *The Technological Society*, translated by J. Wilkinson. New York: Knopf.

Emmerson, Frank. 1979. "Amps: Making It in Canada." *Music Market Canada* 3 (1): 24–25.

Eno, Brian. 1983. "The Studio as Compositional Tool—Part I & II." *Down Beat* 50 (7/8), July and August: 56–57, 50–53, respectively.

Erlhoff, Michael. 1984. "Cassetten Radio—the New Shape of Radio." *Ear Magazine* 8 (5), March: 10.

Ewen, Stuart. 1976. *Captains of Consciousness: Advertising and the Social Roots of the Consumer Culture*. New York: McGraw-Hill.

Fabbri, Franco. 1982. "A Theory of Musical Genres: Two Applications." In *Popular Music Perspectives*, edited by David Horn and Philip Tagg. Göteborg: IASPM, 52–81.

———. 1991. "Copyright—The Dark Side Of The Music Business." *Worldbeat* 1: 109–13.

Faulkner, Robert R. 1971. *Hollywood Studio Musicians*. Chicago: Aldine-Atherton.

Feld, Steven. 1981. " 'Flow Like a Waterfall': The Metaphors of Kaluli Musical Theory." *Yearbook for Traditional Music* 13: 22–47.

———. 1982. *Sound and Sentiment: Birds, Weeping, Poetics, and Song in Kaluli Expression*. Philadelphia: University of Pennsylvania Press.

———. 1984. "Communication, Music, and Speech About Music." *Yearbook for Traditional Music* 16: 1–18.

———. 1988. "Aesthetics as Iconicity of Style, or 'Lift-up-over Sounding': Getting into the Kaluli Groove." *Yearbook for Traditional Music* 20: 74–113.

Fink, Michael. 1989. *Inside the Music Business: Music in Contemporary Life*. New York: Schirmer.

Finlay-Pelinski, Marike. 1983. "Technologies of Technology: A Critique of Procedures of Power and Social Control in Discourses on New Communications Technology." *Working Papers in Communications*. Montreal: McGill University.

Ford, James L. C. 1969. *Magazines for Millions: The Story of Specialized Publications*. Carbondale: Southern Illinois University Press.

Foucault, Michel. 1980a. *The History of Sexuality, Volume I: An Introduction*, translated by Robert Hurley. New York: Vintage Books.

———. 1980b. "The Confession of the Flesh." In *Power/Knowledge: Selected Interviews & Other Writings 1972–1977*, edited and translated by Colin Gordon. New York: Pantheon Books, 194–228.

Fox, Ted. 1986. *In the Groove: The People Behind the Music*. New York: St. Martin's Press.

Frederickson, Jon. 1989. "Technology and Music Performance in the Age of Mechanical Reproduction." *International Review of the Aesthetics and Sociology of Music* 20 (2): 193–220.

Frith, Simon. 1981. *Sound Effects: Youth Leisure, and the Politics of Rock 'n' Roll*. New York: Pantheon.

———. 1986. "Art versus technology: the strange case of popular music." *Media, Culture and Society* 8 (3): 263–79.

———. 1987. "Towards an aesthetic of popular music." In *Music and Society: The politics of composition, performance and reception*, edited by Susan McClary and Richard Leppert. Cambridge: Cambridge University Press, 133–49.

———. 1988. "The Industrialization of Music." In *Music for Pleasure*. New York: Routledge, 11–23.

———. 1989. "Euro pop." *Cultural Studies* 3 (2): 166–72.

Frith, Simon, ed. 1993. *Music and Copyright*. Edinburgh: Edinburgh University Press.

Gaburo, Kenneth. 1985. "The Deterioration of an Ideal, Ideally Deteriorized: Reflections on Pietro Grossi's *Paganini Al Computer*." *Computer Music Journal* 9 (1): 39–44.

Giffen, Peter. 1985. "A Source Of Dissonance." *Maclean's* 98, July 29: 48.

Gomery, J. Douglas. 1976. "The Coming of the Talkies: Invention, Innovation, and Diffusion." In *The American Film Industry*, edited by T. Bacio. Madison: University of Wisconsin Press, 193–211.

Goodwin, Andrew. 1988. "Sample and hold: pop music in the digital age of reproduction." *Critical Quarterly* 30 (3): 34–49.

Goodwin, Andrew, and Joe Gore. 1990. "World Beat and the Cultural Imperialism Debate." *Socialist Review* 20 (3): 63–80.

Gould, Glenn. 1966. "The Prospects of Recording." *High Fidelity* 16, April: 46–63.

Grossberg, Lawrence. 1984. "Another boring day in paradise: rock and roll and the empowerment of everyday life." *Popular Music* 4: 225–58.

Grossberg, L., C. Nelson, and P. A. Treichler, eds. 1992. *Cultural Studies*. New York: Routledge.

Grout, Donald Jay. 1960. *A History of Western Music*. New York: W. W. Norton.

Haddon, Leslie. 1988. "The Home Computer: The Making of a Consumer Electronic." *Science as Culture* 2: 7–51.

Hafner, Katie, and John Markoff. 1991. *Cyberpunk: Outlaws and Hackers on the Computer Frontier*. London: Fourth Estate.

Hall, Stuart. 1980. "Cultural Studies: Two Paradigms." *Media, Culture and Society* 2: 57–72.

———. 1985. "Signification, Representation, Ideology: Althusser and the Post-Structuralist Debates." *Critical Studies in Mass Communication* 2 (2): 91–114.

———. 1992. "Cultural Studies and its Theoretical Legacies." In *Cultural Studies*, edited by L. Grossberg, C. Nelson, and P. A. Treichler. New York: Routledge, 277–94.

Hall, Stuart, and Tony Jefferson, eds. 1976. *Resistance Through Rituals*. London: Hutchinson.

Hammond, Ray. 1983. *The Musician and the Micro*. Poole, U.K.: Blandford Press.

Handelman, David. 1990. "Is It Live Or . . ." *Rolling Stone* 156, Sept. 6: 15–16.

Harley, Ross. 1993. "Beat in the System." In *Rock and Popular Music: Politics, Policies, Institutions*, edited by T. Bennett, S. Frith, L. Grossberg, J. Shepherd, and G. Turner. London: Routledge, 210–30.

Harlow, Alvin F. 1936. *Old Wires and New Waves: The History of the Telegraph, Telephone, and Wireless*. New York: D. Appleton Century.

Harvey, David. 1989. *The Condition of Postmodernity*. Oxford: Basil Blackwell.

Hayes, Dennis. 1990. *Behind the Silicon Curtain*. Montréal: Black Rose.

Hebdige, Dick. 1979. *Subculture: The Meaning of Style*. London: Methuen.

———. 1981. "Object as Image: The Italian Scooter Cycle." *Block* 5: 44–64.

———. 1987. *Cut 'n' Mix: Culture, Identity and Caribbean Music*. London: Comedia.

Hennion, Antoine. 1989. "An Intermediary Between Production and Consumption: The Producer of Popular Music." *Science, Technology, & Human Values* 14 (4): 400–424.

———. 1990. "The Production of Success: An Antimusicology of the Pop Song." In *On Record: Rock, Pop, and the Written Word*, edited by Simon Frith and Andrew Goodwin. New York: Pantheon, 185–206.

Hershey, Cary, Eric Shott, and Howard Hammerman. 1978. "Personal Uses of Mobile Communications: Citizens Band Radio and the Local Community." In *Communications for a Mobile Society: An Assessment of New Technology*, edited by Raymond Bowers, A. M. Lee, and Cary Hershey. Beverly Hills: Sage, 233–55.

Hirsch, Paul. 1969. *The Structure of the Popular Music Industry*. Ann Arbor: Institute for Social Research, The University of Michigan.

Hobart, Mike. 1981. "The Political Economy of Bop." *Media, Culture and Society* 3 (3): 261–79.

Hobsbawm, E. J. (a.k.a. Francis Newton). 1989. *The Jazz Scene* (rev. ed.). London: Weidenfeld and Nicolson.

Holmes, Thomas B. 1985. *Electronic and Experimental Music*. New York: Charles Scribner's Sons.

Hornung, J. L. 1940. *Radio as a Career*. New York: Funk & Wagnalls.

Hortschansky, Klaus. 1983. "The Musician as Music Dealer in the Second Half of the 18th Century." In *The Social Status of the Professional Musician from the Middle Ages to the 19th Century*, edited by Walter Salmen. New York: Pendragon, 189–218.

Howe, Hubert S., Jr. 1975. *Electronic Music Synthesis: Concepts, Facilities, Techniques*. New York: Norton.

Huyssen, Andreas. 1986. *After the Great Divide: Modernism, Mass Culture, Postmodernism*. Bloomington: Indiana University Press.

Ifedi, Fidelis. 1990. "Periodicals Published in Canada." *Focus on Culture* 2 (1): 1–3. Ottawa: Statistics Canada.

Ives, Charles. 1961. *Essays Before a Sonata, The Majority, and Other Writings*. New York: Norton.

Ivey, William. 1982. "Commercialization and Tradition in the Nashville Sound." In *Folk Music and Modern Sound*, edited by W. Ferris and M. L. Hart. Jackson: University Press of Mississippi, 129–38.

Jackson, Blair. 1992. "Ch-Ch-Ch-Changes: Music Recording from the Artist's Perspective." *Mix* 16 (6), June: 28–34.

Jameson, Frederic. 1984. "Postmodernism, or The Cultural Logic of Late Capitalism." *New Left Review* 146: 53–92.

Jones, LeRoi. 1963. *Blues People*. New York: Morrow Quill.

Jones, Steve. 1992. *Rock Formation: Music, Technology, and Mass Communication*. Newbury Park, Cal.: Sage.

Kahn, Douglas. 1990. "Track Organology." *October* 55, winter: 67–78.

Kahrs, Mark. 1989. "Notes on Very-Large-Scale Integration and the Design of Real-Time Digital Sound Processors." In *The Music Machine: Selected Readings from "Computer Music Journal,"* edited by Curtis Roads. Cambridge, Mass.: MIT Press, 623–31. (first published in *Computer Music Journal* 5 (2), summer 1981).

Kallmann, Helmut. 1960. *A History of Music in Canada 1534–1914*. Toronto: University of Toronto Press.

Kallmann, Helmut, Gilles Potvin, and Kenneth Winters, eds. 1981. *Encyclopedia of Music in Canada*. Toronto: University of Toronto Press.

Kaplan, S. Jerrold. 1989. "Developing a Commercial Digital Sound Synthesizer." In *The Music Machine: Selected Readings from "Computer Music Journal,"* edited by Curtis Roads. Cambridge, Mass.: MIT, 611–22. (first published in *Computer Music Journal* 5 (3), fall 1981).

Karlin, Fred, and Rayburn Wright. 1990. *On the Track: A Guide to Contemporary Film Scoring*. New York: Schirmer.

Kasha, Al, and Joel Hirschhorn. 1990. *If They Ask You, You Can Write a Song* (updated ed.). New York: Fireside.

Kawasaki, Guy. 1990. *The Macintosh Way*. New York: HarperCollins.

Kealy, Edward R. 1974. "The real rock revolution: sound mixers, social inequality, and the aesthetics of popular music production." Ph.D. dissertation, Northwestern University.

———. 1979. "From Craft to Art: The case of sound mixers and popular music." *Sociology of Work and Occupations* 6 (1): 3–29.

———. 1982. "Conventions and the Production of the Popular Music Aesthetic." *Journal of Popular Culture* 16 (2): 100–115.

Keightley, Keir. 1994. "'Turn it Down!' she shrieked: Gender, Domestic Space, and High Fidelity, 1948–1959." Paper given at a conference of IASPM-Canada entitled "Music and Identity," Montréal, March 12.

Keil, Charles. 1984. "Music Mediated and Live in Japan." *Ethnomusicology* 28 (1): 91–96.

Keil, Charles, and Steven Feld. 1994. *Music Grooves*. Chicago: University of Chicago Press.

Kerman, Joseph. 1985. *Musicology*. London: Fontana Press.

Keyt, Aaron. 1988. "An Improved Framework For Music Plagiarism Litigation." *California Law Review* 76 (2): 421–64.

Kopytoff, Igor. 1986. "The Cultural Biography of Things: Commoditization as Process." In *The Social Life of Things: Commodities in Cultural Perspective*, edited by Arjun Appadurai. Cambridge: Cambridge University Press, 64–91.

Koza, Julia Eklund. 1991. "Music and the Feminine Sphere: Images of Women as Musicians in *Godey's Lady's Book*, 1830–1877." *The Musical Quarterly* 75 (2), summer: 103–29.

Laing, Dave. 1985. *One Chord Wonders: Power and Meaning in Punk Rock*. Milton Keynes: Open University Press.

Langdon, G., D. Queen, J. McKnight, and R. Campbell. 1982. "Standardization Activity of the AES." *Journal of the Audio Engineering Society* 30 (4): 227–50.

Langer, Susanne. 1953. *Feeling and Form*. New York: Scribner's.

———. 1969. *Philosophy in a New Key*. Cambridge: Harvard University.

Langlois, Tony. 1992. "Can you feel it? DJs and House Music culture in the UK." *Popular Music* 11 (2): 229–38.

Leiss, William. 1972. *The Domination of Nature*. Boston: Beacon.

———. 1976. "Commodities." In *The Limits to Satisfaction: An essay on the problem of needs and commodities* Toronto: University of Toronto Press, 71–92.

Leiss, William, Stephen Kline, and Sut Jhally. 1990. *Social Communication in Advertising: Persons, Products & Images of Well-being* (2d rev. ed.). Scarborough, Ontario: Nelson.

Leopold, Perry. 1987. "MIDI by Modem: The Future is Now." Paper presented at the AES 5th International Conference: Music and Digital Technology, Los Angeles, May 1–3.

Limberis, Alex. 1991. "Synth Evolution." *Electronic Musician* 7 (10), October: 122.

Livesay, Harold C., Marcia L. Rorke, and David S. Lux. 1989. "From Experience: Technical Development and the Innovation Process." *Journal of Product Innovation Management* 6 (4), December: 268–81.

Loesser, Arthur. 1954. *Men, Women & Pianos*. New York: Simon & Schuster.

Lowe Benston, Margaret. 1988. "Women's Voices/Men's Voices: Technology as Language." In *Technology and Women's Voices: Keeping in Touch*, edited by Cheris Kramarae. New York: Routledge & Kegan Paul, 15–28.

Loy, Gareth. 1985. "Musicians Make a Standard: The MIDI Phenomenon." *Computer Music Journal* 9 (4): 8–26.

Lyman, Peter. 1984. "Reading, Writing and Word Processing: Toward a Phenomenology of the Computer Age." *Qualitative Sociology* 7 (1/2), spring/summer: 75–89.

Mackay, Andy. 1981. *Electronic Music*. Toronto: John Wiley & Sons.

Macpherson, C. B. 1973. *Democratic Theory: Essays in Retrieval*. London: Oxford University Press.

Majeski, Brian T., ed. 1990. *A History of the U.S. Music Industry*. Englewood, N.J.: *The Music Trades*, Special Centennial Issue.

Manuel, Peter. 1993. *Cassette Culture: Popular Music and Technology in North India*. Chicago: University of Chicago Press.

Mauchley, J. William, and Albert J. Charpentier. 1987. "Practical consideration in the Design of Music systems using VLSI." In *The Proceedings of the AES 5th International Conference: Music and Digital Technology*, Los Angeles, May 1–3: 28–36.

McBride, James. 1988. "Keyboard Contenders, Ensoniq: A U.S. Firm Takes On the Japanese." *The Washington Post*, January 6: C10.

McCall, George J., and J. L. Simmons, eds. 1969. *Issues in Participant Observation: A Text and Reader*. Reading, Mass.: Addison-Wesley.

McClary, Susan. 1991. *Feminine Endings: Music, Gender, and Sexuality*. Minneapolis: University of Minnesota Press.

McGiverin, Bruce J. 1987. "Digital Sound Sampling, Copyright And Publicity: Protecting Against The Electronic Appropriation Of Sounds." *Columbia Law Review* 87 (8): 1723–45.

McGraw, Molly. 1989. "Sound Sampling Protection And Infringement In Today's Music Industry." *High Technology Law Journal* 4 (1), spring: 147–69.

McRobbie, Angela. 1984. "Dance and Social Fantasy." In *Gender and Generation*, edited by Angela McRobbie and Mica Nava. London: MacMillan, 130–61.

Menuhin, Yehudi, William Primrose, and Denis Stevens. 1976. *Violin and Viola*. New York: Schirmer.

Merriam, Alan P. 1964. *The Anthropology of Music*. Evanston, Ill.: Northwestern University Press.

Miège, Bernard. 1982. "La marchandise culturelle: quelques caractéristiques de son développement récent." *Communication et Information* 4 (2): 47–63.

———. 1986. "Les logiques à l'oeuvre dans les nouvelles industries culturelles." *Cahiers de recherche sociologique* 4 (2), Automne: 93–110.

Milano, Dominic. 1975. "Bob Moog: From theremin to synthesizer." *Contemporary Keyboard* 1 (1), Sept./Oct.: 14–15, 24–25, 37.

———. 1984. "Turmoil in MIDI-Land." *Keyboard* 10 (6): 42–63, 106.

Milkowski, Bill. 1987. "Marcus Miller: Miles' Man in the Studio." *Down Beat* 54 (2): 20–22.

Mitchell, Tony. 1993. "World Music and the Popular Music Industry: An Australian View." *Ethnomusicology* 37 (3), fall: 309–38.

Moog, Bob. 1983a. "On Synthesizers: Why They Don't." *Keyboard* 9 (4), April: 58, 80.

———. 1983b. "M.I.D.I.: What it is, What it means to you." *Keyboard* 9 (7), July: 19–25.

———. 1985. "The Keyboard Explosion: Ten Amazing Years in Music Technology." *Keyboard* 11 (10), October: 36–48.

———. 1989. "You've Come a Long Way MIDI." *Keyboard* 15 (2): 117, 168.

Moore, F. Richard. 1988. "The Dysfunctions of MIDI." *Computer Music Journal* 12 (1): 19–28.

Morita, Akio. 1986. *Made in Japan: Akio Morita and Sony*. New York: E.P. Dutton.

Mosher, Janet E. 1989. "20th Century Music: The Impoverishment in Copyright Law of a Strategy of Forms." *Intellectual Property Journal* 5, August: 51–70.

Mott, Frank Luther. 1957. *A History of American Magazines 1741-1850*. Cambridge, Mass.: Harvard University Press.

Ord-Hume, Arthur W. J. G. 1984. *Pianola: The History of the Self-Playing Piano*. London: George Allen & Unwin.

Oswald, John. 1986. "Plunderphonics or, audio piracy as a compositional prerogative." *Musicworks* 34, spring: 5–8.

———. 1988. "Neither A Borrower Nor A Sampler Prosecute." *Keyboard* 14 (3), March: 12–14.

Pareles, Jon. 1986. "Dissonant Issues Of Sound Sampling." *The New York Times*, October 16: C23.

———. 1987. "Record-It-Yourself Music on Cassette." *The New York Times*, May 11: C13.

Partch, Harry. 1974. *Genesis of a Music* (2d ed.). New York: Da Capo.

Peterson, Richard A. 1982. "Five Constraints on the Production of Culture: Law, Technology, Market, Organizational Structure and Occupational Careers." *Journal of Popular Culture* 16 (2), fall: 143–53.

Peterson, Richard A., and David G. Berger. 1971. "Entrepreneurship in Organizations: Evidence from the Popular Music Industry." *Administrative Quarterly* 16, March: 97–106.

———. 1972. "Three Eras in the Manufacture of Popular Music Lyrics." In *The Sounds of Social Change*, edited by R. S. Denisoff and R. A. Peterson. Chicago: Rand McNally, 282–303.

Peterson, Richard A., and Howard G. White. 1979. "The Simplex Located in Art Worlds." *Urban Life* 7 (4), January: 411–35.

Peterson, Theodore. 1964. *Magazines in the Twentieth Century*. Urbana: University of Illinois Press.

Piatier, André. 1987/88. "Transectorial Innovations and the Transformation of Firms." *The Information Society* 5 (4): 205–31.

Poe, Richard. 1988. "The Sweet Sound of Success." *Venture*, May: 28–29.

Pohlmann, Ken. 1985. "The Miniaturization of Audio." *Mix* 9 (2), February: 22–26.

Porcello, Thomas. 1991. "The Ethics Of Digital Audio-Sampling: Engineers' Discourse." *Popular Music* 10 (1): 69–84.

Rakow, Lana F. 1988. "Women and the Telephone: The Gendering of a Communications Technology." In *Technology and Women's Voices: Keeping in Touch*, edited by Cheris Kramarae. New York: Routledge & Kegan Paul, 207–28.

Rastall, Richard. 1983. *The Notation of Western Music: An Introduction*. London: J.M. Dent & Sons.

Raynor, Henry. 1972. *A Social History of Music*. London: Barrie & Jenkins.

Read, Oliver, and Walter L. Welch. 1976. *From Tin Foil to Stereo* (2d ed.). Indianapolis: Howard W. Sams & Co.

Ressner, Jeffrey. 1990. "Sampling Amok?" *Rolling Stone* 580, June 14: 103–5.

Rice, Ronald E. 1987. "New Patterns of Social Structure in an Information Society." In *Competing Visions, Complex Realities: Social Aspects of the Information Society*, edited by Jorge Reina Schement and Leah A. Lievrouw. Norwood, N.J.: Ablex, 107–20.

Rice, Timothy. 1987. "Toward the Remodeling of Ethnomusicology." *Ethnomusicology* 31 (3): 469–88. (See also various responses to Rice on pp. 489–516.)

Richardson, Lyon N. 1931. *A History of Early American Magazines*. New York: Thomas Nelson & Sons.

Rieger, Eva. 1985. "'*Dolce semplice*'?: On the Changing Role of Women in Music." In *Feminist Aesthetics*, edited by Gisela Ecker and translated by Harriet Anderson. London: Women's Press, 135–49.

Roell, Craig H. 1989. *The Piano in America 1890–1940*. Chapel Hill: University of North Carolina Press.

Rogers, Everett M. 1983. *Diffusion of Innovations* (3d ed.). New York: Free Press.

Rose, Tricia. 1994. *Black Noise: Rap Music and Black Culture in Contemporary America*. Hanover, N.H.: University Press of New England.

Rosenbluth, Jean. 1989. "Indie Pubbery Panel Ponders Sampling Trend Pros & Cons." *Variety*, Nov. 1: 70.

Ross, Andrew. 1991. "Hacking Away at the Counterculture." In *Technoculture*, edited by Constance Penley and Andrew Ross. New York: Routledge, 107–34.

Rossum, Dave. 1987. "Digital Musical Instrument Design: The Art of Compromise." In *The Proceedings of the AES 5th International Conference: Music and Digital Technology*, Los Angeles, May 1–3: 21–25.

Rowland, Dara. 1987. "Jack Long: Managing with Principles, People & Product." *Canadian Music Trades* 9 (6), October: 23, 34–38.

Russcol, Herbert. 1972. *The Liberation of Sound*. Englewood Cliffs, N.J.: Prentice-Hall.

Sachs, Curt. 1940. *The History of Musical Instruments*. New York: W.W. Norton.

Schafer, R. Murray. 1977. *The Tuning of the World*. New York: Alfred A. Knopf.

Schrader, Barry. 1982. *Introduction to Electro-Acoustic Music*. Englewood Cliffs, N.J.: Prentice-Hall.

Schutz, Alfred. 1964. "Making Music Together." In *Collected Papers II: Studies in Social Theory*. The Hague: Martinus Nijhoff, 159–78.

Schwartz, Elliott. 1975. *Electronic Music: A Listener's Guide* (rev. ed.). New York: Praeger.

Seeger, Charles. 1977. "Music and Class Structure in the United States." In *Studies in Musicology 1935–1975*. Berkeley: University of California, 222–36.

Sennett, Richard. 1977. *The Fall of Public Man*. New York: Alfred A. Knopf.

Sievert, Jon. 1978. "Les Paul." In *The Guitar Player Book*, edited by Jim Ferguson. New York: Grove, 184–90.

Slack, Jennifer Daryl. 1984. *Communication Technologies and Society: Conceptions of Causality and the Politics of Technological Intervention*. Norwood, N.J.: Ablex.

Small, Christopher. 1980. *Music, Society, Education* (2d rev. ed.). London: John Calder.

Smith, Dave, and Chet Wood. 1981. "The 'USI', or Universal Synthesizer Interface." Paper presented at the 70th Convention of the Audio Engineering Society, New York, Oct. 30–Nov. 2.

Spigel, Lynn. 1988. "Installing the Television Set: Popular Discourses on Television and Domestic Space, 1948–1955." *Camera Obscura* 16: 11–46.

Stewart, Michael. 1987. "The Feel Factor: Music with Soul." *Electronic Musician* 3 (10), October: 56–65.

Stockhausen, Karlheinz. 1961. "Two Lectures." *Die Reihe* 5: 59–82.

Straw, Will, and Jody Berland. 1992. "Music Industries." In *Encyclopedia of Music in Canada* (2d ed.), edited by H. Kallmann and G. Potvin. Toronto: University of Toronto Press, 908–9.

Sudnow, David. 1978. *Ways of the Hand: The Organization of Improvised Conduct*. Cambridge, Mass.: Harvard University Press.

Sutherland, Fraser. 1989. *The Monthly Epic: A History of Canadian Magazines*. Toronto: Fitzhenry & Whiteside.

Taft, William H. 1982. *American Magazines for the 1980s*. New York: Hastings House.

Tankel, Jonathan David. 1990. "The Practice of Recording Music: Remixing as Recoding." *Journal of Communication* 40 (3), summer: 34–46.

Tarr, Edward. 1988. *The Trumpet*. Translated by S. E. Plank and E. Tarr. London: B.T. Batsford.

Théberge, Paul. 1987. "Technological Rationalization and Musical Practice." M.A. thesis, Concordia University.

———. 1989. "The 'sound' of music: Technological rationalization and the production of popular music." *New Formations* 8, summer: 99–111.

———. 1993. "Technology, Economy and Copyright Reform in Canada." In *Music and Copyright*, edited by Simon Frith. Edinburgh: Edinburgh University Press, 40–66.

Thede, Marion. 1967. *The Fiddle Book*. New York: Oak Publications.

Thornton, Sarah. 1990. "Strategies for Reconstructing the Popular Past." *Popular Music* 9 (1): 87–95.

———. 1994. "Moral Panic, the Media and British Rave Culture." In *Microphone Fiends: Youth Music and Youth Culture*, edited by Andrew Ross and Tricia Rose. New York: Routledge, 176–92.

———. 1996. *Club Cultures: Music, Media and Subcultural Capital*. Hanover, N.H.: Wesleyan University Press.

Toffler, Alvin. 1980. *The Third Wave*. New York: William Morrow.

Tomlyn, Bo. 1986. "Bootleg Synthesizer Programs Hurt Everyone." *Keyboard* 12 (9): 11, 154.

Torchia, Dan. 1987. "Sampling Realities: Frank Zappa's Experience With His Recent Jazz From Hell Album." *Recording Engineer/Producer* 18 (4), April: 64.

Truax, Barry. 1976. "A Communicational Approach to Computer Sound Programs." *Journal of Music Theory* 20 (2), fall: 227–300.

———. 1991. "Capturing Musical Knowledge in Software Systems." *Interface* 20: 217–33.

Turkle, Sherry. 1984. *The Second Self: Computers and the Human Spirit*. New York: Simon & Schuster.

———. 1988. "Computational Reticence: Why Women Fear the Intimate Machine." In *Technology and Women's Voices: Keeping in Touch*, edited by Cheris Kramarae. New York: Routledge & Kegan Paul, 41–61.

Tushman, Michael L., and Philip Anderson. 1986. "Technological Discontinuities and Organizational Environments." *Administrative Science Quarterly* 31: 439–65.

Vail, Mark. 1990. "Vintage Synths: The Roland MC-8 Micro Composer." *Keyboard* 16 (10), October: 116–17.

———. 1991. "Down & Dirty: The B-3's Unbeatable Mechanical Soul." *Keyboard* 17 (11), November: 39–47.

———. 1993. *Vintage Synthesizers*. San Francisco: Miller Freeman Books.

Varèse, Edgard. 1967. "The Liberation of Sound." In *Contemporary Composers on Contemporary Music*, edited by E. Schwartz and B. Childs. New York: Da Capo, 196–208.

von Hippel, Eric. 1988. *The Sources of Innovation*. Oxford: Oxford University.

Wallis, Roger, and Krister Malm. 1984. *Big Sounds from Small Peoples: The Music Industry in Small Countries*. New York: Pendragon.

———. 1988. "Push-pull for the video clip: a systems approach to the relationship between the phonogram-videogram industry and music television." *Popular Music* 7 (3): 267–84.

Walser, Robert. 1993. *Running with the Devil: Power, Gender, and Madness in Heavy Metal Music*. Hanover, N.H.: University Press of New England.

Walton, Mary. 1990. *Deming Management at Work*. New York: G.P. Putnam's Sons.

Wasserman, Neil H. 1985. *From Invention to Innovation: Long-Distance Telephone Transmission at the Turn of the Century*. Baltimore: Johns Hopkins University Press.

Waters, Craig R. 1983. "The Rise & Fall of ARP Instruments." *Keyboard* 9 (4) April: 16–21.

Weber, Max. 1958a. *From Max Weber: Essays in Sociology*. Edited, translated, and introduction by H. H. Gerth and C. W. Mills. New York: Oxford University Press.

———. 1958b. *The Rational and Social Foundations of Music*. Edited and translated by D. Martindale, J. Riedel, and G. Neuwirth. Carbondale: Southern Illinois University Press.

Weber, William. 1975. *Music and the Middle Class*. London: Croom Helm.

———. 1977. "Mass Culture and the Reshaping of European Musical Taste, 1770–1870." *International Review of the Aesthetics and Sociology of Music* 8 (1): 5–21.

Wernick, Andrew. 1985. "Promotional Culture." Paper given at a joint conference session of the Canadian Communication Association and the *Canadian Journal of Political & Social Theory*, Montréal, June 2.

Williams, Raymond. 1958. *Culture and Society 1780–1950*. Middlesex: Penguin Books and Chatto & Windus.

———. 1974. *Television: Technology and Cultural Form*. Glasgow: Fontana/Collins.

———. 1977. *Marxism and Literature*. Oxford: Oxford University Press.

———. 1981. *Culture*. Glasgow: Fontana Paperbacks.

———. 1989. "The Future of Cultural Studies." In *The Politics of Modernism: Against the New Conformists* London: Verso, 151–62.

Wilson, Kevin. 1986. "The videotex industry: social control and the cybernetic commodity of home networking." *Media, Culture and Society* 8: 7–39.

Wolff, Janet. 1981. *The Social Production of Art*. London: Macmillan.

Wright, Robert. 1990. "Music and Canadian Studies." *Journal of Canadian Studies* 25 (2): 160–69.

Wurtzler, Steve. 1992. "'She Sang Live, But The Microphone Was Turned Off': The Live, the Recorded and the *Subject* of Representation." In *Sound Theory/ Sound Practice*, edited by Rick Altman. New York: Routledge, 87–103.

Young, Gayle. 1989. *The Sackbut Blues: Hugh Le Caine, Pioneer in Electronic Music*. Ottawa: National Museum of Science and Technology.

Zemp, Hugo. 1979. "Aspects of 'Are'are Musical Theory." *Ethnomusicology* 23 (1): 5–48.

Directories, Statistics, and Other Sources

Canadian Advertising Rates & Data. 63 (10), October 1990.

CARD Publication Profiles '91. 10, September 1990.

Customer Profile: Home Recording Equipment Buyer. Chicago: American Music Conference, 1988.

Economic Survey of Japan. Economic White Paper, Economic Planning Agency, Japanese Government, 1987–88.

Japan Economic Almanac. Tokyo: *Japan Economic Journal*; Nihon Keizai Shimbun, Inc., 1987.

Music USA 90. Chicago: American Music Conference, 1989.

1988 Music Software Consumer Survey. Chicago: American Music Conference, 1988.

1995 Music USA. Carlsbad, Cal.: National Association of Music Merchants, 1995.

Standard Periodical Directory (for U.S. and Canada). New York: Oxbridge, 1990, 1996.

Stepping into a new century (Company Guide). Hamamatsu: Yamaha Corporation, 1987.

Trends in Technology II (Advertisers' Report). Cupertino, Cal.: Miller Freeman Publications, 1990.

Ulrich's International Periodicals Directory (29th ed.). New York: Reed, 1990/91, 1993/94, 1996.

We Design the Future (Company Guide). Osaka: Roland Corporation, 1989.

Main Periodicals Consulted

Canadian Musician
Canadian Music Trades
Down Beat
Electronic Musician
IMA Bulletin (Official newsletter of the International MIDI Association)
Keyboard (formally *Contemporary Keyboard*)
Mix
Musician
The Music Trades
"Transoniq Hacker" (Independent user group newsletter)

Secondary Periodicals Consulted

Billboard
Computer Music Journal
db, The Sound Engineering Magazine
EQ
Future Music
Guitar Player
Guitar, For the Practicing Musician
Modern Drummer
Musical Merchandise Review
Music & Computers
Music Technology (U.S. and U.K. editions)
Pro Sound News
Recording (formerly *Home & Studio Recording*; U.S. and U.K. editions)
Recording Engineer/Producer
Rhythm
Roland Users Group (Roland Corporation)
Rolling Stone
Spin

Index

✳

Page numbers for illustrations appear in bold type.

Bomb The Bass, 204
Born, Georgina, 257nn2&3
Bourdieu, Pierre, 4, 12, 105, 212, 220–21, 263n4; *habitus*, 166–67; theory of practice, 161, 164, 170, 263n2
Bowen, John, 77
Bowie, David, 253
Bridges, John , 174
Brophy, Philip, 197
Brother International, 62–63
Brown, James, 204, 239
Buchla, Don, 35, 52, 111
Burgess, Jim, 37, 78
Bush, Kate, 123
Busoni, Ferruccio, 157

Cage, John, 189, 226
Canadian Music Trades. See Norris Publications
Canadian Musical Review, 93
Canadian Musician 117–18. *See also* Norris Publications
Carlos, Wendy (née Walter), 52, 123
Carse, Adam, 166, 258n1
Caruso, Enrico, 191
Casio Inc., 32, 34, 73–74, 111, 197
CB-radio (Citizens Band), 136, 262n3
CD-ROM, 75, 79, 200, 202, 247, 253–54, 266n5
CD-I (compact disk-interactive), 253, 266n5
Chambers, Dennis, 4
Chambers, Iain, 172, 252, 257n5
Chanan, Michael, 180
Chapple, Steve, 122, 257n4
Charpentier, Albert J., 64, 67–68
Christgau, Robert, 266n14
Ciamaga, Gustav, 52
cinema. *See* film
Clay, Roger, 88, 145–47, 150
Clearmountain, Bob, 83
Clementi, Muzio, 23–24
Clifford, Matt, 196
Collins, Phil, 239
commodities, 10, 83, 90, 98–100, 130; as "material-symbolic" entities, 112, 139–40, 144, 146, 152
Commodore International, 60, 64–65
community: communications and computer enthusiasts, 136, 144, 152, 262n3; musicians', 89, 103, 106, 113, 121, 126, 129–30, 174, 243. *See also* computer networks; musicians

composition. *See* musical practice
computer music, 157–59, 222–23, 227, 264n8, 265nn5,7&8
Computer Music Journal, 118
computer networks, 90, 108–9, 136–37, 143–45, 244, 253. *See also* musicians; Performing Artist Network (PAN)
Cone, Edward T., 206
Considine, J. D., 266n14
consumerism, 5, 29–30, 69, 90, 148–49, 243, 250; consumer practice, 6, 172, 200–203, 218- 19, 241, 242–45, 254–55; creation of consumers, 75–76, 89, 111, 130, 183–84, 212, 254; creation of needs, 17–18, 119, 153, 250–51; "participatory" consumption, 252–55. *See also* advertising; culture; musicians; sounds (synth & sampled); technology
copyright, 76, 181–82, 202, 215, 235–41, 252, 265n13, 266nn3&14
Craft, Robert, 217
Crane, Jonathan, 205–6
Crockett, Bruce, 64
culture: African-American, 173, 197, 205, 263n6; computer culture and "hackers," 65, 131, 136–37, 139, 146, 152, 226, 234, 244; consumer, 19–20, 27, 129–30, 200–203, 205, 245, 251–55; musical, 19, 32, 40, 42–43, 161, 173–74, 189, 202–4, 215; and social class, 173, 175–76, 183; study of, 8–11, 94, 257n6, 263n3
Curtis Electromusic Specialties, 61

Daley, Dan, 233
dance music, 4, 112, 172–73, 196–97, 204, 219, 224, 229
dancing, 171–72, 188
Darter, Tom, 54, 257n3, 258n1
Davidow, William H., 66, 68
Davies, Hugh, 258n1
Davis, Miles, 168
DeCurtis, Anthony, 266n14
de Lauretis, Teresa, 262n1
Deep Magic Music, 79
Deming, W. Edwards, 67
democratization: among communications enthusiasts and user groups, 131–33, 135–36, 142–43, 144–45, 148, 244; democratic theory, 148–49, 152–53; of the musical instrument market, 29–30, 72–73, 88–89, 126, 149, 215, 247, 250, 260n1
Denisoff, R. Serge, 174, 257n4

Der Manuelian, Michael, 238
Desbarats, Peter, 107
Desjardins, Michel, 236, 239, 266n14
Deutsch, Herbert, 52
Devo, 224
Digidesign Inc., 250, 266n1
di Perna, Alan, 266n5
Disco, 2, 112, 219
Doerschuk, Bob, 195, 246, 260n11
domestic space, **28**, 137, 215, 234–35, 241,
    261n6, 262n4; music and instruments
    in the home, 96, 98, 99–100, 125, 183–
    84, 215, 218, 221, 234, 254. *See also* home
    studio
Dougherty, Philip H., 107
Dowd, Tommy, 192
Down Beat, 105, 109–10, 114
drum machines, 3–4, 82–83, 84, 112, 158,
    168, 179, 198, 222, 224–25, 265n9. *See
    also* sounds (synth & sampled); TR-808
    Drum Machine
drums and drumming, 3, 167–68, 188
Dunlap, Orrin E., Jr., 133, 262nn1&2
Dunsby, Jonathan, 162
Dupler, Steven, 266n14
Durant, Alan, 188, 257n5
DX7 Synthesizer, 73–74, 75–76, 81–82,
    88–89. *See also* Yamaha Corporation
Dyck, Ralph, 214, 223

E-mu Systems, 39, 57, 59, 61, 67–68, 201.
    See also Proteus/3 World Synthesizer
easy-play, 29, 31, 38, 47
Eaton, John, 52
education, 126, 142, 161, 182, 184, 261n3;
    market, 30, 32, 104
Eimert, Herbert, 158
electro-pop, 224, 264n5
electronic/electroacoustic music, 7, 45,
    48–50, 158–59, 226, 257n2, 259n5
Electronic Musician, 106, 123, 126, 129. *See
    also* Mix Publications
Emerson, Keith, 1
Emmerson, Frank, 36
engineers (recording), 83, 107, 114, 117,
    192–93, 207, 216–17, 219–20
Eno, Brian, 216, 242
Ensoniq Corporation, 33, 39, 60–65,
    67–68, 139, 141, 144, 259n9; and user
    groups, 132, 140- 141, 144. *See also*
    Mirage Sampler; *Transoniq Hacker*
Erikson Music, 78
Erlhoff, Michael, 252

ethnomusicology, 6, 162–64, 188, 208,
    263n3
Ewen, Stuart, 12, 111

Fabbri, Franco, 169, 237
Fairlight Computer Musical Instrument,
    68, 86, 247
Faulkner, Robert R., 195, 263n3
Feld, Steven, 162, 168–69, 193, 203, 207,
    224
film: industry, 79, 84, 116, 142, 251, 263n3;
    representation of technology in, 124–
    25; sound in, 201, 188, 191, 192, 201–2,
    237; use of electronic instruments in
    production/post-production, 44, 45,
    195, 223, 247
Finlay-Pelinski, Marike, 119
Foster, David, 219
Fostex Inc., 250
Foucault, Michel, 162, 262n1
Fox, Ted, 192
Frederickson, Jon, 160, 217
Frith, Simon, 2, 4, 112, 158, 192, 202,
    257nn4&5, 266n14

Gabriel, Peter, 253
Gaburo, Kenneth, 157–60, 173, 176
Garofalo, Reebee, 122, 257n4
gender: in magazines, 97–98, 102, 122–26,
    244; in music and dance, 96, 128, 172,
    174–76, 183–85, 205; technology and,
    123, 124–26, 137–38, 229, 232, 261n6,
    262nn1&4. *See also* domestic space
Giffen, Peter, 266n14
Gomery, J. Douglas, 38, 84
Goodwin, Andrew, 119, 202–3, 204, 208,
    257n5
Gore, Joe, 202–3
Gould, Glenn, 253
GPI Publications. *See* Miller Freeman
    Publications
Gray, Christopher S., 67
groove, 193, 204, 207, 224–25. *See also*
    musical practice
Grossberg, Lawrence, 8, 257n6, 262n1
Grout, Donald Jay, 95, 177–78, 258n1
guitar, 173, 263n9; distortion and special
    effects, 1, 158, 187, 210; electric, 2, 32–
    33, 119, 159- 60, 172; players/guitarists,
    1, 114, 159, 175, 187, 211, 263nn1&2

Haddon, Leslie, 262n6, 265n12
Hafner, Katie 134

PAUL THÉBERGE is Assistant Professor of Communication Studies at Concordia University in Montréal as well as a composer. He has published widely on music, technology, and culture and has created sound works for various media, including radio and film.

LIBRARY OF CONGRESS CATALOGING-IN-PUBLICATION DATA
Théberge, Paul.
Any sound you can imagine : making music / consuming technology / Paul Théberge.
p. cm. — (Music / culture)
"Wesleyan University Press."
Includes bibliographical references (p.   ) and index.
ISBN 0–8195–5307–7 (cl : alk. paper). — ISBN 0–8195–6309–9 (pa : alk. paper)
1. Musical instruments, Electronic.   2. Music and technology.
3. Computer sound processing.   I. Title.   II. Series.
ML1092.T38   1997
786.7—dc21   97–5418